APOCALYPTIC AND
MERKAVAH MYSTICISM

INSTITUTUM IUDAICUM, TÜBINGEN

OTTO MICHEL, MARTIN HENGEL, PETER SCHÄFER

ARBEITEN ZUR GESCHICHTE DES ANTIKEN JUDENTUMS UND DES URCHRISTENTUMS

BAND XIV

APOCALYPTIC AND MERKAVAH MYSTICISM

LEIDEN/KÖLN
E. J. BRILL
1980

APOCALYPTIC AND MERKAVAH MYSTICISM

BY

ITHAMAR GRUENWALD

LEIDEN/KÖLN
E. J. BRILL
1980

ISBN 90 04 05959 8

PRINTED IN THE NETHERLANDS

CONTENTS

INTRODUCTION

This book is a description of Jewish Merkavah ("Divine Chariot") mysticism, its history, structure and main thematic features. Merkavah mysticism developed from visions like those described in *Isaiah* vi and *Ezekiel* i, viii and x, though when Merkavah mysticism appeared on the literary scene, it did so in a more complex manner than its historical forefathers. The earliest post-biblical traces of Merkavah mysticism are found in apocalyptic literature and in some of the texts discovered at Qumran. However, the literature that first gives a full-scale presentation of Merkavah mysticism is called the *Hekhalot* ("Divine Palaces") literature, mainly composed in Eretz-Yisrael at the time of the Talmud and the beginning of the Ge'onic period (circa 200-700 C.E.). Other traces of such mysticism are found in the rabbinic writings.

As a creative literary stream the Merkavah tradition ended some time in the Ge'onic period, but references to that tradition are also made in the writings of Jewish medieval mysticism, the Kabbalah. We know, too, that the German Ḥasidim (a movement of Jewish piety that flourished in twelfth- and thirteenth-century Germany) engaged in some forms of Merkavah mysticism and contributed in an important way to the preservation of the *Hekhalot* literature in manuscripts. The term Merkavah mysticism derives from the Hebrew term *Ma'aseh Merkavah* ("The Works of the Divine Chariot"), which usually means the mystical explication of the first chapter of *Ezekiel*. It appears that the mystical speculations about the Merkavah were first developed in the circle of Rabbi Yoḥanan ben Zakkai and his pupils (second half of the first century C.E.), though, as has been said, traces of Merkavah mysticism are already present in the apocalyptic corpus of writings and in the Qumran literature. In rabbinic writings, the *Ma'aseh Merkavah* go hand in hand with the *Ma'aseh Bereshit* ("The Works of the Creation of the World"), that is, Jewish cosmology, and together they form the two branches of the esoteric teachings of ancient Judaism. Interestingly, for Maimonides *Ma'aseh Merkavah* and *Ma'aseh Bereshit* stood, metaphorically, for Aristotelian metaphysics and physics respectively.

The prophet Ezekiel supplied the Merkavah tradition with some of its key notions and visual concepts, and his influence prevailed in the literary history of Jewish mysticism till *Sefer Yetẓirah* ("The Book of Creation/Formation") provided a new imagery and symbolic language. Still, Ezekiel was for a very long time the model for visionaries to follow and imitate. All manner of practices were adapted and invented in order to bring about the realization of mystical experiences like those Ezekiel was thought to have had. Of course, as time passed the Merkavah tradition underwent substantial changes: new modes of mystical experiences were discovered, new ideas and concepts were introduced and new points of emphasis reshaped the material.

The present book is divided into two parts. The first contains an analysis of the major features of the Merkavah tradition. In the second a detailed description is given of all the known *Hekhalot* writings. As for the first part, it begins with a general characterization of some of the qualities of Jewish apocalyptic which were hitherto either wrongly or insufficiently presented by scholars. This prepares the way for the second chapter, which analyses the Merkavah material incorporated in some of the early Jewish and Christian apocalyptic writings. The third chapter contains a discussion of the Merkavah material incorporated in the rabbinic writings. The fourth chapter gives a general characterization of the *Hekhalot* literature. Both parts of the book contain also several notes on the Merkavah material incorporated in the gnostic writings found at Nag Hammadi.

Some readers will probably think that this book could have gained had the writer applied to his study the methods of form criticism. Now an accepted methodology, form criticism could have really helped scholars in orienting themselves to the problems raised by this subject. However, it appears that in spite of the study already carried out in the field of Merkavah mysticism the way is not yet open there for the application of any of the higher forms of criticism. The main reason for this is that we still lack critical editions and commentaries for almost all the texts under discussion. Before such editions and commentaries are at hand, final judgement based on serious textual criticism has to be postponed. Consequently, we have limited ourselves to presenting a comprehensive survey of the Merkavah tradition, and it is hoped that what the book does will outweigh what it cannot yet do.

On the whole, Merkavah mysticism has stimulated most controversial attitudes and utterances. To begin with, The *Mishnah Ḥagigah* ii, 1 forbids the study of the *Ma'aseh Merkavah* in public, to say nothing of the many dangers allegedly involved in the study and realization of Merkavah mysticism as described in the Rabbinic writings and *Hekhalot* literature. In one of his letters to his kabbalistic colleagues in Europe, Shlomel Dresnitz, who came from Strassnitz in Moravia to Safed in the year 1602, wrote that Rabbi Yitzḥaq Luria Ashkenazi, The Holy ʾAri as he is called, regarded the *Hekhalot* literature as being full of errors. However, Shlomel Dresnitz reports, the founder of Lurianic Kabbalah believed these errors were purposely introduced to prevent misuse of the writings for magical purposes. Of course, as the writer of the letter says, the Holy ʾAri could have removed all these errors, but for obvious reasons he did not do so. The evidence contained in that letter, as later incorporated in the small book *Shivḥei Ha-ʾAri* ("The Sacred Deeds of the ʾAri") is only one testimony to the fact that the kind of literature we are discussing in this book persisted to be a controversial issue in the history of Jewish literature for a very long time.

In yet another context we find Maimonides attacking certain books which belong to the *Hekhalot* literature. In the introduction to his commentary to *Mishnah Sanhedrin*, *Pereq Ḥeleq*, Maimonides writes in connection with Rabbi ʿAkiva's view quoted in the *Mishnah* to the effect that "he who reads in the *Sefarim Ḥitzonim* (Apocrypha?) has no share in the world to come": "And *Sefarim Ḥitzonim*—it is said (cf. *Bavli Sanhedrin* 100/b) that they are books written by heretics; and also the book written by Ben Sira (actually Pseudo Ben Sira), who wrote books which contained *inter alia* the subject of physiognomy—all these are worthless books and their study is a waste of time". Now, as we shall see in the second part of our book, the subject of physiognomy is one of the oldest subjects in Jewish esoteric literature, and the attitude shown by Maimonides towards its study is reminiscent of his derogatory attitude towards the *Shiʿur Qomah* tractate. In one of his Halakhic Responsa Maimonides attacked the *Shiʿur Qomah* as a book composed by a non-Jew, and recommended its destruction.

These are only three out of many views expressed in connection with the *Hekhalot* literature. To these one can add the views expressed by modern scholars, to the effect that Merkavah mysticism "constitutes an inner Jewish concomitant to Gnosis" (Scholem), or that in comparison to later developments of Merkavah mysticism, the mysticism of the early Tannaim, among them Rabbi Yoḥanan ben Zakkai and the four sages who entered the *Pardes*, was "an ascetic type of mysticism" (Urbach). Under the circumstances I have found it necessary to try to give as balanced a picture of the subject matter as possible. And if I have been successful in that undertaking, I owe a lot to many people.

First to my wife, Rachel. She followed me in my studies with love and devotion. Fortunately for her, she did not stray too far along the path where my studies lead, but where she stayed I always saw a beacon directing me to safety.

This book also owes a lot to Professor Gershom Scholem and to his writings. I had the honour of being invited by him to spend the academic year 1975/76 at the Institute for Advanced Studies of the Hebrew University of Jerusalem. The stimulating hours and days we spent together there have left their traces in this book.

It is at the Institute for Advanced Studies that I first met Professor Saul Lieberman. The interest he took in my studies is clearly seen in the two appendices which he offered to write for this book. In addition, his great erudition has helped me by clarifying a number of questions and prevented me from falling into pitfalls of ignorance.

In mentioning the Institute for Advanced Studies, it is with great satisfaction that I recall my colleagues there: Professors Daniel Sperber, Shama Friedman and David Winston, with whom I discussed several issues, particularly of the first part of the book.

A word of gratitude is also due to the staff of the Institute for Advanced Studies and its secretaries who typed most of the manuscript. Professor Arieh Devoetzki, the Head of the Institute, encouraged us all in our studies and did everything in his power to further its success.

There are many other colleagues who deserve more than mere words can express. First, Professor Morton Smith of Columbia University, who read great parts of the typewritten manuscript, corrected its style and made many useful suggestions. Professor John Strugnell of Harvard University read parts of the manuscript, and he, too, made several useful suggestions. Professor Bentley Layton of Yale University helped me greatly in matters relating to gnosticism.

The editors of the Series "Arbeiten zur Geschichte des antiken Judentums und des Urchristentums", Professor Dr. Martin Hengel of Tübingen, and Professor Dr. Peter Schäfer of Cologne, read the manuscript chapter by chapter and encouraged my work as it was progressing.

Mrs. Shifrah Danai checked the references and compiled the Index.

All these nice people, and others too, helped me in achieving what I have. If, however, the book contains any shortcomings, I alone am to blame.

Last but not least, I would like to mention my parents and children. They were so eager to see this book in print. Here it is dedicated to them, and to my wife, in love and gratitude.

Jerusalem, June 22, 1977

ABBREVIATIONS

OGIS = *Orientis Graeci Inscriptiones Selectae*
TB = *Talmud Babylonicum*
TP = *Talmud Palaestinense*

TRANSCRIPTIONS

א = ’a
ע = ‘a
ב = v
ו = w
ח = ḥ
ט = ṭ (sometimes: t)
כּ = k
כ = kh
צ = ẓ (sometimes: tz)
ק = q (sometimes: c or k)
ש = sh (sometimes: sch)
ת = t

PART ONE

CHAPTER ONE

TWO ESSENTIAL QUALITIES OF JEWISH APOCALYPTIC

A

In spite of a century of intensive studies, the rise of Jewish apocalyptic still seems to be a riddle. Nothing can better illustrate the uncertainty of modern scholarship with regard to the various problems involved in the study of apocalypticism than the title of Klaus Koch's book: *Ratlos vor der Apokalyptik*.[1] Admittedly, there are many studies which have considerably contributed to our understanding of the phenomenon,[2] but Jewish apocalypticism is still, by and large, a riddle, particularly so if we consider its rather vague origin. No attempt will be made here to lift the mists that overhang its prehistory, though the writer inclines to the view, that Jewish apocalyptic had a considerably long history before it entered the literary stage, which it did about the Hasmonaean period. This chapter will attempt to discuss briefly the place Jewish apocalyptic occupies in the history of Jewish religious thought and literature. We shall focus our attention on two literary genres of Jewish literature—Prophecy and Wisdom—and in their light examine some of the particular qualities of Jewish apocalyptic. Naturally, our discussion of biblical prophetic and wisdom literature does not strive to be exhaustive. We shall touch these two fields only inasmuch as they can help us in outlining what is new and original in apocalypticism.

We shall examine Jewish apocalyptic in the light of its relationship to Scripture.[3] It is natural that whenever the proponents of some

---

[1] Klaus Koch, *Ratlos vor der Apokalyptik*, Gütersloh, Gütersloher Verlag Gerd Mohn, 1970. The German title of the book expresses the idea of perplexity better than that of the English translation, *The Rediscovery of Apocalyptic*, London, SCM Press, 1972. [See now P. D. Hanson, "Prolegomena to the Study of Jewish Apocalyptic", in: *Magnalia Dei: The Mighty Acts of God*, ed. F. M. Cross, *et al.*, New York, Doubleday & Co., 1976, pp. 389-413.]

[2] See particularly, H. H. Rowley, *The Relevance of Apocalyptic*, London, Lutterworth Press, 1963; J. M. Schmidt, *Die Jüdische Apokalyptik*, Neukirchen-Vluyn, Neukirchener Verlag, 1969; *idem*, "Forschung zur jüdischen Apokalyptik", *Beihefte zur Evangelische Theologie Verkündigung und Forschung* I (1969): Altes Testament, S. 44-69.

[3] The problem of Scriptural apocalyptic, which has been variously discussed

new ideas in Jewish religious thought sought to introduce them, they found themselves obliged to do so in the frame of some kind of relationship to the Holy Scriptures. This is the essence of Jewish tradition: people look for the authority of Scripture even in cases where their ideas do not explicitly concur with what Scripture plainly says. In this respect it seems safe to argue that midrashic ways of thinking—whether they involved explicating, or widening and even rewriting Scripture—were much older and more widely spread than is sometimes assumed. This relationship which Jewish religious thought seeks to bear to Scripture does not limit its own relative independence. Quite daring and new modes of thinking could well be introduced on the assumption that they really were the hidden sense of Scripture. Medieval Jewish Kabbalah is a famous example of how completely novel ways of expression and thought could be introduced as the symbolic content of Scripture.[4] But long before that, chiefly during the last two hundred and fifty years of the Second Temple, a kind of literature developed which, in the framework of peculiar religious experiences, brought forward a series of ideas and concepts which, if viewed in their relationship to Scripture, were quite revolutionary.

Revolutionary they were, since they purported to disclose, at least to a select group of believers, things which Scripture did not explicitly say or declared to be beyond the reach of the human intellect. Of course, not everything contained in apocalyptic literature belonged to these two categories, but the material that does belong to them, is from the point of view of Scripture, absolutely rule-breaking. To illustrate our argument we shall first pick up certain features of the *Book of Job* and examine them in the light of what happened to them later on in apocalyptic literature. Whenever the *Book of Job* was composed,[5] it clearly expresses a basic mood found in Scripture, and particularly in the so-called wisdom parts, namely that man cannot understand everything and hence is not justified in questioning the ways of God. According to the *Book of*

---

in recent years, can be left out of consideration in the present context. See further, below n. 42. [See now P. D. Hanson, *The Dawn of Apocalyptic*, Philadelphia, Fortress Press, 1975.]

[4] See G. Scholem, *Zur Kabbala und ihrer Symbolik*, Zürich, Rhein-Verlag, 1960, pp. 49-116, 159-207.

[5] For a brief and recent summary of the views concerning the date and the authorship of the Book of Job see M. H. Pope, *The Anchor Bible*: *Job*, Garden City, New York, Doubleday & Company, 1965, pp. xxx-xxxviii.

Job there is a correlation between man's inability to understand the basic laws of Nature and his inability to understand the principles of God's justice. Time and again, Job's friends draw his attention to the wondrous ways in which Nature operates.[6] When they do so, they mean to imply the conclusion that the human intellect—as is so drastically illustrated by its confrontation with Nature—is incapable of grasping the relation between man's just behaviour and the amount of suffering which befalls him. This is also the conclusion which God wants Job to draw, when He reveals Himself in the storm at the end of the book. In fact, God endorses what has previously been implied by Job's friends.

Briefly, the line of these arguments in the *Book of Job* goes as follows: First, in answer to Job's curse on the day of his birth, Eliphaz says: "...to God would I commit my cause; who does great things and unsearchable, marvelous things without number: He gives rain upon the earth and sends water upon the fields; He sets on high those who are lowly, and those who mourn are lifted to safety" (v,8-11; RSV). God's omnipotence is here illustrated by His wondrous works in Nature and by His care for those who are most in need of it. When Job stresses again that he still expects God to repay accordingly those who trust in Him, and when he expresses his dissatisfaction with what the second of the friends, Bildad the Shuhite, suggests, Zophar comes and, in line with what Eliphaz has already implied, says: "Can you find out the deep things of God? Can you find out the limit of the Almighty? The heights of heaven ... Deeper than Sheol—what can you know?" (xi,7-8). It is impossible to grasp God's wisdom, and so what one has to do is to trust in Him and hope. These and some other arguments are repeatedly brought forward till we reach the turning point of the book. In the speech which begins in chapter xxvii Job once again concludes: "As God lives, who has taken away my right, and the Almighty, who has made my soul bitter" (xxvii,2). That is, Job is absolutely convinced of his integrity. But he is now also ready to accept the fact, that only in God is wisdom to be found and that only He knows what wisdom really is. The conclusion for man is: "...the fear of the Lord, that is wisdom; and to depart from evil is understanding" (xxviii,28). This

[6] G. von Rad, *Weisheit in Israel*, Neukirchen-Vluyn, Neukirchener Verlag, 1970, pp. 267 ff.; *idem*, *Gesammelte Studien zum Alten Testament*, München, Chr. Kaiser Verlag, 1965, pp. 262-271.

conclusion, common in biblical wisdom-literature,[7] could be here interpreted to mean, that since man cannot attain wisdom, he must content himself with the fear of God. The inaccessibility of divine wisdom should not lead to rebellion but to respectful submission.

Since Elihu's discourses do not add anything substantial from our point of view, we may directly turn to God's answer from the storm. Actually, God's "answer" is a long series of questions to which Job is unable to find any answer. Hence he is driven to the conclusion, that there is no point in arguing against God. What Job could find in God's questions is an extensive list of His activities in Nature, activities which man can neither directly experience nor reasonably explain. This long list of activities is in fact a catalogue of deeds or subjects which are supposed to be beyond the reach of the human mind. Under such discouraging conditions man has to give in, as Job actually does: his relative ignorance is a *conditio sine qua non* in any moral argument with the Deity.[8] The solution which the Book of Job, thus, suggests for the problem of human suffering is, in this respect, a "negative" one: no satisfactory explanation can be given from the point of view of the suffering human being. Man has to concede that his intellect allows only a partial, and hence insufficient, understanding of the ways of God. The "happy ending" in the case of Job, if it really belongs to the main body of the book, has an obvious mitigating effect; but it is an indirect way of approaching the painful problem of human suffering. The restoration of happiness and wealth to Job and his family is no answer in principle: it only bids us view Job's case in a broader perspective. In the terms of the "happy ending" the period of suffering becomes an unpleasant interlude, and is no real challenge to the justice of God. Yet, as we are going to see, the Jewish tradition did not see in the suggestions made in the Book of Job a conclusive solution to the problem of the lack of any explainable coordination between moral integrity and human suffering. Time and again the same questions were forced on the minds of the people, and in the framework of different historical circumstances and novel intellectual climates new solutions were approached.

As we have already seen, God challenges Job's competence to argue against Him by asking him a long series of questions about

[7] See J. Maier & J. Schreiner (eds.) *Literatur und Religion des Frühjudentums*, Würzburg, Echter Verlag, 1973, p. 44/5, n. 6; W. Eichrodt, *Theology of the Old Testament*, Vol. II, London, SCM Press, 1967, p. 92.

[8] See I. Gruenwald, "'Knowledge' and 'Vision'", *Israel Oriental Studies* III (1973), p. 69 ff.

the wondrous ways of Nature. These questions include references to the creation of the world (xxxviii,4 ff.), the structure of the universe (xxxviii,15 ff.), meteorological phenomena (xxxviii,22 ff.), astronomical laws (xxxviii,31 ff.), animal life and feeding (xxxix,1 ff.), Behemoth (xl,15 ff.), Leviathan (xl,25 ff.), and ancient mythology (xli,5 ff.). All these items of knowledge are riddles to the mind of man. They reflect the contents of God's wisdom, as it was outlined by Job himself in chapter xxviii. And indeed it is in Job's way of putting the idea that we get a deeper view of how God manifests His wisdom in the performances of Nature: "When He gave to the wind its weight, and meted out the waters by measure; when He made a decree for the rain, and a way for the lightning of the thunder" (xxviii,25/6). God, and only He, knows the right proportions of everything, and only He is able to regulate natural phenomena.[9] A similar idea is expressed by the prophet Isaiah when he refers to the creation of the world: "Who has measured the waters in the hollow of his hand, and marked off the heavens with a span, enclosed the dust of the earth in a measure, and weighed the mountains in scales and the hills in a balance?" [10] The idea that order depends on correct measurement and right proportion is in itself neither unique nor new: it may be found implied in the writings of the Greek philosophers and it still holds true in modern science. What is, nevertheless, noteworthy in biblical thought is the fact, that God is there believed to know, and to be responsible for, these right quantities and proportions, and that they are beyond understanding. It is here that Job sees the essential difference between the capabilities of the human intellect and the wisdom of the Deity. Since scientific research and knowledge begin with the attempt to find out what these quantities and proportions are, it may be inferred, that the

[9] See *art. cit.* (previous note), p. 70, n. 29. To the references cited there one may add *The Wisdom of Solomon* xi,20: "But by measure and number and weight thou didst order all things." As for the weight of the wind see further, *Bereshit Rabbā* (ed. Theodor-Albeck), p. 232: "Rav Huna said: Because of three winds which came out (= from their treasure houses into the world) without weight there came destruction on the world". See also *4 Ezra* iv,5: "Or measure me the measure of the wind".

[10] For the idea of the measurement of the seawater see further *Tal. Bav. Horayot* 10a (end) where two sages who lived in the days of Rabbi Aqiva are mentioned as being able to calculate the number of the drops in the sea, but who nevertheless had nothing to eat and to wear. Cf. also notes 14 and 22 below. See also A. Wasserstein, "Astronomy and Geometry as Propaedeutic Studies in Rabbinic Literature", (in Hebrew), *Tarbiz* XLIII (1973), p. 54.

view expressed in the Book of Job runs counter to the scientifically oriented mind.

The limits put here before the inquisitive faculties of the human intellect should not, however, be interpreted in terms of the supression of all scientific activity and knowledge. The particular position taken by the Book of Job means that since man is limited in his ability to understand the wisdom of God in the various operations of Nature, he should withhold any criticism of God's wisdom in His attitude towards man. This is no direct prohibition of scientific inquiry, but a rather skeptical view of what the human intellect may expect from and attain in such an inquiry. In this light one should view the innovation in the lists of revealed knowledge concerning natural phenomena as found in some of the apocalyptic books, and mainly in the so-called Enoch literature. Once man is to receive information about the principles of divine retribution, there is no reason anymore to withhold from him the secrets of nature. The two go hand in hand: where there is no possibility of knowing the secrets of nature it is assumed that there is no possibility of grasping the ways of God with man; where a revelation of the ways of God with man is given it is simultaneous with a revelation of the secrets of nature. In this respect, apocalyptic revelations claim to effect a substantial expansion of the capabilities of the human intellect not only in matters that pertain to man's understanding of the operation of natural phenomena, but also in his understanding of history and divine retribution.

B

References to items of revealed knowledge concerning natural phenomena can be found in *1 Enoch* (*Ethiopic Enoch*) xvii-xviii; xxii; xxxiii-xxxvi; xli,1; xli,3 ff.; xliii-xliv; lii; lix; lx,11 ff.; lxix; lxxi; lxxii-lxxx; xciii,11-14.[11] In *2 Enoch* (*Slavonic Enoch*)[12] v-vi;

[11] To these one has to add the revelations of secrets by the evil angels in vii, lxix and lxv. For a recent discussion of the various traditions concerning the evil angels and the secrets which they revealed see, D. Dimant, *The Fallen Angels in the Dead Sea Scrolls and in the Apocryphal and Pseudepigraphic Books Related to Them*, Diss., Jerusalem, 1974.

[12] The chapter numbering here is according to the one found in R. H. Charles, *The Apocrypha and Pseudepigrapha of the Old Testament*, and it holds true for the long recension (A). A. Vaillant, *Le Livre des Secrets d'Hénoch*, Paris, Institut d'Études Slaves, 1952, has a different chapter numbering.

xi-xvi; xxiv-xxx; xl; xlvii-xlviii. In *3 Enoch* (*Hebrew Enoch*)[13] xi; xiii; xiv; xvii; xli-xlii; xlviii(d). Similar references may be found also in *2 Baruch* (*Syriac Baruch*) xlviii,2-14; lix,5-11; and also in some of the other apocalyptic writings which will be discussed later on. All these references to the revelation of secrets concerning the operation of the various parts of Nature go hand in hand with revelations concerning the angelic world and the divinity. But our interest for the moment lies in the revelations concerning natural phenomena only, and what is implied by them for our understanding of Jewish apocalyptic in relation to the idea of the inaccessibility of divine wisdom as asserted in the Book of Job.

Reading through the various parts which compose the *Ethiopic Book of Enoch* (*1 Enoch*) one easily observes, that the revelations of all kinds of cosmological secrets occupy a prominent part in the apocalyptic experiences of the writers. The apocalyptic visionaries are said to ascend to heaven and there, with the guidance of different interpreting angels, to see and learn about the operations of a number of natural phenomena. Thus, for instance, the apocalyptist says that he has been taken to see "the places of the luminaries, and the treasuries of the stars and of the thunder... and all the lightnings" (xvii,3). In addition, the apocalyptist says that he saw "the mouths of all the rivers of the earth and the mouth of the deep" (*ibid.*, 8). In chapter xviii even more important things are shown to him and, all in all, it may be said that the apocalyptist receives a pretty comprehensive view of the cosmos. In another vision the apocalyptist sees "how the stars of heaven come forth, and I counted the portals out of which they proceed, and wrote down all their outlets, of each individual star by itself, according to their number and their names, their courses and their positions, and their times and their months, as Uriel the holy angel who was with me showed me" (xxxiii,3). What is particularly noteworthy in these revelations of cosmological secrets is that the visionary learns the laws and rules by which all these phenomena operate: "And I saw the chambers of the sun and moon, whence they proceed and whither they come again, and their glorious return, and how one is superior to the other, and their stately orbit, and how they do not leave their orbit, and they add nothing to their orbit and they take nothing from it, and they keep

[13] Ed. H. Odeberg, *3 Enoch*, with a Prolegomenon by J. C. Greenfield, New York, Ktav Publishing House, 1973.

faith with each other, in accordance with the oath by which they are bound together" (xli,5).[14] Although this passage belongs to a different part of the Book of Enoch (and possibly the latest part of the Book),[15] it still records an essential mood in the whole corpus of the Enoch literature. The visionary is translated to heaven and there is instructed about the rules and laws of Nature. Basically, these rules and laws of Nature are referred to in terms of measurement, weight, quantity and proportion. And apart from the fact that in some instances (as for example in *1 Enoch* lxxii-lxxx: "The Book of the Heavenly Luminaries") the revelation of astronomical secrets comes to further the idea of the sectarian solar calendar, the whole idea is meant to induce the impression of order and regularity in Nature. Where there is disorder there is either wickedness—as the introduction to *1 Enoch* (ch. i-v) so clearly implies—or else the coming of the Day of God (ch. lxxx).

This order and regularity in Nature is sometimes conceived as being bound to a secret oath. We have already seen that in *1 Enoch* xli,5 astronomical order is preserved "in accordance with the oath by which they are bound together". An oath, probably the same one, is later on mentioned in connection with the creation of the world (ch. lxix). Though not everything said there is really as lucid as one could wish, it clearly appears that Michael is in possession of a secret oath, and possibly also of a secret name—the two are not necessarily identical—which sustains the whole work of creation. That there was such a secret element which the ancients believed to be operative in the creation of the world and in its subsequent government is neither new nor unique to the Book of Similitudes (*1 Enoch* xxxvi-lxxi). At any rate, the idea and its parallels are amply documented

---

[14] The regularity in the movements of the planets, and the catastrophes that might occur if that regularity is broken, are also often mentioned in rabbinic literature. See the references given in L. Ginzberg, *The Legends of the Jews*, vol. V, Philadelphia, The Jewish Publication Society of America, 1955, p. 34-36, n. 100. For the ideas of order and regularity in Nature as described in Wisdom literature see P. von der Osten-Sacken, *Die Apokalyptik in ihrem Verhältnis zu Prophetie und Weisheit*, München, Ch. Kaiser Verlag, 1969, pp. 53 ff.

[15] Chapter xxxvii-lxxi, generally referred to as the Book of the Similitudes (or Parables), are not represented in the finds from Qumram. Hence the conclusion, that they probably belong to a post-Qumranic period (Qumran was most certainly destroyed in 68 C.E.). See J. T. Milik, *Ten Years of Discovery in the Wilderness of Judea*, London, SCM Press, 1959, p. 33. More recently M. Black, "The Fragments of the Aramaic Enoch from Qumran", in: *La Littérature Juive* etc. ed. W. C. van Unnik, Leiden, E. J. Brill, 1974, p. 19, argued for a post-Christian & Jewish origin of these chapters.

in post-biblical Jewish literature. Thus, for instance, the main Hekhalot text, *Hekhalot Rabbati* ix,5, contains a brief reference to the "...wondrous and strange and great secret; the name through which the heaven and the earth were created, and all the orders of the creation of the world (Hebrew: *sidrei bereshit*)...were sealed by it".[16] Interestingly, both in the *Ethiopic Book of Enoch* and in *Hekhalot Rabbati* the "secret name" is put in apposition to the "oath" or the "great secret". And indeed, the secret name, or names, of God played a great role in some of the ancient Jewish concepts of creation. Thus we find in the Book of Jubilees xxxvi,7 that Isaac makes his sons swear "a great oath—for there is no oath which is greater than it—by the name glorious and honoured and great and splendid and wonderful and mighty, which created the heavens and the earth and all things together...". Later on, in the third century C.E., we hear from Rav Yehudah in the name of Rav that "Bezal'el (*Exodus* xxxi,2) knew how to form the combinations (Hebrew: *lezaref*) of the letters (of the Alphabet) through which the heaven and the earth had been created".[17] Again, in the *Hebrew Book of Enoch* xli, reference is made to the letters by which the heaven and the earth were created. It is not said what these letters are and how they were combined. In fact, one may find in Jewish writings of the Talmudic times a number of theories with regard to the question: Which were the letters of the Alphabet used by God in the creation of the world? We cannot enter here a full-scale description and analysis of these theories, the most noteworthy of which is that in *Sefer Yezirah*.[18] All these theories lie on the borderline between magic and mysticism,[19] and they might be connected with certain speculations concerning the uttering of the tetragrammaton during the temple service,[20] and also with hellenistic logos-speculations.

[16] See G. Scholem, "Der Name Gottes und die Sprachtheorie der Kabbala", *Judaica III*: *Studien zur jüdischen Mystik*, Frankfurt am Main, Suhrkamp Verlag, 1970, pp. 7 ff.

[17] *Tal. Bav. Berakhot* 55a. The gemarā continues with quotations of verses in which divine wisdom and knowledge are mentioned in connection with the creation of the world. See further G. Quispel, "The Jung Codex and its Significance", in: *Gnostic Studies* I, Istanbul, Nederlands Historisch-Archeologisch Instituut, 1974, pp. 21 ff.

[18] See I. Gruenwald, "Some Critical Notes on the First Part of *Sefer Yezira*", *Revue des Études Juives* CXXXII (1973), pp. 475 ff.

[19] Cf. N. Séd, "Le Sefer Ha-Razim et le Méthode de 'Combination des Lettres'", *Revue des Études Juives* CXXX (1971), pp. 295 ff.

[20] See G. Alon, *Studies in Jewish History* (in Hebrew), vol. I, Tel Aviv, 1957, pp. 194 ff.

All in all, when these secrets and oaths used in the creation of the world and which are operative in sustaining it are mentioned in Jewish post-biblical writings, they reflect a significant change in the religious attitude. Not only do the apocalyptists believe in the possibility that such secrets are accessible to man—at least on certain conditions which will be discussed later on—but the knowledge of these secrets opens the way for man's understanding of divine justice. The restrictions and limitations maintained in such books as *Job* are thus removed and, consequently, man is ready to receive the hitherto wanting explanations for the existence of evil and suffering in a world ruled by a benevolent God. The apocalyptists, who lived in the deep conviction that the days of the eschatological fulfilment were close at hand, believed that whatever had been concealed from man, because of the injustice that reigned in the world, could now be released for the knowledge and benefit of the just. It must be remembered that the apocalyptic writers believed that these secrets had been disclosed long before they were withdrawn from the knowledge of such people as Job. This belief belongs to the heart of apocalypticism as a pseudonymous literary genre. The secrets had been disclosed to the legendary sages of antiquity who in turn put them into books which were sealed away, and in that condition they were preserved till the eschatological time came to open them.[21]

It must be noted that the disclosure of cosmological secrets is not found in all apocalyptic writings. In *4 Ezra* we find the angel Uriel asking the apocalyptist a series of questions concerning natural phenomena, the purpose of which was to induce in Ezra, the apocalyptist, the same conclusion which Job had been induced to reach.[22] Similarly, *1 Enoch* xciii,11-14 contains a list of questions, such as "who is there that can behold all the works of heaven... and who is there of all men that could know what is the breadth and the length of the earth". These questions obviously originated from a different spiritual climate than did many of the experiences described in the

[21] See, for instance, *1 Enoch* lxxxii; *4 Ezra* xii,36-38; xiv,24 ff.; all these in comparison to *Daniel* xii, on the one hand, and *Revelation* x and xxii,10, on the other.

[22] The Armenian text has even a more extensive list of such "impossible" subjects. See J. Issaverdens, *The Uncanonical Writings of the Old Testament Found in the Armenian MSS. of the Library of St. Lazarus*, Venice, Armenian Monastry of St. Lazarus, 1934, pp. 388-391. See the extensive discussion of the nature of such lists by M. Stone, "Lists of Revealed Things in the Apocalyptic Literature", in: *Magnalia Dei* (see above n. 1), pp. 414-454.

other parts of the book. In a different context we meet yet another list of questions. In what in all likelihood is the oldest Hekhalot text we know of, *Hekhalot Zutreti*,[23] there is a list of questions such as "who is there who is able... to explore the world... to combine the letters, to say the names... and to know the lightning". If taken together, these last question-lists can lead to the conclusion that, parallel to the general concept found in apocalyptic literature and according to which there is a strong relationship between man's ability to comprehend the secrets of nature and his ability to understand the ways of God with man, there was a trend within the apocalyptic tradition itself which still stuck to the more Scriptural point of view. Yet, generally speaking, in contradistinction to the view held in Scripture according to which neither Nature nor human suffering is open to the understanding of man, the dominant tone in the apocalyptic tradition was that an understanding of nature and of human suffering is possible in an eschatological context. In this respect one may even consider such questions as in *1 Enoch* xciii,14 —"Or is there anyone who could discern... how great is the number of the stars, and where all the luminaries rest"—as merely rhetorical questions that are explicitly, and affirmatively so, answered in the other parts of the book. If so, no real polemic can be found in apocalyptic circles with regard to the possibility of deciphering the secrets of Nature by apocalyptic methods. In addition, if one compares the questions, "And who is there that can behold the works of heaven? And should there be one who could behold the heaven, and who is there that could understand the things of heaven and see a soul or a spirit and could tell thereof, or ascend and see all their ends and think them or do like them" (*1 Enoch* xciii,11-12) with the ones of *Hekhalot Zutreti*, "And who is there who is able to ascend on high, to descend below... to behold what is on high, and to behold what is below", then the conclusion would appear to follow that—whatever their tone and purpose—certain apocalyptic modes of expression and thought were adapted by the Merkavah mystics.[24]

Yet again, one has to consider that, according to a tradition preserved in *1 Enoch* viii-xi and lxix,1-12, the rebellious angels taught mankind all kinds of secrets, some of which were also shown to the

---

[23] See G. Scholem, *Jewish Gnosticism, Merkabah Mysticism, and Talmudic Tradition*, Second, Improved Edition, New York, The Jewish Theological Seminary of America, 1965, p. 78.

[24] Cf. I. Gruenwald, *art. cit.*, above n. 8, p. 75/6.

apocalyptists.[25] On the other hand, it is stated in *2 Enoch* xxiv,3 [26] that God did not tell the secrets of the creation to His angels. Thus we may once again surmise, that a number of parallel, sometimes even conflicting, traditions with regard to the revelation of cosmological secrets were circulating among the apocalyptists, and one can only speculate as to what made each of them adopt this or that attitude. We know that heavenly ascensions, or descents to the underworld, were practised in many religions in the ancient world. We know, too, that in the intellectual world influenced by Greek thought a deep interest in Nature motivated and directed an intensive philosophical, or scientific, activity. The alleged resentment expressed by some of the apocalyptists with regard to the revelation of cosmological secrets could well have been motivated by a deeply-felt opposition to these kinds of non-Jewish activities. This resentment of all kinds of foreign influence may at least partly be attributed to the fact that some of the apocalyptists were driven by strong nationalistic emotions: those who had a bitter battle to fight for their true national identity were obviously zealous in their preservation of the genuine Jewish spirit.[27] However, what in every case remained was the new understanding which apocalypticism suggested for the problems of evil and human suffering.[28] Seen in a broader, eschatological, context both evil and suffering received different proportions. Their meaning and function was not to be decided anymore in relation to temporary pain and grief, but within the framework of history as a totality regulated by God from creation to salvation.

Thus, we may summarize, within the wisdom tradition of ancient Judaism apocalypticism introduced a number of new ideas and notions. We have followed one of them in detail, namely the revelation

---

[25] See above n. 11.

[26] Both recensions, the long and the short ones (A and B), testify to the same tradition.

[27] See M. Hengel, *Judaism and Hellenism*, London, SCM Press, 1974, pp. 58 ff. Hengel is inclined to discuss apocalypticism within the framework of Hasidism, and it is indeed in such pietistic circles that one has to look for the documentary traces of anti-hellenistic opposition. On the other hand, apocalypticism as such could be a much more widely spread literary phenomenon than is sometimes maintained. For a priestly orientation in the interpretation of apocalypticism see K. Schubert, "*Das Zeitalter der Apokalyptik*", in F. Leist (ed.), *Seine Rede Geschah zu Mir*, München, Manz-Verlag, 1965, pp. 265-285.

[28] It must be left for further consideration whether there were any differences among the apocalyptists with regard to the inclusion of mythical material. At any rate, there are some apocalyptic books, such as *4 Ezra*, which are more reserved in their references to material that came from mythical sources.

of cosmological secrets and its relation to the problem of theodicy. While such books as *2 & 4 Maccabees* already contain an eschatological solution to the problems of evil and suffering,[29] the apocalyptic books which we have reviewed here relate the eschatological solution to the possibilities of enlarging and deepening man's knowledge of the world.[30] This knowledge does not come as a direct result of the inquisitive curiosity and efforts of man, but as a special supernatural revelation. The contents of these supernatural revelations were often seen as an anticipation of what the just ones are to experience in the world to come. Thus, in the so-called Apocalypse of Weeks, *1 Enoch* xci-xciii, it is said that, at the end of the seventh "week" (*i.e.*, unit of seven years), the righteous shall be elected "for true witnesses of the eternal plant of righteousness, to whom shall be given sevenfold wisdom and knowledge".[31] And in another place Enoch summons his family to give them his spiritual testament, and among his prophecies for the eschatological future he mentions the fact that "the righteous shall arise from their sleep, and wisdom shall arise and be given to them".[32] If the wisdom granted to the apocalyptists corresponds to that promised to the righteous in the days to come, then apocalyptic revelation is one of the first, and necessary, stages in the process of salvation. No wonder, then, that the Qumran-psalmist quite often repeats his thanks for the revelation of secrets

[29] Scholars rightly debate over the question, whether *4 Maccabees* really contains the doctrine of the immortality of the soul. At least, the doctrine of the immortality of the soul is not as straightforwardly expressed there as it is in *2 Maccabees*. See, G. W. Buchanan, "Introduction" to R. H. Charles, *Eschatology*, New York, Schocken Books, 1963, p. xviii.

[30] In an interesting passage in *The Wisdom of Solomon* vii,15-21, the author, who hides behind the name of King Solomon, speaks of his great knowledge, and says, among other things: "For He has given me an unerring knowledge of the things that are, to know the constitution of the world, and the operation of the elements." This indeed, comes very close to the apocalyptic concept of revealed knowledge, and that in the context of wisdom literature!

[31] *1 Enoch* xciii,10. The translation here is that of the Aramaic text which has been found at Qumran. See, M. Black, "The Fragments of the Aramaic Enoch from Qumran", in: *La Littérature Juive entre Tenach et Mischna,* ed. W. C. van Unnik, Leiden, E. J. Brill, 1974, p. 24. Charles's translation of the Ethiopic text reads: "And at its close shall be elected the elect righteous of the eternal plant of righteousness, to receive sevenfold instruction concerning all His creation". Notice the difference between the Aramaic and the Ethiopic texts: While the Aramaic refers to "sevenfold wisdom and knowledge" in general, the Ethiopic text specifies and says: "sevenfold instruction concerning all His creation".

[32] *Ibid.*, xci,10. As has been variously observed, the Ethiopic text here preserves a corrupt order of chapter and verses.

granted to him by God.[33] This assumption of a relation between the revelation of secrets to the apocalyptists and the future revelation of knowledge to the righteous approaches the conclusion maintained by the early gnostics, that knowledge is a *conditio sine qua non* for salvation. Although the gnostic concept of knowledge is much more complex and developed than the one we find in apocalypticism, it still seems that the relation between knowledge and salvation was one of the major elements which Jewish apocalyptic contributed to the development of gnosticism.[34]

C

We have begun our discussion of Jewish apocalyptic with some remarks concerning the place it holds within the framework of Jewish wisdom literature. Before we go on with our discussion, it seems fitting to quote yet another source which significantly bears on the problems raised in the previous section. *The Testament of Job*, which is based on the story of the Biblical Book of Job,[35] mentions at one point the following conversation between Baldas (= Bildad) and Job:[36]

Baldas: ...But if you are really in a stable condition, I shall ask you about something, and if you answer me sensibly at first, I will question you a second time... Or who can ever comprehend the deep things of the Lord and His wisdom so that someone dares to ascribe to the Lord an injustice?... And again I say to you... why do we see the sun rising in the east and setting in the west, and again when we get up early we find the same sun rising in the east?...

Job: ...For who are we to be busying ourselves with heavenly matters, seeing that we are fleshly and have our lot in dust and ashes? Therefore... listen to what I ask you: Food through the mouth, and then water through the mouth is swallowed in the same throat. But when the two fall into the latrine, they are then separated from each other.
Who then divides them?

[33] See, for instance, *The Psalms Scroll* (*Hodayot*; *1 QH*), IV, 27-29; XI, 15-17. Cf. W. D. Davies, "Knowledge in the Dead Sea Scrolls and in *Matthew* xi,25-30", *Harvard Theological Review* XLVI (1953), pp. 113-139.

[34] See I. Gruenwald, in: *Israel Oriental Studies* III (1973), pp. 75 ff.

[35] For an "Annotated Chronological Bibliography" of the various problems involved in the study of *The Testament of Job*, cf. R. Spittler, in: *The Testament of Job according to the SV Text, Greek Text and English Translation*, edited by Robert A. Kraft, Society of Biblical Literature & Scholars' Press, 1974, pp. 17-20.

[36] *The Testament of Job* (see previous note), xxxvi,8-xxxviii,8 (5). The dramatized form is mine.

Baldas: I do not know.
Job: If you do not understand the function of the body, how will you understand the heavenly matters.

Although parts of the arguments, the nature of which we have discussed in the previous section, are here put into the mouth of Job, the passage still goes in line with the basic idea which the Book of Job advocates.

The *Testament of Job* was written most probably at a time when Jewish apocalyptic flourished, and it may be asked whether the tones struck by the writer are not in their own way a kind of reaction against the higher kinds of knowledge which some of the apocalyptists claimed to have received. Of course, one may see in the above quoted conversation between Baldad and Job a mere and innocent reflection of the mood which prevails in the Book of Job. But if one holds this conversation against the light thrown by one of the most famous passages from Ben-Sira, then a different way of looking at the conversation becomes plausible. In *Ben-Sira* iii,18-25 we find the following statements:

...Humble thyself in all greatness of the world
And thou wilt find mercy in the sight of God.
For many are the mercies of God,
And to the humble He revealeth His secret.
Seek not (to understand) what is too wonderful for thee,
And search not out that which is hid from thee.
Meditate upon that which thou must grasp
And be not occupied with that which is hid.
Have naught to do with that which is beyond thee,
For more hath been shown to thee than thou canst understand.
For many are the conceits of the sons of men,
And evil imaginations lead astray.
Where there is no apple of the eye, light is lacking,
And where there is no knowledge wisdom is wanting.[37]

Basically, two contrasting interpretations have been suggested for these verses. According to the one, Ben Sira here simply intends to discourage people from engaging in matters and problems that are

[37] The English translation is that of Box and Oesterley in R. H. Charles, *The Apocrypha and Pseudepigrapha of the Old Testament*, vol. I, p. 325/6. For the textual problems involved in these verses see, H. P. Rüger, *Text und Textform im Hebräischen Sirach*, Beiheft CXII zur *Zeitschrift für die alttestamentliche Wissenschaft*, 1970, pp. 30 ff.

beyond their physical or spiritual reach.[38] According to the other interpretation, which is supported by the contexts in which verses 21 and 22 (seek not... is hid) are quoted in talmudic and midrashic sources,[39] these verses are a straightforward call to refrain from exploring the secrets of nature and of the Deity. Both interpretations are in a way justified, and indeed there is no decisive proof in favour of either. It may, however, be argued, that from the way in which Ben Sira refers to the heavenly translation of Enoch [40] and to the vision of Ezekiel [41] one may well infer, that Ben Sira was familiar with some early kinds of apocalyptic or mystical traditions, and that the above quoted verses from chapter iii were therefore an exhortation directed to the general public to refrain from all kinds of speculations which involved apocalyptic experiences.

If so, two conflicting views may be detected in the ancient Jewish Apocrypha and Pseudepigrapha with regard to the question of the revelation of cosmological secrets. According to one view, represented chiefly in the Enoch corpus of writings, man may receive such supernatural revelations concerning natural phenomena. According to the other view, no such revelations are possible, or at least they should not be desired and trusted. Even if they come to men, they have no relevance to the basic problems of man's existence. And, finally, although we do lack clear literary evidence, there are good reasons to believe that the above mentioned conflicting views were much older and more widely spread in Jewish thought than their documented evidence. As we know, the literary prehistory of apocalypticism is rather vague and the attempts to reconstruct it are highly speculative. It is therefore difficult to tell whether the above mentioned conflict began with the rise of apocalypticism itself or whether it is older, in spite of the fact that the literary evidence for it is no more

---

[38] See Y. Gutman, *The Beginnings of Jewish-Hellenistic Literature* (in Hebrew), Jerusalem, Bialik Institute, 1958, vol. I, p. 173.

[39] See M. Z. Segal, *Sefer Ben Sira Ha-Shalem*, Jerusalem, Bialik Institute, 1958, p. 17/8.

[40] *Ben Sira* xliv,16; xliv,14. For the textual problems see Y. Yadin, *The Ben Sira Scroll from Masada*, Jerusalem, The Israel Exploration Society, 1965, p. 38. See further, J. C. Greenfield, "Prolegomenon" to *op. cit.* (above n. 13), p. xlvi, n. 27; D. Lührmann, "Henoch und die Metanoia", *Zeitschrift für die Neutestamentliche Wissenschaft* LXVI (1975), pp. 103 ff.

[41] *Ben Sira* xlix,8. See I. Gruenwald, "Jewish Mysticism in the Time of the Mishnah and Talmud", in: *Compendia Rerum Judaicorum ad Novum Testamentum*. Forthcoming.

in our hands. Furthermore, what in modern scholarship is rather loosely called "biblical apocalyptic" [42] can only be considered with due reservation as the forerunner of post-biblical, pseudonymous, apocalyptic, and in any case it does not contain any descriptions of heavenly ascensions and the secret cosmological knowledge gained in the course of such alleged ascensions. In addition, although it may seem an overstatement, it still does not fall short of the truth to say that some of the basic attitudes maintained in apocalyptic were formed by some degree of confrontation with some of the prevailing ideas found in Scripture. This particularly holds true, as we are going to see immediately, when one examines some of the utterances found in apocalyptic with regard to biblical prophecy. Thus one may look at the apocalyptic ascensions as a kind of challenge to basic beliefs postulated in Scripture. When we read *Psalm* cxv,16—"The heavens are the Lord's heavens, but the earth he has given to the sons of men"—in combination with *Proverbs* xxx,4—"Who has ascended to heaven and come down"—then it clearly appears that these biblical writers were, so-to-speak, geocentrically minded. And indeed the wisdom of Israel was the Torah—"for that will be your wisdom and your understanding in the sight of the peoples" (*Deuteronomy* iv,6) [43] —and the Torah clearly is on earth: "For this commandment... is not in heaven..." (*ibid.* xxx,11-12). Yet, some of the apocalyptists thought otherwise, and as we are going to see later on, the debate over the question whether heavenly ascensions were possible or not was still carried on in tannaitic circles.

D

The attitude of the apocalyptic writers towards biblical prophecy is somewhat provocatively stated in some of the apocalyptic writings, and particularly so in those of the Qumran community. The Qumranites were justifiably called an apocalyptic community,[44] and although, as far as we know, their apocalyptic experiences were of a more literary character, the contents of their revelations were in many respects similar to those received by the other apocalyptists.

[42] See J. Lindblom, *Die Jesaja-Apokalypse*: *Jes. 24-27*, Lund Universitets Arsskrift, N.F. I, 34, 3, Lund und Leipzig, 1938; J. Schreiner, *Alttestamentliche-jüdische Apokalyptik*, München, Kasel Verlag, 1969.

[43] Cf. M. Weinfeld, *Deuteronomy and the deuteronomic School*, Oxford, Clarendon Press, p. 244 ff.

[44] See chiefly, F. M. Cross Jr., *The Ancient Library of Qumran*, Garden City, New York, Doubleday & Company, 1961, pp. 76-78.

Basically, they claimed that among the revelations given them were the correct explications of Scripture.[45] Some of their writings in fact were eschatological commentaries to Scripture, and in them they believed to have uncovered the exclusive inner meaning and terms of reference of the biblical text.[46] The Qumran people devoted much of their time to the study of the Torah,[47] and if we may generalize certain of their rulings, they were so organized as to ensure that in every group of people there should be at least one priest whose duty it was to study the Law and to lay its explication before the members of the group.[48] The Word of God, they appear to have believed, was given in at least two principle stages of revelation: before and after the formation of the New Covenant in the "Desert of Damascus".[49] The New Covenant did not mean the giving of new Scriptures, but the revelation of special methods of discovering the inner and true sense of the old ones. In fact, the Qumran sectarians believed in a series of additional stages in which this inner sense of Scripture came to the fore. Nothing specific is said about the number of these additional stages and when they would be initiated, but the idea is several times stressed in their writings,[50] and it is juxtaposed to the complementary idea about the various individual degrees in knowledge of Scripture.[51]

---

[45] See H. Braun, *Spätjüdisch-häretischer und frühchristlicher Radikalismus*, Tübingen, J. C. B. Mohr (Paul Siebeck), 1957, vol. I; F. F. Bruce, *Biblical Exegesis in the Qumran Texts*, Grand Rapids, Michigan, 1959; O. Betz, *Offenbarung und Schriftforschung in der Qumransekte*, Tübingen, J. C. B. Mohr (Paul Siebeck), 1960.

[46] See I. Gruenwald, "The Jewish Esoteric Literature in the Time of the Mishnah and Talmud", *Immanuel* IV (1974), pp. 37 ff.

[47] According to *1 QS* (= *The Manual of Discipline*) VI,7 each member of the community had to spend at least one third of the nights of the year in the reading of the Book, in the study of the Law and in the communal meals or gatherings.

[48] *1 QS* VI,3; *CD* (= *The Damascus Covenant*) XIII,2 ff. In both cases the number of the members of the group is ten; but in *1 QS* VIII,1 a group consisting of twelve laymen and three priests is mentioned, while *CD* X,4-6 mentions six laymen and four priests. The age of the officiating priests should be between thirty and sixty (*CD* XIV,7).

[49] See mainly the first four pages of *CD*. For a recent discussion of the various theories with regard to the history of the sect cf., J. Murphy-O'Connor, O.P., "The Essenes and their History", *Revue Biblique* LXXXI (1974), pp. 215 ff.

[50] See, for instance, *1 QS* VIII,15/6; IX,12-14,20.

[51] See particularly, *1 QS* V,23; VI,14,18. It seems that, at least among some of the sectarians, additional means of gradation were applied. Thus in *4 Q* 186 astrological, physiognomic and similar techniques are applied in defining the qualities of those who desired to become members of the sect. See I. Gruenwald, "Further Jewish Physiognomic and Chiromantic Fragments", *Tarbiz* XL (1971),

At its face value the attitude of the Qumranites to Scripture can be viewed as a process of bringing Scripture up-to-date. In their *Pesharim* (= commentaries) they interpreted the biblical verses mainly in the light of events happening in their lifetime or of events which they believed were imminent in the near future. Much of what is found in those *Pesharim* is in the form of what was later on called *Midrash*. But in contradistinction to the material found in the rabbinical midrashic literature many of the Qumran *Pesharim* proclaim themselves to be exclusive revelations of secrets. We shall illustrate the Qumranic *Pesharim*-method by referring to a passage from the *Pesher Habakkuk* (1 QpHab) vii,1-13. The passage has been quoted before by various scholars in order to illustrate the Pesharim-method, yet its radical qualities have not always been adequately stressed. Briefly, what the passage says is, that the *Moreh Ha-Ẓedek* ("the Teacher of Righteousness"), the spiritual leader of the Qumran sect, received information about the true meaning of the prophecy which Habakkuk, the prophet, had received. Referring to *Habakkuk* ii,1-3 the Qumran-commentator says:

> And God told Habakkuk to write down that which would happen to the final generation, but He did not make known to him when time would come to an end. And as for that which He said, *That he who reads it may read speedily*, interpreted this concerns the Teacher of Righteousness, to whom God made known all the mysteries of the words of His servants the prophets... the final age shall be prolonged, and shall exceed all that the prophets have said; for the mysteries of God are astounding... For all the ages of God reach their appointed end as He determines for them in the mysteries of His wisdom.[52]

As a careful reading of the passage shows, it is not only the true meaning of Habakkuk's prophecy that the Teacher of Righteousness received, but also some additional information concerning the prolongation of the eschatological end. The words uttered by the prophet contained secrets the revelation of which was reserved for the Teacher of Righteousness. Whether Habakkuk himself was aware of the fact that he was actually talking in riddles or in a code that had to be deciphered, or whether he was quite ignorant of the inner layers of meaning which had to be attached to his prophecy, it is clear that the revelation of that secret meaning had to wait for

pp. 301 ff. See also the thoroughgoing discussion of J. Licht in *Tarbiẓ* XXXV (1966), pp. 18-26.

[52] English translation: G. Vermes, *The Dead Sea Scrolls in English*, Harmondsworth, Penguin Books, 1962, p. 236/7.

the spiritual leader of the sect. All this, the passage repeatedly says, was according to the wondrous secrets of the Deity. What practically made God reveal to the Teacher the inner mysteries of the Habakkuk-prophecies was the approaching time of fulfilment. In the age to which Habakkuk had assumably referred to in his prophecy, the time was ripe for making the necessary exegetical connections between the words of the prophecy and the events to which they were thought to refer.

The prophetic utterances had to await an apocalyptic revelation for their inner truth to be made explicit. For the first time we hear that Scripture cannot, and should not, be read only for its external meaning. This awareness of the existence of an inner truth was complemented by the revelation of that very truth. If there was any crisis with regard to prophecy because people saw that a lot of what was the prophetic word of God remained unfulfilled, then the apocalyptic process of updating prophecy was to remove the scepticism of the people.[53] But to see in the written word of God a vessel containing some inner truth apart from the obvious external meaning —is the essence of the esoteric approach to Scripture. Apocalypticism was often described as being esoteric in nature [54] mainly because it pertained to be an exclusive revelation of secrets.[55] Added to this was the pseudepigraphic way of writing, which was sometimes interpreted as the result of the desire to enhance the element of secrecy. Of course, one cannot altogether dismiss the exclusiveness and the secrecy of the revelation, or even the pseudepigraphic way of writing; they are weighty factors in shaping the special qualities of apocalypticism.[56] But what makes some of the apocalyptic books esoteric as they are, is the special attitude maintained in them regarding their relationship to the previous revelation in Scripture.

"Esotericism", thus, is here taken to mean a special attitude towards Scripture and the explication of its content. The passage from *Pesher Habakkuk* makes it sufficiently clear that Scripture is considered as a code, the indications for the decipherment of which are given in a special revelation. As such, it is a classic example of an esoteric text.

---

[53] See P. von der Osten-Sacken, *op. cit.* (above n. 14), p. 33.

[54] See D. S. Russell, *The Method and Message of Jewish Apocalyptic*, London, SCM Press, 1964, pp. 107 ff.

[55] See A. Böhlig, *Mysterion und Wahrheit*, Leiden, E. J. Brill, 1968, pp. 3-40.

[56] See M. Hengel, "Anonymität, Pseudepigraphie und 'Literarische Fälschung' in der jüdisch-hellenistischen Literatur", *Entretiens sur l'Antiquité Classique* XVIII (1972), pp. 191 ff.

The degree to which the apocalyptic revelation finds itself disentangled from and independent of the biblical text on which it leans varies from one apocalyptic text to the other. In the Qumran *Pesharim* eschatological and messianic meanings are read into the biblical text. In other words, historical references are attributed to texts which seem to lack precise historical specifications. Comparatively speaking, however, the *Pesharim* do not entail too drastic changes or additions to the biblical text. They are the product of a group which believed it lived in an age of the fulfilment of Scripture, and of the desire to view the events of that age as the fulfilment of Scripture.

However, the esoteric element of the *Pesharim* is not as radical as the one we encounter in other, pseudepigraphic, apocalyptic books.[57] A typical example of a pseudepigraphic book in which esotericism receives noteworthy radical dimensions is the Book of Jubilees.[58] The book pretends to be the revelation given by the Angel of the Divine Presence to Moses on Mount Sinai. It tells the story of the world from the days of the creation till the theophany on Mount Sinai, and in many respects it poses as a rival version to the one found in Scripture. It is exactly here that the esoteric qualities of the Book of Jubilees come to the fore. Reading the book, one gets the clear impression that the author wants to convince his readers of the existence of two parallel versions of the biblical story: the one, the exoteric revelation given by God himself and recorded in Scripture, and the other, the esoteric one given by the angel and recorded in the Book of Jubilees. The very fact of the revelation of the Book of Jubilees can be interpreted to mean that there are so-to-speak two complementary versions of the truth: the one given exoterically to the whole of the People of Israel, and the other given esoterically to the initiate alone.

The essential difference between the exoteric revelation of Scripture and the esoteric one in *Jubilees* lies in a variety of details. In the eyes of the author of *Jubilees*, the story found in *Genesis* and in *Exodus* seemed to lack essential details which pointed to a recognizable guiding idea. Hence, it was the task of the Book of Jubilees to dis-

---

[57] The esoteric qualities of the Qumran writings have been discussed also by H. Braun, *op. cit.* (above n. 45). But Braun limits his understanding of esotericism to the exclusiveness of the revelation.

[58] In spite of a considerable number of studies concerned with the dating and the evaluation of the book, many of the more essential problems which the book raises for the scholar are still unsolved.

close those details and inner ideological patterns that were believed to underlie everything that is told in these two books in Scripture. We need not enter here a detailed discussion of these ideological patterns, but it may be safely assumed that the eschatological idea of the purpose and the direction in the history of the world and that of the People of Israel is one of the guiding ideas of the book.[59] Only with the disclosure of those patterns and ideas the scriptural story was believed to receive its true meaning and perspective. This is the theory that underlies the Book of Jubilees. No event in the history of the world and of the People of Israel could be properly understood and evaluated unless it conceptually and practically became part of the underlying scheme the details of which are revealed in the book. A particular sense of direction and purpose which among other things was revealed in the Book of Jubilees was believed to add extra dimensions to the scriptural story. These dimensions were withheld or else not explicitly and manifestly expressed in Scripture. They were revealed in a special way to Moses on Mount Sinai, and henceforth their revelation was restricted to a limited number of those who were to be guided by them in their daily life, beliefs and practices.

Thus, what really gives the Book of Jubilees its unique esoteric character is neither the secrecy of its revelation nor its exclusiveness. Even the pseudepigraphic attribution of the book to the Angel of the Countenance cannot epitomize the esoteric quality of the book. All these factors should be viewed only as formal aspects in qualifying esotericism. Where the real qualities of esotericism come in this case to the fore is in the contents of the new revelations and their relation to the previous revelation in Scripture. The discovery of the underlying structures is the basic component in the new revelation as we find it in *Jubilees*, and it is imposed therein on the biblical story in various forms, such as the periodization into jubilees of history and in the manner of practising the religious Law.[60] In addition, and this certainly is the most crucial point of all, the Book of Jubilees explicitly advocates a solar calendar as opposed to the lunar calendar that was believed to be implied in Scripture and officially practised

---

[59] See G. L. Davenport, *The Eschatology of the Book of Jubilees*, Leiden, E. J. Brill, 1971.

[60] The subject of the Halakhah in the Book of Jubilees was treated in Ch. Albeck, *Das Buch Jubiläen und die Halacha*, Berlin, 1930, see further, G. Vermes, "Sectarian Matrimonial Halakhah in the Damascus Rule", *Journal of Jewish Studies* XXV (1974), pp. 197-202.

in its time.[61] What all this amounts to is a process of rewriting Scripture. And since this rewritten version of the biblical story is revealed to Moses himself, the problems that arise are as sharp and bewildering as one can imagine.

As Professor Scholem has rightly observed,[62] it was only natural for Jewish groups who propagated dissident views to base their views and ideas on Scripture. This was generally done by claiming an exclusive revelation of the true meaning of Scripture. Whether this so-called true meaning of Scripture was presented to the public in the form of a running commentary or in a rewritten version of Scripture makes no real difference, particularly so if both are attributed to some kind of supernatural revelation. Thus it may be concluded that esotericism should be qualified more by virtue of the content of the revelation than by the formal, and mainly literary, modes of presentation. The content of the revelation is mostly connected with Scripture, and claims to expose the latent, inner and exclusive sense of Scripture. The authority of an angel is in this case an almost inevitable ingredient, all the more so when to it is added the authority of one of the illustrious sages of antiquity to whom the angel presented the revelation.

E

It must, however, be noted that not all the pseudepigraphic books are necessarily of an esoteric nature in our sense of the term. A notable example of an apocalyptic book which has no full esoteric qualities is *4 Ezra*. Although the book is pseudepigraphically attributed to Ezra the Scribe, and contains angelic revelations, it nevertheless does not pretend to uncover systematically hidden layers of any specific scriptural passages. In addition, the book contains a well-defined eschatological scheme, but, as it does not always bear a direct relation to Scripture, it cannot be called esoteric in the sense in which we have defined esotericism in *Pesher Habakkuk* and in *Jubilees*.

Apocalyptic, as we saw, could, but did not necessarily, mean the re-writing of Scripture. *Jubilees* certainly rewrites Scripture but so does also *Pseudo-Philo Liber Antiquitatum Biblicarum*,[63] which tells its

---

[61] See most recently, S. Zeitlin, *Studies in the Early History of Judaism*, New York, Ktav Publishing House, vol. I (1973), pp. 183-211; and further vol. II (1974), pp. 116-164.

[62] See above n. 4.

[63] See lately, D. J. Harrington, "The Original Language of *Pseudo Philo's Liber Antiquitatum Biblicarum*", *Harvard Theological Review* LXIII (1970), pp. 503 ff.;

own version of what happened from the days of the creation of the world till the days of King Saul. But, while the Book of Jubilees poses as an angelic revelation, it presses some kind of additional ideological pattern on history and on religious practice, and this by making manifest alleged hidden meanings of Scripture, the Book of the Antiquities is more in the manner of a running midrash, which adds or subtracts from the biblical account of events, but adds no ideological schemes to the manifest content of Scripture. Above all, it does not claim angelic authority for itself. Yet, there are several passages in the Book of Antiquities which freely rewrite Biblical stories,[64] and hence its partial resemblence at least to *Jubilees*. Admittedly, the process of rewriting Scripture was widely spread and applied, and what characterizes the esoteric apocalyptic way of rewriting Scripture therefore is its claim to be an exclusive supernatural revelation regarding the secret meaning and significance of the scriptural text. As a matter of fact, traces of rewriting Scripture can already be detected in Scripture itself: the Deuteronomist and the Chronicler are two famous examples of that. In a wider sense one can regard the writings of Philo as drastic examples of rewriting Scripture, though his allegorical method of exegesis involved additional and complicated ways of interpretation.[65] Even Josephus Flavius, who wanted to reconstruct the ancient history of the People of Israel in his *Jewish Antiquities*, applied to a considerable extent the method of rewriting Scripture. And, finally, the rabbinical midrash-literature contains passages which, *de facto* at least, render Scripture in a rewritten form.[66] But in none of these does the re-written product claim to be a secret, angelic, revelation of the ultimate meaning of Scripture.

The process of rewriting Scripture thus turns out to be a widespread and acknowledged method in biblical exegesis, and is not restricted to esoteric writings. From Judaism the method was trans-

---

idem, *The Hebrew Fragments of Pseudo-Philo's Liber Antiquitatum Biblicarum Preserved in the Chronicles of Jerahmeel*, Missoula, Montana, Society of Biblical Literature, 1974. A. Zeron, "Einige Bemerkungen zu M. F. Collins 'The Hidden Vessels in Samaritan Traditions'", *Journal for the Study of Judaism* IV (1974), pp. 165-168, repeats the theory that one can trace antisamaritan polemic in the book.

[64] Such as the Prayer of Moses in xii,8-9, and more emphatically even in the story of Bilam's blessings in xviii,10 ff.

[65] For a good description of Philo's method of biblical exegesis see, R. Williamson, *Philo and the Epistle to the Hebrews*, Leiden, E. J. Brill, 1970.

[66] This aspect in rabbinical midrash has not yet been studied.

ferred to Christian writers, and especially to the writers of Gnosticism.[67] Several of the major texts of Gnosticism, some of which have been found at Nag Hammadi, based their subject matter on biblical stories, notably those found in the first chapters of *Genesis*, and presented them in a rewritten form.[68] What is more, most of these gnostic texts are in one way or another attributed to supernatural revelations, and at least in one of them we find the angel saying that the new revelation is not as Moses said.[69] It is here that the delicate borderline between esotericism and heresy has been crossed. By attributing the revelation to an angel who pertains to disclose the innermost secrets implied in the scriptural text almost everything that a writer wanted to propagate could be said. Since everything bore the trademark of an exclusive secret there was neither limit nor criterion as to what should or could be said. Thus, to come back to Jewish apocalyptic, a considerable amount of mythical material could find its way into that literature. Generally, as we know, Scripture maintained a reserved and hesitant attitude towards mythological material. At least, very little of ancient mythology found its way into Scripture.[70] Apocalypticism, however, could digest almost everything, particularly so if it contributed to furthering the ideological purposes of the writer, and had the authority of an angel and of antiquity.

Thus, some of the apocalyptists preached the existence of dualistic forces in the world.[71] We find in apocalypticism a well developed angelology which, most likely, derived a good deal of its characteristic features from foreign sources. These sources, whatever their nature and quality, reached the apocalyptists in a variety of ways, most of which are no more recognizable. Yet, the place they succeeded in occupying in apocalyptic is so dominant as to give the whole of this literature some of its idiosyncratic character. What is

---

[67] See R. M. Grant, *Gnosticism and Early Christianity*, New York, Columbia University Press, 1959, pp. 32 ff.

[68] Two important examples are, *The Hypostasis of the Archons*, ed. R. A. Bullard, Berlin, Walter de Gruyter & Co., 1970; and *Die koptisch-gnostische Schrift ohne Titel aus Codex II von Nag Hammadi*, ed. A. Böhlig and P. Labib, Berlin, Akademie Verlag, 1962. See further, below Chapter Four, n. 62.

[69] See *Apocryphon Johannis*, ed. S. Giversen, Copenhagen, Prostant Apud Munksgaard, 1963, plates 61,20; 70,22; 71,3; 77,6.

[70] For a recent discussion of the mythological elements that found their way into Scripture see F. M. Cross, *Canaanite Myth and Hebrew Epic*, Cambridge, Massachusetts, Harvard University Press, 1973.

[71] For a detailed discussion of the dualism of the Qumran sect see, I. Gruenwald in: *Israel Oriental Studies* III (1973), pp. 77 ff.

so outstanding in this mythological material in general and in the angelology in particular is once again the fact that it poses as the real, true and inner meaning of Scripture. Scripture is rewritten in such a way as to include the whole lot of these foreign elements. The legitimation of this material comes, as we saw, from the fact that it has the authority of the angelic revelation, and partly also from the fact that the revelation is—fictitiously so—given to one of the sages of scriptural times.[72]

The conclusion that can be reached from the previous discussion is, that apocalypticism transcended the world of Scripture not only in supplying information which is not explicitly contained therein, but also in attempting to open to man, at least to a chosen elite of the People of Israel, a wider range of emotional and intellectual experience. Whatever purposes apocalypticism consciously served in the eyes of those who cultivated its ideas and forms of expression, it also paved the way for the experiences and literature of the mystical circles from the time of the Tannaim onwards. But before we turn to the Jewish mysticism of the time of the Tannaim and Amoraim, we shall look at the mystical passages found in some of the apocalyptic books.

---

[72] Unfortunately L. Hartman, *Prophesy Interpreted*, Lund, C. W. K. Gleerup, 1966, softens the theological radicalism of apocalyptic, and this mainly because he does not pay full attention to the esoteric qualities of that literature.

CHAPTER TWO

THE MYSTICAL ELEMENTS IN APOCALYPTIC

A

In the previous chapter we discussed several elements of Jewish apocalyptic in the light of some characteristic notions found in biblical Prophecy and Wisdom. It could be noticed that the writer subscribed to the view, that apocalyptic cannot be adequately explained in the light of *either* Prophecy *or* Wisdom.[1] Apocalyptic is much too complex a phenomenon to be explained by an either/or-theory. Nor can justice be done to the phenomenon if only *one* central quality is selected as its more characteristic feature, and the one that best explains it. Prophecy and Wisdom both had their respective share in the formation of apocalyptic, but there were also other factors which contributed in their own ways to endow apocalyptic with its idiosyncratic shape and content. Hence, the present chapter will be devoted to a discussion of the mystical elements in apocalyptic. Particular attention will be given to those apocalyptic books which describe heavenly ascensions and contain relatively detailed accounts of visions in which the God and His hosts of angels appear to the apocalyptists.

These mystical visions too had their antecedents in biblical literature, yet the way these visions are described in apocalyptic, and also the place they occupy there, make it clear that a new religious mood and interest are pervasive in these books. It would be difficult to assess with certainty the role and place that these mystical visions occupied within the general apocalyptic experience. What, in any event, seems safe to say is, that in comparison to the parallel material in Scripture, the mystical visions found in apocalyptic literature are much more intense and elaborate in the embellishment of the description. The passages in Scripture which contain such visions are: *1 Kings* xxii,19;

[1] In recent years it was G. von Rad, *Theologie des Alten Testaments*, München, Ch. Kaiser Verlag, 1966, Band II, p. 327, who advocated the Wisdom-origin of apocalyptic: "die apokalyptischen Schriften . . . in der Überlieferung der Weisheit wurzeln".

Isaiah vi,1 ff.; and *Ezekiel* i; iii,22-24; viii,1 ff.; x.[2] In a broader sense one can include here the theophany at Mount Sinai (*Exodus* xix,16-18; xx,15-18; xxiv,16-18; *Deuteronomy* v,19-24), and the prologue to *Job*. Finally, we find the vision of *Daniel* vii,9-10, which evidently is in line with the visions described in *Isaiah* and *Ezekiel*, but because of its date of composition is already considered as apocalyptic literature. Summing up certain features in the theophany-tradition in the early history of the People of Israel, F. M. Cross says that "It is not coincidental that the language of theophany and the imagery of revelation derived from the mythology of the storm-God largely fell out of use, beginning in the ninth century, and including the two centuries to follow, in prophetic Yahwism. The prophets chose another language, other imagery with which to describe their intercourse with Yahweh, drawn as we have seen from the concept of the messenger of the Council of 'El... Nevertheless, they used a refined or purged language of revelation, because Yahweh, so to say, no longer used the storm as a mode of self-manifestation".[3] Professor Cross obviously has in mind the difference in the language and the imagery between such theophanies as those described in *2 Samuel* xxii,8-16, on the one hand, and those described in *Isaiah* and *Ezekiel*, on the other. But schematizations whenever they are made should be applied with caution, and it seems that *Ezekiel* i,4, for instance, has still something in common with the storm-God theophanies. And although God is described in the theophany of *2 Samuel* xxii as riding the stormy clouds, He still occupies there a Palace (*Hekhal*; *ibid.*, v.7) as He does in *Isaiah* vi,1.[4]

There is a vast literature in which the various types of biblical theophany are extensively discussed.[5] We may, therefore, immediately

[2] A similar vision is referred to in xliii,3-4; but the vision in viii,2 is most probably that of an angel. Compare also *Daniel* x,5-6.

[3] F. M. Cross, *Canaanite Myth and Hebrew Epic*, Cambridge, Mass., Harvard University Press, 1973, p. 191.

[4] It is useless to enter here the discussion whether Isaiah saw the *Hekhal* in heaven or on earth in the temple in Jerusalem. A rather fantastic view on the subject is expressed by A. Aptowitzer in *Tarbiz* II (1931), p. 144/5. According to Aptowitzer, Isaiah actually saw the *Hekhal* in the Jerusalem-Temple but in the course of the vision Isaiah himself translated the whole scenery unto heaven!

[5] Some of the more recent extensive studies of the subject of biblical theophanies are: J. Lindblom, "Theophanies in Holy Places in Hebrew Religion", *Hebrew Union College Annual* XXXII (1961), pp. 91-106; J. Jeremias, *Theophanie: Die Geschichte einer alttestamentlichen Gattung*, Neukirchen-Vluyn, Neukirchener Verlag, 1965; F. M. Cross, *op. cit.*, pp. 147 ff.

turn to those visions in Scripture which are more mystically oriented, that is, visions in which God appears to man in a man-like form and seated upon a throne. The relevant visions in this respect are those in *2 Kings*, in *Isaiah*, in *Ezekiel* and in *Daniel*. Taken together these visions display the following characteristic features:

a. God is sitting on a throne;
b. He has the appearance of a man (*Ezekiel*) and particularly that of an old, white-haired man (*Daniel*);
c. God is sitting in a palace (*2 Kings*, *Isaiah*, and *Daniel*);[6]
d. Fire occupies an important position in the vision (*Ezekiel*, *Daniel* and indirectly also in *Isaiah*);[7]
e. God is accompanied by angels who minister to Him (*2 Kings*, *Isaiah*, *Ezekiel*, and *Daniel*);
f. The angels recite hymns (*Isaiah* and *Ezekiel*).

All these elements became major components in the mystical visions found in apocalyptic and later on in the Merkavah visions of the *Hekhalot* literature (= the mystical writings of the time of the Talmud). If one can speak of a Jewish mystical tradition that had more or less unified qualities, then, it seems, the above enumerated features are the more characteristic ones in that tradition. This is not to say that these elements are all simultaneously found and equally stressed in all the visions we know of. Although later visionaries allowed themselves freedom of imagination, it may be said that they followed some kind of standard, the nature of which was basically modelled on these features.

We shall now turn to an analysis of the various mystical visions in apocalyptic literature. Our attention will be given chiefly to those elements in the visions which were dominant in later developments of Jewish mysticism.

---

[6] As for Isaiah see above n. 4. The visions in *2 Kings* and in *Daniel* do not explicitly mention a palace, but there is nothing in them that contradicts the assumption that a divine palace is actually presupposed there. In *Ezekiel*, however, it is clear that God is moving about in the cosmos. The visions in *Amos* vii,7 and ix,1 seem to belong to a different type of theophany: the allegorical elements in them is predominant.

[7] Decisive in this respect was the theophany on Mount Sinai where God revealed Himself in the Great Fire (*Deuteronomy* iv,7). See E. E. Urbach, "The Traditions about Merkabah Mysticism in the Tannaitic Period", *Studies in Mysticism and Religion Presented to Gershom G. Scholem*, Jerusalem, Magnes Press, 1967, Hebrew Section, pp. 7 ff.—It should be noted that from *Ezekiel* onwards crystal and sapphire play a major role in mystical visions. We shall come back to this point soon.

B

First, we will deal with the two visions contained in the *Ethiopic Enoch* xiv and lxxi. These two visions do not belong to the same literary stratum, and it is generally believed that the second one belongs to the latest part of the book. What, however, they have in common is, that in contradistinction to the mystical visions in Scripture, they maintain that the visions were granted in the course of heavenly ascensions.[8] It has been noted in the previous chapter that according to Scripture nothing attainable to man is to be searched for in heaven. Everything that man should know can be revealed in such a manner that people need not search for extraordinary and supernatural experiences. Unfortunately, lack of literary evidence makes it difficult for us to state with certainty when heavenly ascensions were first systematically practised in Judaism. But, what can be said is, that at least at the time of the composition of the Book of Enoch, the practice was already seriously considered by the people to whom the book was addressed.

The vision of *1 Enoch* xiv comes in the middle of the scene where Enoch is described as having ascended unto heaven to intercede on behalf of the fallen angels. It is introduced in xiv,8 where Enoch says that in his dream-vision he saw himself uplifted to heaven by clouds.[9] The first thing which Enoch says he saw in heaven is "a wall which is built of crystals and surrounded by tongues of fire" (xiv,9). As it turned out to be, the wall surrounded a house. The house, no doubt, is identical with the heavenly divine palace,[10] yet

[8] Aramaic fragments of this vision as they were found in Cave 4 at Qumran are now published by J. T. Milik, *The Books of Enoch: Aramaic Fragments of Qumran Cave 4*, Oxford, Clarendon Press, 1976, pp. 348-351. Unfortunately, the texts are too fragmentary to draw any conclusions from them, and Milik's attempts to reconstruct the text cannot be discussed here. According to J. Daniélou, *Théologie du Judéo-Christianisme*, Tournai, Desclée & Co., 1958, pp. 131 ff., heavenly ascensions are the trade mark of Jewish-Christian apocalyptic. Yet, this view has its obvious tendentious shortcomings.

[9] The details of the ascent are not sufficiently clear, though the whole description most likely derives from *2 Kings* ii,11. See further *1 Enoch* xxxix,3; lii,1; lxx,2; *2 Enoch* iii,1 (version A). In midrashic literature it is told that Moses ascended to heaven in (!) a cloud: *Pesikta Rabbati*, ed. M. Friedmann, 96b (= A. Jellinek, *Bet Ha-Midrasch*, vol. I, p. 59). In *Tanḥumā* (ed. Buber), "*Ẓav*", Parag. 16, it is said that the just ones ascend to heaven in clouds which God supplies for that purpose.

[10] The analysis of this vision as found in H. Bietenhard, *Die himmlische Welt im Urchristentum und Spätjudentum*, Tübingen, J. C. B. Mohr (Paul Siebeck), 1951, p. 54, by no means exhausts the material.

the way it is described requires some comment. The house, its walls, its floor and its groundwork, was built of crystal.[11] Now, this description of the crystal-like appearance of the walls most probably derives from *Ezekiel* i,22, where the prophet says that "Over the heads of the living creatures there was the likeness of a firmament, shining like crystal".[12] This description of what the walls of the house looked like is quite rare, and actually its main parallel is to be found in two places connected with the visions of the *Hekhalot* mystics.[13] What equally strikes the eye in the sight of the walls is the fact, that they are surrounded by fiery flames. Twelve times is the fire mentioned in this vision, and this naturally enhances the numinous quality of the vision.[14] The fact that Enoch went into the tongues of fire without being burned could be reminiscent of *Isaiah* xliii,2—"when you walk through fire you shall not be burned etc."—with all its eschatological connotations. But it also bears resemblance to *2 Enoch* xxii, where it is told of Enoch that he was divested of his earthly garments and clad in heavenly ones so as to protect him against the various

---

[11] The Greek fragments of *1 Enoch* here use two separate terms: of the wall surrounding the house (verse 9) it is said that it was built ἐν λίθοις χαλάζης (= of hailstones; cf. *Isaiah* xxx,30), while of the walls mentioned in verse 10 it is said that they were in the likeness of snow (*Telag* is the Aramaic term used in the text published by Milik). The existence of hailstones in heaven could well be inferred from *Joshuʿa* x,11 and *Job* xxxviii,22; see also *1 Enoch* lxix,23, to say nothing of the fact that hail comes from the sky! See further *Ezekiel* xxxviii,22; *Revelation* xvi,21. Cf. also *Mechilta d'Rabbi Ismael*, ed. Horovitz-Rabin, p. 111. *Job* xxxviii,22 likewise mentions the heavenly origin of snow. In *Bavli Ḥagigah* 12b, the treasuries of snow and hail are said to be found in the sixth heaven, *Makhon*, while *2 Enoch* v,1 locates the treasuries of hail in the first heaven! Rivers of hail and treasuries of snow are also mentioned in *Maʿaseh Merkavah* (ed. G. Scholem, *Jewish Gnosticism, Merkabah Mysticism, and Talmudic Tradition*: Appendix C, pp. 103 ff.) paragraphs 3 (p. 103) and 10 (p. 108; rivers of hail only). See further *Tanḥumā*, "Terumah", Parag. 11. The heavenly snow is actually considered as the material out of which the earth was created: *Pirke de-Rabbi Eliezer*, ch. iii; Rabbi Yoḥannan in *Bereshit Rabbā*, ed. Theodor-Albeck, p. 75. Cf. H. F. Weiss, *Untersuchungen zur Kosmologie des hellenistischen und palästinischen Judentum*, Berlin, Akademie Verlag, 1966, pp. 96-97. The material collected in L. I. J. Stadelmann, *The Hebrew Conception of the World*, Rome, Biblical Institute Press, 1970, pp. 118-119, by no means does justice to the wealth of material available.

[12] Thus according to the LXX. The Hebrew text here implies a slightly different sense: "awesome crystal". All this provided that the Hebrew *qeraḥ* really is the equivalent to the Greek 'krystalos'. See however above n. 8!

[13] *Hekhalot Zutreti* (quoted and translated in G. Scholem, *op. cit.*, p. 15), and *Bavli Ḥagigah* 14b. We shall come back to this point in greater detail in the next chapter.

[14] Urbach, *art. cit.*, p. 18.

dangers that might befall a mortal who is bodily translated onto heaven.[15] Professor Scholem has rightly explained such experiences in terms of a mystical transfiguration,[16] and they certainly belong to the heart of the apocalyptic and mystical experiences.[17] In any event, Enoch had here to pass twice through such fiery flames, first when he passed through the wall and then when he entered the house.

When he entered the house, Enoch was overwhelmed with fright, and typical of a state of extreme terror he felt cold and hot almost simultaneously (verses 14-15).[18] Then, as it turned out, he saw another house, which was within the first one.[19] This second house, Enoch says, "excelled in splendour and magnificence" the first one, but generally speaking, apart from the ceiling, it more or less resembled the first one.[20] The second house contained the Throne of God,

---

[15] See, similarly, *Ascension d'Isaie*, ix,9, ed. E. Tisserant, Paris, 1909. See further J. Maier, "Das Gefärdungsmotiv bei der Himmelsreise in der jüdischen Apokalyptik und 'Gnosis'", *Kairos* V (1963), pp. 18-40.

[16] Scholem, *op. cit.*, p. 60. To the parallel material which Scholem collected there, pp. 56-64 and 132, one should add *Pistis Sophia*, English Translation G. R. S. Mead, London, John M. Watkins, 1963, p. 18, where Jesus is reported to tell his disciples that he had clad himself in special light-vestures by the help of which he succeeded in passing the various heavenly evil-beings without being harmed by them.

[17] M. Smith, *Clement of Alexandria and a Secret Gospel of Mark*, Cambridge, Mass., Harvard University Press, 1973, pp. 243-244, sees in the synoptic tradition about the Transfiguration of Jesus a piece of key information about the mystical activity of Jesus. Yet, the way Professor Smith infers the kind of baptism-mysticism which Jesus alledgedly practised seems to be rather hypothetical and cannot be regarded conclusive.

[18] This terror which seizes the apocalyptic visionary is typical almost of all the apocalyptic and mystical visions. A notable exception to the rule is *Revelation* iv, where no such feeling is reported. We shall come back to this vision later on.

[19] H. Bietenhard, *op. cit.* p. 54 sees in the first house "eine Vorhalle". Yet, from the *Hekhalot* literature we know that the seven palaces in the seventh heaven were like "a room within a room". See, for instance, *Hekhalot Rabbati* xv,1. However, the Aramaic fragments of *1 Enoch* published by Milik (above, n. 8) make the impression that the visionary saw only one "house". Compare the expression *ḥadrei hekhal demamah* in *Hekhalot Rabbati* iii,1 and vii,5. It should be noticed that the term *demamah* does not imply here quietness but a whisper. See E. Y. Kutscher, in: *Archiv of the New Dictionary of Rabbinical Literature*, I, Ramat-Gan, Bar-Ilan University, 1972, pp. 77-78 (in Hebrew). See further *Sifre to Numbers* (ed. Horowitz), p. 56, where the angels are said to speak in low voice.

[20] While it is said of the ceiling of the first house that it was "like the path of the stars and the lightnings, and between them were fiery cherubim, and their heaven was clear as water", the ceiling of the second house is only briefly described: "its ceiling also was flaming fire". It should be noticed (1) that cherubim are seen only in the ceiling of the first house; (2) the "heaven" in connection with the first ceiling is not quite clear; and (3) both descriptions are only loosely

and of it Enoch says: "its appearance was as crystal,[21] and the wheels thereof as the shining sun,[22] and there was the vision of Cherubim" [23] (verse 18). From underneath the throne there came out streams of fire [24] which made it difficult for Enoch to look at the Throne.[25]

From the vision of the Throne Enoch passes on to the vision of the Godhead. He says that "the Great Glory [26] sat thereon, and His raiment shone more brightly than the sun and was whiter than the snow.[27] None of the angels could enter and behold His face by

influenced by the way Ezekiel describes the firmament which he saw above the heads of the Creatures.

[21] The description of the "lofty throne" (θρόνον ὑψηλόν) derives from *Isaiah* vi,1 (LXX: θρόνου ὑψηλου) and also from *Ezekiel* i,26. The "crystal" of which the throne is made of is unique. *Ezekiel* says that the throne was "in appearance like sapphire" (i,26; x,1). Sapphire was the stone which, as a matter of general rule, the throne was described as being made of. See *Exodus* xxiv, 10; *Bavli Ḥulin* 89a: "...and the firmament is like the sapphire, and the sapphire is like the throne of the Glory". Similarly it is said of the rod of Moses that it was made of sapphire; *Tanḥumā*, "*Beshalaḥ*", xxi. The Tablets of the Law were likewise said to be hewn from the Sapphire (*Tanḥumā*, "*Ki Tisā*", xxix). At one place we also hear that the ark was made of sapphire! (*Tanḥumā*, "*Beshalaḥ*", xxi; compare *Exodus* xxv,10 ff.). As for the colour of the sapphire, it is generally considered to be blue (*Bavli Ḥulin* 89a: "... since blue is like the sea, and the sea looks like the firmament, and the firmament is like the sapphire, and the sapphire is like the throne of the Glory"). But in one place (*Lekaḥ Tov, ad Exodus* xxiv,10) it is said that the sapphire is white! See further, G. Scholem, "Farben und ihre Symbolik in der jüdischen Überlieferung und Mystik", in: *Judaica* III, Frankfurt a.M., Suhrkamp Verlag, 1970, pp. 117-119.

[22] See *Ezekiel* i,16 and *Daniel* vii,9.

[23] There is a vast literature dealing with the cherubim. Still relevant is the discussion of W. F. Albright, "What Were the Cherubim", *Biblical Archeologist* I (1938), pp. 1-3. See further P. Schäfer, *Rivalität zwischen Engeln und Menschen*, Berlin, Walter der Gruyter, 1975, pp. 18-20.

[24] *1 Enoch* xiv,19: ποταμοὶ πυρὸς φλεγόμενοι. Compare *Daniel* vii,10, where only one ποταμὸς πυρός is mentioned. In *3 Enoch* xix and xxxiii four and seven streams of fire are mentioned respectively. In *Maʿaseh Merkavah* iii (Scholem, *Jewish Gnosticism* etc., p. 103) twelve thousand streams of fire are referred to, while *Revelation* iv,5 has no streams of fire at all. See also G. Scholem, *ibid.*, pp. 56-57.

[25] The idea that no human being can see the face of God and survive is first expressed in *Exodus* xxxiii,20. *Hekhalot Rabbati* xi,4 contains a beautiful description of how the four Creatures come out from underneath of the Throne and dance before God. It is said there that in the course of their dance they uncover their faces, while God covers His own. In another place there (viii,2) it is said that he who looks at God is immediately destroyed. Even the angels cannot serve Him but for one day "since they were utterly weakened and their face was completely burned; their heart was totally confused and their eyes were darkened". (viii,2).

[26] xiv,20: ἡ δόξα ἡ μεγάλη.

[27] God's raiment is a central theme both in Jewish apocalyptic and in Merkavah

reason of the magnificence of the glory, and no flesh could behold Him.[28] The flaming fire was round about Him, and a great fire stood before Him, and none around could draw nigh Him".[29] At the end, Enoch describes the angels that minister unto God: "ten thousand times ten thousand (stood) before Him, yet He needed no counsellor.[30] And the most holy ones who were nigh to him did not leave by night nor depart from Him".[31]

We have extensively quoted from this vision of Enoch, since it is the oldest Merkavah vision we know of from the literature outside of the canonical Scriptures. It contains, on the one hand, several motives already found in the "Merkavah" visions in Scripture, and, on the other hand, there is already a great deal in this vision that became typical of later Merkavah visions. Indeed, one can consider this particular vision a model-vision of Merkavah mysticism. Although in the *Hekhalot* literature certain magicotheurgic practices are added, the Enoch-vision of chapter xiv contains in principle many important mystical elements. To begin with—as we have already said—it presupposes a heavenly ascent. But—quite unlike other heavenly visions in apocalyptic literature and in the *Hekhalot* mysticism—no angel is reported here to accompany Enoch on his heavenly journey.[32] This fact, that Enoch makes this heavenly trip with no angelic accompaniment, is even more emphatically stressed when Enoch himself says (verse 21): "None of the angels could enter and behold His face".[33] In this respect Enoch is here more privileged than all the angels, and even more so when he finds himself addressed

mysticism. See G. Scholem, *Jewish Gnostisicm* etc., pp. 56 ff. It should be noticed that contrary to *Daniel* vii,9 and *1 Enoch* xlvi,1 and lxxi,10, Enoch does not describe here the hair of God. See further *Revelation* i,14.

[28] See above note 25. See also *Hekhalot Rabbati* iii,4.

[29] Compare *Deuteronomy* iv,36; v,21-24. See also above note 7.

[30] It is interesting to notice, that in both Merkavah visions in *1 Enoch*, here and in lxxi, there is no angelic song mentioned. But there is one in xxxix,12-13.

[31] The presence of angelic beings at night is noteworthy for two reasons: (1) In *Bavli ʿAvodah Zarah* 3b it is said that what God does at night is to hear the song of the Creatures (in *Bavli Ḥulin* 91b another tradition states that the angelic song is recited only at daytime). (2) In *Hekhalot Rabbati* we find that God descends from the eighth heaven to His throne in the seventh only at the hours of prayer of the People of Israel, in the morning and in the afternoon! Cf. *Hekhalot Rabbati* iii,3 and ix-xi. We shall come back to this interesting point later on.

[32] For the function of the *angelus interpres* see P. Schäfer, *op. cit.*, p. 10.

[33] There seems to be some kind of discrepancy between this verse and the next one, where it is said that the angels *do* stand before God.

directly by God (xiv,24-xvi,4). Thus it may be said, that in the eyes of the apocalyptist, Enoch enjoys a qualitative superiority over the angels. However, it is difficult at this stage to say with certainty whether this vision can be considered as the direct source of the Enoch-Metatron speculations, or whether we have to look for their source in a completely different direction.[34] What, however, is certain, is that the remark made in xv,1 about Enoch, who is described as a "righteous man and scribe of righteousness", actually brings this vision of Enoch very close to that Enoch-Metatron tradition.[35] In addition, it should be noticed, that Enoch sees two houses, one inside the other, and this we find later on to be characteristic of the *Hekhalot* visions.[36] Then we also have the terror which overwhelms Enoch just before the climax of the vision is reached. This is typical of many apocalyptic and Merkavah visions,[37] and one may argue that this terror, which results in a swoon, is later on in the Merkavah visions transformed into the danger-theme.[38] Finally, the vision of the Godhead seated on His throne with a great number of angels ministering to Him has since the days of *Daniel* and *Enoch* become classical.

Before we go on to the second central Merkavah vision in *1 Enoch*, that of chapter lxxi, mention should be made of the several minor Merkavah-passages in the book. First, we have the short reference in xviii,8-9 to the "throne of God, of alabaster, and the summit of the throne was sapphire". Here the throne is not in a house, as the throne which Enoch described in chapter xiv, but on the peak of a mountain. This mountain, again, is the middle one in a series of seven mountains which Enoch is allowed to see, and the

---

[34] We need not enter here the difficult problem of the identification of Enoch with the Son of Man, as it occurs in the Book of Similitudes (*1 Enoch* xxxvii-lxxi). See mainly E. Sjöberg, *Der Menschensohn im Äthiopischen Henochbuch*, Lund, 1946. Notice too the detailed discussion in H. Odeberg, *3 Enoch*, Reprint: New York, Ktav Publishing House, 1973, pp. 69 ff., and the commentary there pp. 6 ff.

[35] See also xii,3. Charles in his commentary overlooked the technical implications of the terminology used here in connection with Enoch. Compare *Jubilees* iv,16-17 with the tradition preserved in the *Targum Yerushalmi* to *Genesis* v,24 (version A). Cf. *3 Enoch* viii-xi. See further our discussion of *3 Enoch*, in Part Two of the present book.

[36] See above note 19.

[37] And in this sense it may reflect what R. Otto, *The Idea of the Holy*, Harmondsworth, Pelican Books, 1959, pp. 26 ff., has identified as the "Mysterium Tremendum"-element in religion.

[38] See J. Maier, "Das Gefärdungsmotiv bei der Himmelsreise in der Jüdischen Apokalyptik und 'Gnosis'", *Kairos* V (1963), pp. 18-40.

theophany which Enoch experiences thereon is obviously reminiscent of the theophany on Mount Sinai. Particularly so, since Enoch goes on to say: "And I saw a flaming fire".[39] A similar vision recurs in xxv,3. Here Enoch reaches another place of the earth, where again he sees seven mountains the middle one resembling the throne of God (xxiv,3).[40] When Enoch inquires of the accompanying angel the meaning of what he sees, the angel Raguel,[41] says: "This high mountain which thou hast seen, whose summit is like the throne of God, is His throne, where the Holy Great One, the Lord of Glory, the Eternal King, will sit, when He shall come down to visit the earth with goodness" (xxv,3).[42]

Another of the smaller Merkavah passages in *1 Enoch* belongs to the so-called Book of Similitudes (xxxvi-lxxi). In xxxix Enoch describes his vision of the "dwelling-places of the holy, and the resting-places of the righteous". All this occurred in the course of a heavenly ascent (xxxix,3), which is of great interest for our study. The place to which Enoch is translated is most probably the Paradise of Righteousness (Aramaic: *Pardes Qushtā*),[43] though the term itself occurs only elsewhere: xxxii,3; lx,23 (see also verse 8); and lxxvii,3.[44] Enoch sees there not only the dwelling places of the righteous of Israel, but also the dwelling places of the angels,[45] and, last but not

[39] On the theme of the divine throne and temple situated on mountains see, J. Maier, *Vom Kultus zur Gnosis*, Salzburg, Otto Müller Verlag, 1964, pp. 97 ff.

[40] It should be asked whether this vision is not a duplication of the previous one in xviii. See Charles' commentary *ad* viii,6.

[41] For Raguel see P. Schäfer, *op. cit.*, pp. 11, 22.

[42] For a discussion of the parallels in other Jewish writings see, I. Gruenwald, *Re'uyot Yeḥezkel*, in: *Temirin* I (1972), p. 138.

[43] In Greek: παράδεισος τῆς δικαιοσύνης. See next note.

[44] There is a vast literature dealing with the idea of the Paradise, both from the eschatological and theosophical points of view. See lately, M. Stone, "Paradise in *4 Ezra* iv,8 and vii,36; viii,52", *The Journal of Jewish Studies*, XVII (1966), pp. 85 ff.; M. Gil, "Enoch in the land of Eternal Life", (In Hebrew), *Tarbiz* XXXVIII (1969), pp. 322 ff.—It should be observed that the term "Paradise of Righteousness" is used in apocalyptic literature as the heavenly equivalent for the Garden of Eden in *Genesis* ii. As far as our knowledge goes, Hebrew texts in Tannaitic times, and even later on, always referred to the eschatological "Garden" as the Garden of Eden, while the term "Pardes" was reserved to designate mystical speculations. It seems that the turning point in the use of the word "Paradise", from an eschatological to a mystical sense, could be traced back to *2 Corinthians* xii,4, which should be compared with *Vita Adae et Evae* xxv,3. Compare also the terms "Paradise of God" in *Ezekiel* xxviii,13 and xxxi,8-9 (LXX!) and "Garden of Life" in *1 Enoch* lxi,12. Yet, see *infra* our discussion of *2 Enoch* viii-ix.

[45] The heavenly, and possibly also the earthly, participation of human beings

least, of the Messiah himself.[46] Some scholars have been inclined to detect in the messianic passages in the Book of Similitudes Christian influence; yet, it should be observed that the inclusion of the Messiah in Merkavah visions is also known from the *Hekhalot* literature.[47] Since there is much more in this vision that has its parallel in Jewish sources—such as the notion that "all the righteous and elect before Him shall be shining as fiery lights" [48]—the Christian origin of the Book of Similitudes is not from this point of view as self-evident as some scholars take it to be.[49] In the concluding section to the vision Enoch describes the angels and the doxologies which they recite. There are two doxological formulae mentioned here. The one, "Holy, holy, holy, is the Lord of Spirits: He filleth the earth with spirits", takes as its model the Sanctus of *Isaiah* vi,3; and the other one, "Blessed be thou, and blessed be the name of the Lord for ever and ever", is reminiscent of the Benedictus of *Ezekiel* iii,12. In either case the biblical opening phrases are, as it were, the doxological

---

in the angelic community is one of the most striking features of the eschatology of the Qumran sect. See now P. Schäfer, *op. cit.*, pp. 33 ff.

[46] See xxxix,6: "And in that place mine eyes saw the Elect One ... and I saw his dwelling-place under the wings of the Lord of Spirits." Later on, in Kabbalah-literature, the Messiah was allocated a heavenly (mystical) palace. See G. Scholem, "The Sources for 'The Story of Rabbi Gadi'el, the Infant' in Kabbalistic Literature", (in Hebrew), in: *Devarim Bego*, Tel Aviv, ʿAm Oved, 1975, pp. 270-283. See also the vision described in *1 Enoch* xlvi,1.

[47] See, for instance, the additions to *Hekhalot Rabbati* printed in A. Jellinek, *Bet Ha-Midrash*, V, pp. 167-169. Although these additions apparently belong to a rather late stage in the creation of the *Hekhalot* literature, the idea could well be of a much earlier date. See further, Y. Even-Shemuel, *Midreshei Ge'ulah*, Jerusalem-Tel Aviv, Bialik Institute, 1954, p. 7.

[48] See *Sifre* on *Deuteronomy*, ed. L. Finkelstein, p. 104/5, and parallels. Notice also the famous saying of Rav (*Berakhot* 17a), that in the world to come the righteous will sit peacefully before God with "their diadems on their heads, enjoying the divine Glory (Hebrew: *ziv ha-shekhinah*)". "To enjoy the divine Glory" (Hebrew: *Lehanot mi-ziv ha-shekhinah*) is a technical expression in rabbinical literature and its meaning is: to have all the physical needs supplied from the divine Glory.

[49] The case for the post-Christian origin of the Book of Similitudes has recently gained new momentum: it has been observed that the only part of the Book of Enoch not represented in Qumran is that very Book of Similitudes. See J. T. Milik, *Ten Years of Discovery in the Wilderness of Judaea*, London, SCM Press, 1959, p. 33. Strong as this argument from Qumran may sound, it is still nothing but an *argumentum ex silentio*. And even when the post Christian date of its composition is taken for granted, the Jewish origin of the Book of Similitudes is not necessarily challenged. See E. Sjöberg, *op. cit.* (above note 34), p. 39. See also Chapter One, n. 15.

trade-mark, while the main body of the doxology is more or less in the form of a free variation on the biblical *Vorlagen*.

It goes beyond the purpose of the present study to investigate those doxologies for all their morphological and theological contents. There are, however, one or two points to be made in connection with doxologies and these concern the way these doxologies are tagged on to the above mentioned verses in *Isaiah* and *Ezekiel*.

Although, as has been mentioned before, the opening words are kept, the rest is but loosely and freely connected to the biblical wording. Some scholars have attempted to show that certain principles underlie these changes in and deviations from the biblical models. While to some of the scholars interpretative tendencies could be detected in the post-biblical doxologies,[50] to others theological considerations, both Jewish and Christian, appeared to have determined the variations in the wording.[51] However, if all these examples of angelic doxologies are taken together, it appears that a variety of factors variety will have to be considered.[52] In addition, certain liturgical formulae taken from the Temple service were introduced into these doxologies.[53] What is important for us here is to observe that when the biblical doxologies were not considered as strictly binding in their wording, significant changes could be introduced into them, and the way stood open for the composition of the more elaborate angelological hymns of the kind and lyrical quality found in the *Hekhalot* texts.

We shall have to return later on to a detailed discussion of the *Hekhalot* texts. What can already be said is that certain inner developments in those apocalyptic doxologies could in themselves have paved the way for the lyrical and structurally more complex composition of the *Hekhalot* hymns. A glance, for instance, at the doxologies found in *Revelation* would well show how the doxological elements underwent certain inner developments, both from the point of view of length and of the diversification of themes. But what at

---

[50] See D. Flusser, "Sanktus und Gloria", in: *Abraham unser Vater: Festschrift für Otto Michel*, Leiden, 1963, pp. 129-152.

[51] See the survey of views in E. Werner, *The Sacred Bridge*, New York, Schocken Books, 1970, pp. 282 ff.; see also H. Bietenhard, *op. cit.*, pp. 137 ff.

[52] For a survey of some of the motives that played their respective role in the development of the Jewish *Qedushah*-liturgy see I. Elbogen, *Der jüdische Gottesdienst in seiner geschichtlichen Entwicklung*, Reprint: Hildesheim, Georg Olms, 1962, pp. 61 ff., 521/2.

[53] See E. Werner, *ibid.*, pp. 277-291.

this stage seems to be of much greater importance for our study is the angelological liturgy of the Qumran sect. Professor John Strugnell published in 1960 two fragments from an angelic liturgy found among the manuscripts of the fourth cave at Qumran.[54] Professor Strugnell inclined to date these manuscripts between the years 75 and 50 B.C.E., though the liturgy itself could well go back to an earlier date. In other words, these fragments belong to the flourishing days of Jewish apocalyptic. Professor Strugnell is presently preparing some additional material of the same texts for publication in the series of "Discoveries in the Judaean Desert" (Oxford). When this material becomes available to the public, it will be seen that the Qumranites' interest in heavenly liturgies and hymns was greater than has previously been thought, when only the brief references in the Scrolls themselves and the small published fragments were known.[55] It is difficult to tell from these Qumran texts, whether real heavenly hymns are quoted or whether the Qumran writer only gave picturesque descriptions of the orders of the angels who are said to sing the hymns. The language of these fragments is so rich that it is very often difficult to decide whether a hymn is quoted or only a description of how it is sung is given. The bad condition in which these manuscripts are preserved makes it even more difficult to decide whether a description ends or a possible hymn begins. At any rate, when published, the fragments will be a major contribution to our understanding of one milieu in which the doxologies found in apocalyptic grew and also of the literary and conceptual background of the hymnological material in the *Hekhalot* literature. It now seems that if certain hymnological passages in rabbinic literature [56] are added to the evidence from apocalyptic and Qumran, then the sort of literary sources behind the *Hekhalot* hymns can be fairly well exemplified.

---

[54] J. Strugnell, "The Angelic Liturgy at Qumran, 4Q ...", *Vetus Testamentum Supplement* VII (1960), pp. 318-345. Professor Y. Yadin has unearthed in *Meẓadah* another fragment of the same angelic Shabbat-liturgy.

[55] See, for instance, 1 QH (= *Hodayot*) III,21-23: "... Thou hast made a mere man to share the lot of the Spirits of Knowledge (= the angels) to praise thy name in their chorus ..." (English translation: Th. Gaster, *The Dead Sea Scriptures*, New York, Anchor Books, Doubleday & Co., 1964, p. 145).

[56] See G. Scholem, *Jewish Gnosticism* etc.", pp. 22 ff. It must be remarked that the Song of the Kine quoted *ibid.*, p. 25 is in its form and in its style closer to the angelological liturgy of Qumran than (as Professor Scholem inclines to think) to the *Hekhalot* hymns.

Finally, we come in this series of short Merkavah-like visions in *1 Enoch* to the visions described in xlvii,3 and in lx,1-4. First, in xlvii,3, the visionary says that he saw "the Head of Days when He seated Himself upon the throne of His glory, and the books of the living were opened before Him; and all His Host which is in heaven above and His counsellors stood before Him". Apart from the fact that the description follows in its general lines those found in *1 Kings* xxii,19 and in the Prologue to the Book of Job, a similar vision is recorded in xlvi,1, where the Messiah is included too. What should be noticed in the vision of xlvii,3 is the fact, that the scene is that of the final, eschatological, judgement.[57] The vision described in lx,1-4, however, is interesting for the report it contains of the great excitement of the apocalyptist, and also for the fact that the righteous are described there as standing before God together with the angels. This last point could well fit into the previously mentioned idea stressed in the Qumran writings about the eschatological participation of the angels in the community of the righteous, and, *mutatis mutandis*, of the community of the righteous in the heavenly orders of the angels. It should be noticed, too, that the inclusion of the righteous among those who stand before God is once again stressed in the Merkavah vision in *Revelation* iv. There, apart from the four Creatures, the Messiah and the seven Spirits of God, only the twenty-four elders are present before God. The angels are not mentioned there, which is quite remarkable in comparison with other Merkavah visions.

C

The second major Merkavah vision of *1 Enoch* is the one found in lxxi. Although some of its characteristic features are in a way a repetition of those already found in the first major Merkavah vision (ch. xiv), there are some new items which this vision presents. Most noteworthy is the fact that Enoch is taken into what could be interpreted to be two separate heavens, and the fact that God is described as leaving His palace in order to welcome Enoch. But before we go into the details of that vision, some remarks are in order concerning its place in the book. In chapter lxx the final translation of Enoch is described, that is, the translation after which he did not return down

[57] For the biblical background of the idea see Charles' Commentary *ad locum*. See further H. Bietenhard, *op. cit.*, pp. 116 ff.

to earth.[58] It is, therefore, quite peculiar to hear once again in lxxi about yet another translation of Enoch. Indeed, several of the interpreters of the Book of Enoch have thought this chapter to be an artificial addition to the main body of the book, and there are excellent reasons for accepting arguments that follow this line of thought. However, there is also another way of looking at the problem. *1 Enoch* has long been thought to be composed of at least five main parts. Chapter lxxi was most probably a loose fragment which the editor(s) of the book did not exactly know where to place. Realizing that this fragment bears a number of similarities to the other visions contained in the Book of Similitudes, the editor decided to place it at the end of this part of the whole book. Thus it happens that after Enoch had been finally translated onto heaven, another translation comes in the form of an appendix.

Now to the vision itself. It falls into two parts:[59] verses 1-4 describe Enoch's journey through the first heaven, while verses 5-17 apparently describe his journey through the second heaven.[60] In the first heaven Enoch sees "the holy sons of God",[61] that is, the angels, and his description of them—"their garments were white and their faces shone like snow"—reminds one of the description of the angel

[58] The idea of Enoch being translated at least twice, once in his lifetime and once at his death, is obviously inspired by the twice repeated phrase "Enoch walked with God" in *Genesis* v,22&24. The notion of his final translation derives from the concluding remark in verse 24 to the effect that "he was not, for God took him".

[59] There is no absolute necessity to distinguish between two separate visions in this chapter, as suggested by Charles and others. Yet there is some difficulty in the literary structure of the chapter. In verse 3, Michael is mentioned as the guiding angel of Enoch during the latter's tour in the first heaven. In verse 8 Michael is once again mentioned, but this time as one of the four archangels in the second heaven. In addition, at the end of verse 2 we read: "and I fell on my face before the Lord of the Spirits", though God actually appears only later on in verse 10, that is in the second heaven! It should be noticed in this respect too that in the first part of the chapter God is referred to as the "Lord of the Spirits", while in the second part He is called "the Head of Days". However, if we take verses 2 & 3 to include some later interpolations, then these difficulties could be removed.

[60] Actually this vision of the journey through two separate heavens is nowhere else found in *1 Enoch*, though it is typical of *2 Enoch*, and some other apocalyptic books. This again may account for the fact, that the vision of chapter lxxi found no integral place in the book.

[61] It seems that the derogatory associations in connection with the appellation "Sons of God" given to the evil angels in *Genesis* vi,2 did not persist for long. See *Encyclopaedia Biblica* (in Hebrew), vol. II (1954), coll. 172-174. Still, it is noteworthy, that they are here called "the *holy* Sons of God".

which Daniel saw (*Daniel* x,5-6).[62] Typical of such visions, Enoch sees fire everywhere, though in contradistinction to the vision in chapter xiv Enoch also receives here revelations about the secrets of nature. In verse 5, the second part of the vision begins. Actually it is here that the more interesting Merkavah material of the vision is to be found. Enoch says that the angel Michael "translated my spirit into the heaven of heavens" [63] and that there he saw "a structure built of crystals". This structure obviously corresponds to the house or houses which Enoch saw in the vision of chapter xiv. Once again Enoch saw "tongues of living fire", and he remarks that the house itself was surrounded by "a girdle" of fire. Four classes of angels—Seraphim, Cherubim, Ophanim and ʿIrim—together with countless other angels are present on the scene, the first ones (those distinguished as classes) guarding the throne of God and the second ones encircling the house. There Enoch also sees the four angels, Michael, Raphael, Gabriel and Phanuel, who together with other angels "go in and out of that house". Actually these four angels accompanied by the other angels escort God, called here "the Head of Days", when He comes out of the house to welcome Enoch! The idea of God coming out of His palace to welcome the visionary is found only here in the Merkavah visions we know of. It could be explained as a reflection of some biblical theophanies in which God is said to come out of the heavens.[64] When Enoch sees God, his whole body and soul are transfigured: "and my whole body became relaxed, and

---

[62] Compare *Revelation* i,13-15 and x,1; xviii,1. It seems that the supernatural appearance of the angels, as described in *Daniel* and in other apocalyptic books is a comparatively late development in Jewish angelology. In *Judges* xiii, for instance, where Manoʾaḥ's wife sees the angel and yet confusedly thinks him to be *ʾIsh Elohim*, a man of God (verse 6), an appellation generally given to the prophets. Even Abraham, the Patriarch, seemingly could not distinguish between angels and common men; *Genesis* xviii,1. Nor did Joshuʿa for that matter realise that the man standing before him with his sword drawn was in reality an angel (*Joshuʿa* v,13-14). However, for a different interpretation of the angel-scene in Joshuʿa see A. Rofé, *Israelite Belief in Angels in the Pre-Exilic Period as Evidenced by Biblical Traditions* (Dissertation. In Hebrew), Jerusalem, 1969, pp. 271 ff.

[63] Elsewhere it has been shown by the present writer that the designation 'Heaven of Heavens' (in Hebrew: *Shmei Ha-Shamayim*) is a common one for the second heaven in Palestinian lists of seven heavens. See in *Temirin* (above note 42), pp. 116 ff. If our interpretation of this vision is correct, and it really describes the ascent to two heavens, then this seems to be the first literary evidence for the name given here to the second heaven. But compare *1 Kings* viii,27!

[64] See, for instance, *2 Samuel* xxii,10-11 = *Psalms* xviii,10-11; and also the visions described in *Ezekiel* i & x.

my spirit was transfigured".[65] Consequently, Enoch sings songs of praise to God, a fact not mentioned before in *1 Enoch*. This could therefore be considered to be one of the earliest references to a Merkavah hymn recited not by the angels but by the visionary himself![66] The vision ends with a comparatively long reference to the Son of Man and a description of some of his eschatological functions.

The purpose of this extensive analysis of the so-called Merkavah passages in *1 Enoch* was to stress some of the more characteristic features of these passages in comparison with the parallel biblical material and in anticipation of the corresponding material in the Merkavah literature. In the first chapter of the present book, a general outline has been given of two particular qualities of Jewish apocalyptic in relationship to Scripture. The aim of this chapter is to exhibit yet another quality of Jewish apocalyptic, that is, the special interest it shows in theosophy. It has been shown that certain mystical elements found in Scripture were picked up by the apocalyptists and worked into a, comparatively speaking, full-scale model of mystical experience. Needless to say, this Merkavah material in Jewish apocalyptic had its own important share in shaping the mystical experience of the kind which we find later on in the *Hekhalot* literature. Although it is quite difficult to show the direct historical connection between Jewish apocalyptic and the *Hekhalot* literature, the literary connections between these two types of literature are almost self-evident. It must be admitted that even in the case of the mystical passages in Scripture it is difficult to say that they really and directly gave rise to the mystical preoccupation in Jewish apocalyptic. Although one may well argue even in this case for the presence of real historical connections, literary connections too could in themselves account for the formation of the mystical tradition in Jewish apocalyptic.

A mystical sensibility is a common phenomenon in almost all the religions of the world. The rise of an interest in mystical speculations, or even the mystical experiences themselves, in one age or another, could be explained either by some kind of now unattested traditions which linked the ages, or else by an independent mystical impetus that annexed itself to traditional modes of expression, or most likely by both. Whether we view these connections as merely of a

[65] For a characterisation of such feelings in the course of ecstasies see, E. Underhill, *Mysticism*, London, Methuen, 1960, pp. 359 ff.

[66] A parallel to this is to be found in the *Apocalypse of Abraham*. We shall later on come back to this point in connection with the *Hekhalot* hymns.

literary quality or as real historical affiliations, the fact that the ancient Jewish mystical tradition is mainly focused upon the vision of the divine Merkavah is more telling from the point of view of the historical connections than is sometimes admitted by scholars. More difficult, however, is the question of the connection between the Merkavah mysticism and later medieval developments of Jewish mysticism. The book which marked the change from Merkavah mysticism to the kind of mysticism which was later on designated by the term "Kabbalah" (= literally: tradition), was *Sefer Yeẓirah* or: The Book of the Formation of the World.[67] It was compiled sometime at the beginning of the Islamic period,[68] but some of its more characteristic elements belong to a much earlier period. Although it contains some references to the Merkavah lore (paragraphs 5, 8, 14, and 38), it is the starting point for quite a new language and direction in the history of Jewish mysticism, and hence presents some new historical and literary problems.

Returning to the Merkavah passages in Jewish apocalyptic, they show an extensive interest in mystical experiences, an interest that increased, at least in some Jewish circles, once Jewish apocalyptic was no more in the vogue. In addition, there is still much left for further investigation and thought concerning the place—or as some would like to call it: the "*Sitz im Leben*"—of these mystical scenes in Jewish apocalyptic. But in the present study considerations of the kind known as *Formgeschichte* would lead us off the main track, which is a thematic description of the Merkavah-tradition in Jewish apocalyptic, in the Talmudic literature and in the *Hekhalot* literature. We shall now turn to the Merkavah passages found in some of the other texts of Jewish apocalyptic, and first to the so-called *Slavonic Enoch*, or *2 Enoch*.

[67] There is a vast literature on the book; see G. Scholem, *Kabbalah*, Jerusalem, Keter Publishing House, 1974, pp. 205/6.

[68] Professor N. Allony has recently published a series of articles in Hebrew in which he argued for the post-Islamic origin of *Sefer Yeẓirah*. Allony argues that the linguistic theory embodied in *Sefer Yeẓirah* could be explained only on the ground of the *Kitab al-ʿEin* of the first known Arab lexicographer, Ḥalil ibn Aḥmad (died in 797). It must be admitted, that the arguments presented by Allony cannot be easily dismissed as wrong, yet there is still a lot in the *Sefer Yeẓirah* that has its origin in earlier speculations, and particularly so the doctrine of the ten *Sefirot*. See further the article referred to above in Chapter One, note 18. Whatever its date, the book had a tremendous influence on all later developments of Jewish mysticism. And that part of the book which exercised the greatest conceptual influence is the first one, that is, the older one which deals with the *Sefirot*, and not the second, and later one, which deals with the letters of the alphabet!

D

The Merkavah material in *1 Enoch* belongs to the period preceeding the destruction of the Second Temple. This is probably true also concerning the material found in the so-called Book of Parables (Similitudes), that is, chapters xxxvi-lxxi. Although reasons could be found for dating this particular part of the book to a later period, it seems certain that the Merkavah material contained therein is similar to the Merkavah material included in the earlier parts of the book. But all the other apocalyptic books we are going to discuss hereafter belong to a period which is very close to the destruction of the Temple and it may be said, that the writers had some particularly pressing problems to solve. It has been said in the previous chapter, that some parts of Jewish apocalyptic seem to express a crisis regarding the fulfilment of prophecy. Since a considerable part of the Scriptural prophecies remained unfulfilled, apocalyptic came to reassure people of the validity of biblical prophecy. With the destruction of Jerusalem and the Temple, however, apocalyptic had to face a bitter crisis regarding itself. Indeed, it appears that Jewish apocalyptic hardly overcame this crisis. Within thirty or forty years from the destruction of Jerusalem, Jewish apocalyptic literature disappeared—at least for the time being—from the literary scene.

Yet, before it finally did so, it underwent a noteworthy change. Its natural interest in the world of the divine Merkavah gained more power and significance. Thus one can find in the apocalyptic texts which were written under the tragic impression of the destruction of Jerusalem a marked interest in theosophical subjects. In addition, the very rise of rabbinic Merkavah mysticism was connected with the name of Rabbi Yoḥanan ben Zakkai, who was himself an eyewitness to the events that led to the destruction of Jerusalem. Thus, in a sense, the preoccupation with mystical problems could well be interpreted as being one of the ways in which people reacted to the disasters which befell them. When the cultic centre of the nation was no longer available, some people adapted beliefs and cultivated experiences which in some sense could replace experiences which had once been connected with the now destroyed Temple and with the immanence of God which it had signified. Yet, again, this is not to say that the *Sitz-im-Leben* of Jewish Merkavah mysticism was in the Temple cult.[69] It seems that it would be safer to say that the destruc-

[69] See J. Maier, *Vom Kultus zur Gnosis*, Salzburg, Otto Müller Verlag, *passim*.

tion of the Temple brought about a reaction which could well be characterized as a kind of mystical escapism. The stresses and distresses of reality pushed people to find comfort and consolation in super- or infra realistic realms. Thus we find a marked intensification in the interest in, and in the preoccupation with, mystical speculation. Yet, even here it would be incorrect to interpret this increase in mystical speculation only as a result of the disappointment and grief felt at the destruction of Jerusalem. This intensified interest in mysticism could also, at least partly so, be inspired by parallel phenomena in the hellenistic culture of the period.[70] Other motivations, hitherto only vaguely identified, could also have had their share as contributing factors in instigating the mystical speculations of the period. Thus, internal and external, literary and historical, factors played their respective roles in preparing the conditions necessary for the flourishing of mysticism in the post-destruction period.

We shall now turn to the apocalyptic writings which were, in all likelihood, composed in that period. These apocalypses still reveal a marked interest in eschatology while the curiosity in cosmological and natural phenomena which is so characteristic of *1 Enoch* is somehow suspended. Since the apocalyptic writings of the period which we shall discuss here describe ascents to a number of heavens, one may to some degree be justified in qualifying them as mystical apocalypses, without indeed overlooking their general eschatological interest. The number of the heavens to which the apocalyptist is said to ascend is generally seven, though Paul describes an ascent to the third heaven (*2 Corinthians* xii,2; see also *Testament of Levi* iii). Seven heavens are mentioned or described in *2 Enoch*, in the *Apocalypse of Abraham* (they are referred to in chapter xix), in the *Ascension of Isaiah*, in the *Greek Baruch* (only five heavens are described) and in the fragment of the *Apocalypse of Zephaniah* which was preserved by Clement of Alexandria (only the fifth heaven is briefly described). It seems that only in *Revelation* we find once again the older concept of the existence of one heaven.

As already said, we shall first discuss the Merkavah material in the Slavonic Book of Enoch, or *2 Enoch*. It is quite likely that its date of composition coincided with the events that terminated in the destruction of Jerusalem, yet the historical references in the book are rather vague and leave room for a number of guesses. In addi-

[70] E. R. Dodds, *Pagan and Christian in an Age of Anxiety*, Cambridge University Press, 1968, *passim*.

tion, the book presents some extremely difficult textual problems, the most difficult of which, namely the determination of the original version of the book, has not yet been conclusively solved. In our discussion of the Merkavah material found in the book, we shall pay equal attention to the long (A) and the short (B) recensions as they are printed in Charles, *Apocrypha and Pseudepigrapha*, vol. II, pp. 431 ff.[71] *2 Enoch* contains, among other things, a description of the ascent of the hero to the seven heavens, and the great interest of the description lies in the details it gives of the things which the hero saw in each of the heavens. This extensive description of the contents of the seven heavens has a number of parallels in Jewish apocalyptic literature as well as in later Jewish mystical and cosmological writings.[72] However, not all the details of this description directly belong to our subject; we shall limit ourselves to those details which directly concern us.

Generally speaking, the descriptions of what the seven heavens contain reveal a cosmological, or astronomical, interest. Yet, when it comes to the description of these things, one can always find a basic interest in theosophical matters.[73] Whatever one sees and finds in heaven always has a close connection to the divine and, thus, even the heavens below the seventh include items which are affiliated to the Merkavah material. This, naturally, reminds us of the fact already observed by various scholars, that, in apocalyptic literature and, also, in later mystical literature the interest in cosmological and theosophical matters goes hand in hand.

When we come to *2 Enoch*, the point that should be noticed about chapters viii-ix is the fact that the hero there is said to see Paradise, the place of retribution for the righteous and compassionate ones, in the third heaven. This is interesting for two reasons. Firstly, while in *1 Enoch* this Paradise is just said to be in heaven, here in *2 Enoch* it is located in the third heaven. The location of Paradise in the third heaven is also known from *Apocalypse of Moses* xxxviii,4, and it seems that even in the case of Paul (*2 Corinthians* xii,2; 4) the same holds

---

[71] The best edition still is: A. Vaillant, *Le Livre des Secrets d'Hénoch*, Paris, Institut d'Études Slaves, 1952.

[72] The relevant writings are: *Re'uyot Yeḥezkel*, *Beraita De-Ma'aseh Bereshit*, *Bavli Ḥagigah* 12b, and *Sefer Ha-Razim*. Among the apocalyptic writings, mention should be made in this connection of *Greek Baruch* (= *3 Baruch*) and the fragment of the *Apocalypse of Zephaniah* found in Clement, *Strom.* V 11 77.

[73] See F. Cumont, *Astrology and Religion among the Greeks and Romans*, New York, 1912, particularly pp. 101 ff.

true. Secondly, the word "Paradise" in *2 Enoch* is still a place in heaven and not a *terminus technicus* for theosophical speculations. The technical change in the use of the word can almost certainly be observed in Paul's account (*ibid.*), and it is already taken for granted in the story about the four sages who entered the *Pardes*. Thus it appears that *2 Enoch* was composed either at a time when the shift in the terminological usage, already imminent in Paul, was not yet known, or else by someone who was not aware of the shift.

In some sense, however, the Paradise-description in *2 Enoch* is already connected with the Merkavah lore. It is said in viii,8 (in both versions) that many angels (in A: three hundred) keep the garden and "with incessant sweet singing and never silent voices serve the Lord throughout all days and hours". This is a characteristic feature of *2 Enoch*, where the song of the various angelic beings is repeatedly referred to. Only the angels in the fifth heaven do not sing their celestial song (according to A only!). More important in this respect, however, is the fact that the apocalyptist says that "in the midst of the trees (is) that of life, in that place whereon the Lord rests, when he goes up into Paradise" (viii,3; A and B). As Charles remarks in his notes *ad locum* (p. 434), "this is a familiar feature in Jewish Apocalypse".[74] We may add that wherever this particular idea occurs, it refers to the original abode of *Shekhinah* before the *Shekhinah* ascended to heaven on account of the sins of mankind. Thus, we find in *3 Enoch* v, that "From the day when the Holiness, blessed be He, expelled the first Adam from the Garden of Eden, *Shekhinah* was dwelling upon a *Keruv* under the Tree of Life. And the ministering angels were gathering together and going down from heaven in parties... to do His will in the whole world. And the first man... (was) sitting outside of the gate of the Garden to behold the radiant appearance of the *Shekhinah*".[75] This description has obvious points of connection with the one found in *2 Enoch*, the only difference being that the Paradise described in *2 Enoch* is the celestial abode of retribution while the Garden in *3 Enoch* is still in its original terrestrial environment. Wherever this Paradise is located, either on earth or in heaven, the Tree of Life could be the place on which God rests, and

[74] Cf. indirectly *Ezekiel* xxviii,13, where it appears that the notion of God's abode in the Garden of Eden is an ancient oriental tradition.

[75] English translation in H. Odeberg, *3 Enoch*, Reprint: New York, Ktav Publishing House, 1973, p. 13 ff. See also Odeberg's commentary, *ibid.*, where parallels are quoted.

God's theophany on the Tree of Life is, thus, a counterpart to His theophanies in the Temple and on His Throne of Glory.

Most important, of course, is the description of what happened to Enoch in the seventh heaven.[76] When Enoch reached that heaven with the two men who lifted him up to heaven,[77] he became afraid and began to tremble in great terror. The two men encouraged Enoch and showed him "the Lord from afar, sitting on His very high throne". Around the throne were the various classes of the angelic beings who served God. Then the two men departed and Enoch was left alone in great fear. Consequently, the archangel Gabriel was sent by God to carry Enoch and place him before His face. When Enoch fell prone and worshipped God, he heard God telling Michael to take him "out from his earthly garments, and to anoint him with sweet oil, and (to) clothe him in garments of glory" (version B xxii,8). Michael did so, and consequently Enoch was transfigured and looked "like one of His glorious ones". Then God summoned one of His angels [78] to bring forth books and a reed so that Enoch could write down in them all that had happened to him in heaven together with some other secrets that were revealed to him.

The book contains two additional references of Merkavah material: in chapter xxxi, version A only, a Merkavah vision of Adam is described, and in xxxvii Enoch experiences a final vision of a most fearful angel.

E

After *2 Enoch* let us turn to the *Apocalypse of Abraham*. Chapters ix-xix of the book contain one of the most important Merkavah visions in apocalyptic literature. This Merkavah vision is introduced

---

[76] In version A there seems to be a certain confusion in the enumeration of the heavens. In xx,3 a tenth heaven, Aravat (= ʿAravot; see *Bavli Ḥagigah* 12b), is mentioned; and in xxi,6 the names of Muzaloth (= Mazaloth) and Kuchavim (= Kokhavim) are given to the eighth and the ninth heavens respectively. Only these three heavens are mentioned by name and it thus appears that B, which has only seven heavens, preserves the more original version.

[77] The fact that two men (= angels) escort Enoch in his heavenly journey is quite remarkable since it is similar to the idea of the two angels who carry the Merkavah mystic when he passes from one palace to the other. See *Hekhalot Rabbati* xvii.

[78] The name of the angel is given in A as Pravuil, and in B as Vretil. M. Margalioth, *Sefer Ha-Razim*, p. 56, n. 5, assumes that Pravuil is a corruption of Raziel. Yet, he adds: "This is a mere guess which I suggest with great reservation." However, Margalioth is less careful in suggesting all kinds of other links between *2 Enoch* and *Sefer Ha-Razim*.

in the course of the apocalyptic retelling of the story of the making of the Covenant in *Genesis* xv. In fact, as Box has already remarked in his notes to his translation of the book,[79] *Genesis* xv became a *locus classicus* for the introduction of all kinds of apocalyptic speculations. The *Apocalypse of Abraham*, however, is unique in the significance that it bears also for the study of ancient Jewish mysticism in general.

This part of the *Apocalypse* begins with the description of Abraham being ordered to bring a pure sacrifice to God and being promised that through that sacrifice God would bestow upon him a revelation of future events together with some other "great things which thou hast not seen" (ix). Very soon, however, the story in the *Apocalypse of Abraham* departs from its biblical source and Abraham is told to "abstain from every form of food that proceedeth out of the fire, and from the drinking of wine, and from anointing (thyself) with oil, forty days".[80] These preparatory practices which Abraham was instructed to follow are all well known from other apocalyptic works and in our general discussion of the *Hekhalot* literature (Chapter Four) they will receive proper attention. The narrator goes on to state that Abraham was overwhelmed with fear and, consequently, fell down upon the earth in a trance. Then, Abraham heard a voice speaking to the angel Jaoel telling him to raise Abraham to heaven "by means of the ineffable name".[81] Jaoel came to Abraham, introduced himself, and led him up towards heaven.

---

[79] G. H. Box, *The Apocalypse of Abraham*, London, 1919, p. 44. All my quotations are from that edition. *The Apocalypse of Abraham* has no division into verses.

[80] These forty days are certainly an allusion to the forty days during which Moses stayed on Mount Sinai abstaining from sustenance. See *Deuteronomy* ix,11. As we are going to see in chapter 4, different periods of time were prescribed as a preparation for the apocalyptic and mystical experiences.

[81] This practice of speaking out holy names in order to bring about a mystical experience is well known from the *Hekhalot* literature. In *Heklahot Rabbati* xiv,4-5 we read: "And when a man wants to descend into the Merkavah, he should conjure Suriah, the Prince of the Countenance, and to call him a hundred and twelve times by the name of Tetrasii ... He should be careful neither to add to that number of one hundred and twelve nor to subtract from it; for if he adds or subtracts, he is liable to die: but his mouth should speak out the names and his fingers should count a hundred and twelve. Then, for sure, he descends and masters the Merkavah". In his commentary to *Bavli Ḥagigāh* 14b (s.v., "They entered the Pardes"), Rashi says: "They ascended to heaven by means of a Name". This explanation evidently displays Rashi's acquaintance with the mystical lore. See also Rav Hai Ga'on's *Responsa* in B. Lewin, *Otzar Ha-Geonim*, vol. IV, Jerusalem, 1931, "Tractate Chagiga", pp. 22 ff. See also G. Scholem, *Jewish Gnosticism* etc., p. 54. It should be noticed that in *Mishnah 'Avot* i,13, Hillel the

Some of the things which Jaoel says when he introduces himself to Abraham are of importance to our subject and merit discussion. Jaoel says that he is called by that name "by Him who moveth that which existeth with me on the seventh expanse upon the firmament". The firmament is here, as also in the *Ascension of Isaiah* vii,9, a domain distinct from the seven heavens.[82] Yet, in spite of the fact that Jaoel here mentions the "seventh expanse", Abraham is not described as having in reality experienced an ascent through seven heavens. Only almost at the end of the vision (xix) it is said that Abraham, who was standing on the peak of the Mount Horeb, was granted a vision—from above—of the seven heavens that were so to speak below him. Jaoel also mentions that he possesses "a power in virtue of the Ineffable Name that is dwelling in me". This may well be the earliest occurrence of the idea found also in several places in midrashic literature to the effect that "A tablet with the Name of the Holy One, blessed be He, is engraved on the hearts of the angels . . .".[83] The idea which lies behind this midrashic saying is in all likelihood that the suffix "el" at the end of the names of many angels indicates not only their divine origin, but also the divine power or authority (exousia) which they possess. In the case of Jaoel, his name actually is a combination of the three root-letters of the Tetra-

Elder is reported to have said: "He who uses the Crown (Aramaic: *Tāgā*) is to pass away". According to the explanation found in *ʾAvot de-Rabbi Nathan* (ed. Schechter) version A, chapter xii, the meaning of Hillel's saying is: "He who uses the *Shem Ha-Meforash* (= the Ineffable Name) has no share in the world to come." It should be noticed that while Hillel warns him who "uses the Crown" of real death, the Scholia of *ʾAvot de-Rabbi Nathan* threatens only with the loss of future life. It is a well known fact, not only in the case of Ben ʿAzai who entered the Pardes (see next chapter), but also from the *Hakhalot* literature in general, that people who were not careful enough in their mystical experience were expected to suffer severe affliction and sometimes even death. We know of a certain tradition which speaks of the Name which was pronounced by the priests while reciting their Benediction in the Temple; see *Bavli Qidushin* 71a, where the Gemārā brings two views, the one about the Name which consisted of twelve letters and the other one about the Name which consisted of 42 letters! Now, Hillel, who lived in the days of the Temple, could well have meant that no one who was not authorized should "use" the Names for whatever purpose. He could have had in mind a priest who abuses the knowledge he gained in the Temple for a variety of theurgic purposes which were not connected with the priestly Benediction. Hillel, however, could have likewise meant people who gained knowledge of these Names and who were liable to use them for profane purposes.

[82] In the *Ascension of Isaiah* it is the place where Sammael and his hosts are.

[83] For the discussions of the different versions of this saying see G. Scholem, *Jewish Gnosticism* etc., pp. 71, 133; E. E. Urbach, *The Sages*, pp. 139, 150, 742, 749.

grammaton with the usual "el" ending (the Hebrew spelling of his name would thus most certainly be *Yhwel*). This is what Jaoel seems to imply when he says: "a power in virtue of the Ineffable Name that is dwelling in me".[84]

After Jaoel has introduced himself by name and mentioned the special rank he enjoys among the angels, he proceeds to refer to his functions in heaven. First he says: "I am the one who has been set to restrain, according to His commandment, the threatening attack of the living creatures of the Cherubim against one another". This hostility of the living creatures, the *Ḥayyot*, of the Merkavah is nowhere else mentioned, at least not in those apocalyptic texts that came down to us. Generally, the hostility of the angels is directed only against human beings who ascend to heaven and the idea expressed here in connection with Jaoel is thus quite extraordinary. Yet, it should be remarked that there are some rabbinic sayings to the effect that a certain hostility does in fact exist among the angels,[85] and thus, the tradition preserved in *Apocalypse of Abraham* does not stand altogether alone.[86]

Next Jaoel says that he teaches "those who carry Him the song of

[84] It goes beyond the present discussion to decide whether Jaoel is actually identical with Metatron, who is also called "little Jao" (*3 Enoch* xii; "And He called me The Lesser YHWH"), or whether at this stage Jaoel is still a separate angelic being not connected in any way to the Metatron tradition. See further, G. Scholem, "Über eine Formel in den Koptisch-Gnostischen Schriften und ihren jüdidischen Ursprung", *Zeitschrift für die neutestamentliche Wissenschaft* XXX (1931), pp. 170 ff.

[85] The most striking rabbinical parallel is in *Pesiktā Rabbati*, ed. Friedmann, fol. 97b, where it is told of *Galiẓur* that "his wings are spread out to receive the vapour of the *Ḥayyot*, for if he does not receive it, the ministering angels are burned by that vapour". See also the material collected in the next note.

[86] First we find the saying attributed to Bar Kaparā in *Shir Ha-Shirim Rabbā* viii,11: "Why are the ministering angels called 'fellows' (*Haberim*)?—Because there is neither hatred nor jealousy nor enmity nor hostility ... among them". Whatever its original purpose, this saying has obvious polemical overtones, which can be clearly heard if due attention is given to such sayings as: "Rabbi Yoḥanan said ... 'Dominion and fear are with Him, He makes peace in his high heaven'. (*Job* xxv,2)—'Dominion' this is Michael, and 'Fear' this is Gabriel, 'With Him' and He makes them live in peace, and none of the two does any harm to the other"; *Pesiktā de-Rav-Kahanā*, ed. Mandelbaum, p. 5. In *Devarim Rabbā* (ed. Lieberman, p. 100) Reish Lakish is quoted as explaining this to be the result of the fact that Michael is made of snow while Gabriel is made of fire. See further *Bavli Sanhedrin* 99b: "Rabbi Alexandrei said: He who studies the Torah for its own sake causes peace to reign among those above and those below". See also Rav Safrā's prayer in *Bavli Berakhot* 16b-17a; and *Agadath Shir Hashirim*, ed. Schechter, p. 4.

the seventh hour of the night of man". The references given by Box *ad locum* make it sufficiently clear that there circulated a view according to which the angels did not sing their songs of praise to God during the day-hours, thus avoiding any interference with the prayers of the Sons of Israel. Yet, the more common view, which is also represented in the *Hekhalot* literature, is that the angels wait till the Sons of Israel have finished their day-prayers, notably the *Qedushah*, before they begin their own songs of praise. However, what Jaoel says is not sufficiently clear, and it is only with reservation that it can be viewed as a parallel in apocalyptic literature to the idea that the angelic song is heard only at night.

At the beginning of chapter xi, a detailed description is given of the appearance of Jaoel: "The appearance of his body was like sapphire, and the look of his countenance like chrysolite, and the turban upon his head like the appearance of the rainbow, and the clothing of his garments like purple; and a golden sceptre was in his right hand". This description of Jaoel derives in its essential details from such descriptions of God and of the heavens found, for instance, in *Daniel* x,5-6 and *Joshua* v,13 and its parallels are to be found in several places in apocalyptic literature too.

Then a description follows of Abraham going with Jaoel to Mount Ḥoreb and of the sacrifice which Abraham offered there. Following the sacrifice, Abraham receives certain eschatological revelations and then experiences an ascent to heaven. Abraham says that "the angel took me with the right hand and set me on the right wing of the pigeon, and set himself on the left wing of the turtle dove which had neither been slaughtered nor divided", when Abraham offered his sacrifice. This description of the ascent is quite a peculiar one and its details will be discussed in chapter four.

Upon his arrival in heaven, Abraham experiences the main part of his Merkavah vision. This part of the vision is important for two reasons: First, it contains the longest Merkavah hymn in apocalyptic literature; and second, it contains a detailed description of the Throne of the Glory. We turn first to the Celestial Song, which was recited while Abraham and the angel were still in the air. It is of a composite nature and in spite of the various hymnological elements which it contains, has very little in common with the lyrical and numinous qualities of the *Hekhalot* hymns.[87] In form and content it is more like

[87] See A. Altman, in *Melilah* II (1945/46), pp. 1-24. See further J. Maier,

a liturgical hymn or sapiental psalm which recites the grace of God and His benevolence.[88] The song is, in fact, recited by Jaoel who tells Abraham to join him. From the words which Jaoel addresses to Abraham—"Only worship, Abraham, and utter the song which I have taught thee"—it appears, that the song also had the function of a protective charm. Abraham observes that he actually wanted to fall down upon the earth and thus pay reverence to the voice of the Divinity which he heard, but, since there was "no earth to fall upon", Jaoel told him to "Recite without ceasing".[89]

Next follows the Merkavah vision itself (chapter xviii). In its general form it derives from the description of the vision of Ezekiel, except that Ezekiel did not experience an ascent, which Abraham is here described as having had. This part of the vision begins when Abraham sees a huge flame of fire rising upwards and hears "a voice like the roaring of the sea".[90] When "the fire raised itself up, ascending into the height", Abraham saw "under the fire a throne of fire, and round about it all-seeing ones,[91] reciting the song". Under the throne Abraham saw the four Living Creatures. Yet, although Ezekiel had described them as having each four wings (i,6, 11), Abraham saw them as having six wings, like the Seraphim in *Isaiah* vi,2.[92] Interestingly, Abraham sees from where the six wings grow: from the shoulders, from their sides (?), and from their loins.[93] And he adds:

"Serienbildung und 'Numinoser' Eindruckseffekt in den poetischen Stücken der Hekhalot-Literatur", *Semitics* III (1973), pp. 36 ff.

[88] Because of textual problems, it is quite difficult to tell what in this Celestial Song really belongs to the original and what was later on added.

[89] All the quotations in this paragraph are from chapter xvii.

[90] This could be a reference to *Ezekiel* i,24.

[91] In *Ezekiel* i,18 we find that the backs of the four creatures were full of eyes. This gave rise to a number of similar descriptions in apocalyptic and *Hekhalot* literature. See *3 Enoch* chapters ix; xviii; xxii; xxv; *Hekhalot Rabbati* iii,4; xxii,5; xxiii,1; *Masekhet Hekhalot* (in Jellinek *Bet Ha-Midrasch* II, p. 42) chapter v. In some of the references, the alleged number of those eyes is given as well as their measure.

[92] The Living Creatures in *Revelation* iv,8 likewise have six wings, and it may be argued that in this particular detail, some Christian translator or editor of *Apocalypse of Abraham* adapted the irregularity found in *Revelation*. See further *Bavli Ḥagigah* 13b where an attempt is made to harmonize between the number of the wings described by Isaiah and those described by Ezekiel.

[93] Another interesting description, attested to by some of the MSS, is that each of the Creatures had four faces, "so that the four creatures had sixteen faces". The number of the Creatures' faces was an important issue in Jewish mystical calculations. In *Hekhalot Zutreti* (in Sh. Musajoff, *Merkavah Shelemah*, Jerusalem, 1921, fol. 7a) Rabbi Akiva is quoted as introducing the special secret

"with the (two) wings from their shoulders they covered their faces, and with the (two) wings which (sprang) from their loins they covered their feet, while the (two) middle wings they spread out for flying straightforward".[94] Then the Apocalypse refers once again to the hostility of the Creatures, "And when they had ended the singing, they looked at one another and threatened one another". Jaoel interfered and "turned the countenance of each living creature from the countenance immediately confronting him, in order that they might not see their countenances threatening each other". In addition to that Jaoel "taught them the song of peace". This part of the vision ends with a description of the Throne of the Glory, a description which follows quite closely the one given in *Ezekiel* i. The book ends with an extensive apocalyptic prophecy which tells the story of the Sons of Israel till the eschatological salvation. Before this conclusion of the vision, Abraham says that he was standing, in fact, in the seventh firmament and that God opened to him all the firmaments below.[95]

F

Another vision of the Merkavah is included in *The Ascension of Isaiah*. There it comprises the second part of the book (chapter vi onwards) and from the date given at its beginning it appears that the writer did not intend to identify it with the vision described in *Isaiah*

---

wisdom which deals with the number of the faces and the wings of the *Ḥayyot*. Interestingly, the number of faces is also given in the gnostic so-called *Koptisch-Gnostische Schrift ohne Titel aus Codex II von Nag-Hammadi*, ed. A. Böhlig & P. Labib, Berlin, Akademie Verlag, 1962, p. 52/3. Both in *Hekhalot Zutreti* and in the Aramaic Targum to *Ezekiel* i,6 sixty four faces and two hundred and fifty six wings are mentioned. See further Chapter Four, Section B.

[94] Compare the Aramaic Targum to *Isaiah* vi,2: "with two (wings) they cover their faces so as not to see (the Godhead); and with two they cover their bodies so as not to be seen (in their nakedness), and with two they perform (their) service (to God)". The service referred to here is the Celestial Song which according to a current tradition was voiced with two of their wings. See, for instance, *Bavli Ḥagigah* 13b, where "the wings with which they say the song" are said to have been taken away from the Creatures when the Temple was destroyed. See further, *Tanḥumā*, "Qedoshim". paragraph vi; *Pesikta de-Rav Kahana*, ed. Mandelbaum, p. 151; *Pirkei de-Rav Eliezer* iv; *Bavli Sanhedrin* 37b (Tosafot, s.v. "*Miknaf Ha-ʾAretz*"); *ʿArugat Ha-Bosem*, ed. E. E. Urbach, vol. I, p. 213.

[95] This unique description is reminiscent of what Rabbi Yuda said in the name of Rabbi Yoḥanan about the experience which Abraham had had: "He raised him above the dome (Hebrew: *Kippah*) of the firmament. God told Abraham: 'Look at the heaven', and 'Look' (Hebrew: *Habet*) implies a look from above to below". *Bereshit Rabba*, ed. Theodor-Albeck, p. 432/3.

vi. The vision begins when King Hezekiah and all the people of his court, together with the prophet Isaiah, heard "a door which had opened and the voice of the Holy Spirit" (vi,6).[96] This idea of a door which is heard or seen being opened at the beginning of a mystical vision is also known from *Revelation* iv,1, and it may reflect a mystical interpretation of the words "the heavens were opened" in *Ezekiel* i,1. Yet, while Ezekiel experienced no ascension, such an experience is presupposed in *The Ascension of Isaiah* and in *Revelation*.[97] Indeed, the idea of a door which is opened in heaven is characteristic of the tradition describing heavenly ascensions. Thus the so-called Mithras Liturgy mentions such doors,[98] and in *Hekhalot Zutreti* such a door or gate [99] is said to have been pre-established by God before he made heaven and earth.[100] In *Hekhalot Rabbati*, the gates of the seven palaces and the special means which should be applied in order to pass through them safely become a central theme. However, there are several instances in Jewish mystical literature in which the phrase "the heavens were opened" or "the heavens were torn asunder" occur, but then they do not indicate a heavenly ascension.[101]

Soon Isaiah fell into a trance,[102] and an angel came to show the vision to him. Isaiah goes into some detail when he describes the glory of that angel: he was "a glorious angel not like unto the glory of the angels which I used always to see" (vii,2). Obviously, this remark is directed to distinguish between this vision—which entailed a heavenly ascent—and the one in *Isaiah* vi, which the writer apparently believed to entail no such experience. In fact, the angel said that he

---

[96] This door is only mentioned in the Ethiopic text of the *Ascension of Isaiah* but not in the Latin texts. See R. H. Charles, *The Ascension of Isaiah*, London, 1900, p. 99. See further E. Tisserant, *Ascension d'Isaie*, Paris, 1909, p. 136.

[97] Compare also *Syriac Baruch* xxii,1, where the words of Ezekiel are repeated and again no heavenly ascension is presupposed.

[98] A. Dieterich, *Eine Mithrasliturgie*, Reprint: Darmstadt, Wissenschaftliche Buchgesellschaft, 1966, p. 10/11, lines 19-20.

[99] The word used here is a *hapax-legomenon*. See G. Scholem, *Jewish Gnosticism* etc., p. 78, n. 9. See further, E. Ben Iehuda, *Thesaurus*, vol. IV, p. 1821, s.v. "*Ḥatirah*".

[100] See further *3 Maccabees* vi,18, and *Testament of Levi* v,1.

[101] See G. Scholem, *op. cit.* p. 68. See further *Mark* i,10 (and parallels), and also *Revelation* xix,11: "Then I saw the heaven open", where once again—in contradistinction to iv,1—no heavenly ascension is maintained.

[102] Interestingly, the physical symptoms of that trance are given in the following words: "he became silent, and he saw not the men who stood before him, though his eyes indeed were open. Moreover his lips were silent ... But his breath was in him" (vi,10-12).

had come from the seventh heaven (vi,13) and that he did not want to reveal his name to the visionary (vii,4-5).[103]

Then follows the description of what Isaiah was shown in each of the seven heavens. Before he reached the first heaven, however, he had passed through the firmament which was between the earth and the heaven.[104] Only afterwards did Isaiah reach the first heaven. Generally, the description of each of the first six heavens is more or less the same, only that every new heaven was more glorious than the preceding one. In each of the first five heavens, Isaiah saw "a throne in the midst, and on its right and on its left were angels".[105] This is probably the only occurrence in Jewish apocalyptic of the idea of the existence of a throne, a Merkavah, in each of the heavens. The idea is, however, repeated in an early Merkavah-midrash, *Re'uyot Yeḥezkel*, where Ezekiel is said to have seen a Merkavah in every one of the seven heavens. In *Re'uyot Yeḥzekel*, we also find the idea, which is first mentioned in the *Ascension of Isaiah*, that God is sitting only in the throne of the seventh heaven.[106] In addition, the *Ascension of Isaiah* says that the angels "who stood on the right had the greater glory, and they all praised with one voice...[107] and those who were on the left gave praise after them; but their voice was not such as the voice of those on the right, nor their praise like the praise of those".[108]

Then Isaiah passes upwards to the second heaven. First, however, he remarks that "the height of that heaven is the same as from the

[103] Indirectly, this could reflect the Essene practice of not revealing the names of the angels. See Josephus, *Bellum* II, viii,7. Generally speaking, the apocalyptic writers did keep secret the names of the angels, while of the Merkavah mystics the contrary can be said to be the truth.

[104] This is quite unique a concept. Yet see Charles's commentary *ad locum*.

[105] The present writer slightly differs here from Charles's translation. Charles thinks that the 'throne' is an angel of the class of the θρόνοι and, therefore, translates: "on *his* right and on *his* left...". Yet, according to the Latin, the throne is a throne indeed: *vidi ibi sedem*. The textual evidence for the existence of somebody who sits on the throne from the second heaven upwards is somehow questionable. See further Scholem, *Jewish Gnosticism* etc. p. 18/9.

[106] In *Re'uyoth Yeḥezkel* each of the seven *Merkavot* has a mystical name. See in *Temirin* I (1972), pp. 119 ff. A plurality of chariots is also mentioned in the yet unpublished angelic liturgy found at Qumran and in *Mezadah*.

[107] For the idea of the angels singing in one voice see G. Scholem, *op. cit.*, pp. 30, 129, to which, however, more material could be added.

[108] This lack of equality between those standing on the right and those standing on the left is in a way repeated in *Hekhalot Rabbati* xvii, where it appears that the gate-keepers on the right are more important than those standing on the left.

heaven to the earth". Similar utterances can be found in rabbinic literature [109] and in some of the Merkavah texts.[110] But once again the occurrence of this measure in *The Ascension of Isaiah* could well be taken to be the first of its kind in Jewish apocalyptic and mystical tradition. When Isaiah, the visionary, ascends to the second heaven, he again sees a throne with two groups of angels standing on its right and on its left. However, in contrast to the throne seen in the first heaven, at least some of the manuscripts can be understood here to imply that somebody could be seen sitting in the throne. Yet, as has already been said,[111] the readings in the manuscripts could well be a result of the misunderstanding of the copyists.[112] Yet, the words of the *angelus interpres* in vii,21—"Worship neither throne nor angel which belong to the six heavens"—seem to imply that, after all, the throne did not remain unoccupied and that some kind of angelic being—a 'thronos'—was envisaged as occupying it. Yet, this seems to defy the Jewish tradition that angels cannot fold their legs and, thus, cannot sit.[113] In any event, the "one who sat on the throne" is again mentioned in the third heaven (vii,27), in the fourth heaven (vii,31) and in the fifth (vii,35). In the sixth heaven, however, "there are no longer angels on the left, nor a throne set in the midst" (viii,7).[114]

When Isaiah reached the seventh heaven, he heard a voice saying: "How far will he ascend that dwelleth in the flesh?" (ix,1). This question obviously reflects the traditional theme of the angelic opposition to the ascent of man to heaven.[115] But immediately another

[109] In *Beraita de-Maʿaseh Bereshit* (ed. N. Séd, in: *Revue des Études Juives* CXXIV (1965), p. 58), the distance is given as 502 "years of walk", which equals the total sum of the years which Abraham, Isaac and Jacob lived. These were later on rounded out to become 500 "years of walk". See next note.

[110] See the material collected in my edition of *Re'uyot Yeḥezkel*, in: *Temirin* I, pp. 121 ff.

[111] See above n. 105.

[112] Thus we find in vii,21 that L^2 (in Charles' edition, p. 109) reads "ut *adorem eum*", while S (= the Slavonic version) implies "adoravi eos"! The "eum" could well refer to God who is in the seventh heaven, and not necessarily to the throne, or to the alleged being who is sitting thereon.

[113] See *Bereshit Rabba*, ed. Theodor-Albeck, p. 738, and parallels. See further in *Temirin* I, p. 129. Only Metatron could enjoy the privilege of sitting, and this most probably because he had once been a human being (= Enoch). See *Bavli Ḥagigah* 15a.

[114] The special numinous quality of the sixth heaven reminds us of the special quality of the sixth palace as described in the *Hekhalot* literature.

[115] In the case of *The Ascension of Isaiah*, the voice came from the angel who "is over the praise-giving of the sixth heaven". See further J. Schulz, "Angelic Opposition to the Ascension of Mosis and the Revelation of the Law", *Jewish*

voice was heard to the effect that "It is permitted to the holy Isaiah to ascend hither; for here is his garment" (ix,2). As it turned out, this was God's voice, who here and elsewhere in parallel cases, set out to protect the ascending hero from the wrath of the jealous angels (ix,5). The first thing which Isaiah saw in the seventh heaven were all the righteous, "stript of the garments of the flesh" (ix,9). They were, in fact, like angels, "in their garments of the upper world" [116] (*ibid.*). What strikes Isaiah's attention is the fact that these righteous dwelling in heaven "have received the garment but have not the thrones and the crowns".[117] This is explained by the angel thus: "Crowns and thrones of glory they do not receive, till the Beloved will descend in the form in which you will see Him descend into the world in the last days". This part of the vision obviously belongs to the Christian editor or interpolator of the book and it transforms at least one traditional Jewish theme, the wearing of crowns,[118] into a Christian apocalyptic theologumenon.[119]

Quarterly Review LXI (1970/1971), pp. 282-307. Schulz rightly observes: "Thus there appear to be two lines of thematic development, one in which the angels serve as guides for the ascending hero, the other in which they protest or try to prevent his ascension". (p. 288). In *Pesiktā Rabbati* (ed. Friedmann) p. 96b, the opposing angels are referred to as "angels of destruction" (*Mal'akhei Ḥabbalah*), which obviously means that the author was disturbed by the idea that good angels could oppose the ascension of Moses to receive the Torah. See further P. Schäfer, *Rivalität zwischen Engeln und Menschen*, Berlin, Walter de Gruyter, 1975, pp. 128 ff. For the development of the term *Mal'akhei Ḥabbalah*, see in *Israel Oriental Studies* III (1973), p. 97. See further, *Apocalypse-of Abraham* xiii, where this type of angelic opposition is put into the mouth of Azazel!

[116] These "garments of the upper world" could have two distinct functions: (a) they are the white garments of the righteous as described several times in *Revelation* (see mainly iv,4), and in *Vita Adae et Evae* (Greek version), xl (in: Tischendorf, *Apocalypses Apocryphae*, p. 21). In all these cases they are eschatological garments; but we do have another type of heavenly garments: (b) mystical garments. These garments most likely are to protect the mystical visionary from all kinds of dangers. This could well be the meaning of God's words in *Ascensio Isaiae* ix,2. See further *2 Enoch* xxii, *3 Enoch* xii; *Pesiktā Rabbati*, ed. Friedmann, fol. 98a (= *Bavli Shabbat* 88b). It should also be noted that in one of the liturgical poems of Amram Dare, a Samaritan poet of the fourth century, it is said of Moses' ascension: "And the Good says: 'Let my prophet be exalted. Let the prophet be great and let him be beautiful and let him grow and reach the heaven. Indeed he will be vested by me in a garment that no being is worthy to wear". English translation in: S. Leiter, "Worthiness, Acclamation, and Appointment: Some Rabbinic Terms", *Proceedings of the American Academy for Jewish Research*, Vol. XLI-XLII (1973-1974), p. 156. Unfortunately, Leiter was not aware of the possible mystical connotations of this passage.

[117] Compare *Revelation* iv,4.

[118] *Bavli Berakhot* 17a, see also above n. 48.

[119] In fact, it is quite difficult to state with certainty what in ix,11 ff. actually

In fact, the whole of the description of the seventh heaven in *The Ascension of Isaiah* is impregnated with Christian material and it is quite difficult to differentiate between the Jewish origin and its Christian recasting. What, in any case, should be noticed in this part of the vision is: (a) Isaiah was transformed and became an angel (ix,30);[120] (b) Isaiah could not see the Great Glory, but he noticed that the righteous could (ix,37-38);[121] (c) Isaiah heard the celestial song of praise (ix,40 ff.); (d) Isaiah saw the descent of the Messiah into the terrestrial world (x,8 ff.);[122] and finally (e) Isaiah saw the Messiah ascending again through the heavens and reaching the seventh heaven. The terminology used in (d) and (e) comes very close to the terminology used in some of the texts of gnosticism, and it may, furthermore, be asked whether the Christian part of the book was not recast in some gnosticistic circles.

G

The Merkavah vision in *Revelation* iv is an interesting example of how Jewish Merkavah material was recast in the new Christian environment. It is generally believed that *Revelation* was composed by a certain John who was familiar with the apocalyptic writings of the Jews before the destruction of the Temple. Although the *Apocalypse of John* received its final shape some twenty years after the destruction of the Temple, its Merkavah material is nevertheless typical of its Jewish counterpart before the destruction. There is no plurality of heavens in the book and this might mean that the book was primarily conceived either in circles which had not adapted the idea or by someone who had simply ignored what was becoming a central concept or fashion in Jewish apocalyptic. In addition to that, it is believed that the *Apocalypse of John* is the only one of its

belongs to a Christian editor or interpolator. There are good reasons to believe that the book as a whole is of Jewish origin and that all the clear Christian references belong to a later editor or interpolator. But it is difficult to decide whether everything from ix,11 ff. belongs to him or whether one has even here to try to distinguish between the Jewish origin and the Christian additions.

[120] This, as we have already seen, signifies a mystical transformation. See above n. 16. Compare also the transformation of Enoch into Metatron in *3 Enoch*.

[121] Compare *Sifra*, ed. Weiss, fol. 4a-b. It should be noticed that some of the MSS of the *Ascension of Isaiah* here read "Him" referring to the celestial figure of Jesus and not to God!

[122] The description here comes very close to the description of the descent of the Saviour at the opening pages of *Pistis Sophia*. Yet, it would be beyond the scope of the present discussion to compare in detail *The Ascension of Isaiah* and *Pistis Sophia*.

kind that is not pseudepigraphically attributed to some biblical figure. This may be explained by the fact that the book purports to be a prophecy which should be revealed to the community of the believers (i,3; xxii,6 ff.). There are some discrepancies in the vision described in chapter iv and they, in turn, could be explained by the rather eclectic nature of the material contained in the vision. As we are going to see, the vision brings together several traditions and it could well be asked whether it describes a genuine experience or whether it is a mere compilation of literary motives. Of course, the question of the genuineness of the vision is quite a difficult one, and skeptics could find a great number of reasons to justify their doubts. Generally speaking, however, discussions of this kind do not lead very far in any sincere attempt to understand and evaluate the experience once it is cast as a literary document.

John, the apocalyptist, introduces his vision with the remark that he saw a "door opened in heaven". This expression may, of course, be reminiscent of the opening words used by Ezekiel to describe the beginning of his vision. However, since John does not literally repeat the words of Ezekiel "the heavens were opened" (*Ezekiel* i,1), we may well infer that John here uses technical terminology. Indeed, the reader may remember that the Ethiopic text of *Ascensio Isaiae* vi,9 says that Isaiah heard, not saw, a door being opened and then his vision began.[123] The technical sense in which John's words, "a door opened in heaven", becomes evident when they are compared with another of John's introductory remarks in xix,11. There John, together with Ezekiel, says that he "saw the heaven opened". In this last case, as also in that of Ezekiel, no heavenly ascent is assumed, while the phrase 'a door opened in heaven' usually introduces such an ascent. To be exact, however, the opening of the door in heaven in *Revelation* iv,1 is not directly followed by John's ascension. He first heard a voice, which he had previously heard (i,10), calling

[123] See above n. 96. See also *Testament of Levi* v,1. In *Yerushalmi Sanhedrin* 28c (bottom) we hear of the secret opening which God opened under His throne so as to receive the prayer of the repenting King Manasseh.—The cosmological concept of gates that mark the entrance to the upper world and mainly to the netherworld is, in fact, very old and almost universal. For ancient Greece see G. S. Kirk & J. E. Raven, *The Presocratic Philosophers*, Cambridge University Press, 1973, pp. 10 ff. Scholars are often inclined to see the origin of certain Greek concepts and beliefs in the East and sometimes in Egypt. See the interesting text published in H. Frankfort and others, *Before Philosophy*, Harmondsworth, Penguin Books, 1954, pp. 167 ff. The mystical implication of this cosmological concept, however, becomes evident only in such passages as *Revelation* iv,1.

him to ascend to heaven. Only verse 2 says: "And immediately I was there in spirit". In contradistinction to similar experiences in apocalyptic literature, the writer does not state how he actually arrived,[124] although his manner of imparting what happened to him may well be in line with Paul's description in *2 Corinthians* xii,2 & 3.[125] Then, John says, he saw that "a throne was set in heaven, and on the throne (was) one seated". It is noteworthy that—unlike Ezekiel, Daniel and Enoch—John does not refer to the "one" seated on the throne in anthropomorphic terms. Instead John says that "he that sat was to look upon like a jasper stone and a sardius" (iv,3). While Ezekiel (i,27/8) refers to the appearance of fire in connection with the "one" seated on the throne, Daniel (vii,9) says that the "throne was fiery flames" and that God himself appeared to him as "ancient of days" and that "his raiment was white as snow and the hair of his head like pure wool". Indeed, there are two traditions, so to speak, concerning the description of the appearance of God on His throne. The one, initiated by the vision of Ezekiel, stresses the appearance of fire, while the other refers to God in terms of an old man dressed in white. *1 Enoch* xiv,20 describes "the Great Glory" on the throne thus: "His raiment shone more brightly than the sun and was whiter than any snow". Similarly *1 Enoch* lxxi,10, speaks of the "Head of Days" in terms that are reminiscent of *Daniel* vii: "His head was white as pure wool, and his raiment indescribable". In the *Hekhalot* literature, however, the fiery appearance of God is a key notion, although greater attention is paid there to the separate speculations about His raiment, (Hebrew: *Ḥaluq.*)[126]

Before John continues describing the Throne of God, he is struck by the vision of twenty four elders sitting on twenty four thrones. Who these elders are and what they signify in this particular Merkavah vision is a question often debated among scholars. Their number, twenty four, was considered as pointing to the twenty four divisions of priests as they were first enumerated in *1 Chronicles* xxiv.[127] Indeed,

[124] See our discussion in chapter 4.

[125] For the problems involved in the interpretation of this verse see R. H. Charles, *A Critical and Exegetical Commentary on the Revelation of St. John* (*The International Critical Commentary*) Edinburgh, 1920, Vol. I, pp. 109-111. For the present study, the commentaries of W. Bousset, *Die Offenbarung Johannes*, Reprint: Göttingen, Vandenhoeck & Ruprecht, 1966, and of H. B. Swete, *The Apocalypse of St. John*, Reprint: Ann Arbor, Michigan, Cushing-Malloy, Inc. N.D. have been consulted too.

[126] G. Scholem, *Jewish Gnosticism* etc., pp. 26/7. 58 ff.

[127] Cf. W. Bousset, *op. cit.*, *ad locum*.

their priestly, or levitic, function is further enhanced by the fact that they sing songs of praise (iv,10/1; v,9; vii,12; xi,17; xix,4) just as the levites were used to do in the Temple-service; and the "kithara" which each of the elders holds in his hands (v,8) is reminiscent, again, of the traditional Temple-psalmody.[128] In addition, the golden bowls of incense which they likewise hold in their hands are more than a clue to their priestly function.[129] The same can also be said concerning the white garments in which the elders are clad (iv,4).[130] Generally speaking, however, white garments are taken in the *Apocalypse of John* to signify the special status of those who believe in Jesus [131] and the same kind of garments are also elsewhere mentioned in connection with angels.[132] Indeed, the elders have an angelic function too: the incense which they present before the Lamb (= Jesus) is considered to be "the prayers of the saints" (v,8).[133] As Charles has pointed out in his commentary (p. 145/6), the idea ot an angel, or archangel, offering the prayers of mankind to God is found quite often in apocalyptic literature. In rabbinic literature, however, it is a more complicated issue. In three places in the Bab. Talmud, it is stated that Michael, the archangel (or, in Hebrew, *Sar Ha-Gadol*) is ministering before the altar.[134] In a different context we hear that the angel Syndalphon ties crowns to the head of his Creator (*Bavli Ḥagigah* 13b). S. Lieberman has collected material which shows that in several instances this singular tradition about Syndalphon was interpreted as meaning that the crowns are made of the prayers of the angels.[135] This particular interpretation of the

[128] See H. B. Swete, *op. cit.*, *ad locum*. This could well imply conditions conceivable after the destruction of the Temple. See further x,21/2. Cf. A. Büchler in *Zeitschrift für Alttestamentische Wissenschaft* XIX (1899), pp. 93-133; 329-344; XX (1900), pp. 97-135. In *Hekhalot Rabbati* viii,4 the lute-playing of the Living Creatures is mentioned too.

[129] *Revelation* v,8.

[130] The holy linen garments mentioned in connection with the High Priest in *Leviticus* xvi,4 are called "garments of white" in *Mishnah Yoma* iii,6. See also *Ezekiel* xliv,17.

[131] *Revelation* iii,4/5; vii,13-17; xix,8. Compare *Ecclesiastes* ix,8.

[132] *Ethiopic Enoch* lxxi,1.

[133] Charles, *op. cit.*, *ad locum* (p. 400, n. 3), considers this phrase to be a gloss, but his reasons for doing so, as expounded in his commentary, are not conclusive.

[134] *Tal. Bav. Menaḥot* 110a; *Zevaḥim* 62a; *Ḥagigah* 12b. See Scholem, *op. cit.*, pp. 47 ff. Scholem also discusses there the relationship between the traditions about Michael and Metatron. See further, I. Gruenwald, '*Re'uyot Yeḥezkel*', p. 128/9.

[135] S. Lieberman, *Shkiʿin* (in Hebrew), Jerusalem, 1939, p. 13 f. As for the crowns which the elders put before the throne (*Revelation* iv,10) compare *3 Enoch*

Syndalphon-tradition is very close to the idea of the elders in *Revelation* who offer incense composed of the prayers of the saints. It is, of course, quite difficult to say whether there exists any direct connection between the two ideas or whether what John says is derived only from parallel material found in apocalyptic literature (as collected by Charles). But one thing seems to be clear: John here attributes to the elders an angelic function and this apart from their levitic and priestly functions which we have already discussed. The contamination of these three functions, though it may be explained partly by the kind of Christian-priestly theology developed in the *Epistle to the Hebrews*, is nonetheless highly peculiar. This may again be related to the suggestion made before, to the effect that John's manner of writing (and eventually his visionary imagination) is of a highly eclectic nature.

An additional word must be said about the crowns of gold which the elders wear on their heads. The closest Jewish parallel to this item in the vision is the saying of Rav (third century) describing the eschatological reward of the just: They are sitting before God with crowns (*ʿAtarot*) on their heads (*Bav. Berakhot* 17a). The eschatological context of this saying of Rav is very similar to the vision of the elders in *Revelation* and not unimportant is also the statement in both sources that the elders and the just are actually sitting. We know that according to one tradition, Elishʿa ben ʾAvuya saw Metatron while sitting. (*Bav. Ḥagigah* 15a; *Sefer Hekhalot* [*3 Enoch*] xvi). Knowing that nobody is allowed to sit in heaven, Elishʿa ben ʾAvuya came to the conclusion that there must be two powers in heaven.[136] We also saw that the angels cannot fold their legs into a sitting position.[137] The just and the righteous ones are here described,

xviii. It must be noticed that in *Hekhalot Rabbati* xi,1 the Angel (of the Divine) Countenance (= *Malʾakh Ha-Panim*) ties crowns to the Living Creatures. In xvi,5, moreover, God is called the Lord of the Crowns (= *Adon Ha-Ketarim*). The *Musaf-Qedushah* of Shabbat and Festivals according to the Sepharadic (East European) Prayerbook opens with the words: "A Crown will be offered to you by the multitude of the angels on high together with your people gathered below". —J. N. Epstein, in *Revue des Études Juives* LXXIII (1921), p. 33, drew the attention to the magical implication of the Hebrew term QASHAR. This may well apply to what is said about Syndalphon in *Bav. Ḥagigah* 13b: "He (= Syndalphon) says (a magical) name and the crown of its own goes up and places itself on the head of God". See also *Hekhalot Rabbati* iii,2, where the Living Creatures are called 'those who tie crowns' (= *Qoshrei Ketarim*).

[136] We shall come back to this point in our discussion of *3 Enoch*.

[137] *Bereshit Rabbā*, p. 738: "... there is no sitting in heaven ... they have no joints". *Yerushalmi Berakhot* 2c: "The angels have no joints". Both sayings are

however, as sitting even in the presence of God. This is a privilege that angels do not have.[138] In a different context, moreover, we hear that "In the days to come God is going to sit (in judgement) and the angels offer thrones to the illustrious ones among the People of Israel and they sit, and God, the president of the court, with them, in judgement on the nations of the world".[139] It must, however, be remarked that the elders in the *Apocalypse* have no judiciary function [140] and that what is said about their doxologies is similar to what several sages say about the future heavenly banquet presided over by God and in which the righteous say words of praise to Him.[141] Although the frequent doxologies recited by the elders in the *Apocalypse* may be associated to the Merkavah hymns of the *Hekhalot* literature, they still lack the lyrical pathos of those hymns. On the other hand, the Merkavah hymns serve many purposes,[142] but they definitely lack the eschatological and messianic tones of the doxologies in the Book of Revelation.

Particularly interesting is John's description of the Divine Throne. Although there are many peculiar items in this description, we shall concentrate here on only two of them. It is said, firstly, that the four Living Creatures are "in the midst of the throne and round about the throne". The two phrases are generally considered to be self-contradictory and hence a suggestion was made to see in the first one—"in the midst of the throne"—an interpolation. Logically speaking, this phrase really causes difficulty, yet some kind of solution may be found in Rabbi ʿAkiva's saying in *Sifra* about the throne

---

introduced by Rabbi Ḥaninah b. Andrei in the name of Rabbi Shemuel b. SITIR (*Yerushalmi*: SOTR). Rabbi Ḥaninah could be the same Rabbi Ḥaninah who is quoted as saying that the names of the angels are of Babylonian origin: *Bereshit Rabbā*, p. 485. If so, he most probably belongs to the Palestinian Amoraim of the third century.—In *Wayyikra Rabbah*, (ed. Margolioth) p. 135, Rabbi Shemuel bar Naḥman is quoted as saying that "the angels of destruction (*Malʾakhei Ḥabbalah*) have no joints". See further, *Temirin* I, p. 129, n. 115.

138 See also the quotation from Karaite sources in S. Lieberman, *op. cit.*, p. 14 (bottom). See further our discussion of *Ascensio Isaiae*, above n. 113.

139 *Tanḥumā ad Leviticus*, ed. Buber, p. 72. The midrash is an attempt to explain the plurality of thrones mentioned in *Daniel* vii,9.

140 But compare the scene described in *1 Enoch* lx,2.

141 *Yerushalmi Megilah* 73b. See S. Lieberman, *Hellenism in Jewish Palestine*, New York, The Jewish Theological Seminary of America, 1950, p. 15/6; W. C. van Unnik, "A Note on the Dance of Jesus in the *Acts of John*", *Vigiliae Christianae* XVIII (1964), pp. 1-5.

142 See A. Altman, in: *Melilah* II (1964) (in Hebrew), pp. 1 ff.

and the Living Creatures. In a passage dealing with the question of who may see God, and under what circumstances, it is said (according to the good reading of MS. Vatican 66, fol. 9a): "Even the Living Creatures who are carried in the Merkavah cannot see the Divine Glory". Although Ezekiel clearly says that the Living Creatures carry the firmament over their heads, and it is on this firmament that the Throne of God is placed (*Ezekiel* i,22 ff.), the midrash conceives of the Creatures as being on the same plane as it, and as being carried by the Merkavah. Exactly the same concept is to be found in *Hekhalot Rabbati*, chapter iii. Even in the discussion of the seven heavens and what they contain as it occurs in *Bav. Ḥagigah*, the Creatures are placed on the seventh heaven together with the Divine Throne. Only after *Ezekiel* i,22 was introduced by the Gemārā, in a manner questioning this description, was the tradition of an eighth heaven introduced.[143]

In addition, it is said in *Revelation* iv that the four Living Creatures which were seen by John were like a lion, an ox,[144] a man and a flying eagle. These are the same as those mentioned by Ezekiel, though the latter introduced them in a different order: man, lion, calf, eagle.[145] While Ezekiel stresses the fact that each of the creatures had four faces, nothing explicit is said in the *Apocalypse* about the fourfold structure of the Creatures' faces.[146] Moreover, while Ezekiel mentions that each of the Creatures had four wings, John describes them as having six wings, the number of the wings which the Serafim

---

[143] See also *Hekhalot Rabbati*, iii. For discussions of the traditions about the existence of eight, and not seven, heavens see G. Scholem, *Jewish Gnosticism* etc., pp. 65 ff.; I. Gruenwald, in: *Temirin I*, pp. 116 ff.; *idem*, in *Proceedings of the Sixth World Congress of Jewish Studies*, Jerusalem, 1977, pp. 52 ff.

[144] The distinction made in *Bav. Ḥagigah* 13b between the ox (*Ezekiel* i,10) and the *Keruv* (Cherub) in *Ezekiel* x,14 is midrashic but unjustified from a philological point of view. Though the exact etymology of the word KERUV is not quite clear, there are good reasons to relate it to an ox. See *Encyclopedia Biblica* (Hebrew), vol. IV, coll. 238 ff. In post-biblical Merkavah literature the ox was frequently changed into a calf. The earliest occurrence of this change seems to be in a Midrash on *Ezekiel* i found at Qumran, and which Professor J. Strugnell is preparing for publication. See further, S. Lieberman, in: Scholem, *Jewish Gnosticism* etc., p. 122/3.

[145] The order of appearance of these creatures seemingly did not bother Ezekiel himself. At least there is a change in their order between chapters i and x. In *Bav. Ḥagigah* 13b the order is: lion, calf, eagle, man; and in *Hekhalot Rabbati* xxvi,5 the order is: man, calf, lion, eagle. In the *Apocalypse of Abraham* xviii the order is: lion, man, calf, eagle.

[146] See above n. 93.

of *Isaiah* vi had.[147] Again this blending together of motifs may be proof of the eclectic qualities of our visionary, particularly so since John hears the Creatures sing the Sanctus of Isaiah!

H

Naturally, not every apocalyptic book which contains Merkavah material could be included in our discussion. The choice fell upon the main texts and upon those visions which are most clearly of a Jewish origin. There is still relevant material to be found in such books as the *Testament of Levi*[148] and *3 Baruch*,[149] yet the Merkavah material contained therein does not warrant extensive discussion here. However extensive our discussion of the Merkavah material found in Jewish apocalyptic was, it should be noticed that a number of important philological problems had to be left unsolved. The reason for this is that not all these texts were preserved in their original language of composition. Many changes have in all likelihood been introduced into the texts in the course of the translation and some of the texts were translated at least twice. In addition, most texts suffered from the hands of interpolators, who used the opportunity of introducing Christian *theologumena* into them. Room must likewise be left for the supposition that some Jewish *theologumena* were dropped by those interpolators or translators. However, it stands to reason to assume that the Merkavah sections were less affected by these processes than the rest of the material, particularly

[147] For an attempt to harmonize between the number of the wings of the Seraphim in *Isaiah* vi and the number of the wings of the Creatures in *Ezekiel* see *Bav. Hagigah* 13b.

[148] The *Testaments of the Twelve Patriarchs*, and the *Testament of Levi* among them, are famous for the debate concerning their Jewish or Christian origin. It is here assumed that the *Testaments* are of Jewish origin, although they include obvious Christian interpolations.—In the case of the *Testament of Levi*, the Merkavah material can be briefly summarized thus: Levi describes his ascent to the third heaven where the angels showed him "the holy Temple and upon a throne the glory of the Most High" (v,1). In that Temple, Levi is ordained for his priestly offices. Yet, before this, in the first two heavens, Levi saw the places where all unrighteousness and iniquity is punished.

[149] *3 Baruch*, or the Greek Book of Baruch, contains the description of an ascent to five heavens. It is full of allegorical visions and one may, therefore, assume that in spite of its clear mythological and pagan overtones, the vision of the sun in the third heaven (vi,1-2) actually is an allegorical Merkavah vision. But compare the magical practices in connection with the desire to "see the sun at daytime sitting in the Merkavah and rising", in *Sefer Ha-Razim*, pp. 97 ff. It should be noticed that *3 Baruch* is unique in having a door at the entrance of each heaven. See *Psalms* lxxviii,23.

so since the Church adapted Jewish angelology and the related subjects almost *en bloc*. Thus, we find in one of the first and most important Christian apocalypses, the *Apocalypse of Paul*, which we shall discuss immediately, a statement to the effect that the celestial song is recited in Hebrew!

In fact, the *Apocalypse of Paul*, in spite of its Christian origin, leans heavily on Jewish material. The Apocalypse describes, among other things, two visions of Paradise and it is particularly here that the Jewish material most clearly comes to the fore. In chapter xxx, the visionary asks the guiding angel: "What is Alleluia?",[150] to which the angel replies: "Alleluia is spoken in the Hebrew, that is the speech of God and of the angels". Notwithstanding the controversy found in rabbinical literature as to whether the Torah was given in "Assyrian" (that is, the common Hebrew letters) or in the old "Canaanite" script,[151] it is quite evident from a number of sources, that Hebrew is the language of God.[152] The angel's reply, moreover, mentions Hebrew as the language of the angels too. There are parallel statements in the rabbinical writings, notably the saying of Rabbi Yoḥanan to the effect: "He who prays for the fulfilment of his needs in Aramaic, the ministering angels do not come to his help, since the ministering angels do not understand Aramaic".[153] Elsewhere

---

[150] Thus according to the English translation of M. R. James, *The Apocryphal New Testament*, Oxford, Clarendon Press, 1963, p. 527 ff. The Greek text, however, has here: λέγεται ʽΕβραϊστι θεβελ μαρημματά, λαλιὰ τῳ θεῳ τῳ θεμελιουντι τὰ πάντα . . . The sentence is not very clear, particularly the words θεβελ μαρημματα. On first sight the Greek θεβελ seems to be a transcription of the Hebrew *Thevel* = 'world'. But still the phrase remains unclear. Professor S. Liebermann has suggested to me to interpret θεβελ as a corrupt rendering of the Aramaic *Ṭav El* = 'God is blessed' or 'the good God'. As for μαρημματα, Professor Liebermann again suggests to see in it a corrupt rendering for the Aramaic *Maranā ātā* = 'our Lord will come'. The Syrian version of the *Apocalypse of Paul* here reads: "Hallelujah in the language of the Hebrews means: Praise the Lord. Praise God, who was the first of all. Unto him do the angels, without ceasing, raise Hallelujah, and praise him who sent us salvation and created for us all things". (English translation in Tischendorf, *Apocalypses Apocryphae*, p. 56).

[151] See *Yerushalmi Megilah* 71b-c, and parallels.

[152] See *Jubilees* xii,25-26: "'Open his (= Abraham's) mouth and his ears, that he may hear and speak with his mouth, with the language which has been revealed . . . and I (= Abraham) began to speak with him in Hebrew in the tongue of the creation". For further references see L. Ginzberg, *The Legends of the Jews*, vol. V, Philadelphia, The Jewish Publication Society of America, 1955, p. 205/6.

[153] *Bavli Shabbat* 12b; *Sotah* 33a.

it is explicitly said that the ministering angels speak Hebrew.[154] Such sayings regarding the language which the angels speak and understand could well have had polemical functions, since we know that particularly within those circles which practised magic, angels were conjured in Greek [155] and in Aramaic.[156]

In addition, the guiding angel has also something to say about the way the angelic song is recited: [157] "if any sing Alleluia, and they that are present sing not with him, they commit a sin in that they sing not with him". This passage resembles, though not exactly, the one found at the end of *Hekhalot Rabbati* (chapter xxx) to the effect that the angels sing "in perfect unison, in one voice... and there is no one who preceeds his fellow or follows him in the recital of the song. And he who delays his voice in the spelling out of Your name even at an hair's breadth is turned out and burning fire devours him".[158]

In chapter xliv of the Apocalypse, Paul, the visionary, experiences another vision of the Merkavah: "I beheld and saw the heaven shake like unto a tree that is moved by the wind: and suddenly they [159] cast themselves down upon their faces before the throne: and I saw the four and twenty elders and the four beasts worshipping God". This part of the vision most obviously depends on the vision of *Revelation* iv: particularly so since the twenty four elders are mentioned in both cases. The second part of the vision, however, is even more interesting because of the new material it contains:

[154] *Bavli Ḥagigah* 16a; *mesaprin bilshon ha-qodesh*. See further *Wayyikra Rabbah* (ed. Margulies), p. 28.

[155] Particularly interesting in this respect are the Greek prayers—in Hebrew transcription!—in *Sefer Ha-Razim*, pp. 80, 99. See also *Hekhalot Rabbati*, xix (end), and J. H. Levi, *Studies in Jewish Hellenism* (in Hebrew), Jerusalem, Bialik Institute, 1969, pp 259 ff.

[156] See, for instance, the text published in Scholem, *Jewish Gnosticism* etc., p. 111 (paragraphe 20). See also the *Aramaic Incantation Texts from Nippur*, published by J. Montgomery, Philadelphia, 1913. See further, B. Levine, "The Language of the Magical Bowls", an appendix to J. Neusner, *A History of the Jews in Babylonia*, vol. V, pp. 343-375.

[157] In the additions to *Tanhuma* from MS Oxford 183 Sh. Buber published a passage which refers to the *Takhsisei Ha-Shir*, that is, the "orders" (ταξις) of the angelic song. See Buber's "Introduction", p. 126/7.

[158] See G. Scholem, *Jewish Gnosticism* etc., pp. 29-30, 129. See also *Apocalypse of Paul* xliii (end): "And they, when they heard these words cried out and wept sore, and all said *with one voice*: Have mercy upon us, O Son of God".

[159] It seems that the angels are here implied, though the "they" in text here generally signify those "which say that Christ rose not from the dead, and that this flesh riseth not again" (xlii).

"and I saw the altar and the veil and the throne and all of them were rejoicing, and the smoke of a sweet odour rose up beside the altar of the throne of God". The altar and the veil make it evident that the heavenly Temple is meant. What, however, is the throne of God doing in the heavenly Temple? It may be argued that the visionary here links himself to the vision described in *Isaiah* vi,1, where God is seen sitting on His throne in the Temple. Yet, there are here some peculiar details of the vision not mentioned in *Isaiah*. The altar and the veil are not expressly referred to in *Isaiah*, though their existence there may be self-understood from the context. But apart from *Isaiah* vi the Temple is nowhere mentioned in any Merkavah vision.[160] On the contrary, in the list of the seven heavens and what is contained therein as described in *Bavli Ḥagigah* 12b, the heavenly Temple is said to be in the fourth heaven, *Zevul*. There it is said too that Michael, the archangel, offers sacrifices on the altar found therein.[161] In *Re'uyot Yeḥezkel*, the heavenly Temple is said to be located in the fifth heaven, *Sheḥaqim*.[162] In any event, there is no Temple in the seventh heaven which contains the Throne. Thus, it seems that both in *Revelation* and in the *Apocalypse of Paul*, the visionaries or the writers, brought together inconsistent literary elements which were not found in this manner in other Merkavah visions. This could be well explained by the fact that once "ecstatic" apocalyptic declined, an allegedly new type of apocalyptic arose. In this new type of apocalyptic, mere "literary" motives were blended together. A full discussion of this new type of apocalyptic, however, is not within the scope of the present study.

---

[160] But in *Testament of Levi* v,1, there *is* a Temple in the third heaven, and it contains also the divine Throne.

[161] These sacrifices are generally explained to be the souls of the righteous. See also *Bavli Menaḥot* 110a, *Zevaḥim* 62a. In the *Apocalypse of Paul* only "the smoke of a sweet odour" is mentioned, but it is not said who offers the incense. See further *Revelation* v,8 and Charles's commentary *ad locum*.

[162] See the writer's edition, pp. 128 ff.

CHAPTER THREE

THE ATTITUDE TOWARDS THE MERKAVAH SPECULATIONS IN THE LITERATURE OF THE TANNAIM AND AMORAIM

A

In the previous chapter we discussed the Merkavah material in apocalyptic literature. We shall now turn to the attitude towards the Merkavah speculations in the literature of the *Tannaim* and *Amoraim*. But before doing so, it should be remarked that in considering the mysticism of the period it would be wrong to restrict ourselves only to Merkavah mysticism. There are several utterances in rabbinical literature that refer to the Godhead in quite unusual modes of speech. Consequently, one may ask whether they display a kind of mysticism which is not directly related to the Merkavah tradition.[1] These utterances, few as they are, are highly important and despite the fact that they are sometimes far from clear, they reveal traces of a concept of God that comes close to mysticism.[2] In addition, some of the

[1] There are not many examples which may reflect this kind of apparently non-Merkavah mysticism, but a discussion of them all requires a study in itself. Two examples from the *Mechiltā d'Rabbi Ismael* (ed. Horovitz-Rabin) may give the reader a fairly clear idea of what could be meant by this non-Merkavah mysticism. To the words "And all the people were seeing the sounds" (*Exodus* xx,18) Rabbi Akiva is quoted to have said: "Seeing and hearing that which is given to sight; they saw a word (Hebrew: *Dibber*) of fire coming out of the mouth of the *Gevurah* (= *dynamis*) and being hewed on the Tables" (p. 235). For a discussion of this saying and its parallels in rabbinic literature see what the present writer wrote in *Revue des Études Juives* CXXXII (1973), pp. 501 ff. The other example from the *Mechiltā* concerns the words: "Behold, I will stand before you there on the rock at Horeb" (*Exodus* xvii,6; RSV). The *Mechiltā* says: "God told him (= Moses): wherever you find a place with the imprint of a man's foot, there I am in front of you!" (p. 175). See, however, Scholem, *Jewish Gnosticism* etc., p. 129, who, wrongly it appears, suggests that this version of the saying in *Mechiltā d'Rabbi Ismael* is secondary to the one found in *Mekhilta de-R. Shimon ben Yoḥai*, and which contains a gloss referring to *Ezekiel* i,26. See further the *Targum Yerushalmi to Exodus* xvii,6.

[2] In this respect the various sayings which refer to God in terms of place are of relevance for our discussion. See E. E. Urbach, *The Sages*, Jerusalem, Magnes Press, 1975, pp. 66 ff. See further the various sayings about the *Shekhinah* and the space it metaphorically occupies, in: *Pesiktā de-Rav Kahanā* (ed. Mandelbaum), pp. 1-8. Some of the sayings there are of great importance but were not always correctly interpreted.

utterances in Philo's writings have been taken as evidence of a Jewish hellenistic mystery-mysticism.[3] One may, therefore, speak of a variety of mystical tendencies in the Judaism of the time of the Mishnah and Talmud, the existence of which has not been admitted without controversy, both in the literature of the period and in the scholarly assessment of that literature. We shall now turn to that literature and to the views expressed by some scholars regarding the mystical utterances found therein. Yet, before doing so, it should be remarked that in spite of that controversial attitude later rabbinical writings still persisted in referring to and even quoting from the mystical material found both in rabbinical writings and the so-called *Hekhalot* literature. Thus in post-talmudic times, one can find references to the Merkavah tradition in *Pirkei-de-Rabbi Eliezer* (composed most probably in *Eretz Yisrael* at the beginning of the eighth century) chapters iii-iv, and in some of the writings of the *Ge'onim*, notably in the halakhic and exegetical Responsa of Rav Hai Ga'on (939-1038).[4]

The mystical tradition of the Jews during the talmudic period is called *Ma'aseh Merkavah* (= the work of the divine chariot) and together with the so-called *Ma'aseh Bereshit* (= the work of the creation of the world) it forms the two branches of the so-called esoteric teachings of Judaism at that period. Both terms occur for the first time in *Mishnah Ḥagigah* ii,1 (= *Tosefta Hagigah* ii,1). The term "*Merkavah*", however, was used with reference to the visions of *Ezekiel* (but not by Ezekiel himself) in *Ben Sira* xlix,8. The Hebrew text there reads *Zenei Merkavah* where the Greek has ἅρματος χερουβιν. While the sense of the Greek is clear, the Hebrew, with the Syriac *genasa*, is taken to mean "the kinds of the chariot", which is a little vague.[5] Elsewhere we find the term '*Merkavah*' in the above mentioned fragment of the so-called angelological liturgy of Qumran which was first published by J. Strugnell. The term '*Merkavah*' is also used in *Mishnah Megillah* iv, 10 and applied there to chapter one (and pos-

[3] See especially, E. R. Goodenough, *By Light, Light: The Mystic Gospel of Hellenistic Judaism*, Reprint: Amsterdam, Philo Press, 1969. Goodenough's thesis is not always convincing, and Professor David Winston informs me that he is to take up a new study of the subject.

[4] See B. M. Lewin, *Otzar Ha-Geonim*, vol. IV, Jerusalem, 1931, part 2, pp. 10-24; 53-61.

[5] For the suggestion that *Ezekiel* i originally contained yet another—now lost—vision, see Sh. Spiegel, in *Journal of Biblical Literature*, LIV (1935), p. 168. But see Rashi to *Ezekiel* i,9. For the term *Minei Ha-Kavod* (= the kinds of the Glory) see *Midrash Ha-Gadol* to *Genesis* xvii,22 (and parallels).

sibly also chapters eight and ten) of *Ezekiel*. And finally, the mystics of the time of the Talmud are called *Yoredei Merkavah*, that is, those who descend, so-to-speak, into the mystical vision of the divine chariot.[6]

The central utterance in rabbinic literature with regard to the speculation of the Merkavah is to be found in *Mishnah Ḥagigah* ii,1: "It is forbidden to discourse... on the Creation of the World in the presence of two, and on the *Merkavah* in the presence of one, unless he is wise and able to understand of himself".[7] The ensuing discussion in *Talmud Bavli Ḥagigah* 11b, and also the text of the Mishnah as it is explicated in *Tosefta Ḥagigah* ii,1, make it clear that the meaning of the Mishnah is that "it is forbidden to discourse on the Creation of the World with two (students), nor on the *Merkavah* with one, unless he is wise and able to understand of himself". The technical details as to how this particular kind of discourse on the matters of the Merkavah was conducted in Tannaitic circles is well exemplified in a much discussed and often misunderstood story about Rabban Yoḥanan ben Zakkai and his disciple Rabbi El'azar ben 'Arakh recorded in *Tosefta Ḥagigah* ii,1 and in two major parallel versions in *Yerushalmi Ḥagigah* 77a and *Bavli Ḥagigah* 14b.

The story there tells of Rabban Yoḥanan ben Zakkai who was travelling on a donkey while his disciple El'azar ben 'Arakh was walking behind. At a certain point on their way, the student requested his master to teach him "a chapter in the Work of the Divine Chariot". The master, however, was reluctant to fulfil the student's request and said: "Did I not teach you some time ago that one should not discourse on the Merkavah with a single (student) unless he is wise and able to understand of himself". Rabbi El'azar promptly grasped what his master had implied and, as the version found in *Jer. Ḥagigah* explicitly says, asked for permission to hold a discourse himself before his Rabbi. This was to convince the master of the abilities of his pupil, before the former revealed his knowledge. Soon, Rabban Yoḥanan ben Zakkai descended from the donkey, put on, as the

[6] Cf. the bibliography listed in G. Scholem, *Kabbalah*, Jerusalem, Keter Publishing House, 1974, pp. 204-206; 459. For the earliest recorded occurrence of the term 'Merkavah' in a context relevant for our discussion, see *1 Chronicles* xxviii,18.

[7] For the text of the Mishnah see Y. N. Epstein, *Mavo LeNusah HaMishnah*, Jerusalem, Magnes Press, 1964, p. 1115; *Idem*, *Mevo'ot LeSifrut HaTannaim*, Jerusalem, Magnes Press, 1957, p. 48. [See now also D. J. Halperin, *Merkabah and Ma'aseh Merkabah according to Rabbinic Sources* (Dissertation: University of California, Berkeley), 1977. Halperin's work deserves more attention than can be given to it now].

custom was in many religious and legal practices,[8] his *Tallit* and both of them sat down on a stone in the shade of an olive tree. After Rabbi El'azar ben 'Arakh had finished his discourse, Rabban Yoḥanan stood up and kissed him on his head and blessed him for "knowing how to understand and to discourse in matters pertaining to the Glory (*Kavod*) of his Father in Heaven". In addition, Rabban Yoḥanan praised his student for being one "who discourses well and performs well".

Now, this last sentence, which has been considered not to be in its right place,[9] could well mean in this particular context that Rabbi El'azar ben 'Arakh was not only able to discourse correclty but that he also knew, as the first part of the story so clearly shows, how to introduce such a discourse on the Merkavah. (This notwithstanding the fact that later on Rabbi El'azar ben 'Arakh fell out of grace in the eyes of his colleagues, and Rabbi Yehoshu'a was then considered to be Rabban Yoḥanan ben Zakkai's senior student in the matters of the Merkavah.[10]) The parallel versions of this story about Rabban Yoḥanan ben Zakkai and Rabbi El'azar ben 'Arakh in both Talmuds contain the description of a mystical experience that took place while Rabbi El'azar was discoursing before his master. We shall come back to this experience only after making some additional comments regarding the story as it is told in the *Toseftā*.

The terminology used in this story, like that of the *Mishnah*, clearly indicates that the *Ma'aseh Merkavah* speculations in Tannaitic circles

---

[8] Compare *Toseftā Pisḥa* ii,16 (ed. Lieberman, p. 147 f.).

[9] See E. E. Urbach, "The Traditions about the Merkabah Mysticism in the Tannaitic Period", *Studies in Mysticism and Religion Presented to Gershom G. Scholem on his Seventieth Birthday*, Jerusalem, Magnes Press, 1967, Hebrew Section, p. 3.

[10] *Bavli Ḥagigah* 14b. Here he is said to be one of those who discoursed before their master but before whom nobody later on discoursed. On the ground of several Tannaitic sources (*Kohelet Rabbā* vii,1,7; *Avot de-Rabbi Natan*, Version A, ch. xiv, and Version B, ch. xxix (ed. Schechter, p. 58/9); and *Bavli Shabbat* 147b) it appears that Rabbi El'azar ban 'Arakh did either not follow his master to Yavneh or else that he soon left that place. Rabbi El'azar is reported to have followed his wife to Emmaus, where he forgot all that he had learned. The tragic end of Rabbi El'azar was often discussed by scholars. See recently, J. Neusner, *A Life of Yoḥanan ben Zakkai*, Leiden, E. J. Brill, 1970, p. 249. The change in the attitude of the sages towards Rabbi El'azar ben 'Arakh is best reflected in *Misnah 'Avot* ii,9 where Rabbi El'azar is still considered Rabban Yoḥanan's favourite student, while the preceeding mishnah, ii,8, already considers Rabbi Eli'ezer ben Horkenos as the most deserving of Rabban Yoḥanan's students. Nevertheless, Abba Shaul still tries to insist there on the original attitude towards Rabbi El'azar ben 'Arakh.

primarily were of a midrashic nature. Such terms as *Darash* (discourse), *Shanah* (teach), *Pereq* (a chapter), are terms which clearly show that as a matter of didactic principle there was no substantial difference in the way the Scriptural Merkavah material was studied from the way other biblical passages were handled in rabbinic circles.[11] Yet, there was a major difference between the two, namely, in the number of those allowed to participate in the study. Otherwise, the technical procedure of the study seems to be the customary one in both cases.[12] Moreover, the Babylonian Talmud (*Ḥagigah* 13a) discusses the question: "Which verses (in the first chapter of *Ezekiel*) correspond to the *Maʿaseh Merkavah*". There are two answers given to the question, which vary from verse 28 (according to Rabbi Yehudah Ha-Nasi) to the word *Ha-Ḥashmal* (most likely the one mentioned in v.,27;[13] according to Rabbi Yiẓḥak). Thereafter, several suggestions are made as to how the material in its various parts should be studied: According to one view, till the word "*waʾere*" (*Ez*. i,4) one may teach in the regular manner while from that word onwards only *Rashei Peraqim*[14] should be taught. According to

[11] See my article "Yannai and the Hekhalot Literature" (in Hebrew), *Tarbiz* XXXVI (1967), p. 258/9. We shall later on come back to the "midrashic" terminology found in the *Hekhalot* literature itself.

[12] Except, of course, for the fact, that in the case of the Merkavah-midrashs the student, and not the master, is expected to begin the discourse. As we are going to see, even this procedure was later on reversed.

[13] The Hebrew text here reads: *Ḥashmal* (without the definite article). Doubtless the word *HaḤashmal* (with the definite article) in verse 4 could not be meant here.—The word *Ḥashmal* itself had an interesting role in the rabbinic Merkavah speculations. First, we hear of two cases in which young and inexperienced students discoursed on the word *Ḥashmal* and a fire came out and devoured them (*Bavli Ḥagigah* 13a). Then, we also know that the *Ḥashmal* occupied a special chapter in the *Maʿaseh Merkavah* speculations; see *Midrash Mishlei* x. See also E. E. Urbach, *art. cit.* (above n. 8), p. 26. In addition, the word *Ḥashmal* is interpreted in *Bavli Ḥagigah* 13a-b as indicating the order of the angelic song. Angelic beings called *Ḥashmalim* are quite frequent in Jewish liturgical poetry. In the *Hekhalot* fragments published in *Tarbiz* XXXVIII (1969), p. 370.1.48 we find: "And the *Ḥashmal* is singing before you". Finally, in *Hekhalot Rabbati* xxv,5 a section is inserted which discusses the perils which might befall the unworthy mystic at the gate of the sixth palace. Since at that stage *Hekhalot Rabbati* is already discussing matters that pertain to the seventh palace, this section is to all likelihood to be considered as an interpolation. The section begins with a quotation from *Ezekiel* i,27—"*waʾere keʿein Ḥashmal*"—and may constitute an independent Merkavah-midrash. In some of the MSS. of the *Hekhalot* literature this section is quoted separately, and not in this place in *Hekhalot Rabbati*. It should also be noticed that in no other case in *Hekhalot Rabbati* is any of the sections introduced by the quotation of a scriptural phrase.

[14] For a definition of the term see, *Yerushalmi Megilah* 72a. It appears that

another view in the Gemara, till the word "*wa'ere*" one may teach *Rashei Peraqim* while the rest could be taught only when the student is "wise and able to understand of himself".[15] All these, and also some additional elements which we shall presently discuss, clearly testify to the midrashic character of the Merkavah study in Tannaitic and Amoraic circles. Thus, the principal meaning of *Maʿaseh Merkavah* in these circles was a midrashic explication of the text of the first chapter in *Ezekiel.* Whether any mystical experiences were involved in that study remains to be considered later on in our discussion.

As for the terminology used in the story about Rabban Yoḥanan and Rabbi Elʿazar, it would be best to begin our discussion with the term *PEREQ* (a chapter). As W. Bacher indicated, the term *pereq* designated in Tannaitic literature a section of the oral law [16] and in Amoraic usage it also referred to the chapters of the *Mishnah.*[17] Generally speaking, a *pereq* may well equal a pericope of midrashic exposition, that is, a passage in which a biblical word or phrase is introduced and followed by a midrashic saying. When Rabbi Elʿazar ben ʿArakh asked Rabban Yoḥanan ben Zakkai to teach him one chapter of the *Maʿaseh Merkavah,* he most probably meant that Rabban Yoḥanan should quote any of the biblical phrases found in *Ezekiel* i and offer his own midrashic interpretation to it. Rabban Yoḥanan refused, and as we have seen, Rabbi Elʿazar ben ʿArakh "opened and discoursed",[18] i.e., he cited a biblical phrase and interpreted it accordingly. We do not know what the student discoursed before his master, but we know what his discourse was believed to have brought about. To this part of the story, however, we shall turn only later on.

In the time of the *Amoraim,* the term *pereq* was used in a new com-

---

Rashei Peraqim are the first verses of a biblical chapter in the massoretic division. See also G. Scholem, *Jewish Gnosticism* etc., p. 25 n. 14; Sh. Spiegel, in *Journal of Biblical Literature* LIV (1935), p. 166, n. 7; S. Lieberman, *Toseftā Kifshutah: Shabbat,* p. 104. In the yet unpublished angelic liturgy from Qumran one finds the term *Rashei Tushbaḥot,* which could well correspond to the *Rosh Shirot* found in *Hekhalot Rabbati* ii,4, but may also be a class of angels.

[15] *Bavli Ḥagigah* 13a.

[16] W. Bacher, *Die Exegetische Terminologie der Jüdischen Traditionsliteratur,* Leipzig, 1899, Erster Teil: "Die Bibelexegetische Terminologie der Tannaiten," p. 154.

[17] *Ibid.,* Zweiter (Schluss-) Teil: "Die Bibel- und Traditionsexegetische Terminologie der Amoräer," p. 163 f.

[18] For the technical use of *PATAḤ* see *ibid.,* Erster Teil, p. 162/3; Zweiter Teil, pp. 174 ff.

bination: *Rashei Peraqim*. It is said in *Bavli Ḥagigah* 13a that Rabbi Ḥiyya allowed one to "deliver *Rashei Peraqim*" to a single student who wanted to study the *Ma'aseh Merkavah*. From the way Rabbi Ḥiyya's words are introduced after the quotation from the *Mishnah*, "and not (in the matters of the) Merkavah to a single (student)", it clearly appears that Rabbi Ḥiyya intended to relax the ruling of the Mishnah. He says: "But one may deliver to him *Rashei Peraqim*". This phrase most likely means that the teacher could refer the student to the opening phrases from Scripture upon which the student was then allowed to introduce his own exposition. In giving to the student to the biblical reference, the master already does a great deal, particularly in stimulating the subject of the student's discourse on the matters of the Merkavah. Rabbi Zera (the first, who came from Babylonia), however, could not agree to this procedure and said: "One should deliver *Rashei Peraqim* only to the head of the study-house (*Beit Din*) and to him who sincerely worries".[19] In both cases, what seems to be almost certain is, that at least some of the Amoraim tolerated a more lenient attitude towards the procedure of the study of the *Ma'aseh Merkavah*.[20]

A parallel change in the attitude of the Rabbis towards the Merkavah material can also be seen from the story told about Rabbi Yoḥanan and Rabbi El'azar (both Palestinian *Amoraim* of the third century C.E.). Rabbi Yoḥanan offers to instruct Rabbi El'azar in the *Ma'aseh Merkavah* (*Bavli Ḥagigah* 13a). Rabbi El'azar declines the offer, saying that he is not old enough for that kind of study. No details are given here as to what the proper age for the study of the *Ma'aseh Merkavah* was and it is hardly conceivable that the subjective feeling of the candidate could be accepted in that matter.[21] When Rabbi El'azar

[19] The Gemarā adds here a comment to the effect, that there were some who said that the words "he who sincerely worries" refer back to the head of the studyhouse. Heads of Yeshivot were later on, in Ge'onic times, considered to be recipients of esoteric knowledge. See B. M. Lewin, *Otẓar ha-Geonim*, vol. VI, Jerusalem, 1934, p. 21, where it said that God's secret name of 22 letters was known "in Kabbalah" (oral transmission) to the heads of the Yeshivah. See also *Pirkei de-Rabbi Eli'eẓer*, ch. viii, in comparison to *Bavli Qiddushin* 71 a.

[20] Here the writer agrees with Urbach's contention, *art. cit.* (n. 9), *passim*.

[21] From the text of *Ma'aseh Merkavah* published by G. Scholem, *op. cit.*, p. 108, it appears that the age of thirteen (!) was already considered as the ripe age for the study of esoteric lore. Compare *Mishnah Avot* v,21 where it is said in the name of Yehudah ben Temā that 10 is the proper age for the study of the Mishnah, while 15 was considered as the suitable age for the study of the Talmud. The Qumranites, however, considered the age of 20 as the right age for the esoteric study of the Torah. And finally, the *Sefer Raẓiel* (ed. Amsterdam, 1701) which

reached the right age, Rabbi Yoḥanan died. So Rabbi Assi came forward with a similar offer to Rabbi Elʿazar. Obviously, all this runs counter to the ruling of the Mishnah and, consequently, the Gemārā finds it necessary to state that Rav Yoseph refused to teach the *Maʿaseh Merkavah* to the Elders of Pumbedita, even in exchange for their teaching him the *Maʿaseh Bereshit.* It should be noticed that Rav Yoseph lived in Babylonia, while the other Amoraim mentioned in the Gemārā lived in *Eretẓ Yisrael.* Thus, one may argue that there was some kind of difference in the attitude to the study of the Merkavah lore between those living in Babylonia and those living in *Eretẓ Yisrael.*

Indeed, we find (*Bavli Shabbat* 80b) that a certain Galilean came to Babylonia and was asked by the people there to discourse on the matters of the Merkavah. When he did so, he was afflicted and died. This anecdote speaks for itself, and from yet another saying of the *Talmud Yerushalmi Ḥagigah* 77a it clearly appears, that in *Eretẓ Yisrael* later generations tried to relax the strict ruling of the Mishnah while the sages in Babylonia were less lenient in their obedience to the

collects a good many ancient texts related to magic and Merkavah mysticism says that "this book which is called "The Secrets of Raziel" should be delivered only ... to him who has reached the middle of his life". This is based on *Bavli Qiddushin* 71 a, where the conditions for the revelation of God's secret name are listed. As a matter of fact, 30 was regarded by many to be the earliest date for the study of Jewish Kabbalah. Yet see G. Scholem, *Sabbatai Ṣevi*, Princeton University Press; 1975, p. 114.—The qualities of those who want to study esoteric subjects is variously enumerated in ancient literature. The Qumranites laid great stress on the general demeanour of the candidate, and he had to wait at least two years before he could become full member of the sect and, this, not before he underwent a thorough examination of his moral behaviour and intellectual qualities (I QS VI,13-22). In addition, there was a yearly test of the moral and intellectual qualities of the members of the sect (I QS V,24). According to another text found at Qumran, the candidate had to pass a close examination of his physiognomy in relationship to the astrological signs at his birthtime (4 Q 186). In the *Hekhalot* literature great stress is laid on the perfection of the mystic in the study of the Torah and in his observance of the law (*Hekhalot Rabbati* xiii,2; in: A. Jellinek, *Bet ha-Midrash*, vol. III, p. 93). Among the *Hekhalot* mystics we too find the physiognomic examination of the candidate (G. Scholem, in: *Liber Amicorum ... Bleeker*, Leiden, E. J. Brill, 1969, pp. 175-193; I. Gruenwald, in: *Tarbiẓ* XL (1971), pp. 301-319).—From the days of the Second Temple we hear that the secret name of God was delivered only to "the humble among the priesthood" (*Bavli Kidushin* 71a, and parallels). Finally, Maimonides says that the secrets of physics and metaphysics (in his terminology: *Maʿaseh Bereshit* and *Maʿaseh Merkavah*, respectively) should be studied only by those who have fed themselves with much study of the Law (*Mishneh Torah*, *Sefer ha-Madʿa*, iv,13). See also the discussion in *Bavli Ḥagigah* 14a, concerning those who are allowed to study the secrets of the Torah.

Mishnah. It is said there in *Talmud Yerushalmi*: "How does he do (= how is the study of the *Ma'aseh Merkavah* carried out)?—At the beginning his master opens with the *Rashei Pesuqim* [22] while the pupil listens in silence and examines if his own speculations concur with those of his master". Obviously, this is a procedure that is diametrically opposed to what may be inferred as being what Rabban Yoḥanan ben Zakkai thought was the proper procedure in studying the Merkavah lore.[23] In any event, where the terms *Rashei Peraqim* and *Rashei Pesuqim* are referred to (*Bavli Ḥagigah* 13a and *Yerushalmi Ḥagigah* 77a) one clearly finds a break with the ruling of the Mishnah. Thus, under certain circumstances it was the master who was allowed to open the discussion in the *Ma'aseh Merkavah* with either *Rashei Peraqim* or *Rashei Pesuqim*. One might even go as far as to say that the idea of *Rashei Perqaim* or *Rashei Pesuqim* was introduced to legitimize the deviation from the ruling of the Mishnah.

This less rigorous Palestinian attitude towards the study of the Merkavah lore, as opposed to the strict adherence to the law of the *Mishnah* as it could be observed with some of the Babylonian sages, may be taken to reflect indirectly a more general attitude towards the mysticism of the Merkavah in Amoraic circles. It may be argued that the strict observation of the *Mishnah* as seen in the circle of Rabbi Yoḥanan ben Zakkai's students continued to be the rule as long as the tradition of the Merkavah speculations was a live one in *Eretz Yisrael*. When it ceased to be so, a more lenient attitude was adopted. However, in Babylonia the Merkavah speculations continued to be a most holy subject for a long time, so that even in the days of the later *Amoraim* there the attitude prescribed in the *Mishnah* was still strictly observed. We now know that certain Merkavah texts initially composed in *Eretz Yisrael* were transferred to Babylonia and adapted there for local purposes.[24] There are, therefore, good reasons for

[22] See above, n. 14.

[23] One may suggest that the opposite procedure, namely that the master opens the discourse, was aimed at keeping a uniform procedure of study in the old Yeshivot even in matters of the Merkavah. See *Yerushalmi Bava Metzi'a* 8d: "Who is to be considered one's teacher that taught him wisdom?—Everybody who opened to him the discourse—this is the opinion of Rabbi Me'ir".

[24] In the *Hekhalot* text published by the present writer in *Tarbiz* XXXVIII (1969), pp. 354 ff. mention is made of a certain sage connected to the Merkavah circles who was to occupy a prominent position among the Jews in Babylonia. See, *ibid.*, p. 357, ll. 13 ff. The text is based on *Hekhalot Rabbati*, and in some cases even quotes from it. Yet, it comes even closer to the *Sar Torah*, which is generally appended to *Hekhalot Rabbati* (ch. xxvii-xxx). And in some of the

believing that the Merkavah tradition in Babylonia outlived its counterpart in *Eretz Yisrael.* One may likewise say that the more lenient attitude shown by the *Amoraim* of *Eretz Yisrael* reflects the fact that the Merkavah speculations became known in fairly wide circles and there was no longer the previously felt need to keep these speculations under the most severe restrictions. However, whatever the reasons and whatever the practice, the control required on the part of the master over his students was somehow relaxed, but not altogether cancelled. Finally, whether the above-mentioned difference in the attitude towards the Merkavah-midrashim was also influenced by a parallel attitude towards the *Heklahot* literature or not remains for the moment an open question.

B

We have now to turn to the verbs *DARASH* and *SHANAH* found in the story of Rabban Yoḥanan ben Zakkai and Rabbi El'azar ben 'Arakh. These two verbs, which imply the study of the subject of the *Ma'aseh Merkavah*, are in line with the ruling of the Mishnah: "*'Ein Dorshin*", "one should not discourse". It thus appears that a study and no mystical experience is here involved. These two verbs and the verbs *GAMAR* (to study and to teach), *PATAḤ* (to open a midrashic discourse usually by quoting a biblical verse the relationship of which to the verse under midrashic discussion is the subject of the discourse),[25] and *HIRẒAH* (to lecture), which are repeatedly used in Tractate *Ḥagigah*, in both Talmuds, make it clear that the *Ma'aseh Merkavah* speculations of the *Tannaim* basically were of a midrashic nature. Moreover, from the words "many have discoursed in the Merkavah and have not seen it during their lifetime" (*Toseftā Megilah* iii (iv), 28) it clearly appears that in Tannaitic circles a clear distinction was maintained between the midrashic speculations about

MSS of the *Sar Torah* we find the following passage: "This (i.e. the conjuration of the *Sar Torah*) was done by Rabbi Eliezer and he was answered but did not trust (his success), and it was repeatedly done by myself and I did not trust (my success) either, till I brought a fool who repeated what I had done. (Consequently) they told Rabbi 'Akiva to go abroad ... and when Rabbi 'Akiva descended to Babylonia, and conjured (the angel) and was answered, he returned and told us (of his success) and we rejoiced." The passage obviously stresses the fact that the theurgic practices connected with the conjuration of the *Sar Torah* could be perfected (a) by every layman; and (b) not only in *Eretz Yisrael* but also—and most significantly so—in Babylonia.

[25] See above note 18.

the Merkavah and its mystical perception.[26] In other words, even in these circles one could not completely rule out the possibility of a mystical vision of the Merkavah and this in spite of the fact that no detailed descriptions of such visions were preserved in Tannaitic sources.

However, one may ask whether we can really accept the view as expressed by Prof. E. E. Urbach that the mystical experiences of the *Tannaim* are devoid of any real ecstatic elements and that "the prevailing tone (in the esoteric tradition of the *Tannaim*) is that of an ascetic ecstasy"! [27] Apart from the fact that the idea of an "ascetic ecstasy" is far from being clear, it must be asked what kind of mystical experience did the *Tannaim* after all have and how should the historicity of the documents we have to consult for an answer be judged. In the case of the story about Rabban Yoḥanan and Rabbi El'azar, there are two, almost parallel, interpolations in the versions found in *Talmud Bavli Ḥagigah* 14b and *Talmud Yerushalmi Ḥagigah* 77a.[28] According to the version in the *Yerushalmi*, when Rabbi El'azar began his discourse, Rabban Yoḥanan "descended from the donkey, saying: 'It is not proper for me to hear the Glory of my Creator while I am riding the donkey' ". When both of them sat down beneath a tree, "fire came down from heaven and surrounded them, and the ministering angels were dancing in front of them as groomsmen rejoicing before the bridegroom". It is furthermore reported in *the Yerushalmi* that "one angel was speaking from within of the fire saying: 'It is as you say, Rabbi El'azar ben 'Arakh, this is what the *Ma'aseh Merkavah* is!' ". The end of the story follows, using the same words as in the *Toseftā*. According to the version found in the *Talmud Bavli*, after Rabban Yoḥanan had descended from the donkey, Rabbi El'azar asked him: "Why have you descended from the donkey?"—Rabban Yoḥanan answered: "Is it not improper for me to ride a donkey while you are discoursing in the *Ma'aseh Merkavah*, the Shekhinah is with us, and the ministering angels are accompanying us?". Immediately Rabbi El'azar ben 'Arakh began his discourse in the *Ma'aseh Merkavah*.[29] Only then, as the story in *Tal. Bavli* goes, did

[26] See Urbach, *art. cit.*, p. 7, n. 25.
[27] *Ibid.*, p. 11.
[28] See also *Mekhilta d'Rabbi Sim'on b. Jochai*, ed. Epstein-Melamed, p. 158/9.
[29] According to this version of the Bavli, before Rabban Yoḥannan descended from the donkey Rabbi El'azar asked him for permission to say something which "you have taught me".

the fire come down from heaven and surrounded all the trees in the field. The trees, thereupon, began to sing a song of praise [30] and only afterwards do we hear of the angel who spoke from within of the fire confirming: "This is the *Maʿaseh Merkavah*!" [31]

Although it is quite likely that the version found in *Bavli* is dependent on the one found in *Yerushalmi*, it is equally true to say that both versions are dependent on a common source, introducing their own changes. It remains to be considered what kind of relationship this alleged source and, consequently, the two versions in the Talmudim bear to the story as it is told in the *Toseftā*. According to Professor Urbach, on the one hand, the two versions of the Talmudim reflect the more lenient attitude towards the Merkavah material as it is found in Armoraic circles. Thus, Urbach says, the original version of the story is that of the *Toseftā*: it is short and truly expresses the reserved mood of the mysticism of the *Tannaim*. On the other hand, the present writer has expressed the view that the stories found in the Talmuds, in spite of the differences between them, reflect the mystical mood of the original, while the *Toseftā*, which is more concerned with straightforward halakhic regulations, represents a shortened form of the story.[32] Professor Urbach, furthermore, maintains that the fire-motif which is found in the versions of the Talmuds is not necessarily to be taken as indicating a real ecstatic experience. Urbach quotes several sayings and stories in which the vision of fire by several

[30] Corresponding to *Psalm* cxlviii,7-9.

[31] The *Bavli* adds another story about Rabbi Yehoshuʿa and Rabbi Yossi Ha-Kohen who too discoursed in the matters of the Merkavah. It is told that "Clouds gathered in the sky, and a rainbow was seen, and the angels were gathering and coming to hear, as people who come to watch the festivities performed in honour of the bridegroom and the bride". Rabban Yoḥannan had also a special blessing for these two Rabbis. In *Yerushalmi Ḥagigah* the story is told, with some changes in the account, about Rabbi Yossef Hakohen and Rabbi Shimʿon ben Netanʾel. Urbach, *art. cit.*, p. 7, inclines to distinguish between two branches of the tradition: the one concerning Rabbi Elʿazar ben ʿArakh, and the other about Rabbi Yossi Ha-Kohen and Rabbi Yehoshuʿa. Concerning the rainbow which is seen by the two sages it must be remarked that Ezekiel mentions (i,28) the "appearance of the bow that is in the cloud on the day of rain" (RSV). Hence, the description in the text of *Shiʿur Qomah* (in: *Merkavah Shelemah*, ed. S. Musajoff, Jerusalem; 1921, fol. 38b): "the body (of the Godhead) is like a rainbow". See also *Bavli Berakhot* 59a: "Rabbi Alexandrei in the name of Rabbi Yehoshuʿa ben Levi said: Whosoever sees the rainbow must fall upon his face, as it is said (*Ezekiel* i,28; see above): 'And when I saw it, I fell upon my face'". See also *Bavli Ḥagigah* 16a: "Everybody who looks at three things is liable to lose his eyesight: at the rainbow ...". Compare *Revelation* x,1.

[32] See the article quoted above in n. 11, pp. 260 ff.

sages is introduced in association with the fire seen at the theophany on Mount Sinai. Only the song of the trees which is recorded in both Talmuds is taken by Urbach to express the ecstatic experience of the mystics. It may be argued, however, that fire is always expressive of a mystical experience [33] and the theophany-fire seen on Mount Sinai is, for that matter, no prototypal exception to the rule. Moreover, the present writer finds it difficult to follow Urbach when he argues that the relative freedom of expression of the *Amoraim* when they discussed the *Ma'aseh Merkavah* shows that in comparison to the *Tannaim*, the *Amoraim* were more familiar with the esoteric doctrines of the mystics while the *Tannaim* were more or less ignorant of the writings of the mystics. To begin with, we have already observed a noticeable distinction between the Palestinian and Babylonian *Amoraim* with regard to the attitudes they maintained towards the study of the Merkavah lore. Hence, it would be difficult to generalize concerning the differences between the *Tannaim* and the *Amoraim*, at least not as emphatically as Urbach tries to do. In addition, it is quite risky to reach conclusions about alleged differences of opinion just on the grounds of literary expression,[34] particularly so when we deal with secret lore.

It is really very difficult to guess what the Merkavah speculations of the circle of Rabban Yoḥanan ben Zakkai were like. What is reported concerning these speculations in the rabbinic sources is actually so restrained in matters of content and literary expression that almost everything can be said about it with equal justification. One can say, with Urbach, that what is said is, materially speaking, everything that was known; but one can also maintain that a great deal more than what was said was in fact known. Admittedly, it is quite reasonable to say that the Tannaitic speculations about the Merkavah did not depend on the *Hekhalot* literature which was composed at a later age. But it seems equally reasonable to say that the *Tannaim* did not have to wait for the *Hekhalot* literature to discover the ecstatic potentials for the Merkavah mysticism.

It must, therefore, be admitted that the original version of the story

[33] J. Abelson, *Jewish Mysticism*, London, 1913, pp. 39 ff.

[34] To do so, however, is very much in line with the methods used by those who subscribe to the *Formgeschichte*. *Formgeschichtliche* considerations should, however, be applied in the study of the literature of the Sages with great care, since in the process of oral transmission a lot was changed in the way of expression without necessarily indicating real differences of opinion.

of Rabban Yoḥanan ben Zakkai and Rabbi El'azar ben 'Arakh is hidden within the realm of guesswork. Was it the short version of the *Toseftā*, or was it perhaps a presently unknown source from which both the *Yerushalmi* and the *Bavli* drew their own versions and from which the editor of the *Toseftā* formed his shortened version. Of course, the answer to the question of whether the original story at all contained an ecstatic experience decisively depends on what the original version was. But whatever the conclusion on this particular issue will be, one cannot ignore the possibility that ecstasies still *were* familiar experiences in the *Ma'aseh Merkavah* speculations of the *Tannaim*. A discussion of the famous story about the four sages who "entered the Pardes" will show it to be a good example in which in spite of the lack of straightforward evidence in the talmudic and midrashic sources, one has to assume that the existence of an ecstatic experience was nevertheless implied. The main versions of this story (in *Toseftā Ḥagigah* ii,3; *Yerushalmi Ḥagigah* 77b; *Midrash Rabbā* to *Shir Ha-Shirim*, ed. Vilna, 7d-8a) do not contain any explicit references to an ecstatic experience. But on the ground of the terminology used there, one may reach the conclusion that such an experience was *a priori* assumed. To this, one should add that the version of the story found in *Bavli Ḥagigah* 14b and 15b (bottom) actually contains explicit references to an ecstatic experience of the kind and nature found in the *Hekhalot* literature.

As is well known, the story tells of the four sages, Ben 'Azzai, Ben Zomā, Rabbi 'Akiva and Elisha ben 'Avuyah, who "entered the *Pardes*". It is said that Ben 'Azzai (*Yerushalmi*: Ben Zoma) "cast a glance and died"; Ben Zoma (*Yerushalmi*: Ben 'Azzai) "cast a glance and was afflicted" (Rashi explains: [35] went out of his mind). Elisha ben Avuyah "cast a glance and cut down the saplings"; and only Rabbi 'Akiva "ascended (or, as another version goes: entered) safely and descended (came out) safely". Professor G. Scholem [36] has rightly interpreted this story in terms of the ascension stories known from apocalyptic literature and particularly from the ascension into Paradise described by Paul the Apostle in *2 Corinthians*

[35] Rashi writes here in accordance with the tradition preserved in the Responsa of Rav Hai Ga'on (cf. *Otzar ha-Ge'onim*, vol. IV, to *Ḥagigah*, p. 14/5). Rav Hai Ga'on actually quotes there from *Hekhalot Zutreti* (see the two versions of the text quoted in Scholem, *Jewish Gnosticism* etc., p. 15, notes 2 & 3).

[36] G. Scholem, *Major Trends in Jewish Mysticism*, London, Thames and Hudson, 1955, pp. 52-54; *Idem*, *Jewish Gnosticism* etc., pp. 14-19.

xii,1-4.[37] Even Professor Urbach here admits that the *Pardes* has to be interpreted in terms of the vision of the Merkavah,[38] although he parts ways with Professor Scholem in his interpretation of the words attributed to Rabbi ʻAkiva in *Bavli Ḥagigah* 14b. Rabbi ʻAkiva is reported there as having said to the other sages involved in the experience (or, more generally, to his students): "When you reach the pure marble stones, do not say: 'Water, Water!', as it is said: 'no man who utters lies shall continue in my presence' " (*Psalms* ci,7; RSV). Urbach admits that terms like "enter the *Pardes*", "cast a glance" (Hiẓiẓ), and "ascend" (ʻAlah) evidently point to experiences quite different from those implied by the terms of midrashic activity which we have encountered in the Rabban Yoḥanan story. Still, however, Urbach argues that these terms are worlds apart from "the imaginary compositions about 'ascensions' in apocalyptic literature, in Hellenistic literature, and in the late Merkavah literature".[39] Moreover, Urbach argues that Rabbi ʻAkiva's utterance concerning the marble stones is to be interpreted allegorically as indicating a warning against spiritual processes the likes of which are known as *Sobria Ebrietas* or sober drunkenness.[40] More relevant, however, is Scholem's analysis which interprets Rabbi ʻAkiva's warning in the light of the information which can be gained from the *Hekhalot* literature.

In two of the *Hekhalot* writings, *Hekhalot Zutreti* and *Hekhalot Rabbati* (the Small Book of the Palaces and the Great Book of the Palaces, respectively),[41] there are descriptions of the special experience the mystics are to encounter at the gate of the sixth palace. They see there the glistening marble stones and are warned against crying out "Water, Water!". If they are not able to restrain themselves, the mystics are liable to endanger themselves physically and mentally. Now, this is exactly the context out of which come the words at-

---

[37] Cf. also H. Bietenhard, *Die Himmlische Welt im Urchristentum und Spätjudentum*, Tübingen, J. C. B. Mohr, 1951, pp. 161 ff.

[38] *Art. cit.*, p. 13.

[39] *Ibid.*, p. 14.

[40] *Ibid.*, p. 17, and the references there.

[41] Unfortunately, no definitive critical editions of the Hekhalot literature are yet available. A list of major MSS. and prints of the *Hekhalot* literature is given in Scholem, *Jewish Gnosticism* etc., pp. 5-7; to which one should add the list of texts, published mainly by the present writer, in: *Israel Oriental Studies* III (1973), p. 88/9, n. 4. Compare also J. C. Greenfield, "Prolegomenon" to H. Odeberg, *3 Enoch*, New York, Ktav Publishing House, 1973, pp. xxvii-xx. See also Part Two of the present study.

tributed to Rabbi ʿAkiva. One should, however, notice that Rabbi ʿAkiva merely warns his colleagues, while the descriptions in the *Hekhalot* literature go into the details of what might actually befall the mystics at the gate of the sixth palace. Although Rabbi ʿAkiva does not mention the gate of the sixth palace, as the *Hekhalot* tractates do, the relationship of his words to those found in the *Hekhalot* books seem to be self-evident. The purpose of the descriptions in the *Hekhalot* literature is to warn off those who are not fully qualified mystics from undergoing experiences which they are liable not to survive. Actually, the behaviour of the mystics at the gate of the sixth palace is considered to be the final serious test which they undergo before they are granted right of passage to the sixth and then to the seventh palace found in the seventh heaven. Admittedly, Rabbi ʿAkiva's words are quoted in *Bavli Ḥagigah* out of that particular context, namely as an ordeal at the entrance to the sixth palace, but this fact does not permit us to interpret the whole utterance in allegorical terms. It is, therefore, closer to the truth to maintain with Professor Scholem "that the later Merkavah mystics showed a perfectly correct understanding of the meaning of this passage (= Rabbi ʿAkiva's words), and their interpretation offers striking proof that the tradition of the Tannaitic mysticism and theosophy was really alive among them, although certain details may have originated in a later period".[42] On the grounds of Scholem's presentation of the relationship between the utterance of Rabbi ʿAkiva and the *Hekhalot* literature, it has been suggested by the present writer that the words of Rabbi ʿAkiva actually reflect the same tradition which is incorporated in the above-mentioned passages in the *Hekhalot* literature.[43] It is not, as Professor Scholem argues, that the *Hekhalot* literature contains the correct interpretation of the saying of Rabbi ʿAkiva, but that the words attributed to the sage are words virtually taken from what already was, or was soon to become, the established *Hekhalot* tradition.[44] It should be added that it is a question of a different order whether the words of Rabbi ʿAkiva are authentic or apocryphally attributed to him, as are some of the *Hekhalot* writings themselves.

Since it is unanimously agreed that the entrance into the *Pardes* does correspond to a vision of the Merkavah, it remains to be asked

[42] G. Scholem, *Major Trends in Jewish Mysticism*, p. 52.

[43] *Art. cit.* (n. 10), pp. 261 ff.

[44] Urbach's criticism *art. cit.*, p. 15, n. 62, is therefore unjustified.

what exactly was meant by a mystical vision of the Merkavah in Tannaitic circles. There are some hints to the answer found in the *Talmud Bavli*. The first one has already been discussed and it concerns Rabbi ʿAkiva's utterance about the pure marble stones. The second also centres round the figure of Rabbi ʿAkiva. The *Gemārā* (*Bavli Ḥagigah* 15b, bottom) reports: "And the ministering angels wanted to drive away [or: kill] Rabbi ʿAkiva, too, but God told them: 'Leave that wise man alone, as he is worthy of experiencing my Glory' ".[45] Now, this peculiar sentence reminds us of the hostile attitude the angels showed to Moses when he reached Heaven to receive the Torah[46] and it also reflects the general theme of the angels' hostility to the ascension onto heaven of human beings.[47] This hostility of the angels is known from apocalyptic literature[48] and from the *Hekhalot* literature[49] and it may be said that the gnosticistic concept of the Archons who try to prevent the soul of man from returning to its Source of Light is in many ways inspired by this motif.[50] In our case of Rabbi ʿAkiva, it may again be argued that

[45] For a discussion of the theurgic term "*lehistamesh bakavod*" (literally, to use the Divine Glory) see Scholem, *Jewish Gnosticism* etc., p. 54/5. The parallel text of *Hekhalot Zutreti* here reads "lehistakel bikhvodi" (= to look at my Glory). See Scholem, *ibid.*, p. 77, n. 7.

[46] *Bavli Shabbat* 88b, where Moses is said to have been afraid that the angels were going to burn him with the vapour of their mouths. In a different context it is said that when Moses was due to descend from heaven, angels again came to kill him (*Shemot Rabbā*, ch. xlii,4; and parallels). In *Pesiktā Rabbati*, ed. Friedmann (Wien, 1880), fol. 96b it is told of Qemuʿel, "who was in charge of 12 000 angels of destruction" (*Malʾakhei Ḥabalah*) (see: *Israel Oriental Studies* III (1973), p. 97, n. 36), and of his colleague, Hadarniel, who intimidated Moses upon his ascension to heaven to receive the Torah. *Pesiktā Rabbati* also mentions the name of Galiẓur, who, among his other duties, "stretches out his wings to receive the vapour of the Living Creatures. For if he does not do so, the ministering angels might be burned up by the vapour of the Living Creatures". The hostility of the angels against each other was discussed in Chapter Two in connection to the *Apocalypse of Abraham*, ch. x, and ch. xvii.

[47] See J. Maier, "Das Gefärdungsmotiv bei der Himmelsreise in der jüdischen Apokalyptik und 'Gnosis'", *Kairos* V (1963), pp. 18-40; J. P. Schultz, "Angelic Opposition to the Ascension of Moses and the Revelation of the Law", *Jewish Quarterly Review* LXI (1970/1), pp. 282-307.

[48] Cf., though indirectly, *Apocalypse of Abraham*, ch. xiii, p. 51/2. It is Azazel who speaks there!

[49] Actually the whole of the *Hekhalot* literature is full of accounts which make it clear how dangerous it was for the mystic to carry out his journey in heaven. See specifically *3 Enoch*, ed. Odeberg (Cambridge, 1928; New York, 1973), ch. vi, p. 12 (English translation, p. 20).

[50] Actually, the motif—in various variations—is known from many ancient cultures. See, for instance, N. K. Sandars, *Poems of Heaven and Hell from Ancient*

it belongs to a later tradition than the story of those who entered the *Pardes*, but as the theme was already known in apocalyptic literature which preceded Tannaitic times, it may well be considered as belonging to the original milieu of the *Pardes*-story. The third clue concerns 'Elish'a ben 'Avuyah. It is asked in the *Gemārā* (*Bavli Ḥagigah* 15a): "What did he ('Elish'a ben 'Avuyah) actually do?—He saw Metatron, who was given permission to sit and write the merits of the people of Israel.—He ('Elish'a) said: We have learnt that up in heaven there is no one sitting.., can it be that there are two *reshuyot* (= two Gods)?—So they pulled Metatron out and beat him with sixty lashes of fire. They asked him: 'Why didn't you stand up when you saw him ('Elish'a ben 'Avuya)?' ".[51] Much has been written about the angel Metatron [52] and in spite of all that we now know about the development of the traditions concerning his name,[53] it would be too daring to maintain that this Metatron-passage in connection with the name of 'Elish'a ben 'Avuyah actually belongs to the original phase of the story.

Thus we find in the discussion of the *Pardes* tale in *Talmud Bavli* three passages: one of which (the angelic hostility towards Rabbi 'Akiva) could well go back to Tannaitic times; one (the saying concerning the pure marble stones) which could also go back to Tannaitic times; and one (the Metatron passage) which most probably belongs to a later period. All these passages, however, cannot be taken to be more than fragmentary hints to the solution of the problem what exactly the nature of the Merkavah-experience of the *Tannaim* was.

A more significant answer to the question may be found in the term *Pardes* itself. As we know, the term was used in a mystical context by Paul, and it is thus a crucial one in the characterization of the nature and scope of Jewish mysticism at the time of the early *Tannaim*. Paul says: "I must boast; there is nothing to be gained by it, but I will go on to visions and revelations of the Lord. I know a man in Christ who fourteen years ago was caught up to the third

Mesopotamia, Harmondsworth, Penguin Books, 1971, pp. 117 ff. For the Greek sources cf. W. K. C. Guthrie, *A History of Greek Philosophy*, vol. II, Cambridge Univ. Press, 1974, pp. 9-13.

[51] See also *3 Enoch*, ch. xvi, p. 22/3 (English translation pp. 43-45).

[52] Cf. Scholem, *Kabbalah* (above n. 6), pp. 377-381; M. Black, "the Origins of the Name Metatron", *Vetus Testamentum* I (1951), pp. 217-219. See also Appendix A to the present book.

[53] G. Scholem, *Jewish Gnosticism* etc., pp. 43 ff.

heaven—whether in the body or out of the body I do not know, God knows. And I know that this man was caught up into Paradise—whether in the body or out of the body I do not know, God knows —and he heard things that cannot be told, which man may not utter" (*2 Corinthians* xii,1-4). Assuming that Paul speaks about himself ("a man in Christ") and that verses 2 and 4 reflect one and the same experience, one may conclude that for Paul "Paradise" was a place in the third heaven.[54] Now, this heavenly Paradise was commonly conceived of as the place of divine retribution for the just, or for their souls.[55] It is interesting, however, to notice that Paul, who most probably was aware of the terminology used in apocalyptic literature, did not here use the term found in the Greek translations of apocalyptic literature, "Paradise of Righteousness".[56] He does not even refer to the Aramaic term "Pardes Qushtā", which literally underlies the Greek "Paradise of Righteousness" and which Paul could have known if he read, and it appears that he did, the apocalyptic books in their original.[57] Paul simply uses the word "Paradise" without its qualification, and this brings his experience even closer to the story of the four who entered the *Pardes*. It therefore, seems, safe to maintain, with Scholem, that Paul in his *Epistle to the Corinthians* and the Rabbis who told the story of Rabbi ʿAkiva and his friends spoke the same theosophical language. Thus, we may assume that at a certain point in Jewish thought and terminological usage, the term *Pardes* came to be used not only as the place where the just and the righteous receive their after-life bonus, but also in connection with the apocalyptic experience in which a man saw himself snatched onto or entering heaven to see, *in his lifetime*, that place and all that it contained, including, as we saw in the previous chapter, the

[54] There are various theories about the location of the heavenly Paradise. The clearest parallel to its location in the third heaven, as Paul assumes, is in: *Apocalypsis Mosis* xxxvii,4, in: K. von Tischendorf, *Apocalypses Apocryphae* (Leipzig, 1866), p. 20. See also A. Vaillant, *Le Livre des Secrets d'Hénoch*, Paris, Institut d'Études Slave, 1952, pp. 8-11. The idea of the location of Paradise in the third heaven was later on exchanged for the idea of its location in the seventh heaven.

[55] See D. S. Russell, *The Method and Message of Jewish Apocalyptic*, London, SCM Press, 1964, p. 283/4; M. E. Stone, "Paradise in *4 Ezra* iv,8 and vii,36, viii,52", *Journal of Jewish Studies* XVII (1966), pp. 85-88.

[56] For a discussion of the various references in apocalyptic literature see H. Bientenhard, *op. cit.*, pp. 168 ff.

[57] The Aramaic *Kushtā* translates both Hebrew terms: *Ẓedek* (= righteousness), and *ʾEmet* (= truth). See further M. Gil, "Enoch in the Land of Eternal Life" (in Hebrew), *Tarbiẓ* XXXVIII (1969), p. 329/30. Gil presents a comparative study of the *Pardes*-terminology in Ethiopic, Aramaic and Greek.

Merkavah. No records are left of that particular usage,[58] but this alleged usage might well explain the theosophical usage we encounter in Paul and in the Rabbis, where the *Pardes* is no more a place of retribution.

When Paul uses the term *Pardes*, it already designates the more general "visions and revelations... (and) things that cannot be told, which man may not utter". No further specifications are given and the same holds true concerning the story about the four who entered the *Pardes*. While in the case of Paul almost no clues are given, the *Gemārā* in the *Talmud Bavli* at least tries to make things a little more explicit. Hence, we must conclude that if the term *Pardes* actually relates to an ecstatic experience, its true nature is nowhere explicitly and extensively described. Only on the basis of the three short passages in *Talmud Bavli Ḥagigah* which hint at material that is contained in a more explicit form in the *Hekhalot* literature is it permissible to identify the *Pardes* experience with a mystical vision of the Merkavah. Those, however, who insist on denying the intrinsic connection between the additional material found in *Bavli Ḥagigah* and the story as it appears in its short form in the *Toseftā* are prevented from maintaining even this, namely that the *Pardes*-story is in any way connected to the mystical vision of the Merkavah.

We may, therefore, conclude that both stories, that of Rabban Yoḥanan ben Zakkai and Rabbi El'azar ben 'Arakh and that of the four sages who entered the *Pardes* do not explicitly supply everything one might wish for a clear proof that the Merkavah speculations in Tannaitic circles virtually corresponded to the mystical experiences which one finds in *Hekhalot* literature. What may be maintained with relative certainty is that these mystical speculations of the *Tannaim* entailed ecstatic experiences the nature of which may be surmised from a comparison between (a) the various versions of the stories under discussion and (b) these stories and the *Hekhalot* literature. It should, however, be noticed that while in the case of Rabban Yoḥanan the ecstasy was an experience restricted to an earthly surrounding, the story of the four who entered the *Pardes* allegedly entailed a translation onto heaven.

---

[58] See further J. T. Milik in *Revue Biblique* LXV (1958), pp. 70-77. See also F. Nötscher, *Altorientalischer und Alttestamentlicher Auferstehungsglauben*, Darmstadt, 1970, p. 282 f.

C

We shall now turn to the controversy among the Tannaim regarding the possibility or impossibility, of experiencing heavenly ascensions. On the basis of *Psalm* cxv,16—"The heavens are the Lord's heavens, but the earth he has given to the sons of men"—Rabbi Yossi is quoted as saying: "Neither did Moses and Elijah ascend to heaven nor did the Divine Glory (*Kavod*) descend to earth".[59] This controversial utterance which runs counter to a number of verses in Scripture, becomes the subject of a discussion in *Bavli Sukkah* 5a where it is finally modified to say that Moses ascended to God "but did not come nearer than ten handbreadths", while God descended on Mount Sinai "but did not come nearer than ten handbreadths". Rabbi Yossi probably aimed at a criticism of those who practised heavenly ascensions, or believed in the descriptions and prophecies of those who claimed such ascensions. These could well be either apocalyptic visionaries or practising mystics among the circles of the *Tannaim*, or both. Thus, one could see in the words of Rabbi Yossi a polemical response to the experiences implied by the very term *Pardes*, as it was used by Paul and in the story of the four who entered the *Pardes*. However, Rabbi Yossi, seems to be in the minority among the *Tannaim*, while most of his colleagues appear to have accepted the possibility of heavenly ascensions. The same problem was again raised in the circles of the Palestinian *Amoraim*, this time concerning the figure of Enoch.[60] One may assume that these polemical utterances could have had anti-Christian overtones too, that is, they could be a polemic against the ascension of Jesus.

More relevant to our discussion is the second problem, namely, the controversy among the *Tannaim* as to whether it is possible to see God and, if so, when and under what conditions. In an interesting attempt to define the nature of the prophecy of Moses, it is said that only Moses could hear the voice of God while those standing outside of the Tabernacle heard nothing.[61] Then Rabbi Dosā is quoted: "It is said: '... for man shall not see my face and live' (*Exodus* xxxiii,20)—during their lifetime they do not see, (but) they do see when they die". To this Rabbi 'Akiva makes the following comment:

[59] *Mechilta d'Rabbi Ismael*, ed. Horovitz-Rabin, p. 217. Some of the MSS. drop the name of Moses, and others the name of Elijah.—See also *1 Macc.* ii,58.

[60] *Bereshit Rabba*, ed. Theodor-Albeck, pp. 238-239. See *Israel Oriental Studies* III (1973), pp. 66-67, n. 20.

[61] *Sifrā* (*Torat Kohanim*) quoted from MS. Vatican 66, fol. 9a-b.

"Even the Living Creatures (*Ḥayyot*) which are carried (in the Divine Throne) do not see the Divine Glory (*Kavod*)". To this Rabbi Shim'on ben 'Azzai in turn adds: "Even the ministering angels, whose life is eternal,[62] do not see the Divine Glory".[63] It is certainly in place to notice that two of the *Tannaim* mentioned here, Rabbi 'Akiva and Shim'on ben 'Azzai, were also involved in the above-mentioned *Pardes* experience. This could be interpreted to imply that whatever Rabbi 'Akiva and his colleagues said in the matters of the Merkavah was based on their alleged visions. As a matter of fact, the idea that the mystics and the angels cannot see God is also stressed several times in the *Hekhalot* literature. Despite the daring modes of expression one can find in that literature about the contents of the mystical experience, the possibility of a direct visual encounter with God is generally ruled out.[64] The mystics whose experiences are described in the *Hekhalot* literature, expect to see "the King in (all) His beauty", but when it comes to a face to face meeting with God, one repeatedly hears of what is and should be done in order to avoid the experience.

However, we have seen that Rabbi Dosā said that one can see God after one's death. The belief in the afterlife encounter of the just with God is quite a common idea in midrashic literature.[65] The idea is also previously found in apocalyptic literature and it plays a prominent role in *Revelation*.[66] Yet, a visual encounter with God is also presupposed by the *Shi'ur Qomah* speculations, that is, the speculations concerning the corporeal appearance of God and its definition in terms of length and mystical names.[67] Apart from the texts which specifically deal with the subject,[68] there are quite a number of midrashic sayings based on the *Song of Songs* which Professor Saul Lieberman considers to be related to the *Shi'ur Qomah* specula-

[62] The eternal life of the ministering angels is not always maintained. See, for instance, *Bereshit Rabbā*, p. 916 (and parallels); *3 Enoch*, ch. xlvii; *Hekhalot Rabbati*, ch. xxx.

[63] Compare *Siphre ad Numeros*, ed. Horovitz, p. 55/6 and 101/2. Cf. Urbach, *art. cit.*, p. 19, n. 81. See further *Bavli Yevamot* 49b.

[64] See *Hekhalot Rabbati* iii,3-4.

[65] *Sifre on Deuteronomy*, ed. Finkelstein, p. 18 and 105; *Sifrā* (*Torat Kohanim*) ed. Weiss, p. 111, col. b; *Bavli Sanhedrin* 102a; *Wayyikra Rabbā*, ed. Margulies, p. 32; *ibid.*, pp. 240-242 (and parallels) and, finally, *Matthew* v,8.

[66] *Revelation* iv,4; see also *4 Ezra* vii (v),97/8.

[67] G. Scholem, *Von der mystischen Gestalt der Gottheit*, Zürich, Rhein-Verlag, 1962, pp. 7-47: "*Schi'ur Koma*; die mystische Gestalt der Gottheit"; *idem*, *Jewish Gnosticism* etc., pp. 36-42.

[68] They are printed in S. Musajoff, *Merkavah Shelemah*, Fol. 34a ff.

tions.[69] These particular midrashim to the *Song of Songs* reveal two views: the one, attributed to Rabbi ʿAkiva and his followers, according to which the *Song of Songs* was recited at the theophany on Mount Sinai; and the second, attributed to Rabbi Eliʿezer and his followers, which believes that the *Song of Songs* was said when God revealed Himself personally on the Red Sea. Particularly noteworthy is the saying of Rabbi Eliʿezer: "A maidservant at the Red Sea saw things that were not even seen by Ezekiel... When God revealed Himself on the Red Sea nobody had to ask: 'Who is the King', but as they saw Him, they (immediately) recognized Him".[70] Although there is no exact parallel saying of Rabbi ʿAkiva with regard to the theophany on Mount Sinai, Rabbi ʿAkiva is quoted as saying in a different context: "This (= the renewal of the moon in *Nissan*) is one of the things which God showed Moses as if with His finger!".[71] This saying of Rabbi ʿAkiva may be interpreted as implying that at least Moses saw a certain corporeal manifestation of God. Now, it may be claimed that this saying of Rabbi ʿAkiva contradicts the one we have already seen, to the effect that even the Living Creatures cannot see the Divine Glory. However, the prophecy of Moses was never intended to be a criterion for the prophecy and for the mystical experiences of others. It must be noticed, moreover, that Rabbi ʿAkiva considered the *Song of Songs* to be the holiest book,[72] and that it was recited at the theophany on Mount Sinai. In the light of what has been said, it may be concluded that Rabbi ʿAkiva experienced what he thought was a mystical ascension to the *Pardes*, although this did not entail a direct and immediate vision of the Godhead. What exactly happened could only be guessed on the grounds of the different versions of the *Pardes* tale, mainly those recorded by Paul, in the *Talmud Bavli* and in the *Hekhalot* literature. But it is certainly important

---

[69] G. Scholem, *Jewish Gnosticism* etc., Appendix D, pp. 118-126: "*Mishnath Shir Ha-Shirim*" by Professor Saul Lieberman. See further, J. Maier, *Geschichte der jüdischen Religion*, Berlin & New York, Walter de Gruyter, 1972, p. 201. Maier inclines to date the *Shiʿur Qoma* speculations in "der spättalmudischen und gaonäischen Zeit". From the evidence produced by Scholem and Lieberman it appears that the *Shiʿur Qoma* belongs to the earlier phases of the *Hekhalot* literature.

[70] *Mechilta d'Rabbi Ismael*, p. 126/7. Compare *Mekhilta d'Rabbi Simʿon b. Jochai*, ed. Epstein-Melamed, p. 154/5. Rabbi Eliʿezer seems to extend here the view expressed by his father, Rabbi Yossi Haglili, to the effect that even babies and little children saw the Shekhinah on the Red Sea. *Yerushalmi Sotah* 16c; *Mekhilta d'Rabbi Simʿon b. Jochai*, p. 73/4. See Lieberman in Scholem, *op. cit.*, p. 121.

[71] *Mechilta d'Rabbi Ismael*, p. 6 (emended according to parallels).

[72] *Mishnah Yadayim* iii,5 (and parallels).

to notice that the tones struck by Rabbi ʿAkiva's saying, to the effect that no man can see God,[73] are repeated in the *Hekhalot* literature too. However, as we are going to see, a different view is attributed to Rabbi ʿAkiva in *Shiʿur Qomah*.

In completing this picture of the mystical concepts in the writings of the Tannaitic period, mention should be made of the belief that priests could have special experiences when they took the incense into the Holy of Holies.[74] Thus we hear of the High Priest, Simʿon the Just, who on entering the Holy of Holies used to encounter on every Day of Atonement an old man dressed in white (cf. *Daniel* vii,9);[75] and another High Priest, called Yishmaʿel ben Elishʿa, is reported to have seen God Himself sitting on His throne (cf. *Isaiah* vi,1).[76] Yoḥanan, the High Priest, heard a prophetic utterance from the Holy of Holies [77] and Luke tells of Zacharias, the father of John the Baptist, that an angel appeared to him in the Temple.[78] Naturally, it would go too far to say that all Jewish mysticism from the times of the *Tannaim* onwards derived in many essential ways from the cultic life of the Temple.[79] It must equally be noticed, however, that some of those *Tannaim* who dealt with the *Ma'aseh Merkavah* were priests.[80] At any rate, if the experiences recorded in the Tannaitic

---

[73] It is here that I find myself disagreeing with S. Safrai, *Rabbi ʿAkiva ben Joseph: His Life and Teaching* (in Hebrew), Jerusalem, Bialik Institute, 1970, p. 59. Safrai writes: "The ministering angels do not deserve the privilege of seeing the divine glory, while a human being, who is exalted by his good deeds does deserve the privilege of seeing the divine glory". Rabbi ʿAkiva's words in *Sifrā* are not in opposition to the words of Rabbi Dosa, but, on the contrary, they are complementing them. This is the meaning of the word "even" which introduces Rabbi ʿAkiva's saying to the effect that the living creatures do not see the divine glory.

[74] See J. Z. Lauterbach, "A Significant Controversy between the Saducees and the Pharisees", *Hebrew Union College Annual* IV (1927), pp. 173-205. Lauterbach's Saduceean interpretation of these stories was variously challenged.

[75] *Yerushalmi Yomā* 42c (and parallels). Compare also *Yerushalmi Sotah* 24b.

[76] *Bavli Berakhot* 7a. See Scholem, *Jewish Gnosticism* etc., pp. 51 ff.

[77] *Toseftā Sotah* xiii,5 (and parallels).

[78] *Luke* i,8-22.

[79] J. Maier, *Vom Kultus zur Gnosis*, Salzburg, Otto Müller Verlag, 1964. See K. Schubert, "Das Zeitalter der Apokalyptik", in: F. Leist (ed.), *Seine Rede geschah zu Mir*, München, Manz-Verlag, 1965, pp. 265-285.

[80] Although there were scholars who thought that Rabban Yoḥanan ben Zakkai himself was a priest, it seems safer to maintain with G. Alon, *The History of the Jews in Eretz Yisrael in the Time of the Mishnah and Talmud* (in Hebrew), second edition, Tel Aviv, 1954, vol. I, p. 56, that no conclusive proof could be produced for the priesthood of Rabban Yoḥanan. See further G. Alon, *Studies in Jewish History* (in Hebrew), Tel Aviv, 1957, vol. I, pp. 255-256, where a certain

sources and which refer to the Temple life really occurred, Judaism of that period must have been prepared for the mystical experiences of the kind we find in the *Hekhalot* writings in a manner seriously misrepresented by the scepticism of some of the scholars who have discussed the phenomenon.

---

rift between Rabban Yoḥanan and the priests is discussed. However, Rabbi Yossi and Rabbi Shimʿon ben Netanʾel, who were Rabban Yoḥanan's students and engaged in the Merkavah speculations (*Yerushalmi Ḥagigah* 77a), were both priests, though they seem to have left their master after the destruction of the Temple. See G. Alon, *Studies* etc., vol. I, p. 256, n. 9. In *Bavli Ḥagigah* 14b Rabbi Yehoshuʿa takes the place of Rabbi Shimʿon ben Netanʾel. See above note 11. It must be remembered, that Ezekiel, the prophet, also was a priest.

CHAPTER FOUR

THE HEKHALOT LITERATURE

A

In the present chapter we shall discuss some of the general characteristics of the *Hekhalot* literature. In the second part of the book, a detailed introduction to each of the *Hekhalot* books will be given.

The first scholar who attempted a serious evaluation of the *Hekhalot* literature, and also suggested a historical sequence for its composition, was H. Grätz.[1] In a series of three articles published in the *Monatsschrift für die Geschichte und Wissenschaft des Judenthums* VIII (1859), Grätz reached the conclusion that the so-called *Hekhalot* literature was composed in post-talmudic times, and that the first text in the series was *'Otiyot de-Rabbi 'Akiva*. Grätz's dating of that literature is still considered by some people to be true, though the sequence of the composition of that literature as suggested by him is no more accepted. Professor G. Scholem in a series of studies of that literature, suggested a different order of composition and a much earlier date of composition.[2] Scholem's views on these two issues are here followed, and the discussion which follows deals with some aspects of that literature which still deserve attention. In addition, Scholem's suggestion to interpret the Merkavah mysticism as a Jewish concomitant to gnosticism will be re-examined.[3]

Generally speaking, the three main subjects dealt with in the

[1] Grätz dismisses the chapter dealing with Jewish mysticism in L. Zunz, *Gottesdienstliche Vorträge*, 1832, pp. 165-170, as "so nichtssagend als nur möglich".

[2] See mainly his: *Major Trends in Jewish Mysticism*, London, Thames and Hudson, 1955, pp. 40-79: "Merkabah Mysticism and Jewish Gnosticism"; *Jewish Gnosticism Merkabah Mysticism, and Talmudic Tradition*, Second, Improved Edition, New York, The Jewish Theological Seminary of America, 1965; *Ursprung und Anfänge der Kabbalah*, Berlin, Walter de Gruyter, 1962, pp. 15-20: "Die vor-kabbalistische jüdische Geheimlehre über die Schöpfung und die Merkaba-Literatur der Hekhaloth und jüdische Gnosis"; *Von der mystischen Gestalt der Gottheit*, Zürich, Rhein Verlag, 1962, pp. 7-47: "*Schi'ur Koma*; die mystische Gestalt der Gottheit"; *Kabbalah*, Jerusalem, Keter Publishing House, 1974, pp. 14-22; 373-376.

[3] Here the writer will mainly follow his "'knowledge' and 'vision'—Towards a Clarification of two 'Gnostic' Concepts in the Light of their Alleged Origins", *Israel Oriental Studies* III (1973), especially pp. 88-107; and: "The Jewish Esoteric Literature in the Time of the Mishnah and Talmud", *Immanuel* 4 (1974), pp. 37-46.

Hekhalot literature are: heavenly ascensions, the revelation of cosmological and other secrets, and the special secret method of studying and memorizing the Torah. From the point of view of literary genre, the *Hekhalot* literature falls into two types: the description of heavenly ascensions and the description of the appearance on earth of angels who reveal secrets. A similar distinction with regard to the literary genre can be made concerning apocalyptic literature, but in contradistinction to apocalyptic literature, the *Hekhalot* literature gives detailed descriptions of the various means and practices by which the desired experiences or revelations are gained. In fact, it may be said that the whole of the *Hekhalot* literature might be defined as technical guides, or manuals, for mystics. A lot of the material contained therein is introduced by technical questions. A short paraphrase of some of the *Hekhalot* texts would begin thus: "What is the mystic required to do if he wants to bring about the following mystical experience". These technical details, the "praxis" of the mystical experience, generally consist of special prayers or incantations, of prolonged fasts and special diets, of the utterance of magical names and the use of magical seals, and of the ritual of cleansing the body. Although some of those means are already known from apocalyptic literature, their description in the *Hekhalot* literature is more detailed. They are also known from non-Jewish mysticism and magic.[4]

In contrast to Prophecy, which seems to be spontaneous, and sometimes even comes to those least desiring it, the kinds of experience described in apocalyptic and in Merkavah mysticism necessitated certain preparatory practices.[5] Already in *Daniel* x,2-3, we hear of an extended period of fasting and praying before the visionary received a vision: "In those days I Daniel was mourning for three whole weeks, pleasant food I did not eat, nor did flesh and wine come to my mouth, nor did I anoint myself at all, until the fulfilling of three full weeks".[6] This kind of self-preparation for the apocalyptic

[4] See W. Bousset, *Die Himmelsreise der Seele*, Reprint: Darmstadt, Wissenschaftliche Buchgesellschaft, 1960; A. Dieterich, *Eine Mithrasliturgie*, Reprint: Darmstadt, Wissenschaftliche Buchgesellschaft, 1966; E. R. Dodds, *The Greeks and the Irrational*, University of California Press, 1964, pp. 283-311.

[5] For the question to which extent prophecy was spontaneous or not see, for instance, J. Skinner, *Prophecy and Religion*, Cambridge University Press, 1963, pp. 1 ff. For a discussion of some psychological and phenomenological aspects of prophecy see, J. Lindblom, *Prophecy in Ancient Israel*, Oxford, Blackwell, 1965, pp. 6 ff.

[6] Compare also ix,3. See J. A. Montgomery, *The Book of Daniel* (ICC), p. 407.

experience is also known from later Jewish apocalyptic. Thus we find in *2 (Syriac) Baruch* ix,2 that Baruch and Jeremiah rent their garments, wept, mourned and fasted seven days, before God revealed himself to Baruch.[7] These fasts in apocalyptic literature, whether they meant total abstention from any kind of food or whether they entailed special diets, were usually practised over periods of seven days, and their repetition two or three times. In *4 Ezra* the apocalyptist is told at least three times to fast for seven days (v,13 = v,20; vi,31-35; xii,50).[8] The three books mentioned here, *Daniel*, *2 Baruch* and *4 Ezra*, do not contain heavenly ascents, yet the practice of fasts was also known where ascents were experienced. Thus, as we already saw, in the *Apocalypse of Abraham* ix, Abraham was ordered to "abstain from every form of food that proceedeth out of the fire, and from the drinking of wine... forty days". This period of forty days is likewise known from other cases,[9] and it was most certainly influenced by what we know of Moses [10] and Elijah.[11]

Sometimes instead of prolonged fasts only special diets were prescribed. Thus we hear in *4 Ezra* xii,50 that the apocalyptist sustained himself for one week only on "the flowers of the field... (and) of the herbs". In the Merkavah texts, however, all vegetables are strictly forbidden during the period of time in which the mystic

---

[7] To be exact, these practices were initially performed as a sign of mourning over the destruction of Jerusalem, but it is no mere coincidence that as a result of these, God revealed himself to Baruch. Other fasts are reported in *2 Baruch* in xii,5 and xxi,1.

[8] For further examples of this kind see D. S. Russell, *The Method and Message of Jewish Apocalyptic*, London, SCM Press, 1964, pp. 169-173.

[9] See the text published in Scholem, *Jewish Gnosticism* etc., Appendix C, paragraphs 11, p. 108 and 14, p. 109. In MS. Oxford 1531, 46a we find: "He who wants to study this *Mishnah* and to utter the Holy Name of God should fast for forty days". In both cases no ascent is maintained; but see the Responsum of Rev Hai Ga'on in B. Lewin, *Otzar Ha-Geonim*, vol. IV (Tractate ... Chagigah), p. 14 where fasts are mentioned in connection with ascents to heaven.

[10] *Exodus* xxxiv,28; *Deuteronomy* ix,9,18. In another tradition preserved in *Bavli Yomā* 4a (= *Avot de-Rabbi Nathan* Version A, Chapter i), Rabbi Nathan is quoted as saying that six days had to pass before Moses could receive the word of God. This had to happen "so that he would be cleansed of all the foods and drinks in his bowels, and thus become like the angels". In *Bavli Ḥagigah* 16a we hear that the angels do not eat. See further the discussion between Rabbi ʿAkiva and Rabbi Yishmael in *Bavli Yomā* 75b as to whether the angels eat and of what their nutrition consists.

[11] *1 Kings* xix, 7-8. See further, R. Arbesmann, "Fasting and Prophecy in Pagan and Christian Antiquity", *Traditio* VII (1949/1951), pp. 1-71; S. Lowy, "The Motivation of Fasting in Talmudic Literature", *Journal of Jewish Studies* XIX (1958), pp. 19-38.

prepares himself for his ecstatic experience.[12] In addition, it is said there several times that he should bake his bread himself,[13] and that he should particularly avoid the bread baked by a woman.[14] In the Merkavah texts, fasts and diets go hand in hand and no distinction is drawn between them: "...he should sit in fast for forty days, his morsel should be eaten with salt only" (*Ma'aseh Merkavah*, paragraph 11).[15] Generally, all these ascetic means are also well known from other sources,[16] and even in some rabbinic circles it was maintained that the study of the Torah entailed an ascetic, or austere, way of life.[17] But when we come to the *Hekhalot* literature, and particularly to those sections which describe the practices of conjuring angels to reveal secrets, these ascetic means become a mystical rite.[18]

Together with these diets and fasts we find ritual baths. The initiate preparing himself for his mystical experience is told to take daily ritual baths, preferably every evening before he eats his daily meal. This special procedure is prescribed, again, only in the case of the conjuration of angels in order to come down to earth and to reveal secrets.[19] Sometimes, the number of such ritual baths is given:

---

[12] See, for instance, "Sar Torah" (= *Hekhalot Rabbati*) xxx,1 and in Musajoff, *Merkavah Shelemah* 5a: "He should not taste any vegetables".

[13] "Sar Torah", *ibid.*; *Merkavah Shelemah* 4b.

[14] MS. Oxford 1531, 46b (= MS. Jewish Theological Seminary 828, 25a): "He should not eat bread baked by a woman, nor should he drink water touched by a woman; but he should knead with his own hands, and grind himself, and bake for himself one bread every day and eat" (translated from Aramaic).

[15] In fact, as *Hekhalot Rabbati* xxx,1 explicitly says, one could break one's fast every evening, but then only special kinds of food could be eaten. As we shall soon see, before touching the food, one had to take a ritual bath.

[16] For asceticism as it is viewed by Philo, see H. Leisegang, *Der Heilige Geist*, Darmstadt, Wissenschaftliche Buchgesellschaft, 1967, p. 215.

[17] *Mishnah 'Avot* vi,4: "This is the way of the Torah: A morsel with salt shalt thou eat and water by measure shalt thou drink; and thou shalt lie upon the earth, and thou shalt live a life of hardship, and labour in the Torah". (English translation: R. Travers Herford, *The Ethics of the Fathers*, New York, Schocken Books, 1962, p. 154). For a general summary of the rabbinical views on asceticism, see E. E. Urbach, "Ascesis and Suffering in Talmudic and Midrashic Sources" (In Hebrew), in *I. F. Baer Jubilee Volume*, Jerusalem, 1960, pp. 48-68.

[18] We shall come back to this point in Part Two of our book, where a detailed description of the texts will be given. We also know from rabbinic sources that fasts were in practice when people desired the revelation of Elijah the Prophet; see *Jerushalmi Terumot* viii (46b).

[19] The technical term for this process in Hebrew is: *ZQQ*, literally 'to bind (by an oath)'. See in *Tarbiz* XXXVIII (1969), p. 365, note to line 31.

in one case we find twenty four,[20] and in another seven.[21] In one or two cases specifications are given as to how the ritual baths are to be taken: "at the end of his fast-days and his ritual cleansing he should go and sit in water up to his neck...".[22] Yet, whatever is prescribed in these cases is quite innocent in comparison to the elaborate magical practices known from some of the Greek magical papyri and from the Hebrew magical treatises such as *Sefer Ha-Razim* and *Sefer Ha-Malbush*. In these magical texts, the performer is told to bring animal offerings, wine libations and all kinds of strange instruments and objects which are said to aid the magical performance. It is probably through the influence of these magical performances that we find in some *Hekhalot* texts the idea that certain practices are useful only for bringing about certain experiences at specific dates. Thus we find special practices for mystical experiences and revelations which are to be accomplished on the Feast of Shavuʿot, on New Year Day, at the beginning of every month, etc.[23]

In the *Hekhalot* tractates which deal with heavenly ascents, the theurgic practices which are applied are mainly incantations (or

---

[20] *Maʿaseh Merkavah*, paragraph 11, p. 108. It should be noticed that it is difficult to harmonize between this number—twenty four—and the forty days of fasting prescribed in the same context.

[21] See *Merkavah Rabbā* in: S. Musajoff, *Merkavah Shelemah*, 1b.

[22] *Ibid.* A similar procedure is described in the case of Adam's penitence in *Vita Adae et Evae* vi: Adam was spending forty days fasting and told Eve to "go to the river Tigris and lift up a stone and stand on it in the water up to thy neck in the deep of the river. And let no speech out of thy mouth". Adam also told Eve to "stand in the water of the river thirty seven days". He himself spent forty days in the water of Jordan. In vii,2 it is again said that "Adam walked to the river Jordan and stood on a stone up to his neck in water". A similar tradition is preserved in *Pirkei de-Rabbi Eliezer* xx, where it is told of Adam's penitence that "Adam went to the upper *Giḥon* till the water reached his neck, and he fasted seven weeks ..." For the whole subject see L. Ginzberg, The *Legends of the Jews*, vol. V, pp. 114-115. However, Ginzberg observes that "both sources (= The *Vita* and *Pirkei de-Rabbi Eliezer*) go back to the old Halaka"; yet, as Professor Lieberman pointed out to me, the opposite is the truth. In *Bavli Yomā* 78a (not 87a, as indicated by Ginzberg) Rav Yoseph is quoted as saying that a ritually unclean woman may take a cleansing bath while she is immersed only up to her neck in water. The Gemārā, however, remarks that this is not the accepted ruling (and a woman is cleansed only if she immerses completely into the water; see also *Slavonic Vita Adae et Evae*, xxxvi,4, in Charles, *Pseudepigrapha*, p. 135). See further *Toseftā Kippurim* iv (v),5, and *Bavli Yomā* 77b (twice); *Bavli Berakhot* 25b.

[23] Cf. Ms. Oxford 1531, fol. 67a-b (= Ms. New York 828, fol. 39a).—Compare, for instance, K. Preisendanz, *Papyri Graecae Magicae*, vol. II, Stuttgart, Verlag Teubner, 1974, p. 13, where the days which are unsuitable for magical performance are listed. In *Sefer Ha-Razim* we find several references to the days and hours, which are most suitable for the magical performance.

hymns), the saying of names, charms and magical seals. As for the incantations or hymns, *Hekhalot Rabbati* opens with the question: "What are the incantations which should be said by him who wants to contemplate the vision of the Merkavah, to descend safely and to ascend safely" (i,1). As the last words indicate, the function of these incantations is to conduct the visionary safely through all the dangers which might befall him during his mystical experience. Indeed, we have already seen in the *Apocalypse of Abraham* that the angel Jaoel told the visionary to worship and "to utter the song which I have taught thee". It appears that he did so in order to protect the visionary and to strengthen him against the things he experienced in heaven. The theurgic quality of these incantations also becomes evident from two passages in *Ma'aseh Merkavah.* Both passages are introduced as questions which Rabbi Yishmael asked Rabbi 'Akiva. In the first one, Rabbi Yishmael enquired: "How can a man gain a vision of what is above the Seraphim who stand above Rozaya, Lord God of Israel?". To which Rabbi 'Akiva answered: "When I ascended to the first *Hekhal*, I said a prayer and [then] I saw from the first *Hekhal* in heaven to the seventh *Hekhal*".[24] The second passage brings the question: "How can a man have these visions and see what Rozaya, Lord God of Israel, does?" Rabbi 'Akiva's answer accordingly was: "I prayed a prayer of compassion and thus I was saved".[25]

However, reading these hymns and incantations, their protective function does not immediately come through. On the contrary, some of these hymns are extremely lyrical in their tone and form. They appear to be songs of praise, and only occasionally is a phrase introduced that betrays their real function. Thus, for instance, one of these songs in *Ma'aseh Merkavah* (paragraph 16, p. 110) contains one line which reads: "And rescue me from all these hostile ones (= the angels of destruction) which stand [behind the Holy Creatures], so that they shall become the bearers of my love before You". The theurgic functions come even more directly to the fore in the "five prayers" quoted in *Ma'aseh Merkavah*, paragraphs 26-31. These prayers combine lyrical poetry with magical names. The prayers begin with the remark, attributed to Rabbi Yishmael: "I was praying

[24] Paragraph 33, p. 116.

[25] Paragraph 4, p. 103. See also paragraph 9, p. 107: "I (Rabbi 'Akiva) said the *Qedushah* before him who created and ordered (into being) all the creatures, so that the ministering angels should not consume me". See also there paragraph 17, p. 110.

each of these prayers with its names, both on my descent to and ascent from the Merkavah, and thus no harm was caused to my limbs". Notwithstanding these examples, the general truth remains that these songs were conceived of as songs of praise said by the angelic beings, and even by the Throne of Glory,[26] to God. The mystic who ascended to heaven learnt them in order to apply them also as theurgic means.[27] However, whether these hymns were said as autohypnotic means or whether they were recited in heaven as protective means,[28] their numinous quality [29] establishes them as outstanding specimens of Jewish poetry in Talmudic times.

Even, more important from the magico-theurgic point of view is the saying of names, mainly the secret names of the Deity and of the angels. We already saw that there were various traditions, going back to the ritual practice of the second Temple, which refer to the secret names of God.[30] Thus, we know of the secret name pronounced out by the priests in their blessing.[31] In another place we hear of a secret name that was enunciated in the special oath which God used in the creation of the world.[32] We also know of so-called *nomina barbara* said in adjurations.[33] Finally, mention should also be made of the theurgic material found in the magical papyri,[34] and

---

[26] For the idea that the Throne of Glory adresses God with words see *Hekhalot Rabbati* iii,2. In xxiv,1 we read: "When he (= the mystic) is standing before the Throne of Glory, he opens and says the song which the Throne of Glory sings every day". In MS. Vatican 228 these words are headed by the title: *Shir Kisē*, "The Hymn of the Throne".

[27] See *Hekhalot Rabbati* iv,2 we read: "Rabbi Yishmael said: all these songs Rabbi ʿAkiva heard when he descended to the Merkavah; and he caught and learned them in front of His Throne of Glory when His ministers were singing to him".—For an analysis of these hymns and their theurgic functions see A. Altman, "*Shirei-Qedushah Be-Sifrut Ha-Hekhalot Ha-Qedumah*", in *Melilah* II (1945-6), pp. 1 ff.

[28] See A. Altman, *ibid.*, pp. 2-4.

[29] See G. Scholem, *Jewish Gnosticism* etc., pp. 20 ff.

[30] See G. Scholem, "Der Name Gottes und die Sprachtheorie der Kabbala", in *Judaica III*, Frankfurt am Main, Suhrkamp Verlag, 1970, pp. 7 ff.

[31] See above, Chapter Two, n. 81. See also L. H. Schiffman, "A Forty-Two Letter Divine Name in the Aramaic Magic Bowls", *Bulletin of the Institute of Jewish Studies*, vol. I. (1973), pp. 97 ff. Schiffman's explanation seems rather hypothetical.

[32] *I Enoch* lxix,14 ff. Compare also *Sifre on Deuteronomy*, ed. Finkelstein, paragraph 330, p. 380.

[33] See S. Lieberman, "Some Notes on Adjurations in Israel", *Texts and Studies*, New York, Ktav Publishing House, 1974, pp. 21-28; and more specifically in *Toseftā Ki-Fshutah* to *Shabbat*, pp. 91 ff.

[34] See G. Scholem, *Jewish Gnosticism* etc., pp. 75 ff.: "The Theurgic Elements

which in some respects derived from old Jewish magical practices.[35] In short, there is much in the traditions of the time preceding the *Hekhalot* literature that could well explain the background of the names-praxis of the *Hekhalot* mystics.

Names and adjurations are the two main theurgic means found in the *Hekhalot* literature applied in connection with the descent to the Merkavah and the invocation of angels to come down to earth and to reveal secrets. Most illuminating in this respect is the following passage from *Hekhalot Rabbati*: "When a man wants to descend to the Merkavah, he should call Suriya, the Prince of the Countenance, and conjure him a hundred and twelve times in the name of Tetrasii, Lord God... He should neither add nor subtract from that number of a hundred and twelve, for if he does, he fatally endangers himself. His mouth should utter the names and his fingers should count a hundred and twelve, and he immediately descends and masters the Merkavah" (xiv,4-5). It is interesting to notice that not only does the exact number of the names guarantee the success of the mystical experience, but that in fact any deviation from it is physically endangering the mystic. Similarly, we find in the case of the conjuration of angels that the mystic is told to "pronounce names, and his fingers should count till he reaches the number one hundred and eleven".[36] As we see, the number of names can slightly vary from 112 to 111, but in any event, a deviation from the number prescribed does not only result in failure but virtually works harm on the mystic.

However, there are also other sets of numbers prescribed for the conjurations.[37] In one case,[38] we read that God is conjured by a series

of the *Lesser Hekhaloth* and the Magical Papyri". See also E. E. Urbach, The *Sages*, Chapter Seven, pp. 124 ff. Urbach, however, does not refer to the *Hekhalot* material.

[35] For a recent discussion of the relevant eastern and hellenistic magical material, see J. M. Hull, *Hellenistic Magic and the Synoptic Tradition*, London, SCM Press, 1974. Unfortunately, Hull is not acquainted with the relevant Jewish sources and thus his treatment of the subject is incomplete. More relevant for our discussion, however, is M. Smith, *Clement of Alexandria and a Secret Gospel of Mark*, Harvard University Press, 1973, pp. 220 ff. Most valuable too is E. R. Dodds' article "Theurgy" now reprinted as Appendix II to his *The Greeks and the Irrational*, Berkeley & Los Angeles, University of California Press, 1964, pp. 283 ff.

[36] "*Merkavah Rabbah*", in: Musajoff, *Merkavah Shelemah*, 46. Compare also *Ma'aseh Merkavah*, paragraph 30, p. 114.

[37] In *Ma'aseh Merkavah* paragraph 12, p. 109 we find three names: In *Merkavah Rabbah* (in: *Merkavah Shelemah* 1b), there are fourteen names. In the *Sar Torah* section of *Hekhalot Rabbati* (xxx,4) twelve angels are conjured by their secret names.

[38] *Hekhalot Rabbati* xii,4.

of sixteen names all of which begin with "*tetra*" (or: "*totro*", as some of the Hebrew manuscripts reproduce the name). In addition, it is said there in Aramaic: "And the sign of this *Halakhah* is to learn these Great Names[39] from Tetrasii till Tetrasit: he should learn them in the following sequence...".[40] Interestingly, the importance of the correct sequence is stressed here, but never do we hear anything of the importance of correctly uttering the names. We know of the great importance attached in the magical papyri to the correct pronunciation of the names of the conjured gods (ἐχφώνησις), but nothing of the kind is explicitly said in our texts.

All in all, the theurgic elements of the *Hekhalot* literature have their decisive share in giving this literature its idiosyncratic quality. In contradistinction to the view expressed by A. Jellinek, to the effect that the theurgic content of the *Hekhalot* literature was introduced ("untergeschoben") at a comparatively late period, it must be maintained, with G. Scholem, that that particular element in the *Hekhalot* literature actually belonged to its very heart and this almost from its very beginning.[41] In fact, one of the earliest *Hekhalot* texts we possess, *Re'uyot Yeḥezkel*, explicitly refers to those who are in possession of the mystical secret knowledge as "*Meshamshin Ba-Shum*", which is the Aramaic equivalent for theurgists, that is, those who "acted upon" the gods by the power of their secret names.[42]

Last in this catalogue of mystical practices are the seals. The mystic who descends to the Merkavah has to prepare all kinds of mystical

---

[39] MS. Budapest (Kaufmann) 238, p. 174: *shmahatā ravrevayā*. This is the plural of *shmā rabbā*, the Aramaic equivalent of the Hebrew *shem gadol*, which is to be interpreted as "a most powerful magical name". See the opening three paragraphs of *Hekhalot Zutreti*, (especially nos. 2 & 3) in Scholem, *Jewish Gnosticism* etc., p. 77, n. 6. To this compare also *Hekhalot Rabbati* ix,5 and xxii,1. See further B. A. Levine, "The Language of the Magical Bowls", Appendix to J. Neusner, *A History of the Jews in Babylonia*, vol. V, Leiden, E. J. Brill, 1970, pp. 372-373. The "Great Name" also occurs in a text describing the Ascension of Moses: "The Holy One, blessed be He, said to Michael, Go and teach him (i.e. Moses) my Great Name, so that the flame of the Shekhinah shall not consume him ...'". See, *The Ascension of Moses and the Heavenly Jerusalem*, translated by H. W. Attridge, in: *Studies on the Testament of Moses*, edited by G. W. E. Nickelsburg, Jr., Society of Biblical Literature, Cambridge, Massachusetts, 1973, p. 123. See also *Mishnah Ta'anit* iii,8.

[40] There follow the sixteen letters which correspond to the various endings to the "Tetra" root-form. See also *Ma'aseh Merkavah*, paragraph 30, p. 114, where the "Tetra" root-form was not corrupted.

[41] See A. Jellinek, *Bet Ha-Midrash*, vol. VI, Introduction, p. XXVII f. See further G. Scholem, *ibid.*, p. 75.

[42] Compare E. R. Dodd, *ibid.*, p. 283 seq.

seals which he is told to show to the gate-keepers at the entrance of each *Hekhal*. These seals are to grant him passage through the various gates and to protect him against the hostility of the gate-keepers. Nothing is said in the *Hekhalot* texts about the detailed contents of those seals. What we, however, hear in *Hekhalot Rabbati* xvii, is that at each of the first six gates the mystic has to show two seals, one to the gate-keepers standing to the right and one to those standing on the left. The seals are designated by their mystical names. These names are as unclear as the names uttered in the adjurations and invocations. Professor Scholem has shown that at least in two cases the numerical value of pairs of letters which build up the names of the seals can explain the forms of the names.[43] But, in spite of the fact that some additional formal principles—such as changes in the order of the letters or in the endings of the names—could be pointed out too, the real contents and meaning of these seals are still by and large obscure. Much work has still to be devoted to the deciphering of the names of the seals and of the spells scattered in the literature of the period. As a matter of fact, only the combined efforts of scholars from different branches and fields of knowledge can bring about the desired progress in the study of the magico-theurgic practices found in the magical papyri, in the amulets and bowls, in the writings of gnosticism, and in Jewish mysticism and magic. Only a comprehensive and comparative study of all this vast material will enable us to understand the technique of creating these names and spells, and this notwithstanding the fact that in several cases the names were obscured on purpose, so as to prevent people from using or misusing them. In addition, it should be noticed that errors and confusion were often introduced by careless and ignorant copyists.

What still deserves attention, is the fact that the occurrence of these theurgical practices in the *Hekhalot* literature makes it evident that at least in one of its more central features this literature apparently came under the spell of parallel elements found in the pagan religious syncretism of the time. Indeed, it is quite tempting to argue that in this respect the *Hekhalot* literature virtually betrays indebtedness to pagan and Christian (or gnosticistic) syncretism. If we take into account the fact that the *Hekhalot* mystics were in no way opposed to rabbinic Judaism, then the presence of such syncretistic elements can in no way be taken as a side issue which may be relegated to

---

[43] G. Scholem, *op. cit.*, pp. 65 ff.

carelessness or chance. As Professor Scholem has pointed out, these mystics were learned Jews who greatly valued the study of the Law and advocated strict obedience to its rulings.[44] Thus the magical and theurgical elements in their writings can really be taken to imply a challenge to some of the established views on the nature of Judaism in Talmudic times. Having in mind our short observations concerning the theurgical elements in the *Hekhalot* literature, it seems quite safe to maintain that the last word in the characterization of that Jewry, or at least of certain parts in it, has not yet been said. Later on—in the Introduction to Part Two of our study—we shall have an opportunity to come back to this point. In addition, *Sefer Ha-Razim* confronts us with much graver questions than the ones involved in the discussion of the theurgical elements in the *Hekhalot* literature. At the moment suffice it to say, that the picture of the life and beliefs of the Jews living in the Talmudic times as we are used to viewing it from the commonly studied rabbinic sources, will have to be supplemented from less commonly studied sources among which we include the *Hekhalot* literature.

However, there is nothing new or strange today in the recognition that one form or another of magic was known and practised in the circles of the Jewish sages of the Mishnaic and Talmudic era. There is a lot in the rabbinical sources that points to the fact that magic was not spread among the unlearned and vulgar people alone.[45] It may be argued that magic was almost universally taken for granted, and even practised by many, without the least concern for the fact that Scripture has fought a bitter fight against it and the pagan world-view that it entailed. No wonder, then, that theurgical practices found their way into Merkavah mysticism. Actually, where autohypnotic and autosuggestive experiences were cultivated, one could expect to find the suitable soil for the theurgical and magical seeds to grow. Having in mind these observations, Rashi's commentary to the story of the four who entered the *Pardes* is a most telling one: Rashi explains the words "entered the *Pardes*" by saying: "They ascended to heaven by means of a Name"! [46] The matter-of-fact way in which Rashi introduces his commentary to the story almost succeeds in diverting the attention from the theological problem involved. But

---

[44] G. Scholem, *op. cit.*, pp. 9-13. See also Appendix B, below p. 241f.

[45] Still relevant for this point is L. Blau, *Das Altjüdische Zauberwesen*, Budapest, 1898 (Republished in 1970 by Gregg).

[46] See above Chapter Two, n. 81.

when one gets behind his comment, one discovers a scenery rich in theurgic and magical prescriptions and practices.

Finally, it should be noticed that the theurgical means which we have just discussed were also applied in the cases of the conjuration of angels. Thus we hear in *Ma'aseh Merkavah* (paragraph 12, p. 109) that Arpedes,[47] the Angel of the Countenance, told Rabbi Yishmael that "he who wants to make use of this great secret (= of the *Sar Torah*) should... invoke [48] those three names, and I shall descend".[49] Similarly, seals were also used on such occasions: "Rabbi Yishmael said: I sealed myself with seven seals, when Padkeres, the Angel of the Countenance, descended" (paragraph 15, p. 109). We also have in this text a detailed description of how the mystic put on seven seals: one on his (right?) leg, one on his heart, one on his right arm and one on his left arm, one on the neck, one "to protect my body",[50] and one on the top of his head.[51]

B

All in all, the practices which we have discussed here almost amount to a magical ritual.[52] Yet, we should be careful not to confuse magic with mysticism. In spite of all the similarities between the two, the *Hekhalot* mysticism cannot be classified in terms of magic or theurgy. There are magical and theurgical elements in Merkavah mysticism,

---

[47] The name of an angel Arpada, or Arpeda, is known from *Sefer Ha-Razim*, ed. Margalioth, p. 82, l. 27. It should be noticed that many of the names of the angels occurring in the *Hekhalot* literature do in themselves sound like magical names; and, in any event, those engaged in the study of etymologies may quickly find out that the names of angels are slippery ground.

[48] The verb here used is *qara*. The root QR'A is generally used in the Aramaic and Mandaic incantations in the sense of evil invocation against which one seeks protection. See, for instance, C. H. Gordon, "Aramaic Magical Bowls in the Istanbul and Baghdad Museums", *Archiv Orientalni* VI (1934), p. 324, Text B, line 6; *idem*, "Aramaic and Mandaic Magical Bowls", *Archiv Orientalni* IX (1937), p. 96, Text M, line 11.

[49] There follows a series of nine words whose meaning is not clear. In the next paragraph, mention is again made of "the three names which are said by the Angels of the Glory". Again nine unidentifiable words are given. In addition, this paragraph (13) mentions the "three letters which are uttered by the *Ḥayyot* when they see *Archas* (= Arche?), Lord God of Israel", and also the "three letters which the wheels of the (divine) chariot say when they sing their song to the Throne of the Glory".

[50] Apparently, this seal is put on the chest. See *Song of Songs* viii,6.

[51] See also paragraph 11, p. 108.

[52] See further the comparative references in M. Margalioth, *Sepher Ha-Razim*, Tel-Aviv: 1966, p. 8 ff.

but Merkavah mysticism is neither a magical nor a theurgic experience. E. R. Dodds described theurgy as "magic applied to a religious purpose and resting on a supposed revelation of a religious character".[53] Dodds also remarked that "whereas vulgar magic used names and formulae of religious origin to profane ends, theurgy used the procedures of vulgar magic primarily to a religious end".[54] It should be noted that Dodds here uses the word magic in the sense applied to it in the Greek magical papyri, and not in the sense in which the nineteenth century anthropologists understood it, that is, as a rudimentary form of religion. In any event, practices known from popular magic infiltrated into the various forms of Merkavah mysticism, but this should not be taken to mean that Merkavah mysticism is a form of magic.

In addition, some of these magico-theurgic practices—and specifically ritual baths, seals and names—bear strong resemblance to practices and to the symbolism known from various gnostic writings.[55] It may thus be asked whether the occurrence of these practices in the *Hekhalot* literature is not also indicative of either a real gnostic influence on it, or, at least, of the existence of certain points of connection between the *Hekhalot* mysticism and gnostic beliefs and practices. As we know, it has been argued by Professor Scholem that the *Hekhalot* writings are a Jewish concomitant to gnosticism. The present writer, however, has expressed the view, that since these writings are basically mystical writings with no immediate redemptive claims, they are to be strictly distinguished from the gnostic concepts and writings which have an emphatic redemptive quality.[56] In this respect, one has to distinguish between certain eschatological hopes mentioned in the *Hekhalot* writings or attached to the mystical activity,[57] and the basic redemptive functions of gnosticism and its

---

[53] *Op. cit.*, p. 291.

[54] *Ibid.* See further A. D. Nock, *Essays on Religion and the Ancient World*, Harvard University Press, 1972, vol. I, p. 189, n. 81.

[55] See W. Bousset, *Die Himmelsreise der Seele*, Reprint: Darmstadt, Wissenschaftliche Buchgesellschaft, (n.d.), pp. 5 ff. Bousset's arguments to the effect that the practices applied in ascension-experiences are to be viewed in the light of similar practices known from the Iranic religion are no more acceptable.

[56] Cf. *Israel Oriental Studies* III (1973), pp. 88 ff.

[57] There are clear eschatological passages in the *Hekhalot* writings and the most emphatic eschatological claim, in this respect, is attached to the study of the *Shiʿur Qomah*. See in *Merkavah Shelemah*, fol. 38b, where Rabbi ʿAkiva is quoted as saying that an after-life is promised to everyone who knows the mystical dimensions of the divinity.

writings. While gnosticism by and large means a final escape from the bonds of the material, evil, world, the mysticism of the Merkavah presupposes that the mystic always returns from his celestial adventures to his body on earth. If he fails to do so, that is if he dies in the course of his experience, or as a result of it, this indicates that he did not "deserve to see the King in His beauty", as a common phrase in *Hekhalot* literature goes.[58]

Moreover, the angels who try to stand in the way of the ascending mystic do not share the evil qualities of the Archons (= the evil rulers of this world) who try to capture the soul of the redeemed person and to prevent it from ascending to Incorruptibility, or to the Source of Light. Although these angels in the *Hekhalot* literature —and in the rabbinic literature related to it—are sometimes referred to as 'angels of destruction', they are not in their essence opposed to the divine. On the contrary, they are zealous in their desire to keep God aloft and apart from any undeserving human being. It is only when God personally intervenes on behalf of the visionary, or when the appropriate seals are produced, that passage is granted to the ascending human being. Thus, the relevant material in the *Hekhalot* writings bears at its best only a formal resemblance to concepts and to practices known from gnosticism. However suggestive this resemblance may appear, it does not justify the virtual interpretation of Jewish Merkavah mysticism in terms of gnosticism. Admittedly, in following such an interpretation for a short time we gained a lot in our understanding of certain important details in Merkavah mysticism, but we should now be careful not to follow this interpretation in all directions. We always have to keep in mind that gnosticism was a religious phenomenon diametrically opposed to everything Jewish; in fact, the God of the Jews was considered by the gnostics an evil deity. If we keep this in mind, it becomes clear that the Jewish mystics, who were everything but downright heretics, avoided all conscious contacts with the gnostics, their concepts, their practices and their writings.[59]

On the contrary, in recent years it has increasingly become evident that many of the gnostic writings were in one way or another in-

[58] See S. Leiter, "Worthiness, Acclamation and Appointment: Some Rabbinic Terms", *Proceedings of the American Academy for Jewish Research*, Vol. XLI-XLII (1973-1974), pp. 143 ff.

[59] On this see further, D. Flusser, "Scholem's Recent Book on Merkabah Literature", *The Journal of Jewish Studies* XI (1960), 59-68.

fluenced by Jewish thought and beliefs. Although the exact way these Jewish ideas reached gnosticism is still a riddle, one may assume that certain Jews who underwent conversion to gnosticism brought their knowledge along with them.[60] In addition, Christian writers who were familiar with Jewish writings could have served as literary intermediaries. In any event, it is clear today that a number of Jewish ideas and concepts found their way into gnosticism, and this in spite of the fact that gnosticism totally rejected Judaism. In this manner, we may, for example, understand the occurrence of two Merkavah passages in two of the gnostic writings: in the so-called "Die Schrift ohne Titel vom Ursprung der Welt" [61] and in the "Hypostasis of the Archons".[62] Both texts contain detailed descriptions of the creation of the world. The background of the descriptions is the biblical story in *Genesis* which is interpreted to contain the gnostic truth. Both treatises are strongly interrelated, and it seems that they derive from a third, common, source, which is no longer known to us.[63]

We begin with the "Untitled Work on the Creation of the World". Its declared purpose is to show what had existed before Chaos came into being, what was the nature of that pre-existent entity and what happened to Chaos when it was shaped into the material world. Briefly, the theory developed in the book is that there had been an immense domain of light beneath which a veil (παραπέτασμα) was spread. That veil created a shadow, and in that shadow Chaos came into being. Pistis, who is also called Sophia, and who came from above the veil, created a ruler over that Chaos. This ruler, or Archon, was called Yaldabaoth [64] and he was responsible for the creation of everything that came into being beneath that veil.

[60] See I. Gruenwald, "Jewish Sources for the Gnostic Texts from Nag Hammadi?", *Proceedings of the Sixth World Congress for Jewish Studies*, Jerusalem, 1977, pp. 45 ff. See also the curious statement made by Irenaeus, *Adversus Haereses*, I, xxiv,6, to the effect that the gnostics claim that they are not any longer Jews or Christians.

[61] A. Böhlig and P. Labib, *Die koptisch-gnostische Schrift ohne Titel aus Codex II von Nag-Hammadi*, Berlin, Akademie-Verlag, 1962.

[62] See B. Layton, "The Hypostasis of the Archons", *Harvard Theological Review* LXVII (1974), pp. 351 ff.; and R. A. Bullard, *The Hypostasis of the Archons*, Berlin, Walter de Gruyter, 1970. My quotations, however, are from Layton's English translation of the Coptic text.

[63] J. Doresse, *The Secret Books of the Egyptian Gnostics*, New York, The Viking Press, 1960, p. 163, assumes that "much of this treatise (= *The Hypostasis of the Archons*) is manifestly an abridgement of a certain *Book of Norea*".

[64] The name "Yaldabaoth" has caused difficulties and a number of theories were suggested for its explanation. See most recently G. Scholem, "Jaldabaoth

Among the things which he created were seven archangels, who possessed masculine and feminine qualities and names, and to whom he allocated heavens. These heavens contained, among other things, thrones, temples and chariots (150,11 ff.). When Yaldabaoth saw all the magnificence of his creation, he boasted and declared himself to be the only God (151,12). Pistis, who heard this blasphemy, condemned Yaldabaoth and told him that a 'Son of Light' would come and destroy him and all his Creations. However, Sabaoth, one of the offspring of Yaldabaoth, heard the voice of Pistis, praised her and joined her in her condemnation of his father and mother. As a reward Pistis stretched out her finger and poured over him Light. Consequently, Sabaoth was endowed with great power and became the Lord of all the Powers (152,9). He loathed all his kinsfolk, and they in turn waged war against him in the seven heavens. Pistis, who saw what was going on, sent seven archangels to rescue Sabaoth and they snatched him up to the seventh heaven. There, she erected for him a heavenly kingdom (152,23). In addition, Pistis gave him the Place of Rest (τόπος ἀνάπαυσις) for his repentance (μετάνοια). She also brought to him her daughter Zoe so that she might teach him about all that existed in the Ogdoad, that is, in the eighth heaven (152,26 ff.). Then Sabaoth, who was very powerful indeed, made for himself a dwelling-place which was big and wonderful. In fact, this dwelling-place was even bigger than its counterparts in the other heavens (152,31-35). In front (!) of that dwelling-place he created a

---

Reconsidered", in: *Mélanges d'Histoire des Religions offerts à Henri-Charles Puech* (1974), pp. 405-421. Scholem writes (p. 418): "... Jaldabaoth is a composite of *jald - abaoth*. I propose that it owes its invention to a heretical Jew familiar with Aramaic, the Hebrew Bible and the literature or practice of the magicians, a Jew who, in the context of the Ophitic myth, created it as a secret name of Samael". The element *Yald* designates, according to Scholem, not the son but the begetter (p. 419), and the element *abaoth* "originated as an abridged form, or substitute, of Sabaoth" (p. 420). Scholem's explanation is the best so far, though it may be argued that the 'yald'-element actually conveys Yaldabaoth's double role as the one begotten (by Pistis Sophia, and hence called in the Untitled Work νεανίσκος) and the one who begets! That in the explanation of the alleged etymology of the name Yaldabaoth one should not overlook his status as the *begotten* one becomes evident from the Untitled Work 148,1 ff. (p. 40/1 f.) where among the things mentioned as Yaldabaoth's roles, nothing is said of his role as the one who begets. It is here that Pistis Sophia calls him by the name of νεανίσκος, that is "child", or in Hebrew *Yeled.* Only later on does the Archon discover in himself the desire to create and to beget. Then the shift occurs from the status of the one begotten to the one who begets, or in Aramaic: *Yalda.* If our explanation is correct, then the etymology of the first element in the name actually derives both from Hebrew and from Aramaic.

big throne which was placed on a chariot (ἅρμα = Merkavah!). The chariot had four faces (πρόσωπον), and it was called Cherubin. Now, the Cherubin had four forms (μορφή), one on each of its four corners: lion forms (!) calf forms, human forms, and eagle forms. The number of all the forms thus amounted to sixty-four. Before the throne stood seven archangels. Sabaoth himself was the eighth; thus all the forms amounted to seventy-two, which the Untitled Work assumes is the number which corresponds to the number of the nations of the world.

Before we go on with the description of the installment scene in the Untitled Work, a few remarks are in place concerning the preceding part of the narrative. To begin with, the description of Sabaoth's throne is quite peculiar and causes some difficulties, the main one being how exactly the author conceived of the faces of the "Forms"? He says that each of the four corners of the throne, called "Cherubin", had eight forms, that is, the four forms—the lion, the calf, the human form, and the eagle—which were all placed at every corner had two faces each. This is quite remarkable in itself, and when we multiply the eight faces by four (= corners) we get only thirty two faces, and not sixty four, as the author himself counts (153,9). Elsewhere, in *Hekhalot Zutreti* (in: *Merkavah Shelemah* 7a) we read that each of the Holy Creatures in the divine chariot had four faces, and since there were four Creatures at every corner of the throne there were all in all sixty four faces (4 Creatures × 4 faces × 4 corners = 64!). A similar calculation is preserved in the Targum to *Ezekiel* i,6: every creature had four faces, and there were four creatures at every corner, so that the sum total of the faces was sixty four. Evidently, the tradition preserved in the Untitled Work is dependent on such Merkavah-speculations, and it may be argued that its details should be emended in order to fit the Merkavah material known from *Hekhalot Zutreti* and the Targum to *Ezekiel.* As for the order in which the "Forms" are enumerated in the Untitled Work, it should be noticed that it preserves the order given in *Revelation* iv,7.

Another point which deserves attention is the instruction given by Zoe [65] concerning all that is in the Ogdoad. Though nothing explicit is said in the text about the contents of Zoe's teachings and the

[65] In 154,6, however, it is Pistis Sophia herself who is instructing Sabaoth. Yet, from the parallel passage in the *Hypostasis of the Archons*, it becomes evident that Zoe, and not Pistis Sophia, instructs Sabaoth. See also the Untitled Work 155,4.

Ogdoad, we may conclude that since the Ogdoad represents the domain of light of the Imperishability, the teaching about it is of a theosophical nature, and may also include the secrets of redemption. The idea, that whatever belongs to the Ogdoad is top secret is also found in the Jewish Merkavah speculations. In *Bavli Ḥagigah* 12b a detailed description is given of the seven heavens and what they contain. Then (13a, top) the Gemārā quotes Rabbi ʾAḥa bar Yaʿaqov's question to the effect that there is yet another, eighth heaven, which is above the heads of the *Ḥayyot*. The question refers to *Ezekiel* i,22 ff., where the prophet sees a firmament stretched above the heads of the Holy Creatures. The response given in the Gemārā is: "Till this place (= the seventh heaven) you may discourse, from here onwards (= the eighth heaven) you have no permission to discourse". The Gemārā also refers the student to *Ben-Sira* iii,21-22 which is taken to support the idea. However, it should be noticed that while the Gemārā forbids any speculations of the eighth heaven, the Untitled Work maintains that knowledge of the Ogdoad was granted to Sabaoth. Now, in some respects, Sabaoth in the Untitled Work reminds one of the fate of Enoch who was translated to heaven, transformed into the angel Metatron, and thus received all kinds of honours and revelations of secrets.[66] Both Enoch-Metatron and Sabaoth enjoyed exceptional fates, yet the different contexts of their experiences forbid us from pushing their points of resemblance beyond their formal aspects.

The Merkavah account in the Untitled Work ends with the description of how Sabaoth created above that throne a host of angelic beings (153,16 ff.). One class of the angels was called "Seraphim". Their form was that of serpents [67] and they were always praising Sabaoth.[68] Sabaoth also created a first-born one called "Israel", which in a common etymology of the time [69] was taken to designate "the man

[66] See mainly *3 Enoch*.

[67] This is a rather peculiar—yet typically gnostic—interpretation of *Numbers* xxi,6. See also next note. The Coptic text here uses the Greek word δράκον. In Jewish laws of idolatry, the dragon-form received special attention: *Mishnah ʿAvodah Zarah* iii,3. According to *Talmud Yerushalmi* (fol. 42d), a dragon has spikes growing out of his neck. See further *Bavli ʿAvodah Zarah* 43a.

[68] See *Isaiah* vi,2-3 in comparison to xiv,29 and xxx,6. It is still an open question as to what made Isaiah call the holy angels by a word he uses also for dragons.

[69] See J. G. Kahn, "Israel - *Videns* Deum", (in Hebrew), *Tarbiz* XL (1971), pp. 285-292. Kahn (= Y. Cohen-Yashar), however, was not aware of the existence of the gnostic parallels, as given by A. Böhlig in his notes, p. 54. See also J. Z. Smith, "The Prayer of Joseph", in: *Religions in Antiquity*, ed. J. Neusner, Leiden, E. J. Brill, 1968, pp. 262-268.

who sees God".[70] It is noteworthy that the People of Israel receive in this text a place of honour among the celestial beings. Yet, whatever their status, they still belong to the unredeemed world of the Archons. They are in the hosts of the angels serving Sabaoth, and Sabaoth, to be sure, though he had been transferred to the seventh heaven, did not reach the Domain of Light of the Imperishability. Concerning that Domain, he received only oral instruction. In addition to these angelic beings, Sabaoth created another being called "Jesus Christ", who was like the saviour who was in the Ogdoad. This "Jesus Christ" had a special throne on the right of the throne of Sabaoth,[71] while on its left was sitting the virgin, which represented the holy spirit of Christian theology. Before Sabaoth were also standing seven other virgins in whose hands were zithers, psalteries and trumpets. Finally, Sabaoth himself is described as sitting on a Throne of Light [72] which was surrounded by a great cloud. This description of the throne is familiar from Jewish sources.[73]

As already mentioned before, a similar description of the installment of Sabaoth in the seventh heaven is found in another gnostic text — *The Hypostasis of the Archons*. There, the description is part of the instruction of Eleleth to Norea,[74] after she had resisted the

[70] At the end of *Midrash Conen* (in A. Jellinek, *Bet ha-Midrasch*, vol. II, p. 39) mention is made of one Creature (*Ḥayyah*), called "Yisrael", and which stands in the middle of the firmament and says praises to God. In all likelihood, this Creature is meant to be a mystical representation of the People of Israel in heaven.

[71] This is in line with the Christian interpretation of *Psalm* cx,1.

[72] A literal translation of the Coptic text here reads: upon a throne in the light in a great cloud. As Professor Bentley Layton observed in an English translation of these pages which he has kindly prepared for me, the text seems to be corrupt. Layton suggests to read "a luminous throne" in a great cloud! "A luminous throne" is nothing but the translation of the Hebrew *Kisse Ha-Kavod*, the Throne of (the) Glory.

[73] See *Mechilta d'Rabbi Ismael* to *Exodus* xx,18 (p. 238).—The idea that God is covered from the sight of men and angels by a cloud is also known from a so-called Jewish Orphic poem from the second or third century B.C.E. The poem was preserved in two versions, which were recently re-discussed in Y. Gutman, *The Beginnings of Jewish-Hellenistic Literature* (in Hebrew), Jerusalem, Bialik Institute, 1958, pp. 153 ff. In the first version preserved in *Cohort. ad. gent.*, attributed to Justin Martyr, God's invisibility is accounted for by the cloud which covers him. And in the version attributed to Aristobulus (quoted in Eusebius, *Praeparatio Evangelica* XIII,12) God is hidden from the sight of men by "a tenfold mist" (νέφος . . . δεκάπτυχον). The so-called tenfold mist most likely corresponds to the ten heavens known by the Pythagoreans.—For the Palestinian nomenclature which refers to the fourth heaven by the name of ʿArafel (νέφος), see my edition of *Reʿuyot Yeḥezkel*, p. 118.

[74] For the studies dealing with the figure of Norea see B. Layton, *art. cit.*, p. 388.

temptation of the Archons to lead her astray. In its form and content, the description there is an abridgement of the source from which it drew.[75] In any event, as becomes clear from a number of differences between the two narratives, the account of the installment of Sabaoth in *The Hypostasis of the Archons* does not derive from its counterpart in the Untitled Work. For instance, in contradistinction to the Untitled Work, where to the left of Sabaoth's throne one can find the Virgin of the Holy Spirit, *The Hypostasis of the Archons* reports that on the left of the throne the Angel of Wrath was placed. Thus, one finds Unrighteousness occupying the left of what may be called the sub-Ogdoadian Deity, a fact which implies a symbolism that in a sense draws from the writings of Qumran, and which later on was a key notion in the Kabbalah.[76] Since Sabaoth, in spite of his substantial prominence over the other Archons, still occupies the place which is *beneath* the veil that separates between the Above and the Below, he cannot fully equal the qualities of the God of the Jews in Jewish thought. The degraded Sabaoth here is a gnostic concept and he belongs to the inferior world of the Archons. Thus, even in the conceptual framework of *The Hypostasis of the Archons*, the existence of the Angel of Wrath in the realm of the seventh heaven next to Sabaoth cannot be viewed in such radical dualistic terms as one is used to consider evil in gnostic thought. It has to be noticed too that in the Untitled Work (154,11 ff.) Pistis Sophia places Sabaoth on her right while the Archigenetor (= Yaldabaoth) is called to occupy a place on her left. Thus, both books conceive of evil as being in the vicinity of a divine or semi-divine being. This not only emphasizes the reality of its existence, but also, and even more so, makes it clear that however rebellious the powers of evil may appear, they are still under the control of the supreme divinity. Thus, we once again realize that dualistic religious systems may nontheless be monistic at their very heart.[77]

---

[75] See above n. 63.

[76] In the Untitled Work 154,12 ff. Pistis Sophia is said to call Sabaoth to her right and the Archigenetor (= Yaldabaoth) to her left, thus forming a cosmic scheme of righteousness *versus* unrighteousness. This division comes very close to the one portrayed in the Qumran *Rule of the Community* (1 Q S), III,13 ff. See G. Scholem, "Gut und Böse in der Kabbalah", in *Von der mystischen Gestalt der Gottheit*, Zurich, Rhein Verlag, 1962, pp. 49 ff.—Professor Scholem called my attention to *Masekhet Hekhalot*, in *Bet ha-Midrasch*, vol. II, p. 46, where life and death are placed to the right and left of God respectively.

[77] I have discussed this issue in *Israel Oriental Studies* III, (1973), pp. 77 ff.

We have gone into some detail in our presentation of certain Merkavah-passages in two gnostic writings so as to suggest that just as a number of gnostic elements found their way into Merkavah mysticism so did also certain Merkavah elements find their way into gnosticism. A comparative study of Merkavah mysticism and gnosticism will certainly render important results, one of which will prevent us from overdoing our job by interpreting the one phenomenon in terms of the other. The points of connection between the two can tell us a lot about their own spirit and of the character of the syncretism of the first centuries of the Christian Era. Speaking about "Syncretism", the term can mean many things, yet here it is understood to imply the transference and reception of religious beliefs and practices. The degree of receptivity which some Jewish circles showed to ideas originating from pagan sources is still one of the most bewildering problems which the student of the Judaism of the Talmudic period faces. It will in no way ease the problem if we assume that some Jewish circles timidly and carelessly collected whatever they found in the international market of religions. But it seems equally true to maintain that once foreign ideas had found their way into Judaism they were not—or even could not be—easily swept under the carpet. Although one may argue that in certain cases the Jews were not fully aware of the real qualities—and of the imminent dangers—of the beliefs and practices which they adopted, this argument can hardly explain the whole of the truth. In most cases, however, the impression one gets is that those people were attracted by complex pictures even when these pictures were composed of the most heterogeneous elements. The artificial combination of various and sometimes even conflicting religious elements was the fashion of the day, and if this was believed to enrich one's religious experience, the question of the cost was not raised. On the contrary, the gain appeared to be enormous, and people seem to have been sure that nothing was lost in their own integrity. Thus gnosticism could refer to the Jewish Scripture and "discover" there its own cosmology, while the Jewish mystics partook of rites and practices that grew on the soil of magic and gnosticism. Nontheless, neither side believed that it lost by this anything of its own identity. On the contrary, new sources opened new directions and this in turn resulted in deepening the experience.

C

In the previous section, we discussed some problems in connection with the relationship between gnosticism and Merkavah mysticism. On the whole, it must be remarked that gnosticism owes much more to Judaism than *vice versa*. In fact, there is very little in Judaism that was inspired—even negatively so—by gnosticism. The various sayings, for instance, refuting the two powers (*Shtei Reshuyot*) doctrine need not necessarily be an explicitly anti-gnostic theologumenon. As for the theurgical elements in *Hekhalot* mysticism, it may be argued that they were so common and widely spread in those days that their attribution to gnosticism alone cannot be conclusively proved.

In this section we shall make some additional remarks about the techniques of the ascension, both in apocalyptic and in Merkavah mysticism. In apocalyptic literature we know of at least three kinds of ascensions. The most common description is that of an ascension on clouds in the course of a storm. Thus we find in *1 Enoch* xiv,8-9 the following description: "And the vision was shown to me thus: Behold, in the vision clouds invited me and a mist summoned me and the course of the stars and the lightnings sped and hastened me, and the winds in the vision caused me to fly and lifted me upward, and bore me into heaven".[78] No doubt, the description takes after its model, the ascension of Elijah (*2 Kings* ii.11), but it should be noticed that the visionary here clearly distinguishes between reality (his sleep) and what he saw in his dream-vision (his ascension). Elijah's ascension also left its traces on the description of three other ascensions: on *1 Enoch* lxx,2 ("And he was raised aloft on the chariots of the wind"); on *1 Enoch* xxxix,3 ("and in those days a whirlwind carried me off from the earth") and on lii,1 (". . . I had been carried off in a whirlwind"). Although in the last instances no dream is explicitly mentioned, one may assume that the manner in which the ascension is described in *1 Enoch* xiv,8-9 still holds true in the other cases too. In *2 Enoch* iii, however, the visionary is described as being raised on the wings of two angels.[79] In like manner, as we al-

[78] Compare the description of the ascension of Moses in *Pesikta Rabbati* (ed. Friedmann, 96b): "When Moses was about to ascend to heaven, a cloud came and prostrated itself before him. However, Moses did not know whether to ride on it or to hold it, so the cloud opened and Moses entered . . . and the cloud carried him and he walked in the heaven".

[79] See also *1 Enoch* lxxxvii,2-3: "And I saw in vision, and behold there came

ready saw in the *Apocalypse of Abraham*, both the visionary and his guiding angel were raised to heaven on the wings of a bird. In *Greek Baruch* ii,1 and in the *Ascension of Isaiah* vii,2, it is simply said that an angel carried the visionaries to heaven. In *Testament Levi* ii,6-7 and in *Revelation* iv,1-2, it appears that the visionary did not need any assistence in his ascent. Yet, the expression "and I was there in spirit" (*Revelation* iv,2) apparently was a technical term used to designate experiences which the visionary saw in a trance.[80]

More elaborate, however, are the details given about the ascensions in the *Hekhalot* literature. A recurring image in *Hekhalot Rabbati* is the ladder which the mystic is said to use as a means for his ascension. Thus, we read that the Merkavah mystic is like "a man who has a ladder in his home which he ascends and descends, and nobody can interfere with what he does" (xiii,2; xx,3). In yet another place, mention is made of a "heavenly ladder which stands on earth and reaches up to the right leg of the Throne of Glory" (xiv,1). The idea behind this description evidently is Jacob's ladder (*Genesis* xxviii,12), though the ones climbing it up and down were the angels.[81] In one late *Hekhalot* fragment,[82] we find that the angels climb out of the bath they take in the rivers of fire by help of a "ladder of fire". Another ladder is mentioned in connection with the souls of the righteous ones which are said to climb that ladder in the celestial garden of Eden.[83] Finally, a ladder with seven rungs (κλῖμαξ ἑπτάπυλος), which symbolizes the ascent of the soul through the seven gates of the heaven, is known from the temples of Mithra.[84]

In several instances in the *Hekhalot* literature, various kinds of

---

forth from heaven beings who were like white men ... and those three that had last come forth grasped me by my hand and took me up ..."

[80] See Charles's Commentary *ad loc.*

[81] See A. A. Altman, "The Ladder of Ascension", *Studies in Mysticism and Religion Presented to G. G. Scholem*, p. 1 ff. Altman has brought most of the relevant material from early Jewish mysticism. See further *Bavli Sotah* 35a: "... if Moses is to tell us to make ladders and to ascend to heaven will we not obey him? ...". See also, E. R. Goodenough, *Jewish Symbols in the Greco-Roman Period*, vol. VIII (1958), pp. 148-157. See also the next three notes.

[82] In A. Jellinek, *Bet-ha-Midrasch*, vol. III, p. 162. See also S. A. Wertheimer, *Batei Midrashot*, vol. I, p. 46.

[83] A. Jellinek, *Bet ha-Midrasch*, vol. II, p. 28.

[84] See A. Dieterich, *Eine Mithrasliturgie*, Reprint: Darmstadt, Wissenschaftliche Buchgesellschaft, 1966, pp. 183-184. F. Cumont, *Die Mysterien des Mithra*, Reprint: Darmstadt, Wissenschaftliche Buchgesellschaft, 1963, p. 123. All this material escaped the eyes of J. Danielou, *Théologie du Judéo-Christianisme*, Tournai, 1958, pp. 131-138, where he discussed the subject of L'échelle Cosmique.

wagons or carriages are mentioned. In one instance, *Hekhalot Rabbati* xviii,5-6, we read that Qaẓpiel, one of the angels who stands at the gate of the sixth palace, "brings you a whirlwind, and he places you in a wagon of light".[85] This wagon is used in the course of the passage from the sixth to the seventh *Hekhal*.[86] In *3 Enoch* vi we read of Enoch's translation with the help of ʿAnafiel [87] in a carriage of fire.[88] Once again, we must notice that the idea of the wagon or carriage is inspired by the description of the ascent of Elijah (*2 Kings* ii,11), though it should be equally noticed that in Plato's *Phaedrus* too the soul is described as ascending to heaven in a chariot. Generally, however, the passage from one heavenly palace to the other is performed with the help of two angels who accompany the mystic on both his sides. New accompanying angels take the place of the former ones in every new palace. In two cases, we even find that the mystic is dragged on his knees till he reaches the Throne of Glory.[89]

To end this general introduction to the *Hekhalot* literature, two additional characteristics will be pointed out. We have seen in the previous chapter that the *Maʿaseh Merkavah* speculations in rabbinic circles were subject to severe restrictions regarding the number of those allowed to participate in the study and the manner in which the discourse on the Merkavah should be introduced. Briefly, we saw that the Merkavah material could be studied only in the presence of one student, provided that he was wise and able to understand by himself. At first, it was the student who had to open the discourse, and only later permission was granted to the teacher to introduce the discourse by suggesting the *Rashei Pesuqin* or *Rashei Peraqim*.[90]

[85] See also A. Dieterich, *op. cit.*, p. 183-184; G. Scholem, *Jewish Gnosticism* etc., pp. 18,82. See further the expression "carriages of gold" in *Bavli Kidushin* 76b.

[86] The details of this stage in the mystical ascent are given in *Hekhalot Rabbati*, chh. xix-xxiii.

[87] In *Hekhalot Rabbati* xxii,4 ff. ʿAnafiel is described as a most distinguished angel, and some of his extraordinary qualities actually remind of some of the qualities of Metatron.

[88] See further the so-called *Apocalypsis Mosis* xxxiii, where Adam's body is described to be carried up to heaven after his death in a chariot of light borne by four eagles. In the gnostic *Letter of James* it is said that when the revelations have come to an end Christ rises to Heaven in a Chariot of Pneuma: see G. Quispel, "The Jung Codex and its Significance", in: *Gnostic Studies* I, Istanbul, 1974, p. 8.

[89] See *Hekhalot Rabbati*, iii,1 and the *Hekhalot* text published in *Tarbiz* XXXVIII (1969), p. 359, ll. 30 ff.

[90] Only after the completion of Chapter Three has G. A. Wewers's book, *Geheimnis und Geheimhaltung im rabbinischen Judentum*, Berlin, Walter de Gruyter,

In the *Hekhalot* writings, however, no specific demand for secrecy is included, and even contrary to the tone struck in Jewish apocalyptic, there is no claim for the exclusiveness of the revelation. What one does repeatedly hear in the *Hekhalot* writings are the details of the extraordinary dangers which the mystics have to overcome. Only the most deserving ones will come out safely from the series of ordeals and tests which they have to undergo. The imminent dangers of the *Ma'aseh Merkavah* are already stressed in the discussions found in both Talmuds on the first *Mishnah* of Tractate *Ḥagigah*. In the *Hekhalot* writings, the danger-motif comes even more emphatically to the fore, evidently in order to prevent the undeserving from realizing the experiences described. The theurgic elements in these writings also belong to this aspect of that literature. In fact, the mystic is taught all these theurgic practices and means in order to be able to overcome the dangers which he has to encounter in the course of his mystical experience. Only the knowledge of their correct application is to guarantee him physical and psychical safety.

But, it is interesting to notice that the *Hekhalot* writings do not declare these theurgic means to be secret. In contrast to the reserve felt in the pages of the *Talmuds* with respect to everything relevant to the subject, the *Hekhalot* writings do no even refrain from discussing openly the theurgic means which are to be used in every case. No secrecy is demanded from the initiate, and although we may assume that such secrecy was elementary, one still remains puzzled by the outright manner in which the material is displayed. The fact that people were aware of the extreme dangers involved in such experiences did not guarantee that no leak will be found in the wall of secrecy. Dangerous experiences only arouse the curiosity of people, and in many cases nothing can stop them from trying out the mystical experiences described.[91]

It is hardly conceivable that those who put the *Hekhalot* tractates into writing were not aware of the dangers involved in putting these writings before the ignorant public. And yet they did so. Thus, the question arises if we have to interpret this fact as indicating that the

---

1975, reached me. Unfortunately Wewers' discussion does not add anything substantial to our understanding of the material he handles. Although he touches some of the important problems, his original contribution is quite hypothetical. He could have done better had he made use of the *Hekhalot* literature etc. In addition, Wewers was not aware of a number of studies published in recent years and reference to which could have opened his eyes in many essential points.

[91] See in *Tarbiẓ* XXXVIII (1969), p. 358.

process of putting the *Hekhalot* literature into writing took place only after the *Hekhalot* mysticism had become a memory of the past and decayed so-to-speak into a mere literary phenomenon?

There is very little, if anything at all, in the *Hekhalot* literature that may justify its classification as esoteric, at least not in the sense in which esotericism was applied in Jewish apocalyptic. In our discussion of Jewish apocalyptic, it was pointed out that its esoteric quality was mainly lying in its explicit or implicit claim that what had been revealed to the visionary in many cases was an exclusive angelic revelation, or at least some kind of heavenly inspiration. Although secrets are sometimes referred to in the *Hekhalot* literature, it cannot, thus, be defined as esoteric. The *Hekhalot* writings did not claim secrecy for themselves, and what was assumingly in them that could prevent their contents from being misused were the dangers described therein. In a sense the description of the details of these dangers can be much more effective in restraining people from misapplying the information gained from the *Hekhalot* literature than the mere formal demand to keep its contents secret.

PART TWO

INTRODUCTION

As indicated before, the second part of our book contains detailed introductions to the various *Hekhalot* writings we possess. The first part of the book was devoted to an analysis of some of the major problems involved in the study of the development of the Merkavah tradition in the time of the Mishnah and Talmud. After an attempt had been made to qualify the esoteric features of Jewish apocalyptic (Chapter One), we passed on to examine the place and nature of the Merkavah tradition incorporated in that literature. It was seen that some of the apocalyptic books contain detailed Merkavah visions which follow the Merkavah tradition found in books like *Ezekiel*, *Isaiah* and *Daniel* (Chapter Two). In Chapter Three the attitude of the rabbinical circles to the Merkavah material was examined. Finally, in Chapter Four, a general introduction to the *Hekhalot* writings was presented.

However, two major problems still have to be discussed in a more detailed manner. The first one is the question of the continuity of the Merkavah tradition. It has been shown that there existed at least a thematic continuity between the so-called Merkavah tradition in Scripture and the one in apocalyptic literature. There is even a thematic continuity which can be traced from apocalyptic literature on the one hand to the Merkavah material in rabbinical literature and to the *Hekhalot* writings on the other hand. The question now arises as to whether a historical continuity can be pointed out in addition to this thematic continuity. The answer to this question is particularly difficult for a number of reasons: First, we lack almost all the literary documents which were created between the fifth century B.C.E., that is the days of the last prophets, and the middle of the third century B.C.E., that is the early hellenistic period. This is a long period of silence, and doubtlessly in that period all the foundations were laid for the creation of the Jewish hellenistic literature. Second, we lack any direct evidence that the circles which produced the apocalyptic corpus of writings were historically related to those circles that engaged in Merkavah speculations and experiences from the Tannaitic times onwards. Third, no conclusive proof has yet been found that the *Tannaim* and the *Amoraim* were directly involved in the creation of the *Hekhalot* writings. Although the existence of alleged points of connection between all these circles can be concluded from the thematic affinities which the writings under discussion display, no direct proof has yet been found for the existence of real historical connections between them.

However, when we come to the hellenistic period, we find that at least one of its major works contains a so-called Merkavah vision. The work we have in mind is the play written by Ezekiel, the Tragedian, and which describes events connected with the Exodus from Egypt.[1] Among other things, it contains a dream-vision which Moses experienced when he was wandering with the flocks of Jethro in the desert. In his vision, Moses saw himself on the top of Mount Sinai, and there he saw a high throne which reached to the heaven. On the throne was sitting someone who looked like a man wearing a crown on his head and holding a sceptre in his left hand. With his right hand, the figure on the throne gestured to Moses to come forward and to approach the throne. When Moses stood near the throne the being sitting on it gave him the crown [2] and the sceptre, and

---

[1] Y. Gutman, *The Beginnings of Jewish-Hellenistic Literature* (in Hebrew), vol. II, Jerusalem, Bialik Institute, 1963, pp. 66-69, argues that Ezekiel was a citizen of Berenice in Cyrenaica, and lived there in the first century B.C.E. However, M. Hengel, *Judaism and Hellenism*, Philadelphia, Fortress Press, 1974, vol. I, p. 109, vol. II, p. 109, n. 396, represents the more common view that Ezekiel, the Tragedian, lived in Alexandria in the second century B.C.E. It should be remarked that Gutman's discussion of Ezekiel and his work contains a number of rather hypothetical arguments. For example, in his interpretation of the vision of Moses on Mount Sinai, Gutman argues that the man whom Moses saw sitting on the throne was no divine figure, but a real man. The reason for this Gutman finds in the word φώς used by Ezekiel and which Gutman (probably following a remark in Liddell & Scott s.v. φώς III) takes to be used only "opp. a god". But had Ezekiel used the word ἄνθρωπος, he would not have changed matters in any substantial way. It is only in the Septuaginta and in the New Testament that ἄνθρωπος received its divine or messianic connotations! For the Greek text of *Ezechielus Tragicus*, see A.-M. Denis, *Fragmenta Pseudepigraphorum quae Supersunt Graeca*, Leiden, Brill, 1970, pp. 210-216.

[2] The idea of a crown which was given to Moses, is several times repeated in Jewish literature. It complements, most probably, the description of the skin of his face, which was reported to be shining (*Exodus* xxxiv,29 ff.). The most striking parallel to Ezekiel Tragicus is the Shabbat morning service in which we find that God gave to Moses "a crown of glory [*Kelil Tif'eret*] when he stood before You on Mount Sinai". See further J. Liver, *The House of David* (in Hebrew), Jerusalem, Magnes Press, 1959, p. 100-101, who pointed out the various functions of the *ʿAtarah* (στέφανος) in the ancient Near East. In the Qumran writings, we find that the members of the sect were to be endowed with a "crown of glory" (*Kelil Kavod*) as a sign of their eschatological blessing. See 1 QS IV,7; 1 QH IX,25. See further *Bavli Berakhot* 17a where the righteous are described in the world to come as sitting in the presence of God with crowns (*ʿAtarot*)

pointed to him to take his seat on the big throne. Then the 'man' left the throne, and Moses had from above a vision of the whole earth.[3] Finally, Moses says that he saw the hosts of the heavenly stars falling down on their knees before him,[4] and then marching past his throne. The vision obviously implied the initiation of Moses into the heavenly realms and his nomination to his kingly office. However, it is quite doubtful whether real deification was also implied by it. Deification, as we know, was generally believed to occur only after the hero's death and not during his lifetime. Thus, one may see in the vision a description of the enthronement of Moses as viewed within a mystical, or semi-mystical, framework.[5]

In spite of its obvious mystical setting, the vision described in the scene is certainly no Merkavah vision in the full sense of the term, and it is noteworthy that no angels are described in it.[6] Yet, it is also noteworthy that a Jewish drama written in Greek contains such a vision. This fact is evidently telling something about the public for which the play was written: they apparently expected such a scene or at least found nothing strange in its inclusion. Admittedly, this scene has a tremendous dramatic effect, but it also betrays the fact that people in Alexandria were familiar with such experiences and that they clearly understood what such experiences implied. If so, we may assume that mystical, or semi-mystical, experiences were part of the intellectual milieu of the Jewish-hellenistic world.[7]

---

on their heads. The idea became a current one in Christian theology and is well known from Christian iconography. Professor Morton Smith drew my attention to the fact that the "crowns" were really diadems, that is bands tied around the head, which were the Greco-Roman symbol of royalty.

[3] See Y. Gutman, *op. cit.*, pp. 43-46. This part of the dream could have been the model for the writer of the *Apocalypse of Abraham* xix.

[4] The reference here most certainly is to Joseph's dream in *Genesis* xxxvii,9. See also *Nehemiah* ix,6, where the stars are said to be worshipping God in a similar manner.

[5] For Deification after death, see E. Rohde, *Psyche*, New York, Harcourt, Brace & Co., 1925, pp. 524 ff.—For the motif of the enthronement, see G. Widengren, "Iran and Israel in Parthian Times with Special Regard to the Ethiopic *Book of Enoch*", in: *Religious Syncretism in Antiquity*, ed. Birger A. Pearson, Missoula, Montana, Scholars Press, 1975, p. 126 f. Widengren, who was unaware of Ezekiel the Tragedian, suggests that Indo-Iranian as well as ancient Near-Eastern material was the background of the kind of enthronement described in *1 Enoch* lxxi.

[6] However, the absence of angels from the vision cannot be attributed with certainty to polemical motivations.

[7] See M. P. Nilsson, *Greek Piety*, Oxford, Clarendon Press, 1948, pp. 124 ff., though some of Nilsson's generalizations, particularly those concerning gnos-

This conclusion may also be inferred from Philo, *De Vita Mosis*, 158 where Moses is described as entering "into the darkness where God was, that is into the unseen, invisible, incorporeal and archetypal essence of existing things".[8] The reference here is to *Exodus* xx,21, which in rabbinical literature too was interpreted as implying a special mystical experience.[9] To be sure, what Philo describes in his writings is no Merkavah vision, but it points to a kind of sensibility that in others could, and actually did, induce a Merkavah-imagery. Thus, to come back to the scene in Ezekiel the Tragedian, we hear that Moses saw himself elevated to see God on His throne, a vision that evidently draws its imagery from its counterpart in *Isaiah* vi. Yet, there are already some details in this vision that go beyond and differ from the material presented in *Isaiah* vi. We have already mentioned the fact that unlike the vision which Isaiah saw the being sitting on the throne offered to Moses his crown, sceptre and very throne. In addition, it should be noticed that unlike *Isaiah* vi,1, the scene in Ezekiel's tragedy does not take place in a palace but on the summit of Mount Sinai.[10] Finally, as we already observed, in contradistinction to *Isaiah* no angels were present on the scene. What in later apocalyptic and Merkavah literature—as already in *Isaiah* and *Ezekiel*—was the function of the angels was here performed by the heavenly stars. Nevertheless, all the differences notwithstanding, we may see in the scene in the *Tragedy of Ezekiel* a live link in the development of the Merkavah tradition between Scripture and apocalyptic literature. Thus, the historical continuity of that tradition

ticism, cannot be accepted without criticism. More important, however, for our purposes is the chapter "The Mystic Moses" in E. R. Goodenough, *By Light, Light*, Amsterdam, Philo Press, 1969, pp. 199-234. This is not to say that the present writer agrees with Goodenough's thesis regarding the existence of a fully developed Jewish hellenistic mystery religion.

[8] Similarly in *De Mutatione Nominum*, 7: "So Moses the explorer of nature which lies beyond our vision, Moses who, as the divine oracles tell us, entered into the darkness by which figure they indicate existence invisible and incorporeal, searched everywhere and into everything in his desire to see clearly and plainly Him, the object of our much yearning, Who is good".

[9] See *Mechilta d'Rabbi Ismael*, p. 238. See further Goodenough, *op. cit.*, pp. 212 ff.

[10] Compare *Mechilta d'Rabbi Ismael*, pp. 216 & 238 (= *Bavli Sukkah* 5a) where it becomes clear that the virtual descent of the *Kavod* on Mount Sinai, as also the ascent of Moses, became a controversial subject in Tannaitic literature.—The picture of the divine throne which is placed on the summit of mountains is a familiar one in antiquity; see J. Maier, *Vom Kultus zur Gnosis*, Salzburg, Otto Müller Verlag, 1964, pp. 97 ff.

at least up to apocalyptic literature is more clearly attested to than has hitherto been assumed. In any event, the inclusion of Merkavah material in Jewish apocalyptic is now more solidly accounted for: it is not merely the natural interest in things heavenly which explains the presence of this material in that literature, but also an allegedly live tradition which sought soil for its growth.

The second question to which attention must be given here is: How widespread the Merkavah tradition really was. We have already seen that there were various degrees of secrecy which restricted the discourse in the matters of the Merkavah to a small and highly qualified number of students. No wonder, then, that only few, but choice ones, enjoyed acquaintance with the subject. We saw too that the kind of experiences which the *Hekhalot* writings describe was connected with the knowledge of practices that verged on magic and theurgy. Magic and theurgy evidently were branches of knowledge and ritual that could hardly be tolerated in so-called orthodox circles. One may thus advance the conclusion that Merkavah mysticism was confined to a narrow elite of initiates who let themselves be exposed to practices that could be defined as idolatry. But, can it be maintained that people who lived at the very heart of Judaism of the time participated in practices that fell under the immediate spell of the pagan syncretism of the time? The question is no easy one to answer, and it bears decisively on our understanding and evaluation of the nature of Judaism in Talmudic times. It was variously argued, mainly in connection with the discussion of the problem of Jewish receptivity to customs emanating from idolatry, that the sages had no easy job in their attempts to control and to limit the measure of the exposure of many of their kinsfolk to idolatry. The practices we encounter in the *Hekhalot* writings only add fuel to the fire, and we are faced with the problem that, as it appears, traces of pagan syncretism which broke the rules of the Law, did after all reach the very heart of the Judaism of the period.

Since the *Hekhalot* writings are in no other way opposed to the concepts of the Law and the obedience to it, the question becomes even more difficult to answer. In addition, the *Hekhalot* writings have distinctive literary qualities and from this point of view alone it cannot in any way be maintained that they were produced by illiterate, ignorant, Jews who were not able to pass judgement on their own activities. The insistence found in these writings on the observation of the Law and the preoccupation with the problems of the study of the Law and its memorization make it again evident that the solution to our problem cannot be sought in marginal heterodox groups or associations. The problem thus concerns the very heart of the Judaism of the period, and we may say that the occurrence in these writings of magical and theurgic practices can illuminate things that were to all likelihood going on in circles which were not so tightly controlled by the sages. Naturally, the *Hekhalot* writings contained a refined form of magic and theurgy in comparison with the more vulgar form of these practices as it could be found among those less learned and pious. It therefore seems permissible to infer that certain elements of pagan syncretism penetrated into wide Jewish circles, and this in various degrees of intensity and in a manner that cannot leave us indifferent to the problems involved. It is hardly conceivable that the Jews who practised these things did not really believe in the efficacy of the powers they invoked and of the practices they applied. Thus, when it came to it, certain established standards of behaviour and norms of belief had to be suspended. This is particularly so, where the end was worth justifying the means.

Another point which should be considered here is whether we can define the knowledge of the Merkavah material among the common people as mysticism. The interest in what is going on in heaven is a natural component of religion and should not be too easily identified with mystical practice and speculation. It has been pointed out by Professor David Flusser that Jewish liturgy in the times of the Second Temple contained so-called mystical elaborations to the angelic doxologies quoted in *Isaiah* vi,3 and *Ezekiel* iii,12.[11] Flusser referred to the close connections between the material found in Jewish apocalyptic and in Merkavah mysticism on the one hand and in Jewish and Christian liturgy on the other. Indeed, there were ways in which the liturgy of the synagogue was influenced by apocalyptic and *Hekhalot* material.[12] But it is a question of a different order as to how deep this knowledge of the apocalyptic and *Hekhalot* material really went. It is quite likely that those who composed the

[11] D. Flusser, "Sanktus und Gloria", *Festschrift für Otto Michel*, Leiden, Brill, 1963, pp. 129 ff.

[12] See J. Schirmann, "Hebrew Liturgical Poetry and Christian Hymnology", *The Jewish Quarterly Review* XLIV (1953), particularly pp. 138-140; I. Gruenwald, "Yannai and the Hekhalot Literature" (in Hebrew), *Tarbiz* XXXVI (1967), pp. 257 ff. G. Scholem, *Jewish Gnosticism* etc., pp. 20-30 has investigated some qualities of the Merkavah hymns, yet the subject of the literary qualities of the *Hekhalot* literature still waits a scholarly discussion.

liturgy connected with the three forms of the *Qedushah*[13] were in fact more familiar with the mystical material which was alluded to in their composition than were those who participated in the daily service in the synagogues. And it will not be far from the truth if we assume, that those liturgical poets were responsible—sometimes even more than were the mystics themselves—for the spreading of the mystical Merkavah material. But it would be wrong to say that the common man was really aware of the mystical implications and connotations of the prayers he used to say.

Turning now to the *Hekhalot* writings themselves, it should again be observed that no voices of dissidence are heard in these writings, nor can it be said that they contain any explicit form of criticism towards non-mystical circles. Contrary to some of the writings of Jewish apocalyptic, the *Hekhalot* writings bear no sectarian trademarks. Furthermore, the *Hekhalot* writings do not indulge in apocalyptic visions of the imminent destruction of the world, nor do they display the apocalyptic belief according to which the messianic future is reserved to a small group of the elite. Although there are several instances in which the bliss of the world to come is promised to the *Hekhalot* mystics,[14] the general tone of their writings is not eschatological.

[13] See E. Werner, *The Sacred Bridge*, New York, Schocken Books, 1970, pp. 282 ff.

[14] Thus, for instance, it is said of those who know the *Shi^cur Qomah* that future life is promised to them, "on condition that they study this *Mishnah* (= of the *Shi^cur Qomah*) everyday". See the text published in Musajoff, *Merkavah Shelemah*, 38b.

RE'UYOT YEḤEZKEL

Re'uyot Yeḥezkel, or the Visions of Ezekiel, is listed by Professor Scholem as the earliest Merkavah text we possess.[1] It is not a *Hekhalot* text in the strict sense of the term. In fact, the word *Hekhal* never occurs in the text. Instead, the work enumerates the various things which the prophet Ezekiel allegedly saw in his Merkavah vision. In fact, *Re'uyot Yeḥezkel* is a mystical midrash on the first chapter of the Book of Ezekiel. The names of the rabbinical authorities quoted in the text may justify the conclusion that the text was probably composed in the fourth or the fifth century C.E. In addition, all the names of the rabbinical sages quoted belong to Eretz Yisrael and thus there is good reason to believe that the book was composed and edited there.

The mystical part of the book begins with the statement (p. 106) that "God opened to Ezekiel seven divisions of the lower world and as Ezekiel was looking at them, he saw everything that was in the heaven". The divisions mentioned here by their names are subterrestrial "earths", that is, layers of seven earths which correspond to the seven heavens.[2] In fact, *Re'uyot Yeḥezkel* incorporates elements of cosmological speculations, the nature and significance of which are beyond the common mystical interest.[3] However, cosmological

---

[1] A fragment of the text was first published by Marmorstein in: *Jewish Quarterly Review*, New Series, VIII (1917-1918), pp. 367-378, from a Genizah fragment at the British Museum. Later on, J. Mann and Sh. A. Wertheimer published the whole text in two different editions. All these editions have been shown to be faulty, and the present writer has published a new critical edition and commentary in *Temirin* I (1972), pp. 101-139. The extent to which the previous editions were faulty can best be illustrated by the fact that the text became known as *Re'iyot* (!) *Yeḥezkel*, while the colophons of the manuscripts read *Re'uyot*. Although the term is rare, it can nontheless be explained as: Visions.—[Notice that line 14 in my edition has been misplaced by the printer to become, erroneously, line 10 on p. 104. It should be replaced as the last line of the text on p. 105!].

[2] The names of these divisions as they are given in *Re'uyot Yeḥezkel* are: *'Adamah*, *'Eretz*, *Ḥeled*, *Neshiyah*, *Dumah*, *She'ol*, *Tit Ha-Yaven*. In other rabbinical sources, different names are given. See my edition, pp. 107-108.

[3] There are several Jewish texts which deal with such cosmological speculations. Two of these are the *Beraita de-Ma'aseh Bereshit* (ed. N. Sed, in *Revue des Études Juives* CXXIV (1965), pp. 23-123; with a French translation); and *Midrash Konen* in *Bet ha-Midrasch II*, pp. 23 ff. As for the *Beraita de-Ma'aseh Bereshit*, Sed used all the bad manuscripts which he could find. The pagination of these manuscripts

secrets are frequently referred to in the *Hekhalot* writings, though only with few specifications. Here, in *Re'uyot Yeḥezkel*, the basic structure of the universe is referred to, though, as might be expected, only the celestial world receives extensive attention.

As a matter of mystical technique, Ezekiel is described as looking downward and seeing what is above: "Ezekiel was standing on the River Chebar looking down at the water and the seven heavens were opened to him and he saw the Glory of the Holy One". To illustrate this rather peculiar procedure the text brings the following comparison: "This matter is like the following story: A man entered a barber's shop, and he cut his hair. He gave him a mirror and he looked in it. As he was looking in it, the king passed by. He saw the king and his retinue by the doorway. The hairdresser said to him: 'Turn around and see the king'. He said to him: 'I have already looked in the mirror' ". From a technical point of view this passage is of great interest. It tells something unusual about the apocalyptic and mystical technique: The visionary is standing near a river or a sea and while looking at the water, he sees the reflection of heavenly visions. From Scripture and from apocalyptic literature we know of several instances in which the prophet or the apocalyptist described himself as standing near water or at the banks of a river.[4] The water thus served as a mirror of the things shown in heaven. This is reminiscent of the famous distinction drawn in rabbinical writings between the prophecy of Moses and that of the other prophets. It is said that all the prophets gazed upon nine mirrors while Moses gazed upon one only, or that Moses gazed upon a shining mirror while the other prophets gazed upon an opaque mirror.[5] Looking at the mirror-like surface of the water thus turns out to be—at least in some of the cases—an integral part of the prophetic and apocalyptic technique. This procedure could be a means of avoiding the immediate sight of the Godhead and the heavenly beings. In any event, if our interpretation is correct, the passage under discussion in *Re'uyot Yeḥezkel* sheds light on a most interesting detail in the visual experience of some prophets and apocalyptists.

---

is confused, and Sed was unfortunately unaware of the existence of manuscripts which contain the correct pagination.

[4] *Daniel* vii,2-3; viii,2; x,4-5; *4 Ezra* ix (xi)-xi (xiii); *2 Baruch* xxi,1; *3 Baruch* ii,1. Compare also *1 Enoch* xiii,7. See also G. Scholem, "Tradition und Neuschöpfung im Ritus der Kabbalah", in: *Zur Kabbalah und ihrer Symbolik*, Zürich, Rhein-Verlag, 1960, pp. 182-183.

[5] *Wayyikra Rabbah*, ed. M. Margulies, i,14, p. 30-31; *Bavli Yevamot* 49b.

Looking at the waters of the River Chebar, Ezekiel is said to see the "Holiness" opening to him the seven heavens and thus giving him an opportunity of seeing the "*Gevurah*" (the Dynamis).[6] Furthermore, it is said that Ezekiel not only saw the Divine Glory [7] but also all the heavenly creatures as they were tied to the Merkavah. "They were passing in the heaven and Ezekiel was watching them (reflected) in the water". The names of the seven heavens are given: *Shamayim*, *Shemei Shamayim*, *Zevul*, *'Arafel*, *Sheḥaqim*, *'Aravot*, and *Kissé Kavod*. This is a rather peculiar list, which is nowhere repeated in the various lists of the names of the heavens either in rabbinical writings or in writings connected with the *Hekhalot* literature. The names of the first two heavens make it evident that the list is of Palestinian origin.[8] Interestingly, some of its idiosyncratic names also occur in the liturgical poetry of Yannai.[9] However, the list of the heavens as it is repeated later on in the text includes slight changes: *Raqi'a*, *Shemei Ha-Shamayim*, *Zevul*, *'Arafel*, *Sheḥaqin*, *Makhon*, *'Aravot*, *Kissé Ha-Kavod*. In comparison to the first one, this list mentions *Raqi'a* (instead of *Shamayim*) as the first heaven and it adds the name of another heaven, *Makhon*, thus bringing the total number of the heavens to eight. We shall later on, in our discussion of *Hekhalot Rabbati*, see that the *Hekhalot* mystics actually conceived of the existence of eight heavens. The eighth heaven is the place where God abides while he is not sitting on His throne in the seventh palace in the seventh heaven. But in the second list in *Re'uyot Yeḥezkel*, the eighth heaven is called by the name of *Kissé Ha-Kavod*, which clearly indicates that the throne of God is placed here. Thus, if we harmonize *Re'uyot Yeḥezkel* with *Hekhalot Rabbati*, it follows that

[6] For a discussion of this sentence see Scholem, *Jewish Gnosticism* etc., p. 68. To the references given there for parallel expressions to the phrase "God opened to him the seven heavens" one should add: *Tanḥuma* (ed. Buber), *Toledot*, paragraph 22; *'Agadat Shir Ha-Shirim* (ed. Schechter), p. 39 (line 1134); *The Acts of the Apostles* vii,55-56. See further H. Bietenhard, *Die Himmlische Welt*, pp. 7-8, n. 1, who observes that the plural *ouranoi* in *Acts* should not be interpreted as meaning that a plurality of heavens is maintained. See also L. I. J. Stadelmann, *The Hebrew Conception of the World*, Rome, Biblical Institute Press, 1970, pp. 41-42, where the view is expressed that *Shmei Ha-Shamayim* is "an all-inclusive term to denote the space above the earth" (p. 42). Yet, at least in *Re'uyot Yeḥezkel* the plurality of heavens is clearly said to derive from the plural form of the verb "the heavens were opened" in *Ezekiel* i,1.

[7] The terms *Gevurah* (= dynamis) and *Kavod* (= doxa) are interchangeably used in the text!

[8] See the discussion in my edition pp. 116 ff.

[9] See the present writer's article in *Tarbiz* XXXVI (1967), pp. 269-270.

when God leaves His throne, he ascends to the ninth heaven, or else that *Re'uyot Yeḥezkel* does not conceive of the existence of a so-called super-celestial abode of God.[10]

What is also unique in the seven heavens doctrine as it is displayed in *Re'uyot Yeḥezkel* is the idea, which is quoted in the name of Rabbi Me'ir, to the effect that "God created seven heavens and there are seven chariots (*Merkavot*) in them". This statement, which apart from its clear reference to the existence of seven (!) heavens, is reminiscent also of the idea which we met in *Ascensio Isaiae* (above, Chapter Two), namely that a throne is placed in every heaven. But, in contradistinction to *Ascensio Isaiae*, in *Re'uyot Yeḥezkel* no one is seen as occupying the Merkavah in the first six heavens. In addition, each of the Merkavot in *Re'uyot Yeḥezkel* has a name, and, generally, these names are derived from biblical verses. Only the Merkavah in the heaven *Zevul* has a non-biblical name, Haluyah,[11] and, as we have already said,[12] the heaven *Makhon* has no Merkavah at all. In addition, the text states that "Thus did the Holiness, Blessed be He, say to Ezekiel: 'I am showing the Chariot to you on condition that you expound it to Israel... But you should convey them to the people only as much as the eye can see and the ear hear' ". As we shall see in our discussion of *Hekhalot Rabbati*, there are several utterances in the *Hekhalot* literature which make it clear that no special demand for secrecy was laid down these writings. As we notice here, Ezekiel is called upon to reveal to the People of Israel the content of his mystical vision of the Merkavah, though, of course, with a certain degree of reservation: only what the eye can see and the ear hear.[13] This is a statement which no apocalyptic writer could conceive of. The words addressed to Ezekiel by God are also important from another point of view. God says: "I am showing the Chariot to you...". "To see the Chariot" is used here in its plain sense and has no technical overtones.[14] In the other *Hekhalot* texts, the expression

[10] Interestingly, in contradistinction to the other heavens no Merkavah is mentioned in *Makhon*. This by itself could support the view that *Makhon* was a later addition introduced in order to harmonize between the list in *Re'uyot Yeḥezkel* and the lists found in other sources.

[11] This may well be a corrupt rendering of a name that can no more be identified.

[12] See above n. 10.

[13] A similar expression is found in *Mechilta d'Rabbi Ismael*, p. 235 in connection with the theophany on Mount Sinai. See also the notes in my edition, p. 121.

[14] Compare *Tosefta Megilah* iii,28 (ed. Lieberman, p. 361-362): "They said to him (= to Rabbi Yehudah): many discoursed in the Merkavah but had never

"to see the Chariot" has a technical sense, and stands for the mystical experience as a whole.[15]

When the text turns to the discussion of the seven heavens and what they contain, it does so by quoting an introductory remark in the name of Rabbi Yiẓḥaq: "From the earth to *Raqi'a* there is a distance of a five hundred years' walk". Curiously, the biblical verse quoted as supporting this measure is *Deuteronomy* xi,21: "That your days may be multiplied, and the days of your children, in the [land which the Lord swore unto your fathers to give them, *as the days of the heaven upon the earth*]".[16] The cosmological measure given here in the name of Rabbi Yiẓḥaq is elsewhere[17] attributed to Rabbanan: "(The width of the firmament) is like the years of the lives of the Patriarchs. (As it is written:) 'as the days of the heaven upon the earth' ".[18] The sum total of the years of Abraham, Isaac and Jacob amounts to five hundred and two, and this is also the measure given for the distance between the earth and heaven in *Beraita de-Ma'aseh Bereshit* (ed. Sed, p. 58).[19] The measure of five hundred years' walk is repeated in *Re'uyot Yeḥezkel* as the regular distance between each of the heavens. If we may learn anything from the description of the space between the first and the second heaven, then all the spaces between the heavens are filled with water. It is said: "And the water which is above *Raqi'a* is five hundred years' of walk", and there are good reasons to believe that the same could be said of the other "inter-celestial" spaces too.

It would deflect us from the main course if we were here to discuss all the details of the cosmological speculations of what all the seven heavens contain. In fact, the whole subject deserves a separate study in which justice will be done to the various elements involved. It should be remarked that in addition to a few items which repeat

---

seen it before". See also G. Scholem, *Major Trends in Jewish mysticism*, p. 358, n. 18.

[15] Instead of the present expression "to see the Chariot" we find in later *Hekhalot* writings the expression "to see the King in His beauty". See S. Leiter, "Worthiness, Acclamation, and Appointment: Some Rabbinic Terms", *Proceedings of the American Academy for Jewish Research*" XLI-XLII (1973-1974), pp. 143-145.

[16] The words in square-brackets are not quoted in the text. The underlined words are the most relevant ones to the saying of Rabbi Yiẓḥaq.

[17] In *Yerushalmi Berakhot* i,1 (2c).

[18] Compare also *Yerushalmi Berakhot* ix,1 (12a). There Rabbi Levi gives the distance of 500 years.

[19] In *Midrash Konen* (in: Jellinek, *Bet ha-Midrasch* II, p. 27) the number of the years of the Patriarchs is wrongly given as 500. In any event, 500 years is a round number and was probably preferred to 502 for the sake of convenience.

themselves in all the parallel sources there are many others that vary from source to source. Thus, we shall concentrate here only on those items that bear direct significance to our subject. To begin with, the angels who say the *Qedushah* are said to be in the second heaven. Generally, these angels are described as being in the fifth heaven,[20] and their existence here in the second heaven may reflect an ancient tradition according to which there were only two heavens.[21] Evidently, in this case of the existence of two heavens only, God was abiding in the second heaven and there one expected to find the ministering angels too. Curiously, however, where there were more than two heavens the angels who recite hymns to God were not always located in the same heaven as the one in which the throne of God was said to be located. Considering the seven-heavens system in *Re'uyot Yeḥezkel*, it is noteworthy that the sanctifying angels are located in the second heaven, while the seventh heaven contains, in addition to the Merkavah, only the hooves of the Living Creatures and their wings.

It is also said of these sanctifying angels that their existence in the second heaven is not permanent. In fact, they are renewed everyday. This idea, which is also documented in midrashic literature,[22] might express the notion that apart from God,[23] nothing in the world, not even the angels, enjoys permanent existence. The substantial difference between the Creator and the things which He creates lies in the transiency of the things created. Whether the angels are destroyed because they do not recite their hymns properly,[24] or whether they undergo a process of self-annihilation,[25] they carry out only one message and then new ones are created in their place.[26] According

[20] Thus, for instance, in *Bavli Ḥagigah* 12b.

[21] That tradition is explicitly assumed by Rabbi Yehudah in *Bavli Ḥagigah* 12b. We also saw (in Chapter Two) that *1 Enoch* lxxi,5 ff. could also be interpreted as giving expression to the two-heavens doctrine. Indeed, the angels are described in *1 Enoch* lxxi as being in the second heaven.

[22] See my notes *ad locum* (p. 125). To the literature referred to there add E. E. Urbach, *The Sages*, pp. 181-182. However, Urbach does not discuss the theological implications of this idea.

[23] The Living Creatures, the *Ḥayyot*, and the archangels (Michael, Raphael etc.) also enjoy "immortality".

[24] *Hekhalot Rabbati* xxx (end); *3 Enoch* xl.

[25] *Bavli Ḥagigah* 14a: "Every day the Ministering Angels are created from the River of Fire ('*Nehar di-Nur*') and they utter a song and are annihilated!". In *Hekhalot Rabbati* viii,1-2, it is said that the angels can serve God only once, because their faces and their eyes are burned by the beauty of their King.

[26] We shall later on see that there were two distinct theories concerning the

to *Re'uyot Yeḥezkel*, the angels recite their hymns from sunrise till sunset, an idea that contradicts several midrashic sayings according to which the heavenly beings sing their songs only at night, while at daytime God listens to the prayers of His People.[27]

In the third heaven, *Zevul*, one finds the *Sar*, that is the Heavenly Prince. He is described as filling with his presence the whole of that heaven, and thousands upon thousands of angels are said to serve him. *Daniel* vii,9-10 is quoted as supporting the idea, and one might rightly ask whether the author of *Re'uyot Yeḥezkel* did not think that the *ʿAtiq Yomin* described in the Book of Daniel was identical with the *Sar* of the Heaven *Zevul*. Admittedly, the identification is not explicitly made, but one may assume that it could have been implied when the relevant verses in *Daniel* were quoted in connection with the *Sar* of *Zevul*.[28] A number of names are suggested for this *Sar*, two of which are of particular interest for us.[29] The first of these is Komes,[30] that is a minister in the king's court, and the other is Metatron. Recently,[31] Professor S. Lieberman has suggested that

---

creation of the angels. According to the one, the angels are created from the words which God utters; and according to the other, they are created from the river of fire. See further *3 Enoch* xl.

[27] See *Bavli Ḥagigah* 12b; *ʿAvodah Zarah* 3b. On the other hand, *Bavli Ḥulin* 91b concurs with the idea found in the *Hekhalot* writings that the angels in fact sing also at daytime. They do so in correspondence with the prayers of the People of Israel. In the apocalyptic writings which refer to the song of the angels, no explicit restriction is maintained regarding the singing hours of the angels. However, in *1 Enoch* xxxix,13 we read: "And here my eyes saw all those who sleep not: they stand before Him and bless and say ...". Now, "those who sleep not" are in all likelihood those who say their hymns at night. But as has variously been recognized, "those who sleep not" are a class of angels invented by a mistranslation. *Daniel* iv mentions the Aramaic *ʿIr* and the *ʿIrin* as a class of angels. If the word *ʿIr* means "messenger", then the translation ἐγρήγορος, "wakeful", suggested in the LXX, is wrong. See, however, J. A. Montgomery, *The Book of Daniel* [ICC], Edinburgh, T. & T. Clark, 1964, pp. 231-234. See further *Encyclopedia Judaica* (Jerusalem), s.v. "Song, angelic".

[28] It should be noticed that the *Sar* is mentioned three times in Talmudic writings: *Bavli Ḥagigah* 12b; *Menaḥot* 110a; *Zevaḥim* 62a. In all three cases it is the angel Michael who is called "the Great Prince" (*Ha-Sar Ha-Gadol*), and he is said to offer sacrifices on the heavenly altar. However, the *Sar* in *Re'uyot Yeḥezkel* does not offer sacrifices, and this probably because the heavenly Jerusalem is here described as being in another heaven. The term *Sar Ha-Gadol* derives from *Daniel* xii,1, and is there the appellation given to the Angel Michael.

[29] In any event, the greater number of the names are not clear to us: they seem to be "mystical" names.

[30] In the manuscript wrongly: Kimos.

[31] In a Study Conference devoted to the *Hekhalot* literature and held in the Institute for Advanced Studies in Jerusalem on June 13, 1976. Professor Lieberman publishes his remarks in an appendix to the present book.

Metatron reflects the older form of *synthronos*,[32] that is, the God enthroned alongside with a major deity. This idea of the *synthronos*, or as it was allegedly later on substituted by the *metathron(os)*, is also implied by the name Komes given here to the *Sar*. It should be noticed that the term *Metatron* is frequently qualified by such phrases as "whose name is like that of his master",[33] "whose name is like that of the Dynamis",[34] and even the "Small Yah".[35] All these qualifying phrases stress the close affinity between God and His *Sar*, an affinity that is adequately expressed in the names Komes and Metatron.

The next heaven, *'Arafel*, contains the "Canopy of the Law" and the Merkavah in which God descended on Mount Sinai.[36] The location of these two items in *'Arafel* is easily explained by *Exodus* xx,21 (MT!). The fifth heaven, *Sheḥaqim*, contains the heavenly Jerusalem and all the vessels of the Temple. *Makhon* is the name of the next heaven and it contains the treasuries of snow and hail, and the future rewards for the righteous and the wicked. *'Aravot* is the seventh heaven and it again contains both the treasuries of snow and the future rewards for the righteous and the wicked. This repetition is rather peculiar, and it may perhaps be explained by the fact, that the heaven *Makhon* was interpolated into the text of *Re'uyot Yeḥezkel* by a writer who wanted to harmonize the lists of the heavens in *Re'uyot Yeḥezkel* with those found in other Jewish sources.[37] In any event, apart from these things, *'Aravot* also contains the treasuries of the souls.[38] Finally, the highest heaven, *Kissé Ha-Kavod*, contains the hoofs of the *Ḥayyot* and the edges of their wings as well as the Big Merkavah in which God will descend in order to judge all the nations. The text ends with the remark that God is above the wings of the *Ḥayyot*.[39]

---

[32] See Liddell & Scott, p. 1717. The prefix "syn" was gradually superseded by the prefix "meta", which implied even a closer union than "syn". See Liddell & Scott, p. 1108.

[33] *Bavli Sanhedrin* 38b.

[34] *Re'uyot Yeḥezkel*, which may represent an older tradition than the one given in *Bavli Sanhedrin*. Another name, suggested by the theurgists (*Meshamshin Ba-Shum*) is: SLNS QS BS BS QBS "like the name of the Demiurgos (*Yozer Ha-'Olam*)".

[35] *3 Enoch* xii.

[36] For both details see my commentary *ad locum*, pp. 131-132.

[37] See my commentary, pp. 116-120. It should, however, be noticed that in *Bavli Ḥagigah* 12b, *Makhon* is said to contain the treasuries of snow and hail.

[38] In the list of heavens in *Bavli Ḥagigah*, the treasuries of the souls are likewise found in *'Aravot*.

[39] The fact that the wings of the *Ḥayyot* are mentioned twice in this heaven may be explained as indicating the two pairs of wings mentioned in *Ezekiel* i,6.

HEKHALOT ZUTRETI

Hekhalot Zutreti (or: *Zutrati*) is in all likelihood the oldest *Hekhalot* text proper that we possess. It is a collection of several short Merkavah-passages, some of which are in Aramaic. Professor Jonas Greenfield, who undertook a linguistic study of the Hebrew and Aramaic sections of the book, inclines to locate it in Eretz-Yisrael, most probably in the second or third century C.E. This conclusion concurs with that of Professor Gershom Scholem, who on the basis of an analysis of its contents regards the book as representing the Merkavah lore of the Tannaitic, possibly early Amoraic, period. The text in its entirety has never been published, though about three quarters of the text are printed in Musajoff's collection of Merkavah texts, *Merkavah Shelemah*.[1] However, our discussion here will be based on the texts contained mainly in MSS Oxford 1531 and Jewish Theological Seminary Mic. 8128.

The text begins with a short introduction: "If you want to be singled out in the world and that the secrets of the world and the mysteries of wisdom should be revealed to you, you have to study this Mishnah and be careful about it till the day of your death (?).[2] You should neither try to understand what is behind you, nor inquire into the sayings of your lips.[3] Just understand what is in your heart and keep quiet, so that you will be worthy of the Beauties of the Chariot.[4] You should be careful about the Glory of your Creator, and do not cause Him to descend.[5] And if you have caused Him to

---

[1] See G. Scholem, *Jewish Gnosticism* etc., pp. 6 and 76 ff.

[2] The term used here *Yom Perishah* could also be taken to mean: as long as you are engaged in the ascetic practices connected with the Merkavah experience.

[3] This is a mystical paraphrase of *Ben Sira* iii, 19-21. The phrase "Do not investigate the words of your lips" can be interpreted as meaning that one should not venture explaining words uttered as *glossolalia*. However, the more simple meaning, namely, that there are matters relating to the secret lore which should not be discussed in public, cannot be ruled out. See further S. Lieberman, *Tosefta Ki-Fshutah to Ḥagigah*, p. 1295.

[4] For the expression "the beauties of the Chariot" (*Yofiyot Ha-Merkavah*) see, S. Leiter, "Worthiness, Acclamation and Appointment: Some Rabbinic Terms", *Proceedings of the American Academy for Jewish Research*, XLI-XLII (1973), p. 144.

[5] Professor S. Lieberman suggested to me to see in the Hebrew words *We'al tered lo* (= "and do not make him descend"?) a reference to the saying in *'Avot de-Rabbi Natan* Version B, xxxiii (ed. Schechter, p. 72): "He (= Ben Zoma) used to say: Do not peep into a man's vineyard; and if you peeped into it do not

descend, do not enjoy anything of Him; and if you have enjoyed anything of Him you are likely to be turned out of this world. 'It is the Glory of God to keep (His) word secret',[6] so that you will not be turned out of this world". This passage includes one of the rare occasions in which a claim for secrecy is uttered in the *Hekhalot* literature.

After this introduction, there comes in MS Oxford a short paragraph which is connected with the *Sar-Torah* speculations.[7] It says: "When Moses ascended on high to God, God taught him: Everybody whose heart is going astray,[8] should call the following names...: [9] 'that I may keep in my mind everything that I hear and study... and I shall never forget it, neither in this world nor in the one to come' ". As we shall see later on, the *Sar-Torah* sections incorporated in the *Hekhalot* literature in all likelihood belong to a period when real mystical experiences were no longer practised. If this is true, then the *Sar-Torah* passage in *Hekhalot Zutreti* was introduced into the text at a rather late stage, probably in the sixth century C.E.[10] If not, then this very section was the model for the later *Hekhalot* texts, most of which contain material related to *Sar-Torah*. The gist

---

enter (lit. descend into) it; and if you entered do not look; and if you looked do not touch; and if you touched do not eat. For if a man eats he loses his soul's share both in this world and in that to come". In *Tosefta Ki-Fshutah* to *Ḥagigah*, p. 1291, Lieberman suggests to see in Ben Zoma's words an old parable used by him for mystical purposes. See further *Sifre* to *Numbers* (ed. Horowitz), p. 191, l. 15.

[6] *Proverbs* xxv,2.

[7] See our discussion of *Hekhalot Rabbati* (end).

[8] The Hebrew here reads: *Shogeh*; however, one of the variant readings here has *Shoneh*, that is, studies.

[9] Among the magical names listed here one finds SMOSLM and MARMARAOT. Both names are known from the syncretistic magical papyri and their exact meaning is still under dispute among scholars. See Scholem, *Jewish Gnosticism* etc., pp. 76 and 134. On page 76 Scholem explains the first name as being "perhaps a corruption of the Hebrew *Shemesh ʿOlam* (= Sun of the World)", while on p. 134 (in the Second Edition of the book) he writes: "... the magical name *Semiselam* so frequently used in the magical papyri, seems to come from the Aramaic. The word does not represent the Hebrew *Shemesh ʿOlam*, but rather the Aramaic phrase *Shemi Shelam* which literally means: 'my name is peace' ". In the unpublished *Registers* to K. Preisendanz, *Papyri Graecae Magicae*, p. 230, Preisendanz explains the word as implying "Ewige Sonne" (= Eternal Sun).—I am indebted to Professor Morton Smith for preparing for me a xerox copy of the *Registers*.

[10] Professor Scholem, *op. cit.*, p. 77 likewise assumes that the opening passages of *Hekhalot Zutreti* "may not constitute an original part of the *Urform* of the book." However, since the whole text is rather fragmentary it is quite difficult to decide what really belongs to its original layer of composition.

of the *Sar-Torah* speculations is the secret theurgical method of studying the Law and of its memorization. MS. New York (The Jewish Theological Seminary) later on quotes a longer *Sar-Torah* section, which lists several magical names,[11] and in addition mentions the special qualities of *Hekhalot Zutreti*: "This book is (a book of) wisdom, sagacity and knowledge, and inquiries about the things above and the things below, the hidden things of the Torah and of heaven and of earth, and the mysteries which (God) gave to Moses, the son of ʿAmram,... and revealed it to him on Mount Ḥoreb, and by the means of which the world is sustained. In addition, by the means of (this book) Moses performed all the wonders and the miracles in Egypt, and with its help he beat the Egyptians. It is the fire of the burning-bush. And Metatron revealed himself to Moses...". This passage is interesting for a number of reasons. Briefly, it maintains a secret revelation of a certain mystical or magical book to Moses on Mount Sinai. In this respect, we may go back to the Book of Jubilees which also claims to have been revealed by the angels to Moses on Mount Sinai. In fact, the revelation of a secret lore to Moses in addition to the exoteric Law constituted an important branch in ancient Jewish esotericism.[12] We find it also repeated in other Merkavah texts,[13] and in magical texts.[14] In our case, however,

[11] One of which is YHOEL.

[12] See B. Z. Wacholder, *Eupolemus*, Cincinnati, Hebrew Union College, 1974, pp. 71 ff.: Chapter Three: "The Hellenized Moses—Jewish and Pagan".

[13] See the beginning of the text *Maʿaseh Merkavah* (in Scholem, *Jewish Gnosticism* etc., p. 103, paragraph 1): "Since you have revealed to Moses the secrets and the secrets of the secrets, the mysteries and the mysteries of the mysteries, and Moses [taught] them to (the People of) Israel, so that they can learn with them the Torah and multiply with their help the study of the Torah". See also *3 Enoch* (*Sefer Hekhalot*), xv(b) and xlviii(d).

[14] The famous magical text called "The Sword of Moses" and first published by M. Gaster (London: 1896) begins in MS. Oxford 1531 fol. 35a, with the following statement: "This is the Sword of Moses which was delivered to him in the burning bush, and was (henceforth), revealed to Rabbi Yishmaʾel ben Elishʿa in the Maʿaseh Merkavah!". The "Sword of Moses" is a technical expression for magical practices connected in some way with the staff of Moses, regarding which, we know, several magical and supernatural traditions circulated in midrashic writings. See mainly *Targum Pseudo-Jonathan* to *Exodus* ii,21 and *Pirkei de-Rabbi ʾElieʿzer*, xl. Both texts reflect a rather late stage in the transmission of a tradition that has its origins in tannaitic times. See *Pesikta de-Rav Kahana* (ed. Mandelbaum), p. 308. As for the term "The Sword of Moses" see M. Magalioth, *Sefer Ha-Razim*, pp. 29-31, who rightly refers to the Greek term ξίφος (= sword) as implying also a magical formula. To the secret magical books attributed to Moses which Magalioth lists (p. 30, n. 8) one can add the ἀρχαγγελικὴ βίβλος attributed in one of the Paris amulets to Moses. See R. Reitzen-

we may assume that the book which is meant is none but *Hekhalot Zutreti* itself. The book was believed to contain all the important secrets of the world and of the Torah; at least it was considered to be a magical key to their revelation.

The third paragraph of *Hekhalot Zutreti* introduces the Name which "was revealed to Rabbi ʿAkiva when he contemplated the Maʿaseh Merkavah; and he descended [15] and taught it to his students. He said to them: 'My sons, be careful about the Name; it is a great name,[16] a holy name and a pure name.[17] For whoever uses it in terror, in fright, in purity, in holiness and in meekness—his seed will multiply, and he will be successful [18] in all his ways and his days will be long' ". In fact, a great part of *Hekhalot Zutreti* deals with magical and theurgical names, so that the kind of warning attributed here to Rabbi ʿAkiva is quite in place. It is interesting to notice that in *Hekhalot Rabbati* iv,3 we read that Rabbi Yishmael said: "All these incantations Rabbi ʿAkiva heard when he descended unto the Merkavah: he caught them and taught them from before of His Throne of Glory, when His ministers were singing them to Him". The purpose of such utterances is to show that the theurgical practices of the *Maʿaseh Merkavah* are no human invention but of heavenly origin. Consequently, one has to be particularly careful in their application. The

stein, *Poimandres*, Reprint: Darmstadt, Wissenschaftliche Buchgesellschaft, 1966, p. 292 f. See further in *Tarbiẓ* XXXVIII (1969), p. 355. See also A. Böhlig and P. Labib (eds.), *Die Koptisch-gnostische Schrift ohne Titel aus Codex II von Nag Hammadi*, Berlin, Akademie Verlag, 1962, p. 47. In one of the Aramaic magical bowls published by C. H. Gordon in *Archiv Orientalni* IX (1937), p. 87 we read: "By the Lord and the great throne belonging to the Master and YHWH, the Ineffable Name that was revealed to Moses in the bush" (English translation on p. 88). These are almost the very opening words of the second paragraph of *Hekhalot Zutreti*. See further, G. Scholem, "Der Name Gottes und die Sprachtheorie der kabbala", in: *Judaica III*, Frankfurt am Main, Suhrkamp Verlag, 1973, pp. 7 ff.

[15] Contrary to the more current usage of the verb "to descend" (= to enter into the trance of the Merkavah experience), the verb here implies what was in other texts, designated by "to ascend".

[16] The term "Great Name" is a frequent one in Greek, Aramaic and Hebrew magical texts. It is to be understood in the sense of "a most powerful Name".

[17] "Purity" (*Tohorah*) in connection with magical names implies the fact that this is the real name, in contrast to its corresponding *nomen barabarum*. See further G. Scholem, "Über eine Formel in den koptisch-gnostischen Schriften und ihren jüdischen Ursprung", *Zeitschrift für die Neutestamentliche Wissenschaft* XXX (1931), pp. 170 ff. See also below n. 19.

[18] The Hebrew verb *ẒLḤ* has a special meaning in a magical context. It implies that one's magical charm was efficacious. See further H. Tawil in *Journal of Biblical Literature* xcv (1976), pp. 405-413.

same idea is also implied at the end of our paragraph in *Hekhalot Zutreti* where a blessing is quoted for the purpose "of the sanctification of the Name".[19]

A central place in *Hekhalot Zutreti* is occupied by the story of the four who entered the *Pardes*. Since *Hekhalot Zutreti*, like *Re'uyot Yeḥezkel*, does not mention the seven palaces, it is of particular interest to notice that in the version of this story as it is told in *Hekhalot Zutreti* the sixth palace is mentioned. This can only be explained by the fact, that *Hekhalot Zutreti* is a compilation of mystical passages which represent different layers in the history of the *Hekhalot* literature. It has already been pointed out above in Chapter Three that the version, or, rather, the versions, of the story of the four who entered the *Pardes* as told in *Hekhalot Zutreti* represent the true meaning and possibly also the original setting of Rabbi ʿAkiva's saying in *Bavli Ḥagigah* 14b, to wit: "When you reach the pure marble stones, do not say: 'Water! Water!' ". It would be superfluous to repeat here a full-scale discussion of the relation between the saying in *Ḥagigah* and the story in *Hekhalot Zutreti*. However, what requires additional comment here is the fact that the so-called water-episode is repeated in the manuscripts in three different versions:

(a) Ben ʿAzai cast a glance into the sixth palace and saw the brilliance of the air of the marble stones that were decorating the palace. His body could not endure (i.e., the magnificence of the vision) and he opened his mouth and asked them: [20] "These waters, what are they?" And he died.[21]

(b) Ben Zoma cast a glance at the marble stones and thought that they were (made of) water. His body could endure not to ask them, nevertheless his mind could not. And he went out of his mind.[22]

(c) Rabbi ʿAkiva said: Ben ʿAzai was found worthy and stood at the gate of the sixth *Hekhal*. And he saw the brilliance of the

---

[19] In this respect *Hekhalot Zutreti* constitutes a mystical elaboration on the rulings regarding the transmission and study of the Ineffable Name in priestly circles in the days of the Second Temple. See *Bavli Kidushin* 71a. See also the Responsum in *Otzar Ha-Geonim* to *Ḥagigah*, pp. 22-23. See further E. E. Urbach, *The Sages*, pp. 124 ff.

[20] Probably, the alleged accompanying angels.

[21] MS. New York, 16b.

[22] *Ibid.*

> pure marble stones. He opened his mouth twice and said: 'Water, Water'. Immediately they cut his head off and threw upon him eleven thousand iron bars. This should become a lesson for future generations, that a man should not commit the (same) mistake at the gate of the sixth palace.[23]

As we shall see in our discussion of *Hekhalot Rabbati* xxv, the gate of the sixth palace was the place where the last tests were put before the ascending mystic. The worthiness of the mystics was, in fact, tested at every gate, but the sixth gate entailed some crucial tests and temptations, most of which may be called water-tests. The visionary saw marble stones, and the manner in which he reacted to the vision was taken to be proof of his worthiness to proceed.

After the tale of the four who entered the *Pardes*, Rabbi ʿAkiva is quoted as saying: "At that hour, when I ascended on high, I put a sign at the vestibules of the firmament. There are more of them (in heaven) than in my house, and when I approached the *Pargod*, angels of destruction came out to beat me. But God told them: leave that sage alone, since he is worthy of gazing at my glory". Once again this sentence comes close to something that is said in *Bavli Ḥagigah* 15b (bottom): "The ministering angels even wanted to kill Rabbi ʿAkiva, but God told them: leave that sage alone, since he is worthy of using [24] my glory". Both passages underline in their own particular way the extraordinary qualities of Rabbi ʿAkiva which make him the model Merkavah mystic. In contrast to the apocalyptic writers who selected their fictitious heroes from the gallery of biblical heroes, preferably from antedeluvian times, the Merkavah mystics were more selective in their choice and affiliated themselves to the two great heads of halakhic schools in the Tannaitic period. The purpose of this was, among other things, to find authorization for mystical activities in quarters that had a decisive say in halakhic Judaism. This is not to say that the historical founders of rabbinic Judaism were enstranged to the *res mysticae*. On the contrary, we find that from the days of Rabban Yoḥanan ben Zakkai onwards the leaders of halakhic Judaism were involved in mystical speculations.[25] It is, however, remarkable that from Rabbi ʿAkiva onwards we lose the chain of

---

[23] MS. New York, 23a.

[24] A common variant reading here is (as in *Hekhalot Zutreti*): "gazing". For a discussion of the terms and their meaning see G. Scholem, *Jewish Gnosticism* etc., p. 54.

[25] See *Bavli Hagigah* 14b.

the mystical tradition. But we may well assume that it was continued, in spite of the fact that the links of that tradition seem to us today to be discontinued.

This account of the *Pardes*-story brings to an end the Hebrew section of *Hekhalot Zutreti*. What follows is, first, a list of subjects that are assumingly revealed to the Merkavah mystic.[26] The list contains items relating both to cosmology and to theosophy. In fact, it again becomes clear that in the *Hekhalot* literature the two subjects are closely interrelated, and that he who is worthy of the secrets of the Merkavah is also worthy of the secrets of the cosmos. It should be noticed that these revelations are said to come to the mystic in the course of a heavenly ascent: "Before God made heaven and earth, He had established a vestibule [27] to heaven, to go in and to go out". Through this vestibule the mystic ascends to receive his secrets. But all ascensions reach their climax with the mystical vision of the Deity.

The text continues with a comparatively long discussion of the question how it is possible to have a physical vision of God when it is explicitly said that no man can see God and remain alive. Rabbi ʿAkiva is quoted as settling the issue by saying: "It is as if He resembles us; but He is greater than everything else, and that is His glory which is hidden from us. And Moses says to those and to those: 'Do not reflect upon your own words, since He, blessed be He, is in His place' ". The reference here obviously is to *Ezekiel* iii,12, which in Midrashic literature is interpreted as indicating the fact that God's real place of dwelling is completely unknown.[28]

A central place among the things which are revealed to the mystic is occupied by the appearance of the Holy Creatures. The text calculates how many faces and wings the Creatures have, and what they do with their wings. Then the text describes all that is to be seen between the Creatures and the Throne of Glory. The text ends with a rather long discussion of various magical names, in which the Greek

---

[26] See Scholem, *op. cit.*, p. 78, and our discussion above in Chapter One. See further in *Israel Oriental Studies* III (1973), pp. 70 ff.

[27] See Scholem, *ibid.*, n. 9, to which one may add *Bavli Bava Batra* 74a where it is told in the name of Rava bar bar Ḥanah that a certain Yishmaelite merchant showed him where heaven and earth met together. At that place they also saw the window of heaven (Aramaic: *khwata de-reqiʿa*). In *Shemot Rabbā* xlii,4 it is said that God opened to Moses a small window (*Pishpash*) under the Throne of Glory so that he could escape from the wrath of the angels of destruction.

[28] See, for instance, *Bavli Hagigah* 13b.

elements play a prominent role. This last part of the text is of a highly technical nature, and can hardly be summarized. However, it is of great importance for a comparative study of magic and theurgy, and it may prove to be one of the earliest texts of its kind in that literature.

HEKHALOT RABBATI

This is the major *Hekhalot* tractate we possess. It is preserved in a comparatively great number of manuscripts,[1] and there are a number of printed editions of the text.[2] The main body of the text consists of twenty-six chapters, while the last four, or sometimes five, chapters which are appended to them belong to the *Sar-Torah* speculation, that is to the secret technique of the study of the Law and its memorization.[3]

The text begins with the question: "What are the incantations which should be recited by him who wants to behold the vision of the Merkavah, to descend safely and to ascend safely".[4] This opening

---

[1] The two best manuscripts are: Vatican 228 and Budapest/Kaufmann 238. Other manuscripts are: Oxford, Neubauer 1531 (printed in Jellinek, *Bet ha-Midrasch* III, though in a rather negligent manner: both the man who copied the manuscript for Jellinek and, probably, the printer introduced misreadings and misprints); New York: Jewish Theological Seminary 8128 (this manuscript and the one previously mentioned seem to derive from the circles of the old Ḥasidim in Germany); Firenze Laurentiana 44.13; MS. Jerusalem 4 (Scholem, *Codices Codicum Cabbalisticorum Hebraicorum*, Jerusalem, 1930, p. 22; this is the manuscript which Sh. A. Wertheimer printed in his *Batei Midrashot*, I, p. 67 ff. See next note); Munich 22 & 40. There are also some manuscripts which contain parts of the texts. Several Genizah fragments were preserved too.

[2] The best known texts are those printed by A. Jellinek, *Bet ha-Midrasch* III, pp. 83-108; V, pp. 167-169; and by Sh. A. Wertheimer, *Batei Midrashot* (see previous note). The text printed by Wertheimer has a different chapter division than all other texts known to us, and from xxxii,4-xl,5 it contains an apocalypse which uses old material re-written in circles connected with Sabbatai Ẓevi. A less known publication of *Hekhalot Rabbati* is the one incorporated in the collection of short writings by Isaiah Lev, *Sod ʿEẓ Ha-Daʿat* (= "The Secret of the Tree of Knowledge"), edited by S. Musa[joff], Jerusalem, 1891 (it too contains the text printed by Wertheimer). In spite of its obvious defects, Wertheimer's edition is so far the best available: it contains selective *variae lectiones* and also a commentary.

[3] Other texts which deal with the technique of the *Sar Torah* are: several sections in the text called *Maʿaseh Merkavah* (published by G. Scholem in: *Jewish Gnosticism* etc., pp. 103-117), and parts of the *Merkavah Rabba* (published by Sh. Musajoff in: *Merkavah Shelemah*, fol. 1a-6a). As we saw, *Hekhalot Zutreti* too contained *Sar-Torah* material, and, as we shall see, *Sefer Hekhalot* (*3 Enoch*) too contains *Sar Torah* material.

[4] The English translation is generally made from MS. Vatican 228; however, MS. Budapest/Kaufmann 238 has constantly been consulted. In fact, any future critical edition of the text will have to be based on these two manuscripts. The chapter division in them is the same one as in the text published by Jellinek, though there are slight differences in the numbering of the sections.

question is noteworthy for a number of reasons. First, it stresses the technical aspects of what follows. Indeed, *Hekhalot Rabbati* as also the other *Hekhalot* writings, are cast as mystical manuals, describing at some length what should be done in order to achieve the desired experience and how to overcome the perils that stand in the mystic's way. In this respect the *Hekhalot* writings are not mere descriptions of mystical experiences, but mystical guides to experiences the nature of which is described so-to-speak *en passant*. Second, the opening question makes it clear that mystical incantations occupy a central part in achieving the desired experiences. Third, in iv,3 it is claimed that those incantations were learnt by a mystic ("Rabbi ʿAkiva") during a heavenly ascent.

The opening question is repeated in ii,3 where the incantations are introduced. From i,1(b) to ii,3 the text lists the special accomplishments which are attributed to the Merkavah mystics. The mystics are believed to have all kinds of supernatural knowledge and powers, which are supposed to gain them special social status. The mystic is, for instance, able to identify all kinds of criminals and transgressors of religious law. In addition, his social position is strengthened through his ability to know what will happen to people in the future. Last but not least, supernatural protection against his enemies is offered the Merkavah mystic. All this sounds rather peculiar. If this is no mere propaganda for recruiting novices, it may be argued that this section of the book belongs to a stage, or place, where no real mystical experiences were in the reach of those who believed themselves worthy of having them. Otherwise, it is quite difficult to understand why the mystics had to praise themselves for having all kinds of quasi-magical proficiencies instead of being content with the inner satisfaction which the mystical experience obviously brings.[5] In fact, the opening sections of *Hekhalot Rabbati* may be interpreted as reflecting a stage in which mysticism declined into mere wondermaking. If anything certain can be said regarding the process of editing the texts of the *Hekhalot* literature, one may say that these opening sections are an editorial addition.

As already said, the introductory question is repeated in ii,3: "What is the utterance of the incantations which a man recites when he descends into the Merkavah?" The song which is henceforth

[5] Similar supernatural qualities are attributed to the initiates at the beginning of *Sefer Ha-Razim* and *Sefer Ha-Malbush*, both stemming from circles which claimed to be in possession of magical powers.

quoted maintains, as we have already observed, that the mystic actually recites the same songs of praise that are sung by the angelic beings to Him who sits on the divine throne. It is stated that "All these hymns Rabbi ʿAqiva heard when he descended unto the Merkavah. He absorbed them and learnt them as he was standing in front of the divine throne. (They were the very hymns) which His servants were singing to Him". What originally were the hymns of the angels have become theurgical incantations which help the mystic to achieve his goal.[6] The idea of the mystics sharing the song of the angels comes close to the idea expressed by the Qumran sectarians that the special merit of the believers was to enjoy partnership with the angels.[7] But what the *Hekhalot* mystic actually maintains is that he can use the angelological hymns for his own theurgic purposes. G. Scholem has rightly referred to these incantations as "numinous hymns"'[8] and J. Maier has pointed out some of their poetical characteristics.[9] On the whole, however, the literary qualities of the *Hekhalot* hymns still require systematic study. Such a study will discuss the *Hekhalot* hymns also in the light of the doxologies found in apocalyptic literature, including the Book of Revelation, and in comparison to later developments of Jewish liturgical poetry—some of which was influenced by the *Hekhalot* hymnology.

Chapter iii begins with a short dialogue between God, who is here called Zohurariel (= God of the Shining Light), and the mystic as to why the mystic is so terrified. The mystic answers that he is called before God for six hours every day, and that the angels drag him

---

[6] See A. Altman, in *Melilah* II (1946), pp. 1 ff. Altman, in fact, draws on the conclusions reached by G. Scholem in his analysis of the *Hekhalot* literature in general and of *Hekhalot Rabbati* in particular. See *Major Trends in Jewish Mysticism*, pp. 40 ff. See also M. Smith, "Observations on Hekhalot Rabbati", *Biblical and Other Studies*, ed. A. Altman, Cambridge, Mass., H.U.P., 1963, pp. 142-160. Smith's observations are most valuable to the study of the text, though the present description and analysis of the text differs in a variety of points from that of Morton Smith. See further A. Goldberg, "Einige Bemerkungen zu den Quellen und den Redaktionellen Einheiten der Grossen Hekhalot", *Frankfurter Judaistische Beiträge*, Heft 1 (1973), pp. 1-49, which suffers at times from mistranslations.

[7] See, for instance, 1 QS XI,8; 1 QSb IV,26. M. Weinfeld has recently published a comparative study (in Hebrew) in which the idea of the liturgical partnership between men and angels is traced back to ancient Near Eastern, mainly Sumerian, sources. See *Beth Mikra*, 1974, pp. 136 ff.

[8] *Jewish Gnosticism* etc., p. 21.

[9] See J. Maier, "Serienbildung und 'Numinoser' Eindrucksseffelet in den poetischen Stücken der Hekhalot Literatur", *Semitics* III (1973), pp. 36-66.

on his knees till he reaches the divine throne.[10] When the mystic learns that what the angels do is authorized by their King, he proceeds to describe the magnificence of the divine throne. The throne is described as hovering ever since the creation of the world. The Living Creatures are carrying it, but even they do not place their feet on the ground of the firmament.[11] Then follows a most interesting account of the throne which, so-to-speak, bows down before God, asking Him to be seated on it. The description is extremely interesting, though scholars have unfortunately failed to note its importance. What the throne is here described as doing and saying implies that God is not always present on His throne in the divine palace. When God is absent from the seventh *Hekhal*, where he usually receives the prayers of His People and the songs of His angelic servants and where He is given to mystical contemplation, He, so the text of *Hekhalot Rabbati* evidently assumes, resides in the eighth heaven which is above the heads of the Living Creatures.[12] The seventh *Hekhal* is thus ṭaken to be the official, so-to-say public, court of God. He attends there, as we are going to see, two or three times a day, corresponding to the hours of prayer of the People of Israel. The rest of the time, we must assume, He spends in the eighth heaven. Thus, even the *Hekhalot* literature actually supposes a certain degree of divine transcendence.

The text in *Hekhalot Rabbati* iii which describes God's descent to the seventh *Hekhal* says:

> Wonderful loftiness, strange power,
> Loftiness of grandeur, power of majesty
>
> that the Angel of the Countenance of God behaves thus thrice daily in the heavenly court before Your Throne of Glory, when He comes and

[10] The text here reports of "a thousand times they drag me on my knees till I reach Your Throne of Glory". The *Hekhalot* text published by the present writer in *Tarbiẓ* XXXVIII (1969), p. 359, says of Ben Zoma that he was dragged "a hundred times on the first *Hekhal*, ... two hundred times on the second *Hekhal*, four hundred times on the third *Hekhal*, eight hundred times on the fourth *Hekhal*, one thousand and six hundred on the fifth *Hekhal*, three thousand and two hundred on the sixth *Hekhal*, and six thousand and four hundred on the seventh *hekhal*". The sum total here is: 12700. The text there adds: "However, one does not suffer even one scratch!".

[11] Compare *Pirkei de-Rabbi ʾElieẓʿer* iv: "... and His throne is exalted and suspended above in the air ...".

[12] This is a clear allusion to *Eẓekiel* i,22-23. See also my article, "Jewish Sources for the Gnostic Texts from Nag Hammadi?", in the *Proceedings of the Sixth World Congress for Jewish Studies*, 1977, pp. 45-56.

> arrives on the heavens above the heads of the *Cherubim*, above the heads of the *Ofanim* and above the heads of the heavenly Creatures.[13]
> And the *Cherubim*, *Ofanim* and the heavenly Creatures, bound, stand beneath the Throne of the Glory. And when they see Him coming on the firmament which is above the heads of the *Cherubim*, the *Ofanim* and the Holy Creatures, they retreat and are frightened and fall back in swoon.[14]

Needless to say, this description is unique in the way in which it conceives of the manner in which God enters and departs from His abode in the eighth heaven. When God appears on His throne in the seventh palace, He is clad in His divine garment (*Ḥaluq*).[15]

Let us return for a moment to the description of God's descent to the seventh *Hekhal* in the seventh heaven. As is explicitly stated in *Hekhalot Rabbati* ix, God's descents to His throne correspond to the times of the three daily prayers of the People of Israel. The idea that there is a liturgical and ritual connection between the saying of the *Qedushah* by the People of Israel and the *Sanctus* recited by the angels is a common one in Jewish and Christian sources.[16] What is new here in *Hekhalot Rabbati* is the concept that prayers said even by those who are not consciously practising mystics do in fact have mystical consequences. This adds a novel dimension to prayer, and it was the privilege of the Merkavah mystics to reveal that new aspect of prayer. The mystical aspects of prayer were considerably developed through the Middle Ages, both in Judaism[17] and in Christianity,[18] but attention has not yet been given to this particular significance which the daily prayers have: they are, in fact, taken to be invocations to God to descend to His throne in the seventh *Hekhal*.

To complement this idea of prayer as it is conceived of in *Hekhalot Rabbati*, we must refer to xi,3-4 where God is described as addressing, twice daily, words of blessing to those officiating before Him. In the blessing said in the morning, God asks the angels to be silent so as

---

[13] Originally there was no real difference between the Cherubim and the Living Creatures (*Ḥayyot*). Both terms were synonymously used in the visions in *Ezekiel* i and x.

[14] The English translation here follows the draft-translation of *Hekhalot Rabbati* prepared for me by Mr. Yehoshuʿa Schwartz of Jerusalem.

[15] For a detailed discussion of the theme of the *Ḥaluq* see G. Scholem, *Jewish Gnosticism* etc., pp. 58 ff.

[16] See above, Introduction to Part Two, n. 11.

[17] See I. Tishbi, *The Wisdom of the Zohar* (in Hebrew), vol. II, Jerusalem, Bialik Institute, 1961, pp. 247-306.

[18] See F. Heiler, *Prayer*, New York, Oxford University Press, 1932, pp. 172-202.

to enable Him to listen to the prayers of His People. However, nothing is said about the contents of the blessing said by God at the time of the *Minḥah*-prayer. On the whole, mystical ideas of prayer occupy in *Hekhalot Rabbati* a much more prominent place than has hitherto been noticed. A significant proportion of the description found in the book is in one way or another connected with the appearance of God on His throne. And as we have seen, God descends to the throne from his abode in the eighth heaven at the daily prayer-times of the People of Israel. If this idea is carried to its logical conclusion, it appears that a mystical descent to the Merkavah was carried out only during these official hours of prayer. Indeed, there are several instances in the *Hekhalot* writings that make it relatively clear that the mystical prayers, or invocations, were introduced into or appended to the daily prayers. Furthermore, the various descriptions in *Hekhalot Rabbati* as to how the throne is prepared for that descent (chapters x and xi) are substantially connected with the prayer-times of the People of Israel. Chapter x contains a mystical hymn to encourage the Holy Creatures to perform their heavenly duties, while chapter xi describes what the Prince of the Countenance does when he prepares the throne for God. In addition, chapter xi contains a request of the mystic to the Holy Creatures to carry the throne willingly. In xi,4, the ecstatic ritual dance of the angels before the throne of God is described,[19] while in chapter xii, the office of the angels is extended to include the power to intercede on behalf of the People of Israel.[20] Thus perfect correspondence is achieved between the terrestrial—assumingly even non-mystical—human prayer and the angelic liturgical performance. Consequently, the ideas of the angelological liturgy known from the published and yet unpublished texts from Qumran [21] seem to have undergone a substantial mystical transformation.

We deliberately refrain from referring to the angelological liturgy from Qumran, and, for that matter, to the corresponding angelological material in apocalyptic literature, in full mystical terms. On the one hand, although the Qumranites appear to have possessed clear notions about a certain liturgical correspondence between the "orders of

[19] See also viii,3 which could be interpreted to imply that God's throne itself is revolving.

[20] Later on, in medieval Jewish mysticism, this motive of the intercession of the angels on behalf of the People of Israel became a central issue in the concept of prayer.

[21] See our discussion in Chapter Two, Section B.

men" and the "orders of angels",[22] the texts we have do not prove that they had special mystical practices which enabled them to experience these heavenly scenes. On the other hand, the richness of the style and the vividness of the description may give the impression that, after all, lying behind the text, were real visionary experiences of the sort known from some apocalyptic writings. Compared to the parallel experiences in the *Hekhalot* literature, the relevant experiences found in apocalyptic literature are, so-to-speak, proto-mysticism, that is they contain all the necessary elements which could easily turn into mysticism. But we must remember that it was not the ultimate goal of the apocalyptists to experience the Deity. Some of them experienced heavenly ascensions in the course of which they also had a vision of the Deity. Thus, in contrast to the *Hekhalot* mystics who ascended in order to attain a vision of the Beauties of the Merkavah, the apocalyptists were translated to heaven in order to have first hand contact with the secrets of the world. These secrets generally entailed information about the cosmological order of the world and the historical process that leads from creation to redemption. When a vision of the Deity occurred, this only added a mystical ingredient but did not turn the whole of the apocalyptic experience into mysticism.

Another substantial difference between Merkavah mysticism and apocalyptic comes to the fore in *Hekhalot Rabbati* ix. Here, in relation to the mystical ideas expressed in connection with prayer, God is quoted as asking the mystics, the so-called *Yordei Merkavah*,[23] to "tell my sons what I am doing during the morning and afternoon prayers [24]... teach them and tell them... and testify unto them what you saw me doing to the countenance of the face of Jacob, your patriarch, which is engraven on my throne". Here the mystics are explicitly asked to tell and to reveal to the general public ("to my sons") this element of their vision. This, of course, is not in line with

---

[22] The terms *Seder 'Anashim* and *Seder Mal'akhim* occur in fragments connected with the angelological liturgy.

[23] In spite of the many attempts to explain the term, it has not yet been satisfactorily explained. See G. Scholem, *Jewish Gnosticism*, p. 20, n. 1. See also Ph. Bloch, "Die *Yordei Merkavah*, die Mystiker der Gaonzeit, und ihr Einfluss auf die Liturgie", *Monatsschrift für die Geschichte und Wissenschaft des Judenthums* XXXVII (1893), pp. 22 ff.

[24] Some manuscripts here add the word for the evening prayer too: *'Aravit*. Yet, this addition, also found in some of the quotations of this passage in Halakhic sources discussing the *Qedushah* said in the daily service, seems to be out of place, since the evening prayer never contained the recital of the *Qedushah*.

the idea of secrecy as maintained in apocalyptic, and it speaks for the non-esoteric quality of the rest of the *Hekhalot* literature. This non-esoteric quality of the *Hekhalot* literature is further stressed in x,3, where it is emphatically stated: "May the decree of heaven be upon you, descenders unto the Merkavah, if you do not tell and say what you have heard; and if you do not tell what you have seen upon the countenance of grandeur, might, wonder and glory". And again in xvi,3 and 5, God is described as waiting for the mystics to descend unto the Merkavah so as to be able to "see and tell to the seed of Abraham, His beloved". Of course, one may argue that the ones to whom the mystics have to report their experiences are none other than the members of the mystical group.[25] But, one should notice that the *Hekhalot* writings almost never require secrecy. In addition, no esoteric layers of Scripture are revealed in them. As we have already seen, the dangers described in the *Hekhalot* tractates could prevent unworthy people from undergoing experiences which they could neither physically nor emotionally endure. But no straightforward requirement of secrecy is expressed in them, and, as we just saw, the mystics are told not to keep for themselves the contents of their revelation.

Before we go on with our discussion of *Hekhalot Rabbati*, a word is due regarding the ten-martyrs-apocalypse incorporated in the text (iv,3-vi, end.).[26] It is not clear when this apocalypse was introduced into the text, but it is clear that it belongs to a comparatively early stage of the text. All manuscripts known to the present writer contain the apocalypse, some with a longer version than usual. In addition, the apocalypse is known as a separate composition in a number of manuscripts.[27] Since there are several historical or semi-historical figures alluded to in the text, attempts have been made to date the apocalypse and hence to determine the *termini a quo* and *ad quem* of the whole work.[28] However, it is always difficult to date and locate

[25] See the description of the mystical-"seance" in chapter xviii, and the comments thereon by M. Smith, *art. cit.*, pp. 144 ff.

[26] See Ph. Bloch, "Rom und die Mystiker der Merkavah", *Festschrift für Jacob Guttman* Leipzig: 1915, pp. 113-124; and Scholem's remarks in *Major Trends in Jewish Mysticism*, p. 357, n. 10.

[27] My colleague, Professor Joseph Dan, is now preparing a critical edition of this apocalypse. For the time being see the two versions printed in *Bet ha-Midrasch* vols. II and VI.

[28] See the suggestion concerning the dating of the apocalypse made by Professor Morton Smith. He writes: The "use of the title 'Caesar' for the Emperor (= Lupinus, in the apocalypse) suggests a date prior to Diocletian, the *-inus* ter-

stories of religious persecution, particularly so when the sages of antiquity are called upon to serve as models of religious devotion for later, less illustrious, generations.

The raison d'etre for the apocalypse in *Hekhalot Rabbati* becomes clear from iv,4, where Rabbi Neḥuniah ben Ha-Qanah asks Rabbi Yishmael to descend unto the Merkavah and to find out in heaven the reason for the Roman decree to put to death four of the sages of the People of Israel or eight thousand students as their ransom. The four sager are: Shimʿon ben Gamliʾel, Yishmael ben ʾElishʿa, ʾElʿazar ben Dama and Yehudah ben Bava. Later on, in v,1, it becomes evident that the decree actually concerns ten sages whose names are not always given in the manuscripts.[29] The reason for this savage decree is that the ten martyrs have to expiate the sin of the ten brothers who sold Joseph to the Ishmaelites (*Genesis* xxxvii,27-28). As it is written (*Exodus* xxi,16) "Whoever steals a man, whether he sells

mination and the slaughter of the Roman administrators reflect the troubled years of the midthird century when relations between the emperors and the Senate were particularly bad ... The folk-tale motif of transformation and substitution of persons was popular at the time; we find it, for instance, in the third century strata of the Pseudo-Clementine Homilies". See, *art. cit.*, p. 149. However, this suggestion finds no support in Professor S. Lieberman's summary of the historical and halakhic evidence for alleged religious persecutions in the third and fourth centuries. See his article "*Redifot Dat Yisraʿel*" in: *The S. Baron Jubilee Volume* (Hebrew Part), 1974, pp. 234 ff. Professor Lieberman finds no historical evidence for the existence of religious persecutions in Eretz Yisrael in the third and fourth centuries C.E. If so, the apocalypse of the ten martyrs reflects no real historical situation of religious persecution. Professor Lieberman pointed out to me in a private conversation that Jewish stories of martyrdom could have arisen in the third or fourth century at the time when many Christians had suffered martyrdom. The alleged purpose of these stories was to show that Jews too were ready to pay with lives for their belief and religious practice. Indeed, these stories were pseudepigraphically projected back to the second century, when Jews had really suffered religious persecution mainly at the time of Hadrian. Such historical retrojections were common literary phenomenon in the literature dealing with martyrdom. For the halakhic and historical sources dealing with second century religious persecution see S. Lieberman, *art. cit.*, p. 213-234.

[29] In MS. Vatican 228, for instance, the names were added in the margin by a second hand. Of these names, two, at least, are generally erroneously identified: Rabbi Yishmaʾel and Rabbi Shimʿon known from the rabbinical sources as martyrs were not the sons of ʾElishʿa and Gamliʾel respectively. Their exact identity is unknown though it is clear that they were martyred before Rabbi ʿAkiva suffered martyrdom. See S. Lieberman, *art. cit.*, p. 227. Lists of the martyrs found in rabbinical writings considerably vary one from the other. Compare, for instance, the list found in *Hekhalot Rabbati* with the ones found in *ʾEikhah Rabba* ii (ed. Buber, fol. 50b), and in *Midrash Tehillim* ix (ed. Buber, fol. 45a). See also next note.

him or is found in possession of him, shall be put to death", the ten martyrs have to pay with their lives for the sin of their forefathers. Recently Professor E. E. Urbach rightly traced threads of the legend back to *Jubilees* xxxiv,18-19, and pointed out the occurrence of the idea in some medieval midrashic writings which in turn were probably influenced by the *Hekhalot* literature.[30] Urbach likewise remarks that "when the Temple was destroyed, the sin (of the selling of Joseph) allegedly remained without an atonement, and it appears that the burden of expiation was imposed on the righteous in each generation" (p. 521).[31] However interpreted, the legend and its theological consequences are, to say the least, rather peculiar in Jewish thought, and they certainly contradict the basic Jewish concept of retribution as expounded, for example, in *Deuteronomy* xxiv,16 and in *Ezekiel* xviii.

The rest of this ten-martyrs apocalypse is, in fact, of little concern for our subject, so that we may leave the discussion of the apocalypse at this point. It should be noted, however, that later on (in chapter xiv) [32] the ten martyrs are called together to form a kind of mystical group which participates in the ecstasy of a medium who descends unto the Merkavah. We shall come back to this scene in due course.

Chapters viii-xii give an extensive account of the angelic ceremony in heaven. They include long poetical passages, which are masterpieces of lyrical composition. The description chiefly concerns the manner in which the angelic beings prepare themselves and the divine throne for the appearance of God in the seventh *Hekhal*. Long stretches in these descriptions are devoted to the angelic song and dance.[33] It is repeatedly emphasized that this angelic ceremony takes place when the People of Israel recite their *Qedushah*; thus, the heavenly perfectly corresponds with the earthly ritual. At one point a piece of *Shi'ur Qomah* speculation is introduced: "From the Throne of His Glory the height of God is a hundred and eighty thousand

---

[30] E. E. Urbach, *The Sages*, pp. 521-522 and the notes on p. 921 f., which contain references to further bibliography.

[31] According to *Hekhalot Rabbati* iv,4 the decree is to last till the future day of revenge, when Sama'el, the heavenly prince of Rome, will be slain together with the other heavenly princes. It is said there that they will be lying slain "as lambs and sheep (offered on) the day of atonement". Here the text points back to *Jubilees* xxxiv,18.

[32] See also chapter xviii.

[33] *Hekhalot Rabbati* viii,3. The paragraph can also be taken to mean that the throne revolves around itself. The angelic dance is again described in xi,3.

times ten thousand parasangs and from his right arm to his left arm His width is seventy thousand times ten thousand parasangs" (x,1).[34] These measures (unless interpolated) show that the writer of *Hekhalot Rabbati* was aware of the *Shi'ur Qomah* speculations and that the latter, although little room is given to them in the *Hekhalot* writings, were part of the ancient Jewish mystical tradition.[35]

Not only has the throne of God to be prepared, but so do also the Living Creatures who carry it. In chapter xi, the Angel of the Countenance crowns each of the Living Creatures with thousands upon thousands of "crowns". He falls upon his face every time he puts a "crown" on their heads. When the Living Creatures see that God is, so-to-speak, angry with the People of Israel, they untie their "crowns" and beat them on the ground thus asking forgiveness for the People of Israel (chapter xii).

Chapters xiii-xxvi contain a long and detailed description of the ascent unto the Merkavah.[36] It begins with a pseudohistorical paragraph that links the description with the ten-martyrs apocalypse: "Rabbi Yishma'el said: When Rabbi Neḥunyah ben Ha-Qanah saw Rome planning to destroy the mighty of Israel, he at once revealed the secret of the world: that is the virtue of the one who is worthy of gazing on the king and His throne...".[37] The impression one may gain from this introductory passage is that the revelation of the secrets of the world was made public as a result of religious persecutions. At least on that occasion, as we shall later on see, it became necessary to use the mystical services of a medium. In xiii,2 the virtues of the mystic are given: "What is the technique of the Merkavah mystic like? It is like having a ladder in one's house and being able to go up and down at will. This may be done by anyone who is pure of idolatry, sexual offenses, bloodshed, slander, vain oaths, profanation of the Name, impertinence, and unjustified enmity,

[34] Some of the MSS. contain even a longer *Shi'ur Qomah* passage which quotes a sentence said by Metatron and also several verses from the *Song of Songs* v,10 ff. In any event, the *Shi'ur Qomah* passage in *Hekhalot Rabbati* is only partly known from the largest preserved *Shi'ur Qomah* text. See in *Merkavah Shelemah*, 37b.

[35] See G. Scholem, *Jewish Gnosticism* etc., pp. 36 ff.; *idem*, *Von der Mystischen Gestalt der Gottheit*, Zürich, Rhein-Verlag, 1962, pp. 7 ff.: "Schi'ur Koma ..."; S. Lieberman, "*Mishnat Shir Ha-Shirim*", Appendix D to Scholem, *Jewish Gnosticism* etc., pp. 118-126.

[36] See M. Smith, *art. cit.* (above, n. 6), pp. 144 ff.

[37] The translation is—with some changes—that of Professor Morton Smith.

and who keeps every positive and negative commandment".[38] The ladder-motif which is mentioned here [39] is known both from Greek philosophy [40] and from Islamic philosophy and mysticism,[41] but in our case it could also indicate the angel-like quality of the Merkavah mystic.[42] In any event, the ladder is used here only metaphorically, while the real means of the ascension are different ones.

When Rabbi Yishma'el heard what the qualifications of the Merkavah mystic were, he felt discouraged and said to Rabbi Neḥunyah ben Ha-Qanah: "If so, there is no end to the matter, for there is no living man so pure".[43] In response to that Rabbi Neḥunyah ben Ha-Qanah told Rabbi Yishma'el to gather all the "heroes of the assembly and all the distinguished people of the academy" so that he might tell them the most secret mysteries of "the beam of the web upon which rest the perfection of the world and its beautiful construction. And also the axle of heaven and earth to which are bound, sewed, connected, hung and fastened all the edges of the earth and the universe and also the edges of the celestial firmaments. And also the pathway of the heavenly ladder which leads from earth to the right leg of the Throne of Glory" (xiv,1). This description of the creation of the world is also known from other sources,[44] and its

---

[38] See previous note. This passage among others was interpreted by Professor Scholem as indicating "The Halakhic Character of *Hekhalot* Mysticism"; see *Jewish Gnosticism* etc., pp. 9-13.

[39] See also xiv,1 which should be compared with the text published by L. Ginzberg, *Genizah Studies* I, New York, 1928, pp. 185-187. See also xx,3.

[40] Professor David Winston drew my attention to the following references: Plato, *Symposium*, 211c: Regarding the candidate to be initiated in the mysteries of Love it is said: "... he must for the sake of that highest beauty be ever climbing aloft as on the steps of stairs (ὥσπερ ἐπαναβαθμοῖς χρώμενον) ..."; Philo *De Praemiis et Poenis* 43. Speaking of those who have by the power of their intellect recognized the operation of God in Nature, Philo says; "These no doubt are truly admirable persons and superior to the other classes. They have, as I said, advanced from down to up by a sort of heavenly ladder (διά τινος οὐρανίου κλίμακος) and by reason and reflection happily inferred the Creator from His works". [Both translations are from the Loeb Classics; that of Plato, however, with a slight change according to Liddell & Scott, p. 606, s.v. ἐπαναβαθμός]. See also E. R. Dodds, *Pagan and Christian in an Age of Anxiety*, p. 52.

[41] See A. Altman, "'The Ladder of Ascension'", in: *Studies in Mysticism and Religion Presented to Gershom G. Scholem*, Jerusalem, The Magnes Press, 1967, pp. 1 ff. Although Altman deals mainly with later medieval sources his discussion is most relevant for our passage in *Hekhalot Rabbati*.

[42] See *Genesis* xxviii,12.

[43] See above note 37.

[44] See S. Lieberman, *Tosefta Ki-Fshutah to Tractate Kippurim*, pp. 772-773.

inclusion here again speaks for the close connection between mystical and cosmological speculations. On the other hand, some of the Jewish cosmological texts, such as the *Beraita de-Ma'aseh Bereshit* and *Midrash Konen*, contain important mystical sections. This link between mystical and cosmological speculations has already been shown to be present in some of the Jewish apocalyptic writings and is also characteristic of later Jewish mysticism, the *Kabbalah*. In principle, the secrets of the Deity and the secrets of nature may be classified as two distinct branches of knowledge, but in practice they are usually interrelated, and so they also appear in the *Hekhalot* writings.[45]

To come back to *Hekhalot Rabbati* xiv, when Rabbi Yishma'el heard the request to gather the distinguished members of the academy, he did so and "assembled every Sanhedrin, great or small, at the third gate of the temple. Rabbi Neḥunyah ben Ha-Qanah was sitting on a bench made of pure marble which Elish'a my (= Rabbi Yishma'el's) father gave him from the property of my mother and which had been part of the dowry that she brought to him".[46] In xiv,3 nine names of sages are given who, together with Rabbi Yishma'el, were sitting before Rabbi Neḥunyah ben Ha-Qanah. All the rest of the *Ḥaverim* (colleagues), however, were standing on their feet, because "they saw globes of fire and torches of light separating *us from them*". The italicized words indicate that actually three groups of people were present.[47] The first was a one-man group, and it consisted of Rabbi Neḥunyah ben Ha-Qanah only. The second group consisted of the ten sages, whose names are given. In the third group were those to whom the text refers to as "the multitude of the colleagues" (*hamon ḥaverim*). Only Rabbi Neḥunyah ben Ha-Qanah "was sitting expounding all the matter of the Merkavah, the descent and the ascent, how one descends unto and how one ascends from (the Merkavah)". The others were either carefully listening to him or writing down what he was saying.

See also my article "Jewish Sources for the Gnostic Texts from Nag-Hammadi?", in: *The Proceedings of the Sixth World Congress for Jewish Studies*, Jerusalem, 1977, pp. 45-56 ff.

[45] See also *Hekhalot Rabbati* ix,4, and *3 Enoch* ix *seq.*, where the secrets of the Torah are added to the cosmological and theosophical secrets.

[46] Here M. Smith translates only in a summary form.

[47] Professor Morton Smith informs me that he too noticed that three groups were involved, as can be seen from his translation of the passage: "... and R. Neḥunya sat and instructed the chosen few who sat before him, *while the rest of the scholars* stood at a distance, separated from them by globes of fire and torches of light."

Then follows a detailed description of the "praxis", that is, how the descent should be carried out. This description of the descent unto the Merkavah begins with the words: "When a man wanted to descend to the Merkavah he would call Suriyah, the Prince of the Countenance, and conjure him a hundred and twelve times". In addition, it is said that the mystic should be careful neither to add nor to subtract from that number, for if he does, he might fatally endanger himself. "He should utter the names while his fingers count a hundred and twelve times".[48] Then follows the description of the seven palaces and of the doorkeepers. Rabbi Neḥunyah ben Ha-Qanah says: "Totrosi'i, Lord God of Israel, dwells in seven palaces, one inside the other, and at the gate of each palace there are eight doorkeepers, four on either side" (xv,1). The names of the doorkeepers of the first six palaces are immediately given, while we have to wait till chapter xxii,1 for the names of the doorkeepers standing at the seventh palace.[49] Here it is only said that those standing at the seventh *hekhal* are most fearful ones (xv,8). Chapter xvi goes into some detail about the fearful horses on which those doorkeepers ride, and it is said that in spite of everything the *Yordei Merkavah* ascend (!) and are not harmed. In fact, it is said that God is waiting, almost impatiently, for the mystic to undergo a descent to the Merkavah. The passage through the doors is granted only when two seals are shown, one to those standing on the right and one to those standing on the left (chapter xvii). At the door of the sixth *Hekhal*, however, a slight change is introduced: two seals have to be shown to those standing on the right and one to those on the left (xviii,5-6). Only when the seals are shown, do the doorkeepers accompany the mystic to the next door.

In xvii,6, however, an observation is made by Rabbi Neḥunyah ben Ha-Qanah to the effect that the doorkeepers of the sixth palace are so fearful that they inflict destruction on those who descend unto the Merkavah but are not considered as descenders unto the Merkavah. In spite of the fact that the doorkeepers were severely punished for that—they were burned and replaced—the new ones show no better

[48] In a genizah-fragment found in Leningrad (Antonin Collection 186), and which contains a hitherto unknown Merkavah text it is said: "How does he count?—On every finger he counts ten times; then he repeats and counts ten on his first finger and two on his second one".

[49] In xxii,3 it is said that a difference exists between the names of those who keep the doors on the way in and the names of those who keep the doors on the way out.

qualities. When the members of the mystical group heard this, they asked Rabbi Yishma'el to call Rabbi Neḥunyah ben Ha-Qanah back from his celestial vision, so that he might identify this particular class of mystics called "those who descend unto the Merkavah but do not [really] descend unto the Merkavah". Rabbi Yishma'el fulfilled their wish and woke Rabbi Neḥunyah ben Ha-Qanah from his trance. He did so in the following manner: he put on the knees of Rabbi Neḥunyah ben Ha-Qanah a piece of fine and white wool which had previously been touched very slightly by a menstruating woman who had been declared to be pure by a majority of the rabbinical court. According to Jewish law, menstrual blood renders women unclean, and this uncleanliness is considered to pass over to people and things which are touched by them. We have already pointed out (in Chapter Four) that ritual purity was a necessary prerequisite for any mystical experience. The mystic had to undergo a series of ritual baths before he could begin with the more technical "praxis" of the mystical experience. Now, to wake him from the trance a piece of fine and white wool—*Mela Parhava*—which was generally used in order to examine the blood of menstruating women was put on the knees of Rabbi Neḥunyah ben Ha-Qanah.[50]

In discussing this passage in *Hekhalot Rabbati*, Professor Gershom Scholem referred to it as a "set of fictitious circumstances". However, in an appendix to this book, Professor Saul Lieberman analyses the details of this process of awakening Rabbi Neḥunyah ben Ha-Qanah from his trance, and reaches the conclusion that the story is an ingenious construction of mystical imagination based on halakhic knowledge.[51] When Rabbi Neḥunyah ben Ha-Qanah was "dismissed from before of the throne of Glory where he had been sitting and beholding", he was asked who were those who were called "those who descend unto the Merkavah but do not descend unto the Merkavah". His answer to this was that those people were the ones whom the real *Yordei Merkavah* placed before them, either standing

[50] In *Bavli Niddah* 17a we also find the *mela parhava* as a means of testing the menstrual blood of a woman. It is there identified with a kind of material that is either Pikkulin (cotton?) or pure and soft wool. Rashi, however, explains *mela parhava* as cotton, but brings also a parallel explanation: "a pure and soft wool". As for the *parhava*, it still remains a riddle.

[51] See now L. H. Schiffman, "The Recall of Rabbi Neḥuniah ben Ha-Qanah from Ecstasy in the *Hekhalot Rabbati*", *Association for Jewish Studies Review*, I (1976), pp. 269-281. Schiffman's analysis mistinterprets both the halakhic and magical aspects of the passage!

or sitting, and told them to keep alert and hear and write down all that the mystics said and heard when they reached the throne of Glory.[52] If those people were not worthy of the experience, the door-keepers of the sixth *Hekhal* beat them. It was, therefore, necessary to be very careful in the choice of those who participated in the mystical seance. Although those people were only amanuenses, they had to be men of purity and piety comparable to those of the *Yordei Merkavah* themselves.

The sixth door entails a series of particularly challenging tests for the mystic. Some of the tests are described here and some elsewhere (in xxv,5-6, and in *Hekhalot Zutreti*). The angel in charge of those standing on the right side of the door is Qeẓfiel ("The Wrath of God"), and he holds in his hand a drawn sword. This sword is a most fearful one: lightening bolts come out of it, and it shouts "destruction". On the left side stands Dumi'el ("Divine Silence") about whom the text has some interesting things to say. First, his real name is not Dumi'el but Averghidrihm. This curious name was rightly explained by Professor Johanan H. Levy as a corrupt tran-scription of the three Greek words: ἀήρ, γῆ, ὕδωρ (air, earth and water, respectively). These are three of the four elements in Greek philosophy.[53] It may be argued that the reason for the change in the angel's name could be explained by the fact that an angel bearing a name composed of the three or four elements out of which the world was created could be misunderstood to be the Demiurge. Since we know that the angels themselves were created,[54] their participation in the creation of the world was generally considered in rabbinic thought to be a gnostic blasphemy.[55] The reason which the text, however, gives for the change in the name is: "He should be called Dumi'el after my name: just as I see and remain silent so does he.[56] His post of duty is at the right side of the door-post. But

[52] In this respect they resemble the scribes of the Sanhedrin. See *Mishnah Sanhedrin* iv,3-4.

[53] See J. H. Levy, *Studies in Jewish Hellenism* (in Hebrew), Jerusalem, Bialik Institute, 1969, p. 261. Levy suggests seeing in the rather strange ending of the word a corrupt rendering of the Greek πῦρ, fire.

[54] According to the Book of Jubilees the angels were created on the first day. Later on, however, their creation was said to have taken place on the second or even the fifth day. See *Bereshit Rabba* iii, ed. Theodor-Albeck, p. 24. The theolog-ical difficulties caused by *Genesis* i,26 ("let us make a man") have given rise to a vast literature. See next note.

[55] See E. E. Urbach, *The Sages*, pp. 203 ff.

[56] See *Mechilta d'Rabbi Ismael*, p. 142, line 10, where it is said of God that

Qeẓfiel, the Prince, used to push him aside. Nevertheless, he (= Dumi'el) felt towards him neither malice nor rivalry. Both of them do whatever they do in my honour".

When the mystic shows the proper seals, Qeẓfiel calls a whirlwind for him and puts him in a carriage of light and blows trumpets and horns for him while Dumi'el paces in front carrying a "present" (xix,1).[57] What is this present? It is of pure theurgic function. First of all, it consists of the magical seals which the mystic has to produce at the gates of every one of the seven palaces. But, even more important, it consists also of the document in which the legal knowledge and observance of the mystic is recorded. This document is obtained in the following manner: When the Merkavah mystic arrives at the sixth gate, he is met by Dumi'el who is sitting on a bench made of a pure stone.[58] The angel greets the mystic with a Greek blessing: "*Extraordinary day. Show the seal. Shalom*",[59] and then invites him to take his seat beside him. Then Dumi'el addresses the mystic, warning him that only he who has studied all the various categories of the written and oral law *or* (!) he who strictly observes all that is said therein may pass onward to the seventh *Hekhal*. If the mystic claims that he possesses either of these qualities, Dumi'el calls Gabri'el, the Scribe,[60] and asks him to make a note of this fact on a piece of paper. This paper is hung on a mast [61] on the carriage of light in which the Merkavah mystic is placed before he passes through the sixth *Hekhal*. When the doorkeepers of the seventh *Hekhal* see Dumi'el, Gabri'el and Qeẓfiel walking in front of the carriage of the Merkavah mystic, they cover their faces and sit down. Before, however, they were standing in a most intimidating manner, but

before the time of the future redemption He watches the miserable state of His People without uttering a word. See further J. H. Levy, *op. cit.*, p. 262, who identifies in our paragraph a transcription of the Greek word σιγή, silence. In fact 1 *Kings* xix,12 inspired a number of speculations about the divine silence.

[57] The Hebrew text here uses a Greek loan word : δώρον.

[58] The word used here is λίθικος, which means "of stone". See Liddell & Scott, p. 1048, s.v. λιθ-ίδιον.

[59] See J. H. Levy, *op. cit.*, pp. 260-261. Levy assumes that at least two more words can be identified in the corrupt Hebrew transcription of the Greek words. But upon examination of the good manuscripts, it appears that only three phrases can be deciphered with certainty.

[60] In Jewish apocalyptic and mystical tradition, it is generally Enoch-Metatron who is the heavenly scribe. The allocation of that function to Gabriel in *Hekhalot Rabbati* seems to be unique!

[61] The word used here is SKRIYA. See ʿ*Aruch Completum*, vol. I, p. 199, s.v. ASKRAYA.

now they loosen their drawn bows and return their drawn swords to their sheaths. Nevertheless, the mystic has to show the doorkeepers of the seventh *Hekhal* "a great seal and a fearful crown".[62] When the gatekeepers see all this, they enter the seventh *Hekhal* to fetch all kinds of musical instruments,[63] and thus they escort the Merkavah mystic till they offer him a seat near the heavenly Creatures that carry the Throne of Glory and minister to it.

Chapter xxi begins with a digression: it suddenly turned out that the names of the gatekeepers of the seventh *Hekhal* were not given. When the members of the mystical company appealed to Rabbi Neḥunyah ben Ha-Qanah, he told them that this was on purpose. The names of the gatekeepers of the first six *Hekhalot* could be revealed, and the mystics were allowed to make use of them. But one was allowed neither to mention nor use the names of the gatekeepers of the seventh *Hekhal*. Now that he was asked to reveal their names, Rabbi Neḥunyah agreed to do so, on condition that all the members of the company stood up. However, whenever he uttered a name, they had to fall on their faces. The chapter ends with the remark that immediately all the members of the mystical company "stood on their feet before Rabbi Neḥunyah ben Ha-Qanah: he uttered [the names], and they fell on their faces, and the scribes were writing".

The names of the gatekeepers of the seventh *Hekhal* are given in chapter xxii. It is remarked that there is a difference in the names of those keeping the gates on the way of the descent and the names of those on the way of the ascent. A prominent role among the gatekeepers of the seventh *Hekhal* is given to ʿAnafi'el. "And why is he called ʿAnafi'el?—Because of the branch[64] of the crown of the crowns that was placed on his head and used to cover all the chambers of the palace of the firmament *ʿAravot*. (And in this) he resembles the demiurge.[65] As it is pointed out about the demiurge:

---

[62] In the Greek words, which here follow in the text Levy, *op. cit.*, p. 262, hypothetically identifies the words: θεὸς οὐρανὸς γῆ ὁ δεσπότης. However, Morton Smith, *art. cit.*, p. 146, suggests a slightly different reading. The opening prayer of *Hekhalot Zutreti* is sometimes called "The prayer of the Great Seal and of the fearful crown". See Scholem, *Jewish Gnosticism* etc., p. 6, n. 12; pp. 54-55. [See now P. Schäfer, "Prolegomena zu einer kritischen Edition und Analyse der Merkava Rabba", in: *Frankfurter Judaistische Beiträge*, Heft 5 (1977), pp. 65 ff.]

[63] Literally: "all kinds of music and song".

[64] In Hebrew: *ʿAnaf.*

[65] In Hebrew: *Yoẓer Bereshit.* See Scholem, *Jewish Gnosticism* etc., pp. 28, 34 and 46-48.

'His glory covers the firmament' (*Habakkuk* iii,3),[66] so it is also with ʿAnafiʾel, the minister, who is a servant that is called after the name of his master".[67] For a description of God in similar terms we have to turn to chapter xxiv,3 where it is said: "King of Kings, God of Gods and Lord of Lords / He who is exalted with chains of crowns / Who is encompassed by the branches of the rays of brilliance / Who covers the firmament with the branch of His glory".[68] The "branch" here can well be a metonym for the crown and indeed it seems that ʿAnafiʾel belongs to the category of angels of the highest rank. In this respect he may be viewed as an equal to Metatron, ʾAkatriʾel and Synadelphon.

It is ʿAnafiʾel who opens for the Merkavah mystic the gates of the seventh palace. And when the holy creatures of that palace try to assault the mystic, ʿAnafiʾel assists him, "he and the sixty three gatekeepers of the seven *Hekhalot*".

Chapters xxiv-xxvi contain the so-called "Song of the Throne" [69] which the mystic utters when he stands before the Throne of the Glory. In xxv,5-6, however, a short interpolation describes how those who are not worthy of descending unto the Merkavah are prevented from entering the gates of the palaces. If he is a true Merkavah mystic, then, when he is told to enter the gate, he does not stir. He only enters when he is invited a second time. But the false Merkavah mystic has only to be invited once. He almost tries to force his way into the palace, but the angels stand in his way and throw upon him thousands of iron bars. Another test is the one at the gate of the sixth palace. Here the gatekeepers throw upon the descender unto the Merkavah something that looks like thousands upon thousands waves of water. But in reality there is not even a drop of water there. If he asks: "What are these waters", the angels pursue him and reproach him: "Worthless man, are you of the seed of those who kissed the golden calf,[70] and thus unworthy of beholding

---

[66] Professor G. Scholem has rightly recognized the connection between the Psalm of Habakkuk and the Merkavah speculations.

[67] The last words—"who is called after the name of his master—are frequently found in connection with Metatron. See Scholem, *Jewish Gnosticism* etc., pp. 46 ff.

[68] The English translation is basically that printed in G. Scholem, *Jewish Gnosticism* etc., p. 62, though several changes have been introduced into it.

[69] The term "Song of the Throne" is mentioned in MS. Vatican 228, and in the famous responsum of Rav Haj Gaʾon (in Lewin, *Otzar Ha-Geonim* to *Ḥagigah*, p. 24).

[70] For the picture of Israel kissing the golden calf, see *Pirkei de-Rabbi ʾEliʿezer*,

the King and His Throne?". Thereupon a voice from heaven declares this suspicion to be justified, and they throw upon him thousands of iron bars.[71] A similar test is described in *Hekhalot Zutreti*, and its connection to a saying attributed to Rabbi 'Akiva in *Talmud Bavli Ḥagigah* 14b has already been discussed above in Chapter Three.[72] The text ends with another hymn at the end of which Metatron and his eight secret names are mentioned.[73]

The last part of *Hekhalot Rabbati* does not belong to the main body of the text. With chapter xxvii begins the famous *Sar-Torah* section, which generally consists of five chapters. It deals with the secret, magical method of studying the Torah and memorizing that study. As a number of Merkavah texts deal with that subject, it seems that the problems discussed in the *Sar-Torah* obstinately occupied the minds of the *Hekhalot* mystics. *Sar-Torah* passages are found in *Hekhalot Zutreti*, in *Ma'aseh Merkavah*, in *Merkavah Rabbah*, in *Sefer Hekhalot* (*3 Enoch*) and in the *Hekhalot* fragments published by the present writer. It may be argued that these *Sar-Torah* passages belonged to a period where real mystical experiences were no more practised, and new applications had to be found for the old theurgical practices.[74] The text of *Sar-Torah* in the appendix to *Hekhalot Rabbati* is in the form of a dialogue between God, the People of Israel and the angels. The pseudo-historical circumstances are the days of the construction of the Second Temple.[75] The speakers, however, are once again the pseudepigraphical *Hekhalot* mystics: Rabbi Yishma'el

---

xlv: "Rabbi Yehudah said: Sama'el entered into it (= the golden calf) ... and when Israel saw it, they all kissed it ...". For kissing as a kind of idolatry see *Mishnah Sanhedrin* vii,6.

[71] See *2 Samuel* xii,31.

[72] Professor Z. Werblowski drew my attention to the fact that in the *Amitâyur-Dhyâna-Sûtra*, paragraph 10, a series of meditations is enumerated, the second one of which—after the perception of the sun—is the preception of water, "clear and pure". Then follows the perception of ice, and as "thou seest the ice shining and transparent, thou shouldst imagine the appearance of lapis Lazuli". See *Sacred Books of the East* XLIX part 2, p. 170. See also the writer's article "Mysticism, Science and Art", *Leonardo* VII (1974), pp. 123-130.

[73] The number eight here is certainly significant. See, Scholem, *Jewish Gnosticism* etc., p. 102, n. 6; and D. Sperber, "Ligaturae: Something about Amulets in the Talmudic Period" (in Hebrew), in *The Bar Ilan Yearbook* XIII (1976), p. 128, n. 21.

[74] See E. E. Urbach in *Studies in Mysticism and Religion Presented to Gershom G. Scholem*, Hebrew Section, pp. 23 ff.

[75] The expression used here for the Second Temple—*Ha-Bayit Ha-Aḥaron*—is taken from *Haggai* ii,9.

and Rabbi ʿAkiva, who speaks in the name of Rabbi ʾEliʿezer Ha-Gadol.

The text begins with the statement that although the Torah had been given on Mount Sinai, its splendour and glory were not revealed until the days of the Second Temple. The splendour and glory of the Torah evidently are the oral law. This is a remarkable statement, since the customary Jewish concept of the oral law is that it was given to Moses together with the written law.[76] When the people saw, so the text says, that two tasks—that of building the Temple and that of studying the Torah—were laid upon them simultaneously, they were constrained to complain to their Father in Heaven. The two tasks were too much for them, they said, so they wanted to know which of the two they could abandon. God's answer to that complaint is quite remarkable. God is quoted as saying that as long as His people were in exile they did not study the Torah, and now He desires to hear "the voice of my Torah from your mouth". In addition, it is reported that God told His People that it was improper for them to disobey His commandments and that consequently He had to drive them into exile, and that He repented of His rash judgement against His people. As for their complaint itself, He thinks that it is justified, and is thus ready to compensate them for the extra toil put upon them. They only have to express their wish and God will supply everything from His infinite store-houses. Since God is aware of the fact that the People of Israel wish to study the Torah intensively, He is ready to do everything in His power to make them famous and respected throughout the whole world. For that purpose He gives them "a seal" and "a crown", that is, theurgical means, to use whenever they study the Torah. In this manner neither fool nor stupid man will be found in their number.

But, in contradistinction to the theurgical practices of the descent unto the Merkavah, it is here said that the theurgical practice which should be applied in the study of the Torah is a secret. God remarks that His servants, the angels, are sad about its being revealed. In addition, not only the jealousy of the angels is aroused by that revelation, but actually everybody on earth that is informed about this secret practice becomes envious. In fact, with the knowledge of the Torah come fame, riches and respect. It now becomes clear that

[76] For the development of this concept in Judaism see E. E. Urbach, *The Sages*, pp. 286 ff.

"the People of Israel" to whom God is reportedly speaking are in reality the mystics of the Merkavah, to whom it is promised that they will become the real leaders of the People. With this we actually return to the beginning of *Hekhalot Rabbati* where the qualities and virtues of the mystics are listed. It has been pointed out in our discussion there that these extraordinary qualities which are attributed to the Merkavah mystic probably belong to a period when no real mystical visions were anymore experienced. This alleged devaluation of the mystical experience had to be made up for in some manner, and hence the attempt to allure those who would carry on the tradition, by the promise of special social status and economic security. This part of the *Sar-Torah* ends with God remarking that the angels opposed His decision to reveal these theurgical means.

The essence of the angel's opposition is that if these secrets were revealed, men would actually become like angels. It is proper for the Torah to be studied with great effort; and it is to the glory of the Creator if people, because they forget what they have studied, have to repeat it constantly. People should pray to God to preserve their learning in their minds. "But if you reveal that secret to your sons, a young man will be like an old one, and a fool like a wise man". The angels seem to reflect in their words the opposition of certain Jewish circles who criticized the practices and possibly also the arrogance of the mystics. God, nevertheless, decided to disclose the secret to "the faithful seed", so as to compensate His People for their troubles in the exile. God has already given His People everything that he has in His storehouses: gold, silver, precious stones and all kinds of foods. "But what is the world still lacking?—This secret and this mystery!" After this secret had been revealed, so the story goes, the people returned to building the temple. However, it is stressed that God did not reveal His secret before His People forced Him by an oath to do so. They refrained from putting "one stone upon the other in the temple" before God acceded to their request. The text tells how God descended on His throne into the temple, and this only when the skeleton of the building was finished. This allegedly was to prove Haggai's prophecy (ii,9) that the glory of the second temple would be even greater than that of the first one.

Thus the author of the *Sar-Torah* believes that the revelation of the oral law together with the theurgical means of practising it distinguishes the days of the second temple from those of the first one. The actual theurgical means mentioned in the *Sar-Torah* appended to *Hekhalot Rabbati* are comparatively scanty. Those enumerated in *Merkavah Rabbah* and in *Ma'aseh Merkavah* are much more detailed ones. The essence of them all is that one has to prepare oneself by observing absolute ritual cleanliness and special diets or even fasts. In the *Sar-Torah* of *Hekhalot Rabbati* the preparatory practices are said to last twelve days, during which one has to live in absolute seclusion. Special prayers are to be said three times a day in the course of which the *Sar-Torah* (= the Minister of Law) is conjured by twelve secret names. "And when the twelve days have passed he may engage in every activity he wishes in connection with the study of the Law: whether it is Scripture, the Mishnah or the Talmud, and even beholding the Merkavah. For he now lives in purity and in asceticism. For it is a lesson in our hands, an ordinance of the patriarchs and a tradition of the ancient ones who wrote and issued the decree for future generations to the effect that only modest people may use it. And he who is worthy is answered when using it". It should be noticed that beholding the Merkavah is here considered a part of the *Sar-Torah*!

The last part of the *Sar-Torah* tells how Rabbi 'Eli'ezer Ha-Gadol performed the practice and was answered; but he did not trust its efficacy. Even Rabbi Yishma'el did not trust its efficacy before he brought a stupid man who went through the practice "and he became like me". Then it was performed by simple and unlearned shepherds and they likewise were successful. Finally Rabbi 'Akiva was sent to the diaspora and the secret of the *Sar-Torah* turned out to be efficacious even there. It is quite obvious that this last remark in connection with Rabbi 'Akiva was to indicate that people in Babylonia were anxious to show that the Merkavah practice was not limited to the Country of Israel. On the contrary, there are a number of instances—some of which will be discussed later on—which make it clear that in later days the Merkavah lore was mainly practised in the diaspora, first in Babylonia and then in Italy.[77] It is from Italy that the Merkavah tradition was transmitted to the circles of the German Ḥasidim.[78] Parallel to the transmission of the Merkavah lore to the diaspora we

---

[77] See, for instance, the Merkavah material incorporated in *Megillat Ahima'az*, ed. B. Klar, Jerusalem, Tarshish Books, 1973. The "Scroll" describes events which happened in Oria, in South Italy.

[78] See G. Scholem, *Kabbalah*, Jerusalem, Keter Publishing House, 1974, p. 33.

find the *Sar-Torah* speculations developed in the circles of the Ge'onim and the German Ḥasidim of the Middle Ages.[79]

[79] See G. Scholem, *Jewish Gnosticism* etc., p. 13. Scholem also assumes that "it is ... quite plausible that procedures for getting this angel (= of the *Sar-Torah*) to impart some of his treasures to the students of the Law could have been very old". But he admits that "we may safely assume that many of the injunctions for a perfect knowledge of the Law do in fact belong to a later stage".

MERKAVAH RABBAH

This is a compilation of several technical and difficult Merkavah texts. Its main subject matter is the theurgical techniques of adjuring angels to descend on earth and to reveal secrets to man. In this respect, *Merkavah Rabbah* has a number of similarities to the *Sar-Torah* practices as described in the chapters bearing that name and annexed to *Hekhalot Rabbati*. *Merkavah Rabbah* is printed in Musajoff's collection of Merkavah texts, *Merkavah Shelemah*, and it is also known from a number of manuscripts.[1] Our quotations here are from the manuscripts.

The text begins with a question which Rabbi 'Akiva asks Rabbi Eliezer Ha-Gadol: "How is the Minister of the Countenance adjured to descend on earth and to reveal to man the secrets of heaven and earth...?" Rabbi Eliezer's answer is: "My son, I once caused him to descend and he wanted to destroy the whole world. He is the most magnificent angel in the heavenly family, and is always standing and ministering to God...". What this answer seems to imply is that mystical experiences which are inadequately undertaken are liable to bring disaster. We have already seen that unworthy mystics were liable to endanger themselves in the course of the heavenly journeys which they should not have undertaken. In our case, the adjured angel threatens to bring destruction on "the whole world". However, the words "the whole world" may be understood metaphorically as implying the mystic only. It is not said what had been done wrong that aroused the angel's wrath, but his hostile behaviour is no surprise to those who should know of the angels' hostile attitude to men. However, the text goes into great detail to describe what should be done to control the angel and to protect oneself from his threats. It soon becomes clear that, as in the case of the ascending mystic so also in our case the mystic adjuring angels to descend has to seal himself with special protective magical seals. In our case, the prescribed seal is that of the Name of the Forty-Two Letters,[2] upon

---

[1] See Scholem, *Jewish Gnosticism* etc., p. 6, n. 15.

[2] The question what is the Name of the Forty-Two Letters has not yet been conclusively settled and this in spite of the recent article published on the subject by L. H. Schiffman in the *Bulletin of the Institute of Jewish Studies* I (1973), pp. 97-102. In fact, one can find in magical literature a variety of ways in which the rather enigmatic name of Forty-Two Letters—first mentioned in a tradition that allegedly goes back to temple times—was to be rendered. See *Bavli Qidushin* 71a.

the sealing of which on himself the practitioner has to say a special prayer: "I adjure you and constrain you by an oath to continue to be bound to my will... and fulfil my wish: Do not frighten me, and do not make me tremble... And I shall be strengthened so that the oath shall be pronounced properly and the Name shall be well ordered in my mouth[3]... Thus I shall not be devoured by the fire, by the blaze, by the storm and by the whirlwind which are accompanying you".

But even before the seal is applied and its prayer is said, certain preparations have to be made by the mystic. Again we hear of fasts, ritual baths and incantations which constitute the mystic's practice of self-preparation. Thus, we realize that as a matter of theurgical practice there was no essential difference between the means prescribed in the case of ascensions and those to be followed when angels were adjured to descend on earth. Yet, it seems that in the case of the adjuration of an angel more room is allowed for describing the magical names and their applications. In fact, there are two sets of names: the one which is said in the manner called *Meforash* and the other in the manner referred to as *Kinuy*.[4] The Name—*Meforash* generally is a name of an angel taken from the more or less common inventory of angelic names, while the name in the *Kinuy*-mode is a *nomen barbarum* to which certain combinations of the letters Y, H and W are added.[5] The number of these double-names in our case is

---

[3] The meaning of this request most probably is that the forty-two letters of the Holy Name should be said in the right order.

[4] Professor Scholem explains *Meforash* as "a secret name" while *Kinuy* is understood by him as meaning "a name that may be pronounced". See in *Zeitschrift für die Neutestamentliche Wissenschaft* XXX (1931), p. 175. However, this habit of giving double-names to deities, and then to angels in magical practices, seems to be very old. In Jewish tradition we know that the name of God was pronounced in one way in the temple and in another way out of the temple. See *Mishnah Sotah* vii,6 and *Tamid* vii,2. See also *Mishnah Sanhedrin* vii,5 and the discussions in both Talmuds: *Bavli* 56a ff.; *Yerushalmi* 25a ff. Since there is a vast literature on the subject, so suffice it here to mention only J. Z. Lauterbach, "Substitutes for the Tetragrammaton", *Proceedings of the American Academy for Jewish Research* II (1930-31), p. 39 ff.; and Z. Ben Hayyim in *Sefer Eretz Yisrael* III (1954) p. 147 ff. (in Hebrew). It seems that in later magical literature the magicians, or writers, praised themselves with the knowledge of the double reading of the names without paying to much attention to the fact which of the two was the secret one.

[5] Sometimes, however, the difference between the two kinds of names is hardly discernable. Thus, for example, we find the name *Meforash* KNGIALIYA, and its *Kinuy* ẒẒMKHT SYYHU YH WYHWH. The only difference can be observed in the addition of Y-H-W-element in the case of the *Kinuy*-name.

fourteen, four of which are said to be engraved on the heads of the Holy Creatures, four on the four corners of the Throne, four on the four crowns of the *Ofanim* who stand opposite of the Holy Creatures, and two are engraved on the crown of God. Curiously, the names which are said to be thus engraved are not identical with the ones that are uttered in the course of the previously mentioned adjurations. After the names have been uttered, the mystic repeats his request: "I swear you, I constrain you and bind you to hasten and to descend to me I, N. son of N., you and not your messenger. And when you descend, I should not be driven out of my mind. And reveal to me all the hidden things that are on high and below... as a man who speaks to his friend".

However, it appears, one round of incantations and all that they contain seems not to have had its desired effect, and the mystic is compelled to repeat: "Once again I call you with five names, the holiest ones of your names... you have been ordered by God that when you hear an oath containing these names, you will do honour to your name. And hasten and do the will of the one who adjures you. And if you delay, I shall push you into a river of fire,[6] and replace you by another one who is under your command...". But even this turns out to be insufficient; the angel still seems not to be constrained, so the mystic invokes him again: "I call you once again, in the greatest of your names, a lovely and pleasant (name), (by which you are called) in the name of your Master. Your name has one letter less than His,[7] and by that name He created and founded everything and sealed by it all the work of His hands".[8]The first part of *Merkavah Rabbah* ends with what seems to be a prayer which should be said on the angel's departure: "Ascend in peace, and I shall not be terrified at the hour of your departure from me". Again names are to be uttered in combination with certain phrases from Scripture.

The second part of *Merkavah Rabbah* contains two prayers called

---

[6] The word used here for river, *Rigyon*, is not clear. See Y. Levy, *Studies in Jewish Hellenism* (in Hebrew), Jerusalem, Bialik Institute, 1969, pp. 264-265, who suggests to interpret the word as the stream of lava flowing from a volcano.

[7] In the *Hekhalot* fragments published by the present writer in *Tarbiz* XXXVIII, pp. 257-358, it is said that the secret name of God contains five letters: TNR'EL! In that case the name of the angel here is of four letters.

[8] Again it is said that the name has two modes. This time they are called *Perush* and *Leshon Tohorah*. These two modes are to all likelihood parallel to the ones mentioned before.

"The Great Seal" and "The Awesome Crown".[9] There is nothing particularly magical about these prayers, though it is said in the name of Rabbi Yishmael: "Everybody who practises the Great Seal and Awesome Crown [10] and does not say prayers on each of them is likely to be hurt".

The third part of the book contains a mystical elaboration on the short Synadelphon passage in *Bavli Ḥagigah* 13b. Briefly, the "Secret of Synadelphon", as it is here called, is the theurgical practice that is to bring illumination (*'Or*) into the mystic's heart.[11] In all likelihood, what is here meant is an inner illumination concerning the study of the Torah, that is a practice similar to the one of the *Sar-Torah* which is also sometimes called *Or-Torah* (= the Light of the Torah).[12] New in our passage is the fact that the names of the angels are not only said but also written down. The practice of writing the names of angels for theurgical purposes is also known from the *Sar-Torah* passages in the *Maʿaseh Merkavah* published by G. Scholem[13] and is also frequent in magical texts, such as *Sefer Ha-Razim*.

Following this *Sar Torah* section comes another section which contains a series of prescriptions for magical practices, mainly those performed on certain dates throughout the year. There are prescriptions for practices which are performed on the Jewish Feast of the Weeks (*Shavuʿot*), on New Year Day, on New Moon Day and on the first day of the Month of *'Adar*. It seems that these practices are connected with the prediction of events, at least nothing to the contrary is indicated in the text. The common procedure in all these practices is that the practitioner writes the names on leaves of plants or on his finger nails and then puts them into his mouth so as to delete the holy names with his saliva. Only the practice of the first

---

[9] This part is not printed in *Merkavah Shelemah* 3a. However, the prayer of the Awesome Crown is printed thereafter on page 6a (at the beginning of *Hekhalot Zutreti*). [See also above p. 167), n. 62].

[10] Here the terms are used to indicate certain theurgical practices which are not described in the text. See *Hekhalot Rabbati* xxviii,3-4 (*Sar-Torah*).

[11] In this respect, it is interesting to compare this passage with the ones containing the phrase "to lighten one's heart" and the like in the Qumran writings, 1 QS II,3; IV,2 etc. See now M. Kister, "Levi = Light" (in Hebrew), *Tarbiẓ* XLV (1976), pp. 327-330.

[12] That this is the case can be seen from the five shepherds which are mentioned here and at the end of the *Sar-Torah* sections appended to *Hekhalot Rabbati*.

[13] Interestingly, the angel Synadelphon is also mentioned there—together with Metatron—in a similar context. See *Maʿaseh Merkavah*, paragraph 19, p. 111.

day of the last month of the year, *ʾAdar*,[14] breaks this rule: In this particular case the names are written on the inside of a silver bowl and then wine is poured into it in order to delete the names. It seems that the deletion of the names here is not part of the practice itself, but on the contrary, marks it cessation.[15] The power of the spell or the charm is broken when the names are deleted.[16] But we know from *Sefer Ha-Razim* that in certain cases the ink with which holy names were written was deleted in oil and then a charm was said over that oil.[17]

The next section of the text is again devoted to the *Sar-Torah*.[18] What is of particular interest in this part of the text is that it establishes the alleged sequence of the esoteric tradition in Judaism: God "revealed the secrets of the secrets and the mysteries of the mysteries to Moses, and Moses to Joshuʿa, and Joshuʿa to the Elders, and the Elders to the Prophets, and the Prophets to the *Ḥasidim* (the Pious Ones), and the *Ḥasidim* to those who feared God,[19] and those who feared God to the Men of the Great Assembly, and the Men of the Great Assembly revealed them to all the People of Israel.[20] And the People of Israel were learning with their help the Torah and multiplying its study". The fact that the secret of the *Sar-Torah* was revealed to all the People of Israel reminds of the *Sar-Torah* text appended to

---

[14] It seems that the magical year began in *Nissan*; see *Sefer Ha-Razim*, p. 101 (lines 13-14). New Year Day, however, signifies the first of *Tishri*. See further *Mishnah Rosh Ha-Shanah* i,1. See also S. Lieberman, *Tosefta Ki-Fshutah* to *Rosh Ha-Shanah*, pp. 1017 ff.

[15] However, the unfaithful woman (*Sotah*) is brought to test by drinking the water of bitterness into which the priest washes off curses written on a scroll. These curses contain the Holy Name. See *Numbers* v,16 ff., and *Mishnah Sotah*, chapter ii. The water of bitterness which contains the washed-off ink in which the holy name was written has no holiness whatever and may be spilt, if the woman admits her unfaithfulness before she drinks of it. See *Tosefta Sotah* ii,2.

[16] In *Sefer Ha-Razim* we find magical practices which entail the saying of names or charms on vessels of water. See Margalioth's Introduction p. 5 (where also parallels from the *Papyri Graecae Magicae* are quoted).

[17] See *Sefer Ha-Razim*, pp. 71-72; 102.

[18] In MS. Oxford 1531 it is preceded by the story of the four who entered the Pardes. This version of the story is the same one as the one in *Hekhalot Zutreti*. In *Merkavah Shelemah* we find instead of the Pardes-story an interpolation of a mystical-eschatological nature which is also printed in *Bet Ha-Midrasch* V, pp. 167 ff.; and in *Midreshei Geʾulah* (ed. Even Shemuel), pp. 3 ff.

[19] Obviously, the term "those who feared God" (*Yirʾei Ha-Shem*) is not used here in its ancient technical sense as "half proselytes". On the technical use of the term see, for instance, S. Pines in the *Proceedings of the Israel Academy of Sciences and Humanities* II/7 (1967).

[20] The dependence of this list on *Mishnah ʾAvot* i,1 is self-evident.

Hekhalot Rabbati. However, we saw there that the words "all the People" could be understood in a less democratic way; in fact, they seemed to imply there the "aristocracy" of the Merkavah mystics.

In connection with this *Sar-Torah* section another section dealing with the same subject is introduced.[21] Rabbi Yishma'el tells how at the age of thirteen Rabbi Neḥunyah ben Ha-Qanah saw him "in great grief". The reason for that grief was that Rabbi Yishma'el was quickly forgetting all his studies. Nothing that Rabbi Yishma'el did helped in bringing about a change in that sad condition. He was leading an ascetic way of life and still no change occurred. So Rabbi Neḥunyah ben Ha-Qanah took him from his father's house, brought him to the temple, and there made him take the Oath of the Great Seal. As it happened, this oath was the one of the Secret of the Torah. Immediately, so the pseudohistorical story goes, Rabbi Yishma'el experienced an illumination of the Torah and thus he no longer forgot his studies. Evidently, Rabbi Yishma'el felt himself as if born anew and "everyday it seemed to me as if I was standing before the Throne of the Glory". This last remark is a most interesting one: it betrays the fact that the *Sar-Torah* experience was considered a substitute for the ascension unto the heavenly Merkavah. When Rabbi ʿAkiva saw all this, he told Rabbi Yishma'el to return to Rabbi Neḥunyah ben Ha-Qanah and to ask him to reveal the details of that particular practice. Rabbi Neḥunyah gave the following answer: "Go back and report the following answer: The servants are sworn in the name of their king and the slave [22] is sworn in the name of his master". Rabbi ʿAkiva easily understood this hint and consequently "his mouth pronounced names while his fingers were counting a hundred and eleven times".

Merkavah Rabbah ends with a detailed description, attributed to Rabbi Yishma'el, of how the practice of the *Sar-Torah* should be carried out. It is made clear that the main practice is to be performed in the morning when one gets out of bed. Then one should wash one's hands twice and anoint them with oil. Then one puts on the *Tefilin* and stands before one's bed to pray. It again becomes

---

[21] This section bears strong resemblance to the *Sar-Torah* paragraphs in *Maʿaseh Merkavah*, §§ 11 ff.

[22] It soon becomes clear that the slave, ʿ*Eved*, is Metatron. For the appellation ʿ*Eved* as directed to Metatron, see H. Odeberg, *3 Enoch* x, p. 28, n. (3). The text which Odeberg identifies there as "Hekhalot Zotreti" in the Oxford MS. is in fact—as has already been recognized by G. Scholem—nothing but our *Merkavah Rabbah*.

clear that the theurgical prayers are said in the course of the daily prayers which every Jew is expected to say. In addition to the names and theurgical prayers said in the course of the adjuration of the *Sar-Torah*, one has to lead an ascetic life for forty days. It is important to notice that in one of the concluding sentences of the text it is reported that Rabbi ʿAkiva learnt all this from before of the Throne of Glory and was told to teach the secret to his colleagues. This is reminiscent of what is said in *Hekhalot Rabbati* about Rabbi ʿAkiva and the special manner in which he learnt the heavenly songs.

MA'ASEH MERKAVAH

This is the text which Professor Scholem published in Appendix C to his *Jewish Gnosticism, Merkavah Mysticism and Talmudic Tradition.*[1] The text is an interesting combination of two kinds of Merkavah traditions: heavenly ascents and adjurations of angels in connection with the *Sar-Torah* practices. Our quotations will be according to the paragraph division in Scholem's edition.

The first part of the book consists of paragraphs 1-10. Its main subject matter is the incantations that should be said before and in the course of the ascensions. This part also contains a description of the seven *Hekhalot.* The text begins with a question which Rabbi Yishmael asked Rabbi 'Akiva: "What is the prayer which one should pray when one ascends (!) to the Merkavah?". In answer to that, a short prayer is quoted in which the mystic blesses God for revealing the secrets to Moses. As we know from other texts, the "secrets" mentioned here should be understood in a technical sense: they are magical or theurgical practices. In paragraph 3 Rabbi 'Akiva describes the heavenly bridges on which the singing angels stand. These bridges connect the vestibules of all the *Hekhalot* and they are stretched "like a bridge across the river so that everybody may cross them".[2] There are a hundred and twenty million of such bridges, half of which are stretched above the vestibule and the other half below. There are also rivers of fire, rivers of hailstone, treasuries of snow and wheels of fire—all of which encircle the angels that stand on the bridges.

In paragraph 4 the question is asked: "How can one look at them?" To This Rabbi 'Akiva replies: "I prayed a prayer of compassion, and in this manner I was saved". It is said that he who wants to study

[1] The first edition of the book was published in 1960. Before the publication of the Second Improved Edition the present writer has reexamined the manuscripts from which Professor Scholem printed the text of Appendix C. However, for technical reasons not all the corrections could be introduced into the text. In addition to MSS. Oxford and New York which were used by Professor Scholem, one has to refer to MSS. Munich 22 and 40, both of which contain only parts of the text.

[2] The paragraphs which describe these bridges are also printed separately in *Bet Ha-Midrasch* VI, pp. 153-154, and as chapter 22b and c in Odeberg's edition of *3 Enoch*. See further G. Scholem, *Major Trends in Jewish Mysticism*, p. 71; and *Hekhalot Rabbati* xiii,1.

this secret (of the ascension) should "learn it every day at dawn, and he should clean himself of all injustice, fraud and evil, so that ROZAYA, Lord God of Israel, will do him justice every day in this world... and it is promised that he will enjoy future life". There follows the first of the Merkavah hymns which the text contains. It should be noticed that *Maʿaseh Merkavah* contains two types of hymns: The first type lacks the ecstatic quality of the hymns we meet in *Hekhalot Rabbati* and thus resembles common religious poetry. These hymns are written like Psalms, giving expression to the poet's praise of God and enumerating His omnipotence and omniscience. The mystical setting comes to the fore almost in passing when the angels and their heavenly duties are referred to or described. A typical example of this kind of Merkavah hymns is the famous "*ʿAlenu le-Shabeʿaḥ*" ("we have to give praise") which is also known from the daily Jewish prayerbook.[3] Had it not been for their context, we would not even have noticed the relationship of this type of hymns to the *Hekhalot* literature. The other type of hymns included in *Maʿaseh Merkavah* is that of the series of "prayers" at the end of the book (paragraphs 26-33). These "prayers" are a classic example of Merkavah hymns. What is particularly interesting in them are the long series of magical and theurgical *voces* which they contain. In this respect they resemble the magical prayers, the ἐπαοιδαι, of the magical papyri. In tone and structure these "prayers" also resemble the hymns of *Hekhalot Rabbati*, the only difference being that the latter do not contain the lists of magical names. It may thus be argued that the "prayers" of *Maʿaseh Merkavah* are the only ones of their kind that so clearly expose their theurgical function. In fact, one may argue that what the hymns of *Hekhalot Rabbati* practically lack is that very theurgical element so forcefully displayed in the hymns of *Maʿaseh Merkavah*. Indeed, the question arises whether the *Hekhalot Rabbati* hymns were not actually deprived of those so-to-speak non-poetical elements. If that is so, though there is no evidence for it in any of the manuscripts, then the *Maʿaseh Merkavah* "prayers" represent a more original phase of *Hekhalot* hymnology than do their counterparts in *Hekhalot-Rabbati*.[4]

[3] In *Maʿaseh Merkavah* this prayer is introduced in the singular form *ʿAlai* (I have to) instead of the plural form known from the prayer books. See also I. Elbogen, *Der jüdische Gottesdienst*, Reprint: Hildesheim, Olms, 1962, pp. 80-81, 143.

[4] See, however, A. Altman in *Melilah* II (1946), p. 8 ff. (in Hebrew), who thinks that the second type of the hymns of *Maʿaseh-Merkavah* belongs to a later

The theurgical function of the hymns belonging to the first type is nevertheless indicated in the several utterances which accompany them. Thus, for instance, we read: "Rabbi ʿAkiva said: After I had prayed this prayer, I saw 6400000000 angels of glory standing before the Throne of Glory and I saw the knot of the *Tefillin* of Gedudiya,[5] Lord God of Israel, and I gave praise with all my limbs" (paragraph 5).[6] In another place it is again said in the name of Rabbi ʿAkiva: "Blessed is the man who stands and with all his power sings hymns to Barukhiya, Lord God of Israel. He gazes at the Merkavah and sees all that is done before the Throne of Glory upon which Barukhiya, Lord God of Israel, is sitting" (paragraph 8). And in paragraph 9 we read: "In the sixth palace I said the *Qedushah* before Him who said and created (the world); and He ordered that none of the Angels of the Service should destroy me". This last quotation refers us to one of the most interesting problems connected with the *Hekhalot* hymns. It is generally believed that there is a strong connection between these hymns and the *Qedushah* poems in the prayerbook. That the *Qedushah* (*Isaiah* vi,3 and *Ezekiel* iii,12) is a very old element in Jewish liturgy need not be proved here. We know that one of the first literary documents in which the angelic hymnology was taken as a model for human liturgy is the one in the angelic liturgy at Qumran, which in turn should be viewed within the general context of Jewish apocalyptic.[7] But this does not mean that the idea of the correspondence between celestial hymnology and human liturgical service is a registered patent of the apocalyptists. As far as we know, the apoc-

---

age than the first one. If Scholem's view, that the theurgical elements of the *Hekhalot* literature belong to the earliest stratum of that literature, is correct, then there is no basis for Altman's view. See Scholem, *Jewish Gnosticism* etc., p. 75: "The theurgical element was not a later addition to the texts but a basic component, one which the editors of such books as the Greater Hekhaloth, *3 Enoch*, and the *Massekheth Hekhalot* attempted to minimize or to discard entirely." Scholem recognizes the importance of *Maʿaseh Merkavah*, but I am reluctant to agree with him that the text represents a stage of "a progressive hyperthrophy of this (theurgical) material as to amount to a process of degeneration" (*ibid.*).

[5] Interestingly, the attribute of Synadelphon, who crowns God with the *Tefilin* as described in *Merkavah Rabbah* (based on the story in *Bavli Hagigah* 13b), is *Gedud*. See in *Merkavah Shelemah* 1a (beginning).

[6] In *Bavli Ḥagigah* 13b it is noticed that nobody can see God, and consequently it is impossible to crown God with His *Tefilin*. The solution suggested there is that Synadelphon actually conjures the *Tefilin* and they go up and place themselves on the right spot. In our text, it appears, Rabbi ʿAkiva is described as having been allowed to see more than the angel in *Ḥagigah*.

[7] See our discussion above in Chapter Two.

alyptists were mainly those who developed the *Qedushah* to what it became both in the *Hekhalot* writings and in the daily service. It is likely that those who composed the relevant sections in the prayer-book were familiar with so-called esoteric hymnology, but this again does not mean that everything in the prayer book that refers to the angels derives from apocalyptic or *Hekhalot* writings. On the other hand we may argue that at least in the case of some of the later *Hekhalot* writings, knowledge of the prayer book has to be assumed. But nothing absolutely certain in either direction can be proved and we may leave the issue open at this point assuming that Jewish liturgy and the *Hekhalot* writings were mutually influenced in their concepts of the earthly and heavenly *Qedushah*.

Where the concept of *Hekhalot* hymnology in *Ma'aseh Merkavah* also differs from its counterpart in *Hekhalot Rabbati* is in the fact that according to *Ma'aseh Merkavah* there are thousands upon thousands of chariots in each of the heavenly palaces which are said to give praise to God. The praise they give is not in the form of hymns but in the form of short doxologies, which remind of their counterpart in the various *Qedushah*-sections in the prayer book and in apocalyptic literature (see particularly *Ma'aseh Merkavah*, paragraph 6).

The second part of *Ma'aseh Merkavah* belongs to the *Sar-Torah* practices (paragraphs 11-22). It is probably the longest and most detailed *Sar-Torah* piece that we have, though in paragraph 17 an interesting transition from the *Sar-Torah* to the *Hekhalot* speculations occurs. Like the *Sar-Torah* section in *Merkavah Rabbah*, it begins with a statement made by Rabbi Yishma'el to the effect that everything that he is about to tell happened when at the age of thirteen [8] he was fasting in order to receive the revelation of the *Sar-Torah*. When Rabbi Neḥunyah ben Ha-Qanah disclosed the secrets of the *Sar-Torah*, that is, after Rabbi Yishma'el had received the necessary theurgical information as we find it explicated mainly in *Merkavah Rabbah* and in *Hekhalot Rabbati*, Suriyah, the Prince of the Countenance, revealed himself to Rabbi Yishma'el and told him: "The Prince (= Sar) of the Torah is called Yofiel,[9] and everybody who wants him (to appear) should fast for forty days.[10] He should eat his morsel

---

[8] See *Mishnah 'Avot* v,24.

[9] See S. Leiter, in: *Proceedings of the American Academy for Jewish Research* XLI-XLII (1973-1974), p. 144. However, this place escaped his eye.

[10] The forty days should be reminiscent of the forty days which Moses spent on Mount Sinai to receive the Torah. *Deuteronomy* ix,9: "I remained on the

in salt and eat nothing that defiles the body. He should immerse himself twenty-four times,[11] and he should not gaze on any coloured clothes.[12] He should cast his eyes at the ground only.[13] He should say his prayer with all his might, and concentrate himself on his prayer. He should seal himself with his seals and say twelve spells".[14]

Particular attention in the *Sar-Torah* practices of *Maʿaseh Merkavah* deserve the things which the mystic has to do in order to guard himself against evil demons (*Maziqim*). In fact, our text is one of the rare examples in the *Hekhalot* literature that refers to the evil spirits. Generally, we know, the mystic has to protect himself against the angels of destruction. These angels have no demonic role, and it is, thus, noteworthy that in *Maʿaseh Merkavah* special performances are devoted to the protection against those evil spirits. Thus, for example, we read: "He should lift his eyes to heaven so that he might not die. He should stand up and say a name and give praise, so that all his limbs should be sealed. Wisdom and insight are in his heart. He should offer a prayer to the *Sar-Torah.* And he should draw a circle on the ground [15] and stand in its midst, so that the evil spirits shall not come and appear to him as angels and kill him"! (paragraph 11, end). In another place, the practitioner asks for protection against destructive angels and evil spirits alike: "And I said three names... so that the angels and the evil spirits should not touch me" (paragraph 15, end).

---

mountain forty days and forty nights; I neither ate bread nor drank water". See also *1 Kings* xix,8. See also the discussion, above in Chapter Four.

[11] I find it difficult to account for that number.

[12] See *Mishnah Megillah* iv,8. It should, however, be noticed that coloured clothes worn by women were considered as having a tempting effect on men. See *Mishnah Zavin* ii,2; *Bavli Yevamot* 76a; *Bavli ʿAvodah Zarah* 20a-b. See also *Yalkut Shimʿoni* to *Bereshit*, paragraph 44. Compare *Ethiopic Enoch* viii,1 (Greek Version).

[13] For that kind of posture, see Scholem, *Major Trends in Jewish Mysticism*, p. 49.

[14] The Hebrew word used here is *Davar*, which in a magical context always means "a spell" or "a charm".

[15] The drawing of circles for magical purposes is a widespread technique. However, in the *Hekhalot* literature this is the only occurence of that particular practice. We know of Ḥoni, the circle maker, who drew a circle before he prayed to God for rain: "... I swear by Your great name that I shall not move until You have had mercy upon Your children". See *Mishnah Taʿanit* iii,8. In the light of what we have seen in the present study, the magical functions of Ḥoni's practice and prayer need no further comment. See A. Büchler, *Types of Jewish-Palestinian Piety*, Reprint: New York, Ktav Publishing House, 1968, pp. 196 ff. Büchler collected many relevant sources but was not aware of their connection to popular magic. See also the discussion in G. Alon, *Studies in Jewish History* I, Tel Aviv: 1957, pp. 194 ff. (in Hebrew).

In paragraph 14 Rabbi Yishma'el reports of an interesting, though somewhat terrifying, experience he has had: "I was fasting for twelve days, and when I realized that I could not endure it any longer, I used the name of forty-two letters and the angel PDKRS descended in anger. He said to me: 'You most disgraceful man, I am not going to give in before you sit (in fast) for forty days'. I was shocked and said three letters and he ascended... And I was fasting for forty days, praying three prayers in the morning, three at noon time and three in the evening, and every time I said twelve theurgical formulae. On the last day I prayed three times and said twelve "words". Consequently PDKRS, the Angel of the Countenance, and some angels of compassion, descended and planted wisdom into my heart".

Another theurgical practice is described in the Aramaic part of the book (paragraphs 18-20). It is again connected with the secret of the *Sar-Torah*, and in contradistinction to the other *Sar-Torah* practices this one should be performed at the beginning of the Month of *Sivan*. Here too the mystic has to perform the usual practices of fasting, special diets, immersion and praying. However, in this particular case new elements are added. First, it is said that the mystic should not sleep alone, so that he will not be harmed. This may be due to the role the evil spirits played in the mind of the writer(s) of this text. Then, the mystic has to take a leaf of a fig tree, three olive-leaves,[16] a silver goblet, some wine and an egg.[17] With everyone of these objects he has to perform magical practices. For example, the practitioner has to say the following adjuration on the leaf taken from the fig tree: "I adjure you, Synadelphon, the angel who ties a crown to his master, that you shall go up (!) and tell those two angels, Metatron and ʿAGMITYA, that they should (plant) wisdom into the heart of that man (= that is, the practitioner himself), so that I shall know and be wise, learn without forgetting, study without forgetting...". The other objects are used in similar manner.

Already before this Aramaic part of the book the text quotes another of Rabbi Yishma'el's questions: "I asked Rabbi Neḥunyah ben Ha-Qanah: when one says the twelve words how can one gaze at the glory of the *Shekhinah*?" [18] Here an interesting transition occurs:

---

[16] On the writing on olive-leaves see S. Lieberman, *Toseftā Ki-Fshutah to Shabbat*, p. 176, n. 29.

[17] For the use of eggs in magical practices see S. Daiches, *Babylonian Oil Magic in the Talmud and in Later Jewish Literature*, London, 1913, pp. 7 ff.

[18] Paragraph 17.

Rabbi Yishma'el inquires if the theurgical practice used in the case of the *Sar-Torah* is also applicable in the case of the descent unto the Merkavah. We have already observed that the *Sar-Torah* apparently developed from the Merkavah practices and that it probably was a substitute to the latter ones. Here we see that the mystic wants to reverse the process: from *Sar-Torah* theurgy to the Merkavah vision. Indeed, the subject of the Merkavah vision is again taken up in paragraph 21, but in paragraph 22 the two subjects are for a moment linked together again: "Rabbi Yishma'el said: When I received this information from Rabbi Neḥunyah ben Ha-Qanah I stood on my feet and asked him all the names of the ministers of wisdom (*Sarei HaHokhmah*).[19] As a result of that question I saw light in my heart comparable to the light of the first days of the creation of the world".[20] When Rabbi Yishma'el stood up and saw his face shining with his wisdom,[21] he uttered the names of all the angels that were guarding the seven palaces. However, the names of these angels are only seldom identical with the ones listed in *Hekhalot Rabbati* xv. The differences could be explained either by the existence of parallel traditions, or by the fact that in the course of their oral or written transmission these lists underwent changes. In addition, the distinction made in *Hekhalot Rabbati* as to the alternate lists of angels on the way in and on the way out is not repeated here.

The third part of *Ma'aseh Merkavah* is mainly devoted to the five prayers that should be said during the descent to and ascent from the Merkavah.[22] As already indicated above, these prayers include marked theurgical elements. The flow of each hymn is broken in the middle by lists of theurgical names and words. The text ends with two additional hymns which help the mystic gaze at the *Shekhinah* (paragraphs 32-33).

---

[19] This is a clear reference to the procedure described in *Hakhalot Rabbati* xxi,3.

[20] The literal translation here would be: "light . . . like the days of the heavens". However, my translation takes into account the aggadic sayings about the storing away of the light that was shining before the fourth day of the creation. See *Bereshit Rabba*, p. 21 and parallels.

[21] See *Sifre* to *Numbers* (ed. Horowitz), p. 44, paragraph 41 (beginning).

[22] Paragraphs 26-31.

"HEKHALOT" FRAGMENTS

These "*Hekhalot*" Fragments, published by the present writer in *Tarbiz* XXXVIII (1969), pp. 354-372,[1] from *Genizah* fragments at the University Library at Cambridge, are a clear proof that not all the once extant Merkavah texts reached us. Apparently, some of the writings were altogether lost; others were only fragmentarily preserved.[2] However, it seems that the basic texts, which had a wider circulation than the others, were preserved. The "*Hekhalot*" fragments which we shall discuss here seem to be part of two different compositions, and they are of special interest for a number of reasons. Firstly, although they extensively quote from *Hekhalot Rabbati*, they contain material that was hitherto unknown to us. Secondly, these fragments, at least the first one, contain historical—though enigmatic—references. Finally, they claim to be a systematic angelic revelation: it is the angel who describes the celestial world to the mystic, and not the mystic who experiences a heavenly ascent. The angel teaches the mystic "the study of the descent unto the Merkavah". It seems that the complete texts described the details of the descent from the very beginning, that is, from the stages of the preparation, until the entrance into the seventh *Hekhal*. Unfortunately, what was preserved of the texts belongs only to the last stage of the ascent. To make the loss even more painful, some of the lines are badly damaged and it is almost impossible to reconstruct them.

The MS begins with some mutilated lines which make no sense. Then follows a description of the creation of the world in the metaphorical terms of the weaver's work. The description derives from *Hekhalot Rabbati* xiv,1,[3] though some interesting details are added.[4] Then comes a considerably long passage (lines 13-23) which—in a

---

[1] Additional notes were published in *Tarbiz* XXXIX (1969), pp. 216-217.

[2] The present writer knows of more Genizah material relating to the *Hekhalot* literature which he hopes to publish in due course.

[3] See our discussion there.

[4] What is added is mainly the description of the whip with which God is described to have beaten heaven and earth after their creation. Professor S. Lieberman suggested to me that this part of the description is a reference to the stick which the weaver uses to harden the finished piece of cloth. See *Tosefta Shabbat* viii(ix),2, and S. Lieberman, *Tosefta Ki-Fshutah* to *Shabbat*, p. 107. However, the description as a whole still seems to be unclear.

highly enigmatic manner—refers to one of the leaders of Babylonian Jewry whose name, consisting of five letters, has been fixed from the days of the creation of the world. The whole passage sounds like political propaganda in favour of a certain leader who seeks divine support for the position for which he is campaigning, or else has to defend himself against some unidentified opponents (cf. *Hekhalot Rabbati* xxviii, 5).

In line 23 the angel turns to the Merkavah mystic and says: "And now return, my friend, to the study of the descent unto the Merkavah which I was explicating to you and teaching you: thus one descends and thus one ascends; this is the quality of the first *Hekhal*; and thus does one conjure, and thus does one adjure. For I have interrupted you! And now write it down and leave the seal of the descent unto the Merkavah to all the people of the world, and to everybody who wants to descend and cast a glance at the King and at His Beauty. He will take that path and see without being hurt. I have written it for you on a scroll, and you saw it, and then you descended and saw. You tried it out without being hurt, because I made all the paths of the Merkavah to you like light...". The passage speaks for itself. Here a unique procedure is recorded: the angel had taught the Merkavah mystic all the necessary things in connection with the mystical ascent; the mystic then followed his instructions, and afterwards the angel and the mystic met for a further discussion of the matters involved. No similar procedure is known from any of the other *Hekhalot* writings.

Then follows a long section (lines 28-38) which describes the various dangers and temptations that might befall the Merkavah mystic in his passage from one *Hekhal* to the other. In fact, the mystic resembles a man who loses his way in a wood and suddenly arrives at a place full of all kinds of beasts which attack him and threaten to tear him to pieces. However, the mystic who uses his seals correctly is not hurt. In line 38 we find the angel turning to the mystic: "And return, my friend, to the theurgical means,[5] about which you have been warned concerning the sixth *Hekhal*... so that you shall not be destroyed". The angel describes the various kinds of fires emerging from the seventh *Hekhal*, and he tells the mystic that when he sees

[5] The term used here is *Siman*, (Greek: σῆμα) which may be taken here to refer to the seal(s) with which the mystic protects himself against the hostile angels. However, similar terminology is used in *Hekhalot Zutreti* (in MS. New York [Jewish Theological Seminary] Mic. 8128, fol. 23a), and there the *Siman* is used in the sense of warning.

these fires, he should step aside and not stand in the middle of the doorway. However, knowing that the mystic will be frightened by that vision, the angel gives him the following instructions. "If you are standing, sit; and if you are sitting, lie down; and if you are lying on your back, lie with your face down; and if you are lying with your face down, stick the nails of your fingers and your toes into the ground of the firmament. And put cotton in your ears, and cotton in your nose, and cotton in your rectum so that your soul shall not depart from your body until I come [to your rescue]...!" This again is a most extraordinary description, and no parallel to it is found in any of the other *Hekhalot* texts.

The greatest part of the text (pp. 361-367) describes what is happening in the seventh *Hekhal*. Again, many lines in the manuscript are badly damaged, but their subject matter seems to be the various steps the angel takes to rescue the mystic. When the mystic enters the seventh *Hekhal* he sees Metatron (*Na'ar*) coming from behind the Throne of Glory. His appearance is a most wonderful one, and he places the mystic on a seat before the Throne of Glory. A great deal that is said in the text hereafter is in the form of short remarks on various mystical subjects. Among the subjects mentioned is the *Sar-Torah* (p. 366, lines 36-37).[6] In another place (p. 369, line 20) the *Sar-Talmud* is mentioned. It appears that our text maintained the traditional connection between the Merkavah material and the *Sar-Torah* speculation. We cannot end this short description of the text without pointing out its elaborate angelology. Many of the names of the angels mentioned in the text are unknown from other sources. In addition, some of the mystical names attributed to God in our text are likewise unknown from parallel sources.

With all its curiosities and oddities, the "*Hekhalot*" Fragments seem to represent a hitherto unknown line of development within the Merkavah tradition. On the one hand, we find in it long quotations from *Hekhalot Rabbati*,[7] and on the other hand great portions of the text display completely new *Hekhalot* material. The colophon, which is partly preserved, mentions the "seven great and little palaces", which could well be a reference to *Hekhalot Rabbati* ("The Greater *Hekhalot*") and to *Hekhalot Zutreti* ("The Smaller *Hekhalot*"), thus indicating some of the sources of the text or its all-encompassing quality.

---

[6] See also p. 371, lines 10-12; and p. 372, lines 20-28.

[7] There are also references to short quotations from other *Hekhalot* writings; e.g. p. 370, line 48.

SEFER HEKHALOT (3 ENOCH)

Sefer Hekhalot, or as it became known: *3 Enoch*, is probably the best known *Hekhalot* text. Odeberg's famous edition of the book, which also contains an English translation and commentary, made the book available to the scholarly world. In spite of all its deficiencies,[1] Odeberg's edition has done justice to the subject, and in many cases his commentary and long introduction contain interesting and valuable material. *Sefer Hekhalot* is the longest and most complex of the *Hekhalot* writings, and by the manner in which it fuses together a number of esoteric traditions it can be viewed as a romance or grand summary of the Jewish apocalyptic and mystical traditions.

Although it is clear that the book draws its material from a variety of sources, it is not always possible to identify them and to assess the special manner in which the book uses them. Even in the case of the *Hekhalot* material incorporated in the book it is not always easy to show where it derived from. From the manner in which the writer, or compiler, of the book put his material together we may conclude that it is not an original work, as for example *Hekhalot Rabbati* or even *Sefer Ha-Razim* are. In fact, *Sefer Hekhalot* fuses traditions together in a rather artificial way, and one is justified in characterizing it as an eclectic composition. In addition, the writer, or compiler, of the book used his terminology in a rather loose, even careless, manner, and the reader sometimes wonders at the degree of literary degeneration the *Hekhalot* literature has reached with *Sefer Hekhalot*. In fact, none of the original components of the *Hekhalot* writings are present in *Sefer Hekhalot*. Nothing is said in it about the special technique of the ascent; it lacks any reference to the theurgical means which protect the mystic on his journey in heaven; and it contains no *Hekhalot* hymns. However, in spite of all its literary shortcomings, the book is a treasure-house of information about the

[1] For an excellent summary of the main problems of the book as they are seen by a modern scholar, see J. Greenfield's "Prolegomenon" to the Ktav Publishing House Reprint (1973) of H. Odeberg, *3 Enoch*. In spite of all its deficiencies Odeberg's is still the only *Hekhalot* text that received scholarly treatment. A new translation and commentary is now being prepared by Dr. Philip Alexander of Manchester for Doubleday, New York. My translations here follow mainly those of Odeberg, though at times I differed from him, mainly because his text is based on completely wrong textual presuppositions.

esoteric traditions at the time of its writing. The book seems to have been written, or compiled, in post-talmudic times, probably in the 6th century C.E. In any event, it is clear that it was composed at a rather late stage in the creation of the *Hekhalot* literature. However, J. T. Milik's attribution of the book to the Kabbalistic literature of the twelfth or thirteenth centuries only shows how little Milik knows of both the *Hekhalot* literature and of the Cabbalah.[2]

From a literary point of view, the book is affiliated to the ancient Enoch tradition, and it appears that in spite of its late date of composition it contains a great deal that derives from the early Enoch tradition and literature. The book may be divided into several parts, and this division may help us in analyzing and understanding the special manner in which the writer handled his material. The first part of the book (chapters 1-12) describes Enoch's translation unto heaven and his transformation into the angel Metatron. However, in order to affiliate itself to the Merkavah tradition, the book begins with a description of the mystical ascent of Rabbi Yishma'el to behold the vision of the Merkavah (chapters 1-2). This description of Rabbi Yishma'el's ascent is a literary device, which defines the setting of the book: it is a rewritten version of the Enoch tradition in terms of the Merkavah tradition. In this way many of the original traits of the apocalyptic Enoch tradition are preserved, though they are recast in a story that was to become part of the Merkavah tradition.

In line with the common Merkavah tradition, Rabbi Yishma'el is described as having passed from palace to palace until he reached the seventh palace. Before he entered the seventh *Hekhal*, he had said a prayer so that he might be saved from the wrath of Qeẓfiel and his retinue. We already met Qeẓfiel in *Hekhalot Rabbati* xviii, where he was one of the gatekeepers of the sixth *Hekhal*. His new post in

[2] See J. T. Milik, *The Books of Enoch: Aramaic Fragments of Qumran Cave 4*, Oxford, Clarendon Press, 1976, pp. 125-135. There is nothing in *Sefer Hekhalot* that betrays either the style or the symbolism of Jewish medieval Kabbalah. Milik's contention that the identification of Enoch with Metatron does not "appear in Western Europe until the twelfth century" (p. 134) has no basis. Equally strange is Milik's dating of the Greek original of the *Slavonic Enoch* (*2 Enoch*) "to the ninth if not tenth century" (p. 126). A post-Byzantine dating of *2 Enoch* is simply inconceivable to anyone who has the slightest idea of the history of literature. In addition, Milik's explanation of the name Metatron as deriving "from the Latin *metator* through the Greek μητάτωρ, μιτάτωρ" (p. 131) has very little, if any, substantiation. A closer study of the *Hekhalot* literature and its relationship to Jewish apocalyptic could have saved Milik from falling into many pitfalls.

Sefer Hekhalot at the gate of the seventh *Hekhal* may of course be explained by the occasional inconsistencies in the *Hekhalot* literature regarding the names of the angels and their roles in heaven. But we may also argue that Qeẓfiel's post at the seventh gate is a characteristic example of the idiosyncratic manner in which the writer of the book used his sources. We shall have several occasions to show this idiosyncrasy of the writer, or compiler, of the book. As said, Rabbi Yishma'el prayed that Qeẓfiel might not "get power over me and throw me down from heaven". Although this appears to be the only case in the book in which any theurgical practices are referred to, there is something in this prayer that gives reason for speculation. Usually in the *Hekhalot* writings the angels threaten to kill the mystic or to chase and hurt him, but nothing is said of throwing the mystic down from heaven. We may, therefore, see in Rabbi Yishma'el's prayer an echo or interpretation of sayings like: "The ministering angels wanted to push Rabbi ʿAkiva away" (*Bavli Ḥagigah* 15b).[3] In any event, the prayer is characteristic of late mystical literature and one of its literary parallels is to be found in Midrash *Maʿayan Ḥokhmah* (= *Pesikta Rabbati* 97a) where Moses expresses his wish to fall down from the cloud on which he has ascended to heaven.

On hearing Rabbi Yishma'el's prayer, God called Metatron to his rescue. Metatron came "with great joy... to meet me so as to save me from their hands". He took Rabbi Yishma'el by his hand and said to him: "Enter in peace before the high and exalted King and behold the picture[4] of the Merkavah". However, when Rabbi Yishma'el entered the seventh *Hekhal*, he encountered other angelic beings who frightened him. Metatron again came to his rescue, but this time Rabbi Yishma'el was completely exhausted. As he himself says: "there was not in me strength enough to say a song before the

[3] However, it should be noticed that "to push him away" is a literal translation of the Hebrew verb used here *DAḤAF*. But as can be seen from *Bavli Sanhedrin* 103(b) (bottom), the real meaning of the phrase is "to kill".

[4] The Hebrew word which is used here is *Demut*, which is a synonym of *Ẓelem*. Both terms indicate the corporeal appearance of God or man. See *Genesis* i,26; v,3. Here, as elsewhere in the text, terms which are loaded with meanings and associations are somewhat profusely used, or at least they appear to be arbitrarily introduced into new contexts and combinations. The term *Demut Ha-Merkavah* does not occur in the *Hekhalot* writings which we have hitherto discussed. The equivalent technical term which we met in *Hekhalot Zutreti* was *Yofiot Ha-Merkavah* ("The Beauties of the Chariot"). In *Hekhalot Rabbati* we frequently find the expression "to look at the King and His Throne" (xiii,1; xviii,5; xxv,6) [*le-histakel ba-melekh We-kis'o*].

Throne of Glory". However, after a short while, Rabbi Yishma'el recovered his senses and he was able to recite the proper song, which was promptly answered by the *Qedushah* of the angels.

The kind of reception Metatron gave Rabbi Yishma'el aroused the envy and resentment of the angelic beings ministering to the Throne of Glory. They asked Metatron why he let a human being look at the celestial Merkavah. Metatron replied that Rabbi Yishma'el was from the tribe of Levi, and from the seed of Aaron, that is, Rabbi Yishma'el was a priest. This apparently convinced the angels and they said: "Indeed, this man is worthy of beholding the Merkavah". Professor Scholem rightly pointed out that the tradition that presents Rabbi Yishma'el of the *Hekhalot* literature as a priest, is a fiction.[5] However, we have already referred to the fact that according to an ancient Jewish tradition, high priests could experience visions of the Divine Presence in the Holy of Holies. Consequently Rabbi Yishma'el, the alleged high priest, would also gaze at the divine Merkavah.[6]

To sum up our observations on the first two chapters of *Sefer Hekhalot*, we may say that they are a typical example of the kind of work the compiler of the book did. He put together a great number of literary elements which were collected from a variety of sources. The ascent of Rabbi Yishma'el needs no further comment, though as we saw, the description lacks many of the technical characteristics that are present in parallel descriptions in the *Hekhalot* literature. The angel Qeẓfiel, is known from *Hekhalot Rabbati*, though what he attempts to do in our text does not exactly follow the same lines as his actions in *Hekhalot Rabbati*. While in *Hekhalot Rabbati* Qeẓfiel is one of the three angels that escort the wagon of the Merkavah mystic into the sixth *Hekhal* (xviii,5 ff.), he appears here as the leader of a group of angels that stand in the mystic's way. In *Hekhalot Rabbati* Qeẓfiel is appeased by the seal that the mystic shows him, but in *Sefer Hekhalot*—which mentions no protective seals—his opposition has to be overcome by another angelic being, namely Metatron. Also the manner, in which the angels express their objection to Rabbi Yishma'el's ascent has no parallel in other *Hekhalot* writings. As we saw in our discussion of *Hekhalot Rabbati*, the gatekeepers were appointed to check the passage of the mystic from palace to palace.

[5] See G. Scholem, *Major Trends in Jewish Mysticism*, p. 356, h. 3.

[6] The fact that Ezekiel himself was a priest was certainly a major factor in the development of that tradition.

The mystic had to show his seals and also convince them of his moral and intellectual accomplishments. The gatekeepers rarely speak. All this theurgical procedure is missing from *Sefer Hekhalot*. There are no gatekeepers and no seals to be shown to them. Instead the angels express their verbal opposition to the mystic's ascent. What they say is in line with similar utterances in *aggadic* literature, but unlike what they do in the *Hekhalot* literature. Finally, it should be noted that although Metatron is mentioned in other *Hekhalot* writings, he is nowhere else identified with the transfigured Enoch. In his case, *Sefer Hekhalot* blends together apocalyptic and mystical traditions.

Speaking about Metatron, not all the problems connected with his name, status and offices, have satisfactorily been solved. To begin with, we have to consider the name "Metatron" and its etymology. In an appendix to the present book, Professor Lieberman suggests that the name Metatron is a derivation from an earlier form: *Synthronos*. A *Synthronos* was, Professor Lieberman argues, a title given to someone whose throne stood alongside the throne of a king or a deity. Professor Lieberman maintains that the word *Synthronos* could be used either as a substantive or as an adjective, and that whatever we find about Metatron in our sources, both in midrashic literature and in the Merkavah writings, very well fits the idea of the ancient *Synthronos*, that is, the one who is seated on a throne alongside God. Professor Lieberman's explanation is fully acceptable from the point of view of its concern with the etymology of the name. One may, of course, argue that no *Synthronos* is found in any of the extant Jewish writings, but Professor Lieberman has shown that the idea of a *Synthronos* obviously lies behind the story of ʾElishʿa ben ʾAvuyah's blasphemy as described in *Bavli Ḥagigah* 15a and *Sefer Hekhalot* xvi. The story there tells of how ʾElishʿa ben ʾAvuyah saw Metatron sitting in heaven. Knowing that the angels cannot sit, ʾElishʿa ben ʾAvuyah was led to the false conclusion that there were two powers in heaven. And, indeed, the name of Metatron is also elsewhere mentioned in relation to the two-powers heresy (*Bavli Sanhedrin* 38b). The status and offices of Metatron in heaven could really induce impressions of the kind ʾElishʿa ben ʾAvuyah had. In order to avoid such false impressions, so the story reports, Metatron was beaten with sixty lashes of fire and reproached for not standing up in the face of ʾElishʿa ben ʾAvuyah. However, *Sefer Hekhalot* x suggests a different solution to the problem: Metatron received a throne not in the seventh palace itself, alongside the Throne of Glory, but at the gate of that palace. True to his method of mixing up traditions, the writer of *Sefer Hekhalot* was not content with that solution, and when he retold the story of ʾElishʿa ben ʾAvuyah in chapter xvi, he again changed the story. In its new "improved" version, ʾElishʿa ben ʾAvuyah's heresy was not induced by the mere fact that he saw Metatron *sitting* (see *Bavli Ḥagigah*), but by the fact that he saw Metatron "sitting upon a throne like a king with all the ministering angels standing by me (Metatron) as my servants and all the princes of the kingdoms adorned with crowns surrounding me".

In short, the name "Metatron" signified the office and status of the angel who acts as a vice-regent or divine plenipotentiary. Finally, it should be noticed that in *Bavli Sanhedrin* 38b Rav Idi, who is described as an authority in the disputations between Jews and heretics (*Minim*), told one of the heretics with whom he argued over the status of Metatron, that he would not even accept him as a (divine) messenger (the term used here for mission is the Persian word Parwanka = Parwanak). In this office, Metatron may be viewed as the Jewish counterpart to Hermes, who was the divine messenger in Greek mythology. It is interesting to notice in this connection that in one of the *Aramaic Incantation Texts* published by James Montgomery, Hermes and Metatron are mentioned side by side.[7]

Sefer Hekhalot also refers to Metatron with the appellations *Yahweh Ha-Qatan* (Yahweh the Smaller, or: the Lesser Yahweh) and *Naʿar* (Youth). As Professor Scholem has shown,[8] the first appellation, *Yahweh Ha-Qatan*, may derive from the early tradition concerning the angel Yahoʾel. And indeed, Yahoʾel occurs as one of Metatron's names not only in the list of the seventy names of Metatron,[9] but also in the Aramaic Incantation Bowls.[10] The term *Yahweh Ha-*

[7] See J. A. Montgomery, *Aramaic Incantation Texts from Nippur*, Philadelphia, 1913, p. 123; J. T. Milik, *op. cit.*, pp. 128-131. However, the reading Hermes is not certain!

[8] In *Jewish Gnosticism* etc., p. 43.

[9] *Sefer Hekhalot* xlviii (D). The first two names there are Yahoʾel Yah and Yahoʾel. Compare also *Hekhalot Rabbati* xxvi,8.

[10] Misled by Montgomery, his followers, (including H. Odeberg, *3 Enoch*, p. 110) read Yeḥiʾel instead of Yahoel. See Plate XXIV (Text 25), line 7; Ch. D. Isbell, *Corpus of the Aramaic Incantation Bowls*, Missoula, Montana, Scholars Press, 1975, has added nothing but his own mistakes to the First Editions and Publications of the Bowls. Thus he repeats on p. 87 Montgomery's misreading: Yeḥiʾel. It also appears that the Bowl of the Ashmolean Museum, No. 1932.620, first studied by C. Gordon, in *Orientalia* X (1941), p. 280, and re-studied by J. T. Milik, *op. cit.*, pp. 129-130, contains the name of Yahoʾel and not of Yeḥiʾel. Admittedly, Montgomery in his notes to Text 25 (p. 208) raises the possibility

Qatan apparently signifies—as Professor Lieberman thinks—"a smaller god" (*deus minor*) or the semi-divine status of Metatron. It should be remembered that according to the story told in *Sefer Hekhalot*, Metatron had formerly been the man Enoch,[11] and thus whatever his status in heaven his previous human existence should not be forgotten.[12] As Metatron he was raised to a very high position among the angelic beings; in fact, he was made their superior. He was not deified, but was turned into an angel. By calling him *Yahweh Ha-Qatan* one probably wanted to indicate the authority which the appellation lent. This authority is clearly implied by relating the term *Yahweh Ha-Qatan* to *Exodus* xxiii,21: "For my name is in him" (*Sefer Hekhalot* xii).[13] It is true that the Christian gnostics referred to a divine figure called "the little Jao, the Good".[14] But unlike "the little Jao" of the gnostics, Metatron, or *Yahweh Ha-Qatan* as he is called in *Sefer Hekhalot*, is the mystically transformed Enoch! We may well assume

---

that the correct reading is Yahoʾel and not Yeḥiʾel. This may explain Epstein's silence on the issue in his "Gloses Babylo-Araméennes", *Revue des Études Juives* LXXIII (1921), p. 53. Isbell and Milik could have avoided repeating the erroneous reading had they consulted J. C. Greenfield, "Notes on some Aramaic and Mandaic Magic Bowls", *Gaster Festschrift* [*The Journal of the Ancient Near Eastern Society of Columbia University* V (1973)], p. 156, n. 40. It should be noticed that Greenfield also discusses the alleged and real "Enochian echoes in the magical bowls" (pp. 150 ff.).

[11] The most important parallel to this identification of Enoch with Metatron is to be found in Targum of Jonathan to *Genesis* v,24. Milik, *op. cit.*, p. 128, remarks on the end of the verse ("and He called his name Metatron, the Great Scribe"): "But the second part of this passage is certainly, in my opinion, a very late addition, as it does not appear in other Palestinian Targums". Could Milik really overlook a tradition that dates back to *Jubilees* iv?

[12] It may be due to his previous human existence that Metatron is able to sit. Other angels, as we saw, could not fold their legs into a sitting position! It should be noted, however, that the class of the angels called *Shotrim* in *Sefer Ha-Razim* had chairs to sit upon. It is interesting to notice that one of the appellations given to Metatron in the Aramaic Magical Bowls is: *Metatron ʾIsara Rabba de-Kurseh* ("Metatron the Great Prince of the Throne"); cf. C. H. Gordon, "Aramaic Magical Bowls in the Istanbul and Baghdad Museums", *Archiv Orientalni* VI (1934), pp. 328-329.

[13] The same verse is quoted in relation to Metatron in *Bavli Sanhedrin* 38b. As G. Scholem, *Major Trends in Jewish Mysticism*, p. 366, n. 107, pointed out, the Qaraite author Qirqisani quoted the passage in *Sanhedrin* as saying: "... Metatron is *Yahweh Qatan*". Scholem remarks that "the name *Yahweh Qatan* was deliberately eliminated from the Talmudic manuscripts because of its heretical connotations". However, I incline to agree with E. E. Urbach, *The Sages*, p. 743, n. 15, that it was Qirqisani who interpolated the name into the Talmudic passage and not *vice versa*.

[14] Cf. *Pistis Sophia* vii (in G. R. S. Meads edition, p. 9); in chapter cxl we find several times the term "the little Sabbaoth, the Good"!

that the appellation *Yahweh Ha-Qatan* was given to Metatron by people who knew of "the little Jao" of the gnostics, but when they did so they had in mind the special authority given to the angel and not his divine essence.

The other appellation given to Metatron is *Na'ar* (Youth). This appellation was probably inspired by *Exodus* xxxiii,11, and if so, it could imply the status of a chief servant and even of a deputy.[15] The explanation given in *Sefer Hekhalot* to the appellation tells the story of the ascent of Enoch to heaven and his transformation into Metatron (chapter iv). As the story there tells, God elevated Enoch to heaven in the days preceding the Flood. When God saw the evil deeds of the generation of the Flood, He took Enoch up to heaven so that he could be preserved as a witness against the sinful people of that generation.[16] What Enoch was expected to testify against was that not only did the people of his generation rebel against God but that their animals shared their sinful behaviour. Thus no injustice was done to anyone in the Flood.[17] As far as we know, this part of the story derives from apocalyptic literature;[18] however, the second part of the story adds new tones to the original Enoch tradition. It is said that when Enoch came up to heaven, three angels, 'Uzah, 'Azah and 'Azael, [19] came forth and claimed before God that it was improper for a human being to ascend to heaven. Their claim was not solely directed against Enoch, but against the whole of mankind, of which he was to become the representative. Man is a sinful being and should not have been created, and now he is even permitted into heaven. In their objections, the angels combined two traditions of the angelic opposition to man. The first tradition speaks of the opposition of the angels to the creation of man,[20] while the second speaks of their

[15] Obviously, this verse which refers to Yehoshu'a ben Nun could not be quoted in relation to Metatron, and thus we find later sources quoting *Psalm* xxxvii,25 and *Proverbs* xxii,6, as biblical references to Metatron.

[16] Compare *Mishnah Sanhedrin* x,3 and parallels.

[17] Compare *Jubilees* v,2; *Bereshit Rabba* (ed. Theodor-Albeck) p. 266.

[18] See *Jubilees* iv,22-24 and parallels.

[19] Some of the manuscripts give only two names: 'Aza and 'Aza'el, and this appears to be the better reading. See Odeberg's note to the place (pp. 10 ff.). For the various spellings of the names of these angels see D. Dimant, "*The Fallen Angels" in the Dead Sea Scrolls and in the Apocryphal and Pseudepigraphic Books Related to Them* (Dissertation, in Hebrew), Jerusalem, 1974, pp. 55 ff.

[20] See P. Schäfer, *Rivalität zwischen Engeln und Menschen*, Walter de Gruyter, Berlin, 1975, pp. 75 ff.

opposition to the ascent of human beings to heaven.[21] As we saw, the blending together of traditions is a typical trait of the compiler of *Sefer Hekhalot*, and it appears that he misses no opportunity of doing so.

God's answer to the angels' claim is resolute: He wants Enoch to be in heaven and to become their superior. In accepting Enoch into heaven, and in transforming him into Metatron, God may be said to declare that He wants the chief angelic being in heaven to be of human origin. From a human point of view, this may be interpreted to imply the idea that mankind has a representative in heaven; this representative was even raised to occupy the highest angelic position. However, once Enoch had left his earthly existence to become a celestial being, he had in fact nothing to do with mankind. He is the *Naʿar* of God,[22] and in charge of whatever the angels do. However, Enoch-Metatron himself explains his appellation thus: "And because I am small and a youth among them... therefore they call me *Naʿar*" (chapter iv, end). In point of fact, however, only God calls Metatron by that appellation, while the other heavenly beings call him by the seventy names he has, corresponding to the seventy languages in the world.[23] In our discussion of *Merkavah Rabbah* we saw that some of the angels have at least two names. There is an exoteric and an esoteric mode of the angels' names. Metatron, however, has many names and appellations. In *Reʾuyot Yeḥezkel* we met the *Sar* who dwells in the heaven *Zevul*. Several, mostly esoteric, names were suggested there for that *Sar*, one of which was: "Metatron, like the name of the *Gevurah*" ("Dynamis").[24] In *Hekhalot Rabbati* xxvi,8 Metatron is said to have eight names. In the Aramaic Magical Bowls Metatron is called *ʾIsara Rabba* ("the great minister"), and in an ancient *Shiʿur Qomah* fragment Metatron is called *Shamasha Reḥima Sara Rabba de-Sahaduta* ("the beloved servant, the great prince of testimony").[25] This last appellation clearly includes the various

---

[21] See J. Schultz, "Angelic Opposition to the Ascension of Moses and the Revelation of the Law", *Jewish Quarterly Review* LXI (1970/71), pp. 282-307.

[22] Notable exceptions to this rule are: *Bavli ʿAvodah Zarah* 3b where Metatron is said to teach Torah to the souls of dead infants, and *Bemidbar Rabba* xii,12 where Metatron is said to sacrifice in the heavenly temple the souls of the righteous ones (compare *Bavli Menaḥot* 100a where the angel Michaʾel is described offering sacrifices on the heavenly altar).

[23] In chapter xvii the parallel tradition of 72 languages is mentioned. The seventy names of Metatron are enumerated in xlviii(d).

[24] See G. Scholem, *Jewish Gnosticism* etc., p. 46, notes 13 and 14.

[25] *Ibid.*, p. 50.

aspects of Metatron: he is God's choice servant; [26] he is the Great Prince; [27] and he is to bear testimony against the generation of the Flood.[28]

We cannot enter here a detailed discussion of everything that the book says about Metatron and what he told and showed Rabbi Yishma'el. Sometimes parallel and conflicting episodes are piled one upon the other, as for example in chapters iv and vi where two different accounts are given of the angelic opposition to the ascent of Enoch. The one, as we noticed, was put in the mouth of the evil angels, and the other, in the more traditional manner, was attributed to the angels of service. However, the eclecticism of the compiler may be viewed as his *felix culpa*: it enables us to have a panoramic view of the esoteric traditions in the post-Talmudic period. In this respect, it is interesting that Metatron is identified with Enoch. Nowhere [29] in Jewish midrashic and Talmudic literature are the two, Metatron and Enoch, identified. On the contrary, we find that some of the Palestinian sages of the third century expressed negative views about Enoch.[30] These views, which were expressed as polemical utterances in disputes with *Minim* ("heretics"), may be viewed as reflecting anti-Christian positions. Since Enoch and his like who experienced heavenly ascensions could have pre-figured the Ascension of the Christ,[31] some sages found themselves obliged to clear Jewish tradition from the events and experiences which served the early Christians in building up their religion. If one claimed, as these sages did, that Enoch was not entered in the book of the righteous and that he was not translated unto heaven but died a natural death, one clearly aimed at depriving the Christians of some of their alleged roots in the Jewish religion. The sages who undermined the righteousness of Enoch could hardly comply with books such as *Sefer Hekhalot*. Yet, even from their point of view the identification of Enoch with Metatron could have served in their alleged anti-Christian polemic. Enoch was not a messianic figure who was translated to heaven in order to

---

[26] See *Sefer Hekhalot* viii: "... Metatron ... said to me: Before He appointed me to attend (*le-shamesh*) the Throne of Glory"; and chapter x: "... This is Metatron, my servant ...".

[27] Cf. *Re'uyot Yeḥezkel.*

[28] *Sefer Hekhalot* iv.

[29] *Targum Yerushalmi* to *Genesis* v,25 is the only exception to the rule.

[30] In *Bereshit Rabba* (ed. Theodor-Albeck, pp. 238-239).

[31] See *Hebrews* xi,5, though the context there is not the question of the Ascension but of belief. Compare also *Jude* 14; and particularly *1 Clement* ix,3.

complement his mission and function as Son of Man, as the Christians thought of their Christ, but a man who ascended to heaven to become an *angel*. Thus, one may see in the Enoch's metamorphosis into the *angel* Metatron an attempt to overcome the so-called Christian overtones which the apocalyptic legends about Enoch had. By merging apocalyptic and mystical traditions, the Enoch-Metatron legends could have helped, theologically speaking, certain esoteric groups in finding legitimation for a tradition which, under the circumstances, was no longer as fashionable as it had once been in esoteric circles.

In chapter v Metatron tells Rabbi Yishma'el another version of how he ascended to heaven. The story begins with Adam's expulsion from the Garden of Eden. At that time God was dwelling upon a *Keruv* under the Tree of Life. God's initial presence in the Garden of Eden is a constant theme in aggadic literature.[32] But, in contrast to the aggadic utterances which state that God already ascended to the first heaven after the Original Sin had been committed, *Sefer Hekhalot* tells a different story: God ascended only later on, in the days of Enosh (Genesis iv,26),[33] when the angels convinced Him that it would be improper for Him to stay on earth among sinful people. It should be noticed that the subject of God's ascent from earth to heaven is an aggadic theme and has nothing to do with the subject dealt with in the *Hekhalot* literature. Even in apocalyptic literature God is always conceived of as dwelling in heaven, and His presence in Paradise, as described in *Apocalypsis Mosis* xxii,3-4, is an exception to the rule. What, then, is the purpose of this extraordinary chapter in *Sefer Hekhalot*? Odeberg may be right in saying (see his commentary, p. 13) that this chapter provides another explanation for the translation of Enoch into heaven. There is nothing that can prevent the writer of *Sefer Hekhalot* from introducing yet another explanation for this translation, an explanation that does not concur with the one given in chapter iv. Odeberg is, thus, certainly right when he comments (p. 13): "As regards the relationship between ch. iv on the one hand and chs. v and vi on the other, it might be safe to assume that they represent respectively two different lines of tradition as to the translation of Enoch".

---

[32] See *Pesikta de-Rav Kahana* (ed. Mandelbaum), pp. 1-3, and parallels. See also Odeberg's notes, p. 14.

[33] According to *Pesikta de-Rav Kahana*, in the days of Enosh God ascended to the second heaven, while the generation of the Flood caused God to ascend to the third heaven.

However, Odeberg was not sufficiently aware of the problems emerging from the eclectic method which the writer of *Sefer Hekhalot* applies in his book. Thus, for example, in chapter vi we hear that ʿAnafiʾel was sent to fetch Enoch up to heaven. In discussing this chapter Odeberg quotes a number of literary parallels without qualifying and analyzing them. For instance, Odeberg should have noticed that this practice of sending an angel down to earth to fetch the visionary up to heaven is characteristic of some apocalyptic writings, but is never the case in the *Hekhalot* literature. In *2 Enoch* i-iii we hear of the two angels who came to take Enoch up to heaven, and in the *Apocalypse of Abraham* x we read that Jaoʾel was sent to raise the visionary to heaven. But already in *1 Enoch* no angel comes down to fetch the visionary up to heaven; there are only angels who guide him in the course of his heavenly journeys. However, in *Sefer Hekhalot* ʿAnafiʾel was sent to bring Enoch to heaven. We already met ʿAnafiʾel in *Hekhalot Rabbati* xxii-xxiii where he is described as one of the gatekeepers of the seventh *Hekhal*. It should be observed that some of the things that are said there about ʿAnafiʾel are actually found elsewhere in connection with Metatron,[34] and it may be argued that Metatron received the status and offices of ʿAnafiʾel. Nevertheless, it is still an extraordinary fact that in *Sefer Hekhalot* ʿAnafiʾel is described as the divine herald who brought Enoch up to heaven. Since in *Hekhalot Rabbati* ʿAnafiʾel is described as ushering the Merkavah mystic into the seventh *Hekhal*, it appears that the writer of *Sefer Hekhalot* could not find a more distinguished angel to carry out the mission of translating Enoch onto heaven. As it were, Enoch ascended to heaven upon a fiery chariot with fiery horses, and in that he resembled Elijah (*2 Kings* ii,11).[35] But Enoch and ʿAnafiʾel

---

[34] Just to give two or three examples: (1) It is said of ʿAnafiʾel (*Hekhalot Rabbati* xxii,4) that he is the "ʿ*Eved* ('Servant') who is called after the name of his master". We know that similar words are used in connection with Metatron (*Hekhalot Rabbati* xxvi,8; *Sefer Hekhalot* x). (2) ʿAnafiʾel bears the ring which has the seal of heaven and earth on it (*Hekhalot Rabbati* xxii,1), and we read of Metatron's name being "written in one letter with which heaven and earth were created and which was sealed by the ring of ʾEheyeh ʾasher ʾEheyeh" (*Shiʿur Qomah* in: *Merkavah Shelemah* 39b). (3) The angels worship ʿAnafiʾel (*Hekhalot Rabbati* xxii,2) as they worship Metatron (*Sefer Hekhalot* xiv).

[35] See also Odeberg's notes *ad locum*. It should be noticed that in chapter vii Enoch says that he was raised on the wings of the storm. See *1 Enoch* xiv,8 as compared to lxx,2.

were not alone on that occasion: "And he lifted me up to the high heavens together with the *Shekhinah*".[36]

When Enoch reached heaven, the angels gave expression to their "traditional" opposition to the ascent of man. But, as was customary on such occasions, God silenced them, saying: "But this one whom I have taken from among them (the children of men) is a choice one... and he is equal to all of them in faith, righteousness and perfection of deed".

From chapter viii onwards Metatron describes the special gifts and qualities which God bestowed upon him. God adorned Metatron with special angelic features and attributes, and placed him on a throne at the gate of the seventh palace. This throne was made in the likeness of the Throne of Glory. Chapter viii describes the great wisdom bestowed upon Metatron. The chapter is written in the form of a *Hekhalot* hymn. Chapter ix describes how Enoch-Metatron was transformed into a huge angel. In chapter x Metatron tells Rabbi Yishma'el how he was appointed as God's representative and ruler over all the celestial princes of the kingdoms. However, Metatron was not appointed over the eight high princes called by the name of the Ineffable Name. The names of these angels are not mentioned in the text, and all the attempts made by Odeberg to identify them either by their office of by their names only add to the confusion.[37] However, it appears that what the writer had in mind were the seven archangels described in chapter xvii, and which, together with 'Anafi'el, were appointed over the seven heavens. In addition, Metatron was appointed over secret knowledge and sciences; in fact, nothing was hidden away from him (chapter xi). God made for Metatron a garment of glory and put a royal crown on his head (chapter xii).

Most interesting is the description of Metatron's crown (chapter xiii). It is said that God wrote on it with his finger the letters with which he had created heaven and earth and all that they contain. The letters of the alphabet which were used by God in the creation of the world played a prominent role in Jewish mysticism,[38] but it is only here that it is said that they are written on Metatron's crown.

---

[36] This is, of course, incompatible with the earlier description (chapter v) according to which God ascended to heaven in the days of 'Enosh.

[37] The nearest parallel to our passage can be found in *Hekhalot Rabbati* xxvi,8, where the *eight names* of Metatron himself are enumerated.

[38] See G. Scholem, *Judaica 3*, Frankfurt am Main, Suhrkamp Verlag, 1970, pp. 7 ff.: "Der Name Gottes und die Sprachtheorie der Kabbala".

In this respect, it may be true to say that Metatron's crown contained the mystical or magical formula of creation. A similar idea is found in *Shi'ur Qomah* where it is said that Metatron's name was written in "one letter with which heaven and earth were created".[39] This idea is later (in chapter xiv) complemented by the idea of the celestial curtain, *Pargod*, which is said to be spread before the Holy One and upon which are engraved "all the generations of the world and all their doings".

Chapter xiv is the first of a series of chapters which contain a most elaborate angelological system. It should be observed that very few of the angels mentioned in the other *Hekhalot* writings are also found in *Sefer Hekhalot*. In fact, *Sefer Hekhalot* has a different kind of angelology than do the other *Hekhalot* tractates. Most of the angels mentioned in our text perform cosmological duties, and their names derive from the Hebrew names of the objects and phenomena in Nature over the function of which they are appointed. Thus, for example, the angels appointed over the day and the night are called *Shemeshi'el* and *Laila'el*, *Shemesh* being the Hebrew word for sun and *Lailah* the Hebrew for night. It may thus be argued that the angelology of *Sefer Hekhalot* is of a cosmological nature. This type of angelology is known from the apocalyptic Enoch literature and it should be distinguished from yet another type of angelology—magical angelology—which is found in *Sefer Ha-Razim* and in the Magical Papyri. Since the whole subject of Jewish angelology still requires a systematic study, the three types of angelology referred to here (cosmological, mystical and magical angelologies) should be considered only as a provisional classification. Although general classifications can never be conclusive, they are helpful in pointing out essential differences of context and function.

Curiously, in chapter xv we return to the mystical metamorphosis of Enoch into Metatron. A more suitable place for this chapter would have been after chapter viii, principally because chapter ix already described the huge angelic dimensions of Metatron. The opening words of chapters viii and xv are almost identical, and indeed the two chapters are artificially separated. In both chapters we hear of what had happened to Enoch before he became the chief servant before the Throne of Glory. The sequence of the chapters in *Sefer Hekhalot*, particularly in the first part of the book, raises a

[39] See in *Merkavah Shelemah*, 39b.

number of questions, which, unfortunately, have to be left unanswered. Since we do not know the literary sources used by the compiler of the book, we cannot determine the method he applied in organizing his material. The only thing that may be said with some certainty is that the book betrays the fact that it was compiled from a number of sources, which were put together in a manner that leaves the reader with many questions. One also has to take into account the fact that some of the manuscripts add to the confusion by introducing heterogeneous material. Thus, for instance, we find that some manuscripts interpolate into chapter xv a fragment which describes the ascent of Moses! [40] As for the details of the mystical metamorphosis itself, they recall what is said in *2 Enoch* xxii about Enoch's mystical transformation, although a basic difference still exists between the two descriptions. In *2 Enoch* the hero is anointed with special oils so as to enable him to stand in the presence of God, while in our text Enoch is said to be turned into a fiery angel.

Chapter xvi tells the story of ʾElishʿa ben ʾAvuyah's apostasy. The story derives from *Bavli Ḥagigah* 15a, though, as we already saw, several details are changed or added. Unlike the story in *Ḥagigah*, the story here is told as seen from the point of view of Metatron, and, most significantly, it is said that ʿAnafiʾel was the one who treated Metatron with sixty lashes of fire. We have already pointed out the fact that in contrast to *Ḥagigah* where ʾElishʿa ben ʾAvuyah only saw Metatron sitting, in our text it is said that he also noticed the special services rendered him by the angels. Chapter xvii describes the seven archangels who are nominated over the seven heavens and the five angels who are appointed over the astral world. In chapter xviii a description is given of the special manner in which the angels pay homage to their superiors, first the angels of the seven heavens and then the angels of the seven *Hekhalot*. The description appears to derive from *Hekhalot Rabbati* xi,1, though it is implied there (xxii,2) that the angels do not pay homage to one another. According to *Hekhalot Rabbati*, only before the *Sar Ha-Panim* may the angels fall down, and this only by a special permission from God (*Hekhalot*

[40] Printed in Odeberg's edition as chapter xv/b. It describes Moses' ascent to heaven, and it may be considered a mystical version of the story found in *Bavli Shabbat* 88b. Another mystical version of the same story is found in *Pesikta Rabbati* (ed. Friedmann), 96b-98b. A slightly different version of the story found in *Pesikta Rabbati* is known as *Maʿayan Ḥokhmah*; see A. Jellinek, *Bet ha-Midrasch*, I, pp. 58-61.

Rabbati xxii,2). The writer of *Sefer Hekhalot* may have overlooked this fact, but one may also argue that the writer of our text did not feel himself dogmatically bound to concepts and notions which he found in the sources that he used. The obligation he felt towards his literary sources should not be overestimated. As we saw, he felt free to invent new mystical situations and unknown classes of angels. For instance, he describes the angels which inhabit the seventh *Hekhal*, and among the names which he mentions we find several ones that in *Hekhalot Rabbati* and in *Ma'aseh Merkavah* are said to be stationed in other places in heaven.[41] To give only one example of this process of shifting angels from one station to the other in heaven, we may mention the angel Gevurati'el, who, according to *Hekhalot Rabbati* xv,5, is one of the gatekeepers of the fourth *Hekhal* and in *Sefer Hekhalot* xviii he was promoted to be one of the angels of the seventh *Hekhal*.

Referring to its angelology, it should be observed that the book is rich in angelological etymologies. It is not clear whether the compiler invented these etymologies or whether he found them in the sources he used. Comparatively speaking, the other *Hekhalot* writings only seldom engage in etymologies, and, thus, the practice of our compiler deserves special attention. Chapters xix-xxii describe more angels who are stationed in the seventh palace before the Throne of Glory and their roles and duties. These chapters are distinguished by their poetical richness. They are interrupted by two chapters—xxiii-xxiv—which enumerate the various kinds of spirits (*Ruḥot*) and chariots of God. Chapter xxv again takes up the subject of the angels. First we hear of Ofafani'el, the prince of the 'Ofanim, and later (chapter xxvi) of Sarafi'el, the prince of the Serafim. The physical description of Sarafi'el is strongly influenced by the *Shi'ur Qomah* terminology. In connection with Sarafi'el, an interesting etymology is brought to explain the word "Serafim": "Why are they called Serafim?—Because they burn (*sorfim*) the writing tables of Satan. Every day Satan is sitting together with Samael, the Prince of Rome, and with Dubiel, the Prince of Persia, and they write the iniquities of Israel on writing tables which they hand over to the *Serafim*, in order that they may present them before the Holiness, blessed be He, so that He may destroy Israel from the

[41] It must however be admitted that in this respect there are even substantial differences between *Hekhalot Rabbati* and *Ma'aseh Merkavah*. Compare, for instance, *Hekhalot Rabbati* xv with *Ma'aseh Merkavah* paragraph 23!

world. But the *Serafim* know the secrets of the Holiness, blessed be He, that He desires not that the people of Israel should perish. What do the *Serafim* do?—Every day they take them from Satan and burn them in the burning fire which burns in front of the high and exalted Throne".

The presence of Satan here is rather unusual. Satan does not figure in the *Hekhalot* texts known to us, but Samael—who is generally taken to be his main configuration—is mentioned in the Martyrs-Apocalypse in *Hekhalot Rabbati*. The person of Satan is also rarely mentioned in the rabbinic writings of the Tannaitic and Amoraic periods. Living in an age in which Christianity and gnosticism flourished, the rabbis probably felt that too much of the Satan would draw attention in the wrong direction. It is noteworthy that according to *Sefer Hekhalot* the powers of Satan have access to heaven.[42] In fact, nothing is said of their Fall.[43] In comparison with later developments of Jewish mysticism, it may be said that the *Hekhalot* literature had almost nothing to say about the powers of evil. As we saw, *Ma'aseh Merkavah* mentions the demons and here Satan and some of his powers are referred to, but these two exceptions to the rule cannot but bring us back to the conclusion that *Hekhalot* mysticism was only indirectly influenced by gnosticism.

The subject of the heavenly court is carried on until chapter xxxiii, and in chapter xxxiv a new angelological section is introduced. Its main subject matter is the heavenly *Qedushah*. A great deal is said concerning the details of the ritual, but no hymns are quoted. This section ends with chapter xl, and in xli Metatron reveals to Rabbi Yishma'el a series of cosmological secrets. The descriptions here resemble those of the heavenly journeys known from apocalyptic literature, notably in the Enoch writings, though several details borrowed from the Merkavah writings are added. These descriptions practically lead to the end of the book (chapter xlviii), where some of the manuscripts add a number of appendices. It should be noticed that chapter xlviii contains several references to the future redemption.

---

[42] Odeberg in his notes (p. 93) rightly observes that a similar concept is found in *1 Enoch* xl,7.

[43] See also *Sefer Hekhalot* iv and v, where 'Uza and 'Azael are twice mentioned in heaven. Compare *Bavli Yoma* 67b: "It was learnt according to Rabbi Yishma'el: 'Azazel (*Leviticus* xvi,6 ff.) [is called by that name] because he atones for the deeds of 'Uza and 'Aza'el". See Rashi to the place. Compare also *Sifra* (ed. Weiss) 43c (letter c), and L. Ginzberg, *Genizah Studies*, Vol. I (New York, 1928), p. 83 and *Pesikta Rabbati* 191a.

One of these appendices, printed in Odeberg's edition as chapter xlviii (d), is an interesting résumé of the Metatron legend.[44] Among other things this résumé contains the list of the seventy names of Metatron, and it ends with a section that links Metatron with the *Sar-Torah*. After Moses had suddenly forgotten all that he had learnt from the mouth of God, Metatron is said to have revealed the secrets of the Torah to Moses on Mount Sinai.[45] This is a typical *Sar-Torah* episode, and its inclusion at the end of the book was probably aimed at reminding the reader of the parallel ending of *Hekhalot Rabbati*.

---

[44] A similar résumé is also known from *ʾOtiyot de-Rabbi ʿAkiva*, Version A, Letter Aleph.

[45] Compare *Maʿaseh Merkavah*, paragraph 1.

MASEKHET HEKHALOT

Masekhet Hekhalot is the most frequently published *Hekhalot* text we have,[1] and there are also many manuscripts of the text.[2] The text is also known as *Ma'aseh Merkavah* or *Pirkei Hekhalot*, and it consists of seven chapters. The first chapter is divided into two: the first part enumerates six names by which both God and His Throne are called. Biblical verses are quoted to substantiate this parallelism in the nomenclature. In the second part of the chapter the question is asked: "How many thrones does God have?", in answer to which eleven names are given together with the biblical verses from which they allegedly derive. The material in this chapter bears the marks of a free midrashic composition, and it has almost nothing to do with the material found in the other *Hekhalot* writings. It is neither said where the eleven thrones are placed, nor is any explanation offered for the different number of thrones given in the first part of the chapter and the one given in the second part.

The second chapter describes the huge dimensions of the Throne. In fact the beginning of this chapter may be described as the *Shi'ur Qomah* of the Throne. In addition, it is said that God has "seventy thrones of kingdoms... which are like his own Throne". These thrones correspond to the seventy kingdoms of the world. God also has seventy crowns of glory and seventy sceptres, and thus all the kings of the world are under His dominion. They depend on God for all the glory that they have. It should be noticed, in comparison, that in *Sefer Hekhalot* (*3 Enoch*) Metatron is appointed over the kingdoms of the world. Chapter iii goes on in describing the magnificence of the Throne of Glory. The appearance of the Throne "is like *Ḥashmal*", which the writer of the text explains as meaning that "three hundred and seventy-eight [3] kinds of light" are fixed in the throne. The throne is covered by a garment from which emanate all kinds of

---

[1] See, for instance, A. Jellinek, *Bet ha-Midrasch* II, pp. 40-47; and Sh. A. Wertheimer, *Batei Midrashot,* I, pp. 51-62 and 387-390. The text published by Wertheimer is much better than that published by Jellinek, but even Wertheimer's text should be amended according to the MSS. mentioned in the next note.

[2] From the great number of manuscripts which the present writer has examined it seems that MSS. Firenze-Laurentiana 44/2, fol. 159a-162a, and Parma 3531 (Stern 91) [no pagination] are the best.

[3] This is the numerical value of the Hebrew term *Ḥashmal.*

light. Thus none of the heavenly beings can look at the throne and at God. This garment is reminiscent of the *Pargod* which according to *Sefer Hekhalot* xlv is said to be spread before the Throne of Glory. However, it is interesting to note that the writer of *Masekhet Hekhalot* does not use the term *Pargod* (curtain),[4] but the rather strange term *Beged* (garment). It appears that by doing so he wanted to allude either to the *Ḥaluq* (garment) of God which is described in *Hekhalot Rabbati* iii,4 and iv,2, or to the "cloth of all blue" (*Beged Kelil Tekhelet*) with which the ark of the testimony was covered when carried from place to place (*Numbers* iv,6).[5]

Chapter iv introduces more familiar and interesting Merkavah material than that contained in the first three chapters. The chapter begins with a description of the seven heavens and their luminous light. Particular attention is given to the seventh heaven, *Aravot*. It is said that four walls of fire—the names of which are given—encircle the Throne of Glory. Within these walls of fire there are the seven *Hekhalot*, but the text does not explicate how these seven palaces are situated among the four walls of fire.[6] Every palace has 8766 gates of lightnings, which correspond to the number of the hours of one year of 365 days.[7] Every such gate has 365,000 kinds of light, and in every gate stand 3,650,000,000 angels. It seems that like the writer of *Sefer Hekhalot* our writer allowed himself a considerable amount of freedom in his descriptions. He did not feel himself bound by the *Hekhalot* texts which he knew, and there are good reasons to consider him an epigone who looked for artificial means of decorating his subject matter. His manner of writing may betray his origin: he probably belonged to the circles of German *Ḥasidim* (about 1150-1250). According to the writer of *Masekhet Hekhalot*, not only the angels sing their celestial song but also their horses. We have already met celestial horses in *Hekhalot Rabbati* xvi, where only their fearful appearance is described. In *Masekhet Hekhalot*, however, these horses are said to have four wings, like the angels

[4] The MSS. mentioned in note 2 contain in chapter vi a short sentence which refers to the *Parokhet* (curtain) that is spread before the Throne of God.

[5] It should be noted that in *Hekhalot Rabbati* xi,4 a different procedure is recorded: when the angels uncover their faces to look at God, God covers His face. No garment or curtain is mentioned there. We shall come back to this point in our discussion of chapter vi.

[6] It is unlikely that the writer of *Masekhet Hekhalot* conceived of four sets of seven palaces.

[7] In reality, only 8760 divided into 365 makes 24!

who ride them, and like the angels they speak seventy languages! The chapter ends with a description of the eight very important angels who stand at the gates of the seventh palace, and who check all those who enter to see the Throne of Glory.[8]

Chapter v describes in some detail the seventh palace and all that it contains. We find in it a long list of the classes of angels who minister in this palace, some of which are not known from the other *Hekhalot* writings.[9] In chapter vi more angelological material is introduced. Its main subject matter is the details of the celestial *Qedushah*. Among other things it is said that clouds of fire envelop the faces of the angels, so that they should not look at the vision of the *Shekhinah*. This remark is particularly interesting, since the text already said (chapter iii) that God is hidden away from the angels by the "garment" that is spread over the Throne of Glory. This discrepancy can be explained by the fact that the writer of the text used different sources, or else that he invented new details without paying too much attention as to how these details harmonized. In any event, the writer also mentions the fact that a *Parokhet* (curtain) is spread before the Throne. Seven angels, those who were first born, are said to serve God. In addition, a detailed description of the *Ḥayyot* is given. Parts of that description seem to be the result of the writer's misunderstanding of his literary sources.[10] The chapter ends with another angelological section, which describes a variety of angelological hierarchies.

The seventh chapter describes *Me'onah*,[11] which is the firmament above the heads of the *Ḥayyot*. Although the writer does not explicitly allude to it, it appears that he has in mind the eighth heaven.[12] How-

---

[8] In fact, the chapter has a short epilogue: a passage is quoted from *Bavli Hagigah* 13a in which the limbs of the Hayyot are described.

[9] Thus, for instance, we find a class of angels called *Ḥadudei Panim* ("the angels with the shining faces"). For *Ḥadudim* in the sense of rays of light see "Livre de Noé" in: *Discoveries in the Judaean Desert I*: *Qumran Cave I*, ed. D. Barthélémy and J. T. Milik, Oxford, Clarendon Press, 1955, p. 85. See also E. Kimron, in *Lešonenu* XXXVII (1973), pp. 96-98, to which one has to add the expression *Ẓinorei Shemesh* (rays of the sun) in *Sefer Ha-Razim*, p. 92, l. 5.

[10] Thus, for instance, the writer says that each *Ḥayyah* has "four faces within four faces, and four wings within four wings". He may have used *Hekhalot Zutreti*, but obviously his interpretation of the relevant passage there will not fit the calculation of the number of faces and wings as it is explicated in *Hekhalot Zutreti*.

[11] The name, which is unknown from other sources, derives from *Deuteronomy* xxxiii, 27.

[12] See our discussion of *Re'uyot Yeḥezkel*.

ever, what the writer says about this heaven is not very clear, and he seems to have used descriptions of the seventh heaven which he found in different sources. He mainly used *Hekhalot Rabbati*, where he rightly noticed the fact that God descends from the eighth heaven to His Throne in the seventh palace in the seventh heaven. However, the manner in which he refers to *Hekhalot Rabbati* is another proof of the freedom he allowed himself in handling his material. Among other things, he assumes that a dialogue is held between the Angels of Idolatry [13] and the Angels of the Synagogues and Study Houses, as to who God is. Naturally, the Angels of Idolatry are unable to recognize God when He descends from the upper heaven. They ask "Who is the King of Glory?", to which the guardian angels of Israel answer: "The Lord of hosts, he is the King of glory".[14] The chapter ends with a series of quotations from midrashic and *Hekhalot* sources which discuss the creation of the world [15] and the Throne of Glory.[16] Once again, the writer handles his sources in a free manner, as can easily be seen from the way he quotes *Hekhalot Rabbati* iv,3 in the concluding sentence of his text.

---

[13] *Sarei ʿAvodah Zarah*, which in this particular context seem to be the guardian angels of Christianity.

[14] The reference is to *Psalms* xxiv,8-10. I cannot find a parallel or source to this interpretation of the biblical text.

[15] First he quotes *Bereshit Rabba* xii (ed. Theodor-Albeck, pp. 108-109) on the creation of the world with the two letters *Yod* and *Hei*. Then he quotes *Sefer Yeẓirah* i,13 (ed. I. Gruenwald, in: *Israel Oriental Studies*, I (1971), p. 146, paragraph 15). Between the quotations from *Bereshit Rabba* and that from *Sefer Yeẓirah* a number of short aggadic sayings are introduced.

[16] See *Hekhalot Rabbati* iii,2.

SHIʿUR QOMAH

With *Shiʿur Qomah* we begin the discussion of a series of texts which are not *Hekhalot* writings in the narrow sense of the word, but which belong to the ancient Merkavah tradition.[1] Among these texts *Shiʿur Qomah* is the most controversial one.[2] It describes the physical measures of God's limbs and gives their mystical names. In contrast to the *Hekhalot* tradition which refers back to the terminology and imagery of Ezekiel, the *Shiʿur Qomah* speculations attach themselves to the *Song of Songs*.[3] The term *Shiʿur Qomah* means "The Measurement of the Body", and it derives from the *Song of Songs* vii,8. It is first found in Tannaitic literature in connection with the vessels of the Temple.[4] However, *2 Enoch* xxxix,6 may contain the first reference to the *Shiʿur Qomah* of God.[5] In the Middle Ages the *Shiʿur Qomah* was one of the targets which the Qaraites attacked in rabbinic Judaism.[6] Even some of the rabbis were not happy with those provocative speculations.[7] Interesting in this respect was the position taken by Maimonides: in his youth he believed in the book, while in his later days he nervously rejected its Jewish origin.[8]

Since the book abounds in mystical names and measurements, its contents are difficult to convey. The only full text is printed in Musajoff's *Merkavah Shelemah*, and it contains textual information

---

[1] For the connections between the *Hekhalot* tradition and the *Shiʿur Qomah* speculations, see G. Scholem, *Jewish Gnosticism* etc., pp. 36-42.

[2] For the various theological problems involved in the *Shiʿur Qomah* speculations, see G. Scholem, *Von der Mystischen Gestalt der Gottheit*, Zürich, Rhein-Verlag, 1962, pp. 7 ff. For a survey of the medieval controversy over *Shiʿur Qomah* see A. Altmann, "Moses Narboni's Epistle on Shiʿur Qoma", in: *Jewish Medieval and Renaissance Studies*, ed. A. Altmann, Harvard University Press, 1967, pp. 225 ff.

[3] See S. Lieberman in G. Scholem, *Jewish Gnosticism* etc., pp. 118-126.

[4] *Yerushalmi Shabbat* 2d in the name of the ʾAmora, Rabbi Ḥananiah bar Shemuʾel.

[5] The visionary says: "I have seen the measureless and harmonious (B: incomparable) form of the Lord. To Him there is no end".

[6] See, for instance, Salmon ben Jeruchim, *The Book of the Wars of the Lord*, ed. I. Davidson, New York: 1934, pp. 114-124. See further, L. Nemoy, "Al-Qirqisani Account of the Jewish Sects and Christianity", *Hebrew Union College Annual* VII (1930), pp. 331, 350 ff.

[7] See above n. 2.

[8] See S. Lieberman in Scholem, *Jewish Gnosticism* etc., p. 124.

gleaned from a number of sources.[9] The text begins in a manner familiar from the *Hekhalot* literature: "Rabbi Yishma'el said: I saw the King of the Kings sitting on a high and exalted throne, and His servants were attending Him on His right and on His left". Metatron appears and reveals to Rabbi Yishma'el the measurement of God's body. The description begins from the feet and goes up to the head. Every limb is measured by parasangs. On page 38a the fantastic size of these parasangs is given: "Every parasang equals three miles, and every mile equals ten thousand ells, and every ell equals three small fingers. The small finger is that of God, and His small finger fills the whole world".

It is hard to say whether any method lies behind these measures, but we may assume that originally the measures aimed at conveying the notion of ideal proportions. These proportions were shared by God and man alike: "Rabbi Natan, Rabbi Yishma'el's student, said: He (Rabbi Yishma'el) gave me the measure of the nose too, from the right and from the left. And also (the measure of) the lips and (of) the cheekbones... the width of the forehead equals the height of the neck; the shoulder is as long as the nose (?), and the nose is as long as the small finger,[10] and the height of the cheekbones is like the hemisphere of the head. And this is also the size of every man". Since man was created in the image of God, those interested in the subject felt entitled to make inferences from the physical proportions of the human body to that of God.

Every limb has also a mystical name. This may be explained in different ways: First, we already saw that according to *Merkavah Rabbah* the angels have two parallel sets, or modes, of names. Allegedly, one is their exoteric, official name and the other is the esoteric, mystical, appellation. We may thus assume that in the case of the *Shi'ur Qomah* a similar concept was employed. But we may also say that since nobody was allowed to conceive the corporeal configuration of the Deity,[11] the mystics had to use mystical metonyms when they described His corporeal features. Thus the mystical language which was invented for that purpose aimed at circumventing the anthropomorphic problem. But there is yet another way of looking

[9] The text printed there on pages 30a-36a comes from the sources of the German Ḥasidim. However, we shall refer here only to the text printed on pages 36a-44a.

[10] See S. Lieberman, *Shkiin*, Jerusalem, 1939, p. 12.

[11] See *Exodus* xxxiii,20.

at these mystical names. At one stage the text says: "The appearance of the face is like that of the cheekbones, and the appearance of the cheekbones and the face is in the likeness of the spirit and in the form of the soul. Nobody can recognize Him. His body is like the *Tarshish*,[12] and His glory flashes in an awesome manner from out of the darkness. Clouds and mists encircle Him... We do not possess any measure, but only the names are revealed to us".[13] If taken literally, these sentences, and particularly the last one, indicate that the mystical names replace the measures. Thus the mystical name may refer to a particular limb and also indicate its measurement.

The degree of anthropomorphism maintained in *Shiʿur Qomah* is really remarkable. At one point the measure of God's beard is given (37a) and at another that of His eyebrows and of His curls (38b). Naturally, Rabbi Yishmaʾel was shocked by all that Metatron had revealed to him, so Rabbi ʿAkiva felt it necessary to strengthen Rabbi Yishmaʾel's self-confidence: "Everybody who knows this measure of our Creator and His corporeal configuration[14] which is hidden from the people, is promised life in the world to come..." (38b). Apparently, these words had their expected calming effect and Rabbi Yishmaʾel turned to his pupils: "I and Rabbi ʿAkiva give our pledge that he who knows this measure of our Creator and the corporeal configuration of the Lord is promised life in the world to come, on condition that he studies it every day". The condition expressed in the last words is reminiscent of the *Sar-Torah* speculations which, as we saw, should be studied or said daily.

The second part of *Shiʿur Qomah* (38b-39a bottom) extends the principle to God's arrows, sword, Throne and Living Creatures. Each of them has its secret mystical name as well as its huge dimensions. The second part of the text ends with an interesting remark. Referring to the Living Creatures which have just been described, it says: "Those are the ones who say the *Sanctus* and those are the ones who say the *Benedictus*. As it is said (*Psalms* cxlvii,19): 'He declares His word to Jacob'.[15] And everybody who does not conclude

---

[12] The reference here is to *Daniel* x,6, which describes one of the angels which Daniel saw. As for the *Tarshish* itself, it is generally believed to indicate the sea. See M. Mishor in *Lešonenu* XXXIV (1969-70), pp. 318-319.

[13] *Merkavah Shelemah* 37a.

[14] The Hebrew term used here is *Shevaḥ*, and it resembles the Arabic *Shabaḥ*, meaning "human figure indistinctly seen from a distance". See also A. Altmann, *art. cit.*, pp. 228-229.

[15] It is not made clear why this particular verse is quoted at this place. The

with the 'order of the work of creation' (*Seder Maʿaseh Bereshit*) errs concerning God's glory (*Shogeh be-tifʾarto shel Ha-Qodesh Barukh Hu*)". Similar words to the last ones are introduced when earlier the *locus classicus* of the *Shiʿur Qomah* speculations, *Song of Songs* v,10 ff., is quoted: "And everybody who does not conclude with this verse errs". There probably was an established procedure according to which the *Shiʿur Qomah* speculations were explicated. Every deviation from this customary order of explication was a grave mistake. However, in contrast to the *Hekhalot* writings, nothing is said regarding what might befall the erring mystic.

The third part of the text (39a bottom-40a) is devoted to a description of the celestial *Qedushah*. It begins with the words: "His glory fills everything" (*Tifʾarto melo ha-kol*). The words obviously refer to the Glory of God which has just been mentioned in connection with the erring mystic, but it is not clear whether this part of the text really belongs to the original *Shiʿur Qomah*. In several manuscripts this part, and the one following, are reproduced out of their present context as parts of *Shiʿur Qomah*. However, the *raison d'être* for their inclusion here is clear: Metatron who revealed the secrets of the *Shiʿur Qomah* to Rabbi Yishmaʾel is playing a major role in organizing the celestial *Qedushah*. In addition, the concluding sentences of the second part of the text already refer to the celestial *Qedushah* said by the *Ḥayyot*. This (third) part of the text is divided into two sections. In the first section a description is given of how Metatron and the angels perform the ritual of the heavenly *Qedushah*, while in the second part, Merkavah hymns [16] and Psalms [17] form the hymnological conclusion of the text. One point in this description of the celestial *Qedushah* is particularly noteworthy: Metatron is described putting "the fire of deafness" into the ears of the *Ḥayyot* so that they might not hear the voice of God and the Ineffable Name which Metatron utters. We do not know of a similar procedure in any of the other *Hekhalot* writings, and even *Sefer Hekhalot* (*3 Enoch*) which describes

---

same verse is also quoted before (37a) in connection with the "Shiʿur Qomah" of the tongue. However, *Psalm* cxlvii contains another verse (5) which is also taken to refer to God's "Shiʿur Qomah". See Scholem, *Von der mystischen Gestalt der Gottheit*, p. 16. Was *Psalm* cxlvii believed to be a "Shiʿur Qomah" psalm? Though the sources do not bear direct evidence to this, it is noteworthy that two verses are quoted from that psalm in the same connection.

[16] One section of these hymns equals the "Seventh Heaven" of *Sefer Ha-Razim*. See Margalioth's edition of *Sefer Ha-Razim*, p. 107, n. 1.

[17] *Psalms* xxix, xxiv, *Neḥemiah* ix,6-8, and *1 Chronicles* xxix,11-13.

Metatron's role in the celestial *Qedushah* has no reference to that effect.[18] It appears that the compiler of *Sefer Hekhalot* was ignorant of this part of the *Shiʿur Qomah* text, since nothing of it is quoted in his text. Towards the end of these hymns a short personal prayer is introduced (42a-42b), in which the Merkavah mystic asks for several personal favours.

[18] However, *Sefer Hekhalot* xv(b) contains a paraphrase of this passage. But this part of the book, which refers to Moses, is no integral part of it.

PHYSIOGNOMY, CHIROMANCY AND METOPOSCOPY

In our discussion of *Shi'ur Qomah* we noticed that underlying it possibly was a certain theory regarding the ideal proportions of the human body. These proportions were assumed to be shared by God and man alike. Naturally, man who was created in the image of God reflected the same ideal physical proportions as God. And, *mutatis mutandi*, those who engaged in speculations regarding the anthropomorphic features of God could use their observations about the structure of the human body in relation to what they believed was the corporeal configuration of God. However, the human body was not only conceived as revealing a secret mystical doctrine of the *corpus Dei*, but also supplied necessary information about man's character and future fate. This information was gained by examining the shape and relative size of several parts of the body.

The earliest Jewish source known to us that refers to the examination of the human body in order to define the moral and spiritual qualities of a person is a cryptic document from Qumran now published as 4Q 186.[1] The quintessence of this document is that man's moral and spiritual qualities can be defined through an examination of the size and shape of his thighs, toes, fingers, hair, eyes, beard, teeth and height. Even the quality of his voice has something to tell about his righteousness or wickedness. When the information gained through such an examination is added to the zodiacal sign of a man's birth, a perfect sketch of the moral and spiritual qualities of that man may be drawn. According to the theory maintained in that document, man has a share either in the House of Light or in the House of Darkness and that share is determined by a total number of nine points. The ratio of 4:5 is always the critical one in the decision to which of the two Houses he belongs. As Professor J. Licht rightly observed,[2] the information gained by such an examination together with the annual tests of a man's intellectual accomplishments was to help the leaders of the Qumran sect to decide who was worthy of sharing the sect's lot, and who had either to quit or be rejected.

Another document found at Qumran (Cave 4), written in Aramaic,

---

[1] See: *Discoveries in the Judaean Desert. V*: *Qumran Cave 4*, ed. J. M. Allegro, Oxford, Clarendon Press, 1968, pp. 88-91.

[2] In *Tarbiz* XXXV (1966), p. 18 ff.

possibly defines the corporeal features of the future Messiah.[3] Since these Qumran texts were preserved in a rather fragmentary condition, much that could help us in defining the scope and origin of their underlying theory is missing. However, we know that similar theories were spread in the ancient Near East, and since it has recently been argued that at least a certain fraction of the Qumran sect came from Babylonia,[4] it is quite likely that the Qumranites adapted in this case an ancient Babylonian theory and practice. Unfortunately, no traces of such a theory are preserved in either the pseudepigraphical corpus of writings or in the rabbinical writings. Admittedly, there are a few instances in these writings that could be interpreted as indicating a similar theory, but their true meaning could also lie elsewhere. To begin with, *Ben Sira* xix,29-30 says: "A man is known by his appearance, / And the wise man recognizeth him by his look / ... / And his gait showeth what he is".[5] Indeed, these verses of Ben Sira can only be a paraphrase of *Isaiah* iii,9,[6] but the words *Hakarat Panim* mentioned in this verse became a technical term for metoposcopy, the art of reading the lines of the forehead, and for the art of reading special signs on one's face in general. In addition, we find in *Testament Shim'on* v,1: "For some of the trouble of the spirit the face manifesteth". But this can, of course, be only a general statement with no technical overtones.

In rabbinical writings we find at least two cases in which certain corporeal features were singled out to determine certain halakhic problems. In the first case we have the abortion of an embryo. His degree of development is determined by the possibility of recognizing on him what the *Mishnah*[7] calls *Ẓurat Adam*, the shape of man. Referring to the same *Mishnah*, the *Tosefta*[8] uses the term *Ẓurat Panim*, the shape of the face, and the *Talmud Yerushalmi*[9] uses the

[3] J. Carmignac, "Les Horoscopes de Qumran", *Revue de Qumran* V (1965), pp. 206-217.

[4] See J. Murphy-O'Connor, "The Essenes and their History", *Revue Biblique* LXXXI (1974), p. 215 ff.

[5] The text was preserved only in Greek. The English translation is that of Box & Oesterley in Charles, *Apocrypha*, p. 384. See the translators' note *ad locum*.

[6] It should, however, be noticed that the Greek of *Ben Sira* does not repeat the LXX of *Isaiah* iii,9.

[7] *Mishnah Niddah* iii,2. Compare *Mishnah Bekhorot* viii,1.

[8] *Tosefta Niddah* iv,6-7; see also *Bavli Niddah* 25b.

[9] *Yerushalmi Niddah* 20c. The terms *Hakarat Panim*, *Parẓuf Panim* (*Mishnah Yevamot* xvi,3) and *Qelaster Panim* (*Wayyikra Rabba*, ch. xviii, ed. Margalioth, p. 391), are all synonyms.

term *Hakarat Panim*, that by which the individual features of the face are recognized. In another case, the finding of a corpse, the *Hakarat Panim* is determined by means of the nose, the cheekbones and the forehead.[10] As Professor Scholem rightly remarked, this material can only be taken as a general background to the esoteric material which we shall presently discuss.[11]

We now know that the Merkavah mystics engaged in detailed speculations about what can be learnt from the various parts of a man's body concerning his moral quality, his social and economic status, his health, his family, and his future lot in general. A number of texts, published by G. Scholem [12] and the present writer,[13] give a fairly wide picture of the scope of these speculations among the Merkavah mystics. Unfortunately, however, what is said in these texts is of a highly enigmatic character. The technical terminology used in the text is nowhere graphically displayed and analysed, so that the reader has to guess what the various signs really imply. Particular importance is attached in these texts to the lines found on one's palm and forehead. These lines, and particularly those of the palm, have long been subject to all kinds of theories, and some modern psychologists of the Jungian school find them helpful in their psychological diagnosis of their patients. The science of looking at the lines of the palm is called chiromancy, while the observation of the lines of the forehead—the younger of the two sciences—is called metoposcopy. However, the Merkavah mystics did not confine themselves to the hand and the forehead, but added speculations about the other parts of the body, including the sex organs. On the

---

[10] See *Mishnah Yevamot* xvi,3. The Mishnah states that the dead man's identity is determined by his face (*Parzuf Ha-Panim*) together with his nose. In *Yerushalmi Yevamot* 15c Rav Yehudah is quoted as saying that the nose together with the cheekbones determine the dead man's identity, while Rabbi Yirmiyah in the name of Rav quotes *Isaiah* iii,19 and infers that the *Hakarat Panim* is qualified by the nose only. A similar view to the last one is brought there also in the name of Rabbi ʾAbba bar Kahana. In *Bavli Yevamot* 120a Rabbanan are quoted as saying that the dead man's identity is determined by either the forehead or the *Parzuf Panim* and the nose. In any event, the nose is taken to be the most important part of the face to determine the identity of a dead man. In *Yerushalmi Niddah* 20c it is said that the degree of development of an embryo is determined by an examination of the following "signs": the forehead, the eye-brows, the eye, the ear, the cheekbone, the nose, the cheeks (lit. the beard), and the jaw-bone. Rabbi Shimʿon ben Yohai adds even the fingernails.

[11] See G. Scholem in *Sefer Assaf* (in Hebrew), Jerusalem, 1953, p. 462.

[12] See previous note.

[13] In *Tarbiz* XL (1971), pp. 301 ff.

whole, the discipline that is displayed in these texts is that of an occult science, by the help of which the Merkavah mystics either exhibited their superior modes of knowledge [14] or tested the qualities of those who wanted to join their ranks.[15]

The physiognomic and chiromantic texts of the Merkavah mystics raise a number of interesting problems. We shall refer here only to those problems not discussed in the studies which Professor Scholem published on these texts.[16] The first problem concerns the historical continuity of the physiognomic and chiromantic tradition in Judaism. Scholem states that "Chiromancy appears first in Judaism in the circle of Merkabah mysticism".[17] From what we saw in the Qumran writings it appears that the physiognomic tradition in Judaism is much older than Merkavah mysticism. If the *Responsa* of Hai Ga'on and his father, Sherira Ga'on,[18] supply the necessary documentary bridge between the chiromantic writings of the Merkavah mystics and the physiognomic and chiromantic passages in the *Zohar*,[19] no such links are known to exist between the relevant texts of the Qumran people and the chiromantic texts of the Merkavah mystics. Admittedly, we found in some of the rabbinic writings certain terms that later on became key notions in the chiromantic texts of the Merkavah mystics. But while these terms as they appear in the rabbinic writings only indicate general physiognomic notions, the Merkavah mystics were in possession of fully developed disciplines of chiromancy and metoposcopy.

However, it was already noticed that several technical terms used in the Qumran texts do reappear in the chiromantic texts of the Merkavah mystics.[20] This fact may be interpreted as indicating the

[14] See *Hekhalot Rabbati* i-ii, where the recurring phrase *Yode'a umakir bo* may be taken to indicate familiarity with the physiognomic tradition and terminology.

[15] See G. Scholem, in *Sefer Assaf*, p. 459.

[16] Apart from the article published in *Sefer 'Assaf* Scholem published "Ein Fragment zur Physiognomik und Chiromantik aus der Spätantiken jüdischen Esoterik" in: *Liber Amicorum: Studies in Honour of Professor Dr. C. J. Bleeker*, Leiden: 1969, pp. 175 ff.; and the article "Chiromancy" in: *Kabbalah*, Jerusalem, Keter Publishing House, 1974, pp. 317-319. "Ein Fragment etc." is a revised and updated German version of the article in *Sefer Assaf*; and the article "Chiromancy", which should have been an updated version of Scholem's article on that subject in *Encyclopedia Judaica Jerusalem*, was, unfortunately, printed without the additional notes.

[17] See *Kabbalah* (see previous note), p. 317.

[18] Scholem, *ibid.*

[19] See I. Gruenwald in *Tarbiz* XL (1971), p. 301, n. 3.

[20] See my discussion in *Tarbiz* XL (1971), pp. 304-305. See also J. Greenfield, "Prolegomenon" to *3 Enoch*, pp. XXXV-XXXVII.

existence of a historical continuity between these two facets of the physiognomic and chiromantic tradition. In discussing certain striking similarities between the Qumran documents and the Qaraite writings, Professor N. Wieder observed: "It may reasonably be assumed that the remnants of the Qumranites formed one of the dissident elements that went into the formation of the Qaraite sect, and that the Qumran element was able, either through sheer spiritual and intellectual weight, or through numbers, or both, to exert a preponderant influence on the medley of heterogeneous groups and individuals that rallied to 'Anan's banner".[21] However, Wieder had to admit that in "the absence of documentary data we are naturally thrown back upon theory and hypothesis, but, fortunately, not upon blind conjecture".[22] Wieder's words stating the relationship between the Judaean Scrolls and Qaraism ideally fit the problem of the transmission of esoteric traditions in general. Esoteric traditions appear and disappear and the assumed underground streams that connect them give rise to speculations. Hundreds of years passed between the composition of the Qumran texts and the relevant ones of the Merkavah mystics. Yet, one wonders whether it is merely coincidence that the Merkavah mystics repeated some of the technical terms of the Qumranites. Or do we have to assume that hitherto unidentified underground links are to account for the continuation of the physiognomic tradition through the ages.

Turning to the physiognomic texts of the Merkavah mystics, it should be noted that it is difficult to discover in them a coherent system. In fact, certain irregularities can easily be pointed out. For example, the texts frequently refer to certain letters of the alphabet the shape of which is believed to be inscribed in various parts of the human body. Neither is there any regularity in the enumeration of these letters, nor can any coherency be found regarding the part of the body in which these letters appear to be inscribed.[23] Since these letters appear to belong to the heart of this kind of

---

[21] N. Wieder, *The Judean Scrolls and Karaism*, London, East and West Library, 1962, pp. 254-255.

[22] *Ibid.*, p. 254.

[23] See I. Gruenwald in *Tarbiz* XL (1971), p. 307, n. 16. It should be noticed in this connection that some scholars claimed that they discovered certain secret letters in the Qumran Rule of Discipline. See, for instance, E. Ettisch, "Eschatologisch-Astrologische Vorstellungen in der Gemeinderegel (X,1-8)", *Revue de Qumran* II (1959), pp. 3-19. However, almost everything that was said about the letters in question appears to be of a highly speculative nature.

esoteric physiognomy and chiromancy—they are also mentioned in the chiromantic and physiognomic passages of the *Zohar*—it is to be expected that particularly in their case a fixed system should be discovered. However, this is not the case, and the impression one gets is of casualness and arbitrariness. In another case, we find that a certain terminology is differently used in two texts.[24] And in yet another case the same fate is obtained from two different signs of the body.[25] One may easily explain such discrepancies by the existence of parallel traditions or differences of opinion regarding the identification of the signs and their meaning. And it may be argued that in the case of such a popular science no absolute consistency is to be expected. What really mattered in the eyes of those people was the practice itself and its various functions, but not the methodological consistency of the technique.

Another problem that concerns the physiognomic texts of the Merkavah mystics is the inclusion of astrological speculations in some of these texts.[26] Judaism considered astrology as idolatry, and from biblical times onward it fiercely fought all kinds of astral beliefs. However, we know that there were times in which the popular belief in astrology was stronger than the laws forbidding its practice. In many countries and for a long time astrology was the queen of the sciences, so that it was almost inevitable that Judaism of Talmudic times should succumb to the general—pagan—fashion of the time. There are a great number of utterances in rabbinic writings about the efficacy of the astral bodies and the dependence of man on their powers.[27] But it would be wrong to think that Judaism of Talmudic times shared the pagan astrological beliefs without any reservation. On the contrary, there are some sharp utterances against the belief in astrology. On the whole, it may be argued that Judaism of that time maintained an ambivalent attitude towards astrology. On the one hand one finds attempts towards a systematization of this belief;[28] on the other hand one finds views which, in spite of their recognition of the efficacy of astrology, deny its power over an obedient Jew.[29]

---

[24] See Gruenwald, *art. cit.*, p. 311, n. 19.

[25] *Ibid.*, p. 312, n. 7.

[26] Particularly in the first text published by the present writer in *Tarbiz* XL (1971).

[27] Despite many attempts to deal with the subject, there is still room for a comprehensive study of the various Jewish attitudes towards astrology.

[28] See particularly *Bavli Shabbat* 156a.

[29] See in *Tarbiz* XL (1971), pp. 302-303. To which one should add Tosafot *ʿAvodah Zarah* 3b (s.v. *Shomer Nafsho*).

However, in our text, it appears, no room is left for ambivalence: astrology is taken to support and to complement chiromancy and metoposcopy in their prognostic faculty. In fact, if the whole text had been preserved it could have been a grand display of these occult disciplines. Unfortunately, only small parts of what seems to have been a detailed treatise on these subjects have come down to us, and from the few small pages a great deal has to be inferred.

SEFER HA-RAZIM

The publication in 1967 of the *Sefer Ha-Razim* by the late Professor M. Margalioth drew the attention of the scholarly world to the existence in Hebrew of a fully developed magical literature. The nature and scope of that literature in Hebrew does not fall short of the parallel Greek magical papyri and the Aramaic Incantation Bowls. In fact, in addition to *Sefer Ha-Razim* we know of the existence of a great number of Hebrew manuscripts which contain similar material of no less importance than the *Sefer Ha-Razim*.[1] The subject matter of *Sefer Ha-Razim* consists mainly of magical prescriptions for a great variety of purposes: medicine, subjugation of one's enemies, discourse with supernatural powers, etc. The technical term for these practices is *Baqashah* (Request), and most of them begin with the words *'Im Biqashta* (If you expressed the wish). The technical terms used in the book for magic, or the magical practice, are *Davar*, *'Eseq* and *Ḥefeẓ*. The common Hebrew term for magic, *Keshafim*, is only used twice in the book (p. 86, l. 95; p. 94, l. 42), and this only when the magical practice of one's enemy is mentioned. This is probably to say that the book does not designate itself as an inferior kind of pagan or idolatrous magic. This is no black magic for subduing people to the powers of the devil, but white magic used for allegedly constructive purposes.

Although we have dealt extensively in the present book with theurgical and magical practices, magic as such does not directly belong to our subject matter. In fact, the whole question of Jewish magic still deserves a full-scale study which will take into account the details of the relationship between Jewish magic and the Greek magical papyri on the one hand, and the Aramaic Incantation Bowls on the other. Despite L. Blau's monograph, *Das Alt-jüdische Zauberwesen*, first published in 1898 and still a notable cornerstone in the study of Jewish magic, and the many subsequent studies, we still await a comprehensive study of Jewish magic and its connections with other

[1] Two such manuscripts—Sassoon 290 (now sold) and Gaster 177 (now in Manchester)—are described by M. Benayahu in *Temirin* I, (in Hebrew), Jerusalem: 1972, pp. 187 ff. Although the manuscripts are comparatively late—probably of the 16th century—they contain versions of *Sefer Ha-Razim*, *Ḥarba De-Moshe*, *Sefer Ha-Malbush*, etc.

magical systems.[2] Our concern with *Sefer Ha-Razim* results mainly from its unique combination of magic and Merkavah material and our comments revolve around this curious combination of literary elements.

One of the magical practices of the book contains a historical reference,[3] on the basis of which attempts have been made to date the book as belonging to either the third or fourth century C.E.[4] However, it appears that despite the fact that the book contains some early elements, it was compiled rather late (6th or 7th century C.E.) by a compiler who did not always understand the material available to him.[5] In any event, the book presents a unique combination of esoteric beliefs and practices which permeated certain circles in the Judaism of Talmudic times. In this respect, it gives us an opportunity to look back and reconsider some of the problems which have been discussed in the present book.

Before we begin our discussion of *Sefer Ha-Razim*, a few words must be said about Margalioth's edition. To begin with, Margalioth published an eclectic text. The book should not therefore be quoted without a close study of the *variae lectiones* printed at the end of the text. In addition, Margalioth tampered with the text, in some cases even where the manuscripts supply good and interesting readings.[6] After a careful study of the book the present writer came to the conclusion that a new critical edition is required. In a new edi-

---

[2] To give one example of what we have in mind we can mention John M. Hull, *Hellenistic Magic and the Synoptic Tradition*, London, SCM Press, 1974. In spite of the fact that Hull's book was published seven years after the publication of *Sefer Ha-Razim*, the latter is not mentioned in Hull's discussion and survey of Jewish and hellenistic magic! And this is not the only shortcoming of that book.

[3] See *Sefer Ha-Razim*, p. 68, ll. 27-28: "These are the angels who attend to the magical practice in the first and in the second year of the cycle of fifteen years reckoned by the 'Kings of Greece'". See next note.

[4] In a letter to the editor of the book, Professor A. Rosenthal interpreted the date quoted in the previous note as referring to the cycle of the *Indictiones* started by Diocletian in Egypt in 297, and by Constantine in 312. Professor Rosenthal inclines to date the book in the fourth century C.E., while Margalioth himself argues for an earlier date (in the third century C.E.). See, Margalioth's "Introduction", pp. 24-26.

[5] This is particularly true in the case of the many Greek words which the book contains. Not all the corrupt transcriptions can be attributed to careless copyists.

[6] To give just one or two examples: On p. 66, l. 27 he omitted the word *Ha-Razim* after the third word in the line. In line 30 Margalioth changed the clear *Taskil* into the curious *Taskit*.

tion a commentary should be added and the *indices* enlarged and improved.[7]

Sefer Ha-Razim begins with an Introduction which tells the history of the transmission of magic from the days of Noah. That Noah was selected to be the first recipient of magic may be due to the tradition that goes back to *Jubilees* x,12-14, where the angels teach Noah how to cure all kinds of illnesses. Noah writes everything down in a book. However, it should be noted that *Sefer Ha-Razim* was given to Noah before the Flood, while *Jubilees* x,12-14 refers to events that took place after the Flood. The Introduction lists all the things that can be known or achieved with the help of magic. Yet, very little of what the Introduction lists as the efficacy of magic is later displayed in practice in the course of the book. In fact, the Introduction is also known from other books,[8] and its omnibus catalogue of subjects could indeed fit a number of purposes. The Introduction begins with the statement that *Sefer Ha-Razim* was revealed to Noah by the angel Raziel before the former entered his ark. From Noah the book was transmitted down the many generations until it reached King Solomon. As a matter of fact, the Introduction speaks about a plurality of *Sifrei Ha-Razim* ("Books of Mysteries"). Our *Sefer Ha-Razim* is thus only one in a series of such books, and according to the Introduction, it was one of the magical books which King Solomon allegedly possessed.[9]

Reading the details of the Introduction, one can see that the efficacy of magic stretches over the whole of Nature. Magic may help man to gain all kinds of secret knowledge, to divine the future, and to influence the course of events. Magic is efficacious in astronomy, in astrology, in meteorology, and so on. All that one has to do is to study the *Sefer Ha-Razim* and to learn its practices and prescriptions.

---

[7] It is a curious fact that all those who reviewed Margalioth's edition did not refer to its obvious textual shortcomings. Attempts have already been made to translate the book, or parts of it, into English, French and German. None of the translators were aware of the fact, that the text published by Margalioth cannot be trusted without checking the variant readings! Only half of the book is contained in the Genizah fragments, the discovery of which made Margalioth announce it as a sensation.

[8] See A. Jellinek's remarks in *Bet ha-Midrasch* III, pp. XXX-XXXIII.

[9] As far as I can see, the first writer who attributed the knowledge of magic to King Solomon was Josephus Flavius in *Antiquities* VIII, 45-48. At least, Josephus is the first datable written source to the tradition that was variously dispersed in antiquity. See further, J. Doresse, *The Secret Books of the Egyptian Gnostics*, New York, The Viking Press, 1960, pp. 170-172.

Indeed, the existence of such a book in Hebrew could cause its editor severe dogmatic difficulties. Magic was strictly forbidden in Judaism. Even in apocalyptic literature the teaching of magic to mankind was attributed to the evil angels.[10] However, in rabbinic literature a more complex view was held on magic. We cannot include here a detailed summary on the rabbinic view of magic,[11] but it may briefly be said that some of the sages were familiar with certain magical practices and others also practised magic. The official reason for this deviation from the obvious biblical prohibition to practise magic was that one may study—and perform—magic for the purpose of familiarizing oneself with the subject. We may well assume that the common people were less conscientious in restricting their use of magic.

When it comes to *Sefer Ha-Razim*, we find magical practices organized in what appears to be a systematic magical manual. From an orthodox Jewish point of view this is all the more perplexing, since the *Sefer Ha-Razim* is the only systematic magical treatise we know of in (post) Talmudic times. Neither the magical papyri nor the Aramaic Incantation Bowls, to say nothing of the various kinds of magical amulets and gems, are in any sense of the word magical books.[12] All these magical documents are shorter or longer collections of magical practices, and no attempt is made in them to organize the material in any coherent method or system. The way *Sefer Ha-Razim* organizes its magical subject matter is thus rather interesting. The book is divided into seven parts, corresponding to the seven heavens. The names of two of these heavens resemble those found in the so-called Palestinian lists of heavens,[13] a fact that underlines the assumption that the book was composed in *Erez-Yisrael*, or at least by a Jew who was familiar with peculiarities of the Palestinian Merkavah tradition. The organization of this Merkavah material is particularly interesting. The "First Heaven" contains no Merkavah material at all. From the "Second Heaven" onwards, the higher we proceed in the "Heavens" the more Merkavah material, and the less

---

[10] See, for instance, *1 Enoch* vi-viii, and lxix.

[11] See E. E. Urbach, *The Sages*, Chapters vi-vii.

[12] It should be noticed that magical books are sometimes referred to in the Greek magical papyri published by Karl Preisendanz.

[13] See I. Gruenwald, in *Tarbiz* XXXVI (1967), pp. 269-270. More evidence for the Palestinian origin of the book is supplied by Margalioth, though he inclines to locate its place of composition in Alexandria.

magical material is introduced. In the "Seventh Heaven" no magical material is found at all.

Sefer Ha-Razim contains a rather elaborate angelology which in itself underlines the structure of the book. In the "First Heaven" we find a class of angels, called *Shotrim*, ("Scribes"), sitting (!) on seven thrones and presiding over seven camps of angels who serve them. Each camp of angels is responsible for a certain magical activity. In the course of his magical performance, the magician has to call out the names of the proper angels or to write them down—usually in blood—and thus send them on their magical mission. In this sense, one may see the angels as magical apprentices. The number of the angels varies from camp to camp. Although some of the manuscripts mention certain numbers, the actual number of names does not always correspond to the number given in the manuscripts. The reason for this discrepancy lies in copyists' errors. Because the names of the angels in *Sefer Ha-Razim* are rather unusual and mostly incomprehensible, the copyists had difficulty in dividing those completely incomprehensible chains of letters into words. Nothing could direct them as to how to split groups of letters into words. Only in cases where the names had the usual—'el—ending did the copyists find themselves on safe ground.

The "Second Heaven" is formally divided into twelve classes of angels. They are called *Maʿalot* ("Steps"), since, like the Levites in the Temple, they stood on twelve steps in the "Second Heaven". Although many of these angels have the traditional—'el—ending, their names are almost as incomprehensible as the names which do not have that ending. Three angels are in charge of the "Third Heaven". As in the previous two heavens, these angels too preside over groups of angels. Accordingly, this "Heaven" is sub-divided into three parts. The "Fourth Heaven" is divided into two parts corresponding to the two classes of angels that inhabit it: the angels of the day and the angels of the night. In the "Fifth Heaven" there are the twelve angels called The Presidents of Glory (*Nesiʾei Ha-Kavod*). The number corresponds to the twelve months of the year. Evidently, these angels are in charge of information of what may happen in the respective months over which they preside. However, the "Fifth Heaven" is not subdivided into twelve corresponding parts. It contains only a general instruction of what one should do in order to know in which month one will die. The "Sixth Heaven" is once again divided into two parts, corresponding to the two groups of angels inhabiting the west and the east of that Heaven. Since the "Seventh Heaven" does not contain any magical practices, no specific classes of angels are mentioned therein.

When it comes to the magical practices described in the book, a number of interesting features should be emphasized. To begin with, the conjuration of the angels is frequently connected with ritual performances which, according to traditional standards, are downright idolatry. One is expected to offer libations to the angels and incense to the astral bodies.[14] In one case one even has to sacrifice a white cock to the moon and stars.[15] Most surprising is the prayer to Helios, which one has to say if one desires to see the sun rising in its chariot.[16] These and other idolatrous practices described in the book led Margalioth to the conclusion that *Sefer Ha-Razim* is in fact a heretical book.[17] And indeed a book that contains a magical practice for necromancy [18] cannot but arouse orthodox antagonism.[19] In the enlarged Hebrew edition of his book *Greek and Hellenism in Jewish Palestine* (pp. 73 ff.), Professor Saul Lieberman discussed the problem of the penetration of heathen and pagan beliefs in astrology and magic into the world of the Jews in Talmudic times. According to Professor Lieberman, it cannot be denied that the Jews of Talmudic times were influenced by the beliefs and practices maintained and performed among their non-Jewish neighbours. However, according to Professor Lieberman, the Jews absorbed from that world only that which was commonplace in everyday life. Thus, the magical and astrological information contained in rabbinic writings still bears the marks of the strong resentment felt by the rabbis towards that kind of material.

Yet, it may be asked whether a book like *Sefer Ha-Razim*, and similar material contained in manuscripts, does not betray, in a more reliable manner than do the rabbinic writings, the nature and scope of these occult practices among the common people. After all, the rabbis and those who put their sayings into writing had certain standards to maintain. Their responsibility and obligations as religious and social leaders imposed on them restrictions and modes of ex-

---

[14] See Margalioth, "Introduction", pp. 10-11.

[15] *Ibid.*, p. 12.

[16] *Ibid.*, pp. 12-13.

[17] *Ibid.*, p. 14 ff. Margalioth quotes Church Fathers who attacked the Jews for (a) praying not to God but to angels and (b) practising magic.

[18] "First Heaven", ll. 176 ff.

[19] *Leviticus* xix,31; *Deuteronomy* xviii,10-11.

pression that were not always applied among the common unlearned people. Despite the distinctive literary qualities of *Sefer Ha-Razim* which may suggest that its origin was in literate and educated circles, it still seems to represent the popular spirit of the time which engaged in magic and astrology. Magic and astrology, we should remember, were respected sciences. In practising these sciences, the Jews of the time were only following the intellectual fashion of the day. If this is true, then halakhic and doctrinal considerations were suspended in the light of the practical functions these sciences played in everyday life.

In spite of the fact that *Sefer Ha-Razim* bears strong points of resemblance to the Greek magical papyri, one should not view it as a mere Hebrew imitation of the magical material contained in those papyri. There are some outstanding characteristics in the book which make it an original contribution in the history of magical literature. The writer, or compiler, of the book was in all probability familiar with the material found in the magical papyri—he even uses several Greek technical terms found in them—but this fact makes his own contribution to the subject all the more interesting. In contrast to many of the magical practices found in the magical papyri, *Sefer Ha-Razim* repeatedly stresses the importance of the preparatory steps, which, similar to the preparatory stages in the *Hekhalot* mysticism, insist on the ritual purity of the performer and on the special diets he has to keep. In addition, *Sefer Ha-Razim* sometimes refers to the special magical signs and letters—the so-called *kharakteres* of the magical papyri—but it totally omits any reference to the magical words and formulae of the magical papyri. Instead, *Sefer Ha-Razim* displays a highly developed angelology, and the invocation of these angels comes in the place of the magical formulae (*Zauberwörte*) in the magical papyri. It is also interesting to note in this connection that the names of many angels in *Sefer Ha-Razim* sound like magical words, a fact that may be due not to the mere caprice of the writer of the book, but may rather reveal his desire to judaize certain essential elements of the magical papyri.

The magical papyri contain prayers and applications to the various magical spirits and demons which are invoked. These magical prayers are sometimes replaced in *Sefer Ha-Razim* by semi-Merkavah hymns. The Merkavah material in *Sefer Ha-Razim* is interesting for a number of reasons. On close examination, its poetical quality is of a different nature from the hymns in the *Hekhalot* writings. It lacks the ecstatic tone of the *Hekhalot* hymns, and in its style and form it resembles the liturgical poetry, the *Piyyutim*. Although the Merkavah material of *Sefer Ha-Razim* apparently derived from mystical sources that sprang, if not exclusively, from the *Hekhalot* literature, one may see in this Merkavah material a more or less independent development of the *Hekhalot* literature.

As previously mentioned, there is no Merkavah material in the so-called "First Heaven". The "Second Heaven" begins with a description of what it contains: "Frost,[20] treasure-houses of snow, treasure-houses of hail, angels of fire, angels of fright, spirits of fear and spirits of awe". We know of similar lists which enumerate what each of the heavens contains (*Bavli Ḥagigah* 12b-13a; *Re'uyot Yeḥezkel*; *Beraita de-Ma'aseh Bereshit*; etc.). There are significant differences between these lists regarding what is contained in each of the heavens. *Sefer Ha-Razim* does not follow any of the parallel lists, and it may be said that the writer of the book was not seriously interested in cosmological problems. The incorporation of cosmological material into his book probably followed the fashion of the day. *Ma'aseh Bereshit* (cosmology) and *Ma'aseh Merkavah* went hand in hand, but the manner in which the writer of *Sefer Ha-Razim* used them for his magical purposes is rather unique. To give one example of the use the writer made of the cosmological material, one may refer to his description of what the first two heavens contain. In the parallel cosmological lists we find that the first two heavens are always connected with the operation of the heavenly luminaries. However, in *Sefer Ha-Razim* nothing is said about the first heaven apart from the fact that it is inhabited by the seven *Shotrim* ("Scribes"). The second heaven in *Sefer Ha-Razim* contains elements which in the other lists are contained in the sixth and seventh heavens. It should be noted too that the treasure-houses of snow and of dew are found, according to *2 Enoch* iv-vi, in the first heaven. It thus appears that *Sefer Ha-Razim* was not the first to break established facts of cosmological descriptions.

The "Second Heaven" also contains twelve groups of angels which are described at some length. For example, the first group is described in the following manner: "They stand in a frightening position. / They are wrapped up in wrath. / They are girdled with fear. / / They are encircled by trembling. / Their garment is like that of fire. /

[20] The text uses two words, *Kefor* and *Qitor*, which appear to be synonyms.

Their face is like the vision of lightning. / Their mouth does not cease from many things. / But their voice is not heard. / Since their job is to silence and to terrify and to frighten him who stands up against the one who conjures them in ritual purity". The twelfth group is described thus: "They are encircled by justice. / And they have rays of glory on their heads. / They are full of sagacity. / They are qualified by their song. / They stand in two groups. / Half of them sing, and half of them say the response. / There is healing in their tongue and binding up in their speech. / And you shall be successful in everything that they are conjured for". This is more or less the style and form of the Merkavah material in the Second, Third, Fourth, Fifth and Sixth Heavens. It mainly concerns the angels, their features and their activity in heaven.

In the 'Seventh Heaven', which contains no magical material, a description is given of God sitting on His Throne of Glory. The degree to which the writer was familiar with the *Hekhalot* literature is clearly seen from the fact that no palaces are mentioned in that heaven. Instead, God is said to be sitting in His Holy Abode, *Me'on Qodsho*, a term that derives from *Deuteronomy* xxvi,15. Books of fire are said to be opened before Him,[21] and streams of fire are pouring forth from underneath the Throne.[22] God is not even seen by His angels. He is carried by the *Ḥayyot*. Before the angels sing the *Qedushah*, they immerse in "streams of purity" (*Naharei Ṭohorah*) and wrap themselves up in garments of white fire.[23] The description ends with a Merkavah hymn, the phraseology of which is strongly influenced by biblical images. In contrast to the *Hekhalot* hymns, the lyrical elements of *Sefer Ha-Razim* owe a great deal to the poetry of Scripture. In fact, whole biblical verses are quoted in the Merkavah hymns of *Sefer Ha-Razim*, and in this respect we may repeat that the Merkavah material of the book comes closer to the *Piyyutim* than to the *Hekhalot* hymns. In any event, most of them lack the ecstatic tone and style of the *Hekhalot* hymns.

To sum up, *Sefer Ha-Razim* was included in our discussion of the *Hekhalot* writings because of the Merkavah material it contains. It is

---

21 Compare *Sefer Ha-Razim*, p. 89, ll. 142-143; *3 Enoch* xxvii, xxviii, xxx, xxxii, xliv. See *Daniel* vii,10.

22 Compare *Sefer Ha-Razim*, p. 96, l. 3. Heavenly streams (of fire) are also mentioned in *Ma'aseh Merkavah*, paragraphs 2 and 10, and in *3 Enoch*, *passim*. Needless to say, the idea derives from *Daniel* vii,10.

23 For the parallels in the *Hekhalot* literature, see the writer's notes to *Re'uyot Yeḥezkel*, pp. 126-127, n. 65. See also *Sefer Ha-Razim*, p. 96, ll. 6-7.

no mystical treatise in the proper sense of the term, but it is an interesting example of the interplay of magic and mysticism in antiquity. The book still deserves a full-scale revaluation, but not before a new critical edition of the book is available. Then the whole subject of Jewish and pagan magic will be re-opened in light of the material found in the Greek and Coptic magical writings on the one hand, and the Aramaic and Mandaic Incantation Bowls on the other.[24]

---

[24] See E. R. Goodenough, *Jewish Symbols in the Greco-Roman Period*, vol. II (1953), pp. 153-295. Goodenough gives an English translation of several magical papyri and bowls, but his discussion of the material he quotes *in extenso* is far from satisfactory. [After the completion of this book, P. Schäfer drew my attention to J. H. Niggemeyer, *Beschwörungsformeln aus dem 'Buch der Geheimnisse'*, Georg Olms Verlag, Hildesheim & New York, 1975. Niggemeyer produced a systematic and serious work.]

APPENDICES

by Saul Lieberman

1. *Metatron, the meaning of his name and his functions*

The origin of the name מיטטרון was discussed by many scholars. The whole material was collected by H. Odeberg in his edition of *3 Enoch*, p. 137 ff. He first quotes the conjecture that Metatron is "equivalent to σύνθρονος, co-occupant of the Divine Throne", and he then cites a number of other theories. In conclusion he summarizes : "Of these different modes of interpretation that regarding Metatron as equivalent to σύνθρονος can be easily dismissed. There is not a single instance in any known Jewish source of Metatron being represented as the co-occupant of the Divine Throne".

The scholars took for granted that the use of σύνθρονος is similar to the use of σύνναος (sharing the same temple), i.e. sharing the same throne. Professor G. Scholem was therefore quite right in rejecting (*Major Trends in Jewish Mysticism*, p. 60-70) all the conjectures cited by Odeberg. However, the exact meaning of σύνθρονος was misunderstood by Odeberg and his predecessors. E. Cornemann (*Klio* I, p. 55) correctly pointed out that *living* dignitaries were often called σύνθρονοι θεοί, the technical expression for such honors was ἰσοθεοὶ τιμαί.[1] It appears that in our sources Μετάθρονος (= σύνθρονος) is a mere title, [ἄγγελος] μετάθρονος, as he is frequently called in *3 Enoch* : מטטרון מלאך.[2] This last source correctly understood that the chair of the angel stood alongside the Throne of his Master.[3] *Genesis* (41 :43) says about Joseph, the viceroy of Pharaoh : "*And he* (i.e. Pharaoh) *made him ride in the second chariot* etc." which Rashi correctly understood to mean that Joseph rode alongside Pharaoh's chariot. *Test. Levi* (xiii,9) uses the following expression : σύνθρονος ἔσται βασιλέων, ὥσπερ Ἰωσὴφ ὁ ἀδελφός μου. Lucianus in his mockery oracle [4] maintains : ἥρωα μέγιστον σύνθρονον Ἡφαίστῳ

---

[1] Comp. also the material adduced by A. D. Nock, *Essays in Religion* etc., p. 135 and notes *ibid.*

[2] And not מיטטרון המלאך!

[3] See *3 Enoch* ch. 7 and ch. 10. In ch. 48, p. 66 it is explicitly stated: ועשיתי לו כסא כנגד כסאי. In later literature σύνθρονος is simply a πάρεδρος, assessor. See further Liddell and Scott, s.v. σύν !

[4] *de mor. Peregrini* 29.

καὶ Ἡρακλῆϊ ἄνακτι. Peregrinus was eager that his throne should stand alongside the throne of Heracles, as Lucianus said above :[5] συνοδεύει παρὰ τὸν Ἡρακλέα.[6] For our purpose it is important to note that σύνθρονος is a common feature in the heathen temples (*heikhaloth*). In the earlier sources σύνθρονος represents the highest personalities in the temples, mostly the *living* emperors, or their immediate families.[7]

We shall cite here two inscriptions.[8] An inscription of the first century C.E. mentions [9] a "priestess of Athena Nikephoros and Athena Polias and Julia, *enthroned with her*, as *Young Nikephoros*, daughter of Germanicus Caesar".[10]

And again an inscription published by A. von Premerstein [11] contains an order of the Athenian people that an image of the empress Julia Domna be dedicated under the same roof as Polias, in order that she should be synthronos with the god.[12]

Depicting a *noisy* heathen procession, the rabbis describe [13] it as follows : "They carry a *great god* to a *small god*",[14] i.e. when the pagans want to increase the prestige of a temple they introduce a great god alongside with the smaller god dwelling in the temple. The rabbis were familiar with the term "small god". And indeed, the heathen temples were replete with gods and godesses, great gods and small gods (*di maiores* and *di minores*), half gods and even "small gods among the lesser gods".[15] The sources sometimes do

---

[5] *Ibid.*, 24.

[6] But, of course, after being cremated he might have aspired to become an equal of the gods, to become a god himself.

[7] See Liddell and Scott, s.v. σύνθρονος.

[8] Not referred to by Liddell and Scott, but one of them is listed in the Index of *OGIS*, the other is referred to by Nock, *Essays*, etc., p. 229, n. 155.

[9] *OGIS* 474 : ἱέρειαν . . . τῆς Νικηφόρου καὶ Πολιάδος ['Αθηνᾶς καὶ] 'Ιουλίας συνθρόνου, νέας Νικη[φόρου, Γερμα]νικοῦ καίσαρος θυγατρός.

[10] On νέοι θεοί (like: νέος Διόνυσος, νέος 'Απόλλων, etc.), see Nock, *ibid.*, p. 43, n. 84, p. 149, n. 73, p. 151, n. 82. On the meaning of νέος θεός, see *ibid.*, p. 149 and n. 73 *ibid.* Similarly Metathronos (= Synthronos), like our Julia Synthronos, was also styled יה קטן (see below, n. 24). In biblical Hebrew it could signify: Νέος Ιάω.

[11] *Jahreshefte d. Österreichishen Arch. Inst.* XVI (1913), p. 250.

[12] ἵνα σύνθρονος ᾖ τῇ θεῷ. See *ibid.*, p. 254.

[13] TP *ʿAboda Zarah* II, 3, 41b. Comp. Lucretius II. 608 ff.

[14] מוליכין עבודה זרה גדולה אצל עבודה זרה קטנה. The reading of the text is sure. It is also corroborated by the commentary of Rabbenu Hananel TB *ibid.* 32b. Rabinovitz *Shaare Torath Eretz Israel*, p. 562, needlessly emends the text. He misunderstood the purport of the procession.

[15] *Anthol. Pal.* IX 334: τὸν ἐν σμικροῖς ὀλίγον θεόν.

not deign to mention the names of the subordinate gods,[16] but simply state: Διὶ 'Ογμήνῳ καὶ τοῖς σὺν αὐτῷ θεοῖς [17] exactly as it frequently appears in the legal documents: [18] ὁ δεῖνα καὶ οἱ σὺν τῷ αὐτῷ.

The ancients were much less sensitive to the term god than our modern society. Mortals are styled "gods" during their lifetime. The Jews living in a polytheistic society were very well aware of it. The term "small god" would be shocking to us, but it was not so to the ancient mind. As long as no worship is involved the "small god" remains a mere title (see below).

One rabbi maintained [19] that Moses was a ἡμιθεός, a semi-god, his upper half a god, his lower half a man. According to other rabbis, he was sometimes a man and sometimes a god.[20]

Again, we read in *Ps.* 8:6: "*Yet Thou hast made him but little lower than God, and hast crowned him with glory and honor* etc." The rabbis understood [21] this verse as referring to Moses and God.[22] Symmachus translates the verse: καὶ ἐλαττώσεις αὐτὸν ὀλίγον παρὰ θεόν.[23]

Similarly, Metatron was called [24] a minor god,[25] his name being like that of his master.[26] He is also styled in Palestinian Targum **ספרא רבה**, "the great scribe",[27] a very important title.[28] He is cred-

---

[16] Comp. Lieberman, *Hellenism in Jewish Palestine*, p. 115.

[17] *Journal of Hellenic Studies* X, p. 227, cited by Nock, *Essays in Religion*, etc., p. 239.

[18] See Preisigke, *Wörterbuch* II, p. 521, s.v. σύν.

[19] *Debarim Rabba* xi,4.

[20] *Ibid.* and *Pesikta de Rav Kahana* (towards the end), ed. Mandelbaum, p. 443 ff. and parallels.

[21] TB *Nedarim* 38a.

[22] And not angels.

[23] TB *ibid.* explains that Moses was only a little lower than God, because he was endowed with forty nine "gates of Binah". Comp. *3 Enoch*, ch. 48c, p. 67, in the variants.

[24] See Scholem, *Major Trends*, p. 366 *passim*, *Jewish Gnosticism* etc., p. 47.

[25] In heathen literature, Enoch would never be able to escape this title. Any mortal who was taken up (bodily) to heaven becomes a god, See Bickerman, *Entretiens sur l'Antiquité Classique*, vol. XIX, 1973, p. 14-15. A monotheist would never accept it, but this mortal may become almost a god, a small god.

[26] See Scholem, *ibid.*, p. 68, p. 366, n. 103. Comp. *Aggadath Shir Hashirim*, ed. Schechter, p. 9 and Brüll *Jahrbücher* I, p. 224 and n. 6, *ibid.* The association of the number "seventy" with that of the languages is a later speculation.

[27] The same title is given to Moses in the Talmud and *Targumim*, See Lieberman **יוונית ויוונות באי**, p. 212, and notes *ibid.* Add: *Vayyikra Rabba* I,3, p. 12: **הסופר שהיה ספרן של ישראל** The argument of Krauss in **הגורן** VII, p. 29 ff. is childish. Comp. Ezra 7:11 *passim.*

[28] See Lieberman *ibid.* The wording in TB *Hagiggah* 15a is probably a later

ited [29] with the task of teaching babies [who died in their infancy]. *3 Enoch* [30] is more specific : "He is teaching the souls of the embryos that died in their mothers' womb etc.".[31] This is a very old legend. Clemens of Alexandria [32] cites the Apocalypse of Petrus which in his turn asserts : "The *Scripture* saith (ἡ γραφή φησι) that the children who have been exposed are delivered to a care-taking angel, by whom they are educated and brought up etc.". The same fate is allotted to *abortive* babies,[33] exactly like in the tradition of *3 Enoch*. According to one tradition of the Talmud [34] this function of Metatron was subsequently taken over by the Lord himself.

Here we have to note that there is no contradiction [35] between the different titles of Metatron. The rabbis saw a great similarity between the hierarchy of the kingdom on earth and that of the kingdom on heaven.[36] At a certain period during the imperial times the slaves and the *libertini* of the emperors exercised a great power over the empire, or, as the rabbis put it : "A slave of a king is a king".[37] However, at the very same time they could be humiliated and even decapitated at the whim of their master. A small god might wield a lot of power over mortals, but the greater god could destroy him at his will.

A *synthronos* could be the most powerful figure (call him : the Prince of the world), a minor god, but at the same time he is a servant, a slave of his master.[38] Metatron, the great prince (שׂרא רבא), the *Synthronos*, was also styled a נער, a servant,[39] in the same sense as "*And his servant Joshua the son of Nun, the attendant* (נער), *did*

---

sophistication, Comp. Scholem, *Gnosticism*, etc. p. 51, n. 24. With regard to the prophet Elijah, see V. Aptowitzer in *Tarbiz* II (1931), p. 260, n. 7.

[29] TB *ʿAbodah Zarah* 3b.

[30] Ch. 48c, p. 70; *Midrash Othioth de R. Akiba*, ed. Wertheimer, 1914, p. 11.

[31] See Lieberman, *H. A. Wolfson Jubilee volume*, p. 523 ff.

[32] *Eclogae Proph.* 41.

[33] *Ibid.* 48: τὰ βρέφει <τὰ> ἐξαμβλωθέντα.

[34] *Ibid.* (above n. 29).

[35] As a rule, (repeated many times in Geonic literature, see Lieberman, *Shkiin*, p. 83) we do not ask questions with regard to contradictions in *Haggadic* (legendary) literature. Inconsistency is part of the very essence of that literature. But in our case there is not the slightest conflict between the functions of Metatron, as we shall presently see.

[36] TB *Berakhoth* 58a.

[37] *Sifre Deuteronomy* 6, p. 15.

[38] Moses was a slave of God (*Deut.* 34:5), and it was considered a great compliment. See *Sifre* a.l. 357, p. 428.

[39] See Scholem, *Gnosticism* etc., p. 50, n. 23.

not budge from the tent" (*Ex.* 33:11). "He was tied to Moses".[40] Metatron was a servant, a קימוס (read קמיס)[41] an attendant,[42] and a great prince. The rabbis did not see any discrepancy in those terms; they were well aware of the realities of the Roman government.

However, the people could be sometimes inclined to consider the *synthronos* as an equal to his master. Diodorus Siculus (XVI, 92 and 95) stated that the image of Philip of Macedon (while alive) was borne alongside the twelve gods,[43] insinuating the arrogance of such behavior. The master would certainly not tolerate such confusion. We may cite two anecdotes to this effect. Midrash *Bereshith Rabba*[44] records in the name of Rabbi Hoshaya:[45] "When the Holiness blessed be He created Adam, the angels were about to recite the *Trisagion* to him. This [situation] could be likened to a king and an eparchus sitting together in one chariot[46] (קרוכין, καρροῦχα) and the people wanted to acclaim one of them '*Domine*', but they did not know which one of them was the king. What did the king do? He pushed the eparchus, and threw him out of the chariot". In other words, the people did now realize who is the *synthronos*[47] and who is his master. By being thrown out of the chariot the subordinate position of the *synthronos* was revealed.

We find exactly the same situation with regard to Metatron. The Babylonian Talmud relates[48] that Aḥer (Elisha the son of Abuyah) once found Metatron *sitting*[49] and recording the merits of Israel.

---

[40] TP *Yebamoth* IV. 2, 6a, *Nidda* I, 4, 49b.

[41] *Visions of Ezekiel*, ed. Grünwald in *Temirin* I, p. 129. See note *ibid.*

[42] In the new fragments of *Heikhaloth literature*, published by Grünwald in *Tarbiz*, vol. 38, 1969, p. 367 (last line) קברקליאל השר is mentioned. Since the differences between ר and י are indistinguishable in many manuscripts (see *Tosefta Kifshuta* IV, p. 583, note, p. 607 *passim*), we may perhaps read קביקליאל *Cubicularius.*

[43] σύνθρονον . . . τοῖς δώδεκα θεοῖς. See Nock, *Essays*, etc. p. 247, and Nock's conjecture with regard to Alexander, *ibid.* p. 135.

[44] VIII, 9, p. 63.

[45] Fl. in the beginning of the third century C.E.

[46] i.e. the eparchus was the *synthronos* of the king. Socrates (*Eccl. Hist.* II, 16) depicts the following scene: Μακεδόνιος ἐν τῷ ὀχήματι σύνθρονος τῷ ἐπάρχῳ κτλ. Makedonios was *synthronos* of the eparchus in the chariot.

[47] See above n. 46.

[48] *Hagiggah* 15a. Comp. *3 Enoch* ch. 16, p. 23.

[49] The Talmud does not designate explicitly the place from where he was taken out. But *Arukh* s.v. $פלס_3$ quotes מאחורי הפרגוד. From a new fragment of the *Hekhaloth literature*, published by I. Grünwald (*Tarbiz* 38, 1969, p. 362, line 13 ff.) it also appears that he was sitting in the ἄδυτον. He was therefore carried out from "behind the curtain", and was flogged, exactly like the angel

He remarked to himself: We have a tradition that there is no "sitting on high",[50] perhaps there are two Powers? Whereupon Metatron was carried out and administered sixty fiery lashes.[51] This passage of the Talmud and the parable in the Midrash reflect the same situation. The Master showed who is the Master and who is the *synthronos*.[52]

To summarize: We may say that when we combine all the sources, the earlier and the later ones, we gain the definite impression that Metatron is a title, and it could be used both as a substantive and an adjective (exactly like *synthronos*).[53] Metatron might have originally borne another name, but subsequently he was raised to the rank of Metatron, and finally assumed this name as a substantive. This is, of course, a matter of speculation, and we leave it to the specialists.

As for the spelling of מיטטרון,[54] it is perfectly normal. מיטטרון = μετάτρονος = μετάθρονος = σύνθρονος. The Semites transliterating Greek words which contain both a τ and a θ often spelled them with two ט, like טיאטרון (instead of תיאטרון) and אנטיפוטה (instead of אנתיפוטה).[55]

Gavriel, according to TB *Yoma* 77a (in the uncensored editions). However it is evident from the parallel passage in *Vayyikra Rabba* XXVI, 8, p. 608-609, that Gavriel was never admitted "behind the curtain".

[50] Comp. also *Bereshith Rabba* LXV, 21, p. 738. But the privilege of "sitting" was also granted to Moses, as it is explicitly stated in *Midrash Tannaim*, ed. Hoffmann, p. 19. Comp. also *Sifre* Deut. 305, p. 326, and parallels. See further Gruenwald, in *Tarbiz* XXXVIII (1969), p. 362, l. 13, and p. 363, l. 17.

[51] Comp. *3 Enoch* ch. 28, p. 47, ch. 44, p. 57. This is of course, a *topos*, comp. above, n. 49. The same is said about Elijah the Prophet in TB *Baba Mezi'a* 85b, as a punishment for revealing heavenly secrets. However, other angels were exiled from their compartments for a period of one hundred and thirty eight years for the same misdemeanor, but were not flogged.

[52] Rabbenu Hananel (a.l. 16a) records in the name of a *Gaon* that the purpose of the lashes was only to show that there is a Master over Metatron.

[53] See Sophocles, s.v. σύνθρονος.

[54] The י in מיטטרון indicates that it should be pronounced Metatron with an E (see Lieberman, *Tosefet Rishonim* II, p. 227, line 22; Epstein, *Introduction to the Text of the Mishnah*, p. 1242, p. 1243 s.v. ויוד אחרי ש), and not Mtatron. This is especially true in the transliteration of Greek words, see Krauss LW I, p. 16, § 24, A. 2-3. It is more frequently used in the middle of words like (μετάξιον) מיטכסון נומירון (μελία) מילה, מיליניה מיטון, מיתורין, טיטרפלין, טיטרטון and many other words.

[55] In Syriac it is also spelled אנטיפוטה. See also Odeberg, p. 140. For the interchange of θ and τ in Byzantine literature, see S. B. Psaltes, Grammatik der Byzantinischen Chroniken, p. 69. Compare also Liddell and Scott, s.v. κολοκύνθη.

The use of Metathronos instead of Synthronos appears to be a special feature of the κοινή. It was already established by A. Thumb that the κοινή abounds in Ionic and poetic elements.[56] Let us cite two instances which are very similar to our term. The usual Greek use for sitting together is συνίζειν. However, Homer (Odyss. XVI, 362) uses μεταΐζειν.[57] Again, the normal verb for dwelling together is συνναίειν, but the Homeric hymns (*Ad Cer.* 87) use : μετναιετάειν. Similarly, in the Theogony ascribed to Hesiod 401 we read : μετα-ναίετας. The Jews might have had serious reasons for avoiding the term Synthronos with regard to an angel. It was used by the Christians as a title for Jesus,[58] and it is not surprising that the Jews shunned this term as an appellation of the Angel.

2. *The Knowledge of* Halakha *by the Author* (*or Authors*) *of the* Heikhaloth

Chapter 18 of the *Heikhaloth* retains a puzzling and enigmatic passage. It can be understood only in the light of the specific, detailed, and minute laws governing the rules with regard to the impurity of a menstruant woman. According to the strict *Halakha* such a woman imparts impurity to any man who touches her body, or the cloth *on her body.*

Similarly, any cloth (or any object which is fit for sitting, or lying) on which this woman sits, or presses (leans against) with the greatest part of her weight [59] imparts impurity to any man who touches or carries it.[60] However, those objects which were merely touched by that woman (without sitting or leaning on them) do not impart impurity to either man or vessel.

However, we possess a strange book,[61] in which these laws are pushed to the very extreme. Although this source is replete with absurdities and nonsense, many medieval rabbinic authorities

---

56 See the references by Lieberman, *Greek in Jewish Palestine*, p. 48, n. 111, p. 63, n. 226.

57 The Greek lexicons quote it as a *hapax*.

58 See the numerous references by G. W. H. Lampe, *A Patristic Greek Lexicon*, p. 1331, s.v. σύνθρονος. 2. We may add the Christian epigram in *Anthol. Palat.* I, 24.: σύνθρονε καὶ συνάναρχε τεῷ πατρί.

59 Mishnah *Zabim* IV, 5.

60 *Ibid.* V, 5, *Ahiloth* I, 5, *passim*.

61 *Beraitha de Massekheth Niddah V*, (hereafter = *Beraitha d'Niddah*), ed. Ch. M. Horowitz 1890. The work was composed not later than the Geonic period (see below).

treated it very seriously.[62] It cannot therefore be ignored, since this work was current in rabbinic circles. We must add that this book contains some mystic elements,[63] and it stands to reason that the mystics considered the stringent laws of that source binding on persons who pretended to be admitted to the different precincts of heaven. According to that book the very sand on which a menstruating woman treads imparts uncleanliness to man.[64]

Now let us proceed with the explanation of the above mentioned cryptic passage of the *Heikhaloth*. Its essence consists of a plot devised by a group of rabbis which aimed at luring Rabbi Neḥunya ben Ha-Qanah out of his place in heaven. The surest way would be by bestowing impurity upon him, and then he would automatically be removed from his place. But, firstly, it is not permitted to convey uncleanliness to a man sitting in heaven, and, secondly, there is a risk that the rabbi might become aware of it and prevent the action.

In order to understand the plot and its denouement we must bear in mind the following laws and situations. The law requires women with fixed periods of menstruation to examine themselves at the beginning of those periods in order to learn whether they became impure. However if a woman neglected to do so, but subsequently tested herself and found that she is now pure, her status is questionable. According to the majority opinion she is considered ritually pure, but a minority, and it includes Rabbi Eliezer, dissented.[65]

It could be expected that Jewish women would undergo ritual immersion in such cases,[66] but, under circumstances of inconvenience, they would certainly stick to the opinion of the majority.[67] The group of rabbis conceived the following plan. They instructed

---

[62] See the sources adduced by Horowitz *ibid.* IV (פתחי נדה) p. 7 ff. V. Aptowitzer (in his book מחקרים בתקופת הגאונים, Jerusalem, 1941, p. 168) bitterly complained against modern writers who treated the book earnestly. However, I know no modern scholar who acted in such way. The only exception is, apparently, Aptowitzer himself. See his notes to his edition of the *Sefer Rabiah* I, Berlin 1912, p. 45, notes 10-12. But here we are interested in medieval authorities only.

[63] See *Beraithah d'Niddah*, *ibid.*, p. 45.

[64] *Ibid.*, p. 13. It appears that the source *mistakenly* compared the sand on which the woman trode to the מסמא stone (*Mishnah Kelim* i,3, and *Tosefta Parah* viii,2, *passim*), and it considered the sand as *Midras*, thus imparting uncleanliness to both man and vessel. Compare also below n. 79.

[65] TB *Niddah* 16a. Comp. *Tosafoth* a.l. s.v. ורב.

[66] In order not to involve themselves in doubtful laws.

[67] See *Tur Yoreh De'ah* 184.

the slave of Rabbi Akiba to put a strip of Parhaba [68] woolen cloth [on the ground] next to a woman who underwent ritual immersion that turned out to be invalid.[69] According to the stringent laws of *Beraitha d'Niddah* the cloth would become unclean even if it was not touched by the woman.[70] The slave was then ordered to immerse the strip of cloth in ritual water to render it pure. This procedure was necessary in order to indicate that the immersion was performed with direct intention to purify it from stringent impurity (טומאה חמורה). In such way the cloth would be declared pure even in the opinion of those rabbis who followed the strictest views of these laws.[71] The woman was then advised to approach the rabbis and explain to them the ways of her periods. The result of the enquiry would be that the majority (i.e. of the group mentioned in the *Heikhaloth* ch. XIV) would declare her "pure".[72] But one of that group would rule her "unclean",[73] and since her previous immersion was invalid, she is now impure.

They instructed the woman to touch the strip of cloth with the tip of her middle finger, but to be careful not to press it, but to touch it slightly, with "a light gesture, like a man who removes something that fell into his eye".[74] But here again they run a certain risk. Some of the rabbis were able to detect menstrual blood by its odor,[75] and Rabbi Neḥunya might belong to this body of experts,[76] and he might be able to discover in time that the strip was touched by an impure woman. He would never permit the placing of that kind of cloth on his knees.

What did Rabbi Ishmael do? He pressed a myrtle twig full of *foliatum* soaked in pure balsam (אפלסמון, βάλσαμον) into this

---

[68] The etymology of the word is obscure (see Geiger *apud* Krauss in his *Additamenta ad Librum Aruch Completum*, p. 337, s.v. פרהבא), but it is evident from TB *Niddah* 17a that it is a white soft piece of wool.

[69] The slightest interposition between the nude body and the water would invalidate the immersion. See Mishnah *Mikwaoth* IX,1-4 *passim*.

[70] See above, n. 64.

[71] With regard to "intention" in immersion, see Lieberman *Tosefta Ki-fshuta* V, p. 1307 ff.

[72] I.e. that immersion was not necessary, and it is therefore immaterial whether her previous immersion was valid or not.

[73] The "one" is Rabbi Eliezer, see TB *Nidah* 16a.

[74] The rabbis took precautions to instruct the woman not to press and lean against the cloth in order not to confer on it *Midras* (מדרס) impurity.

[75] TB *Niddah* 20b.

[76] Comp. *Baraitha d'Niddah*, p. 9. Rabbi Ḥanina ben ha-Kanah is certainly identical with Rabbi Neḥunya ben ha-Kanah.

strip. This balsam was famous for its pleasant and very strong odor,[77] and the strip of cloth having been permeated with this balsam would repress any other odor. The rabbi would never be able to detect the suspicious odor. The plot was safe. The strip of cloth was placed on the knees of Rabbi Neḥunya, and he was immediately dismissed from his seat.

The rabbis legitimately achieved their purpose. According to the *Halakha* prevailing on earth no impurity was imparted to Rabbi Neḥunya. The woman was ritually pure, for such was the ruling of the majority of the rabbis. Moreover, even if the woman would be impure she would not confer *Midras* (מדרס) impurity on the cloth by merely touching it. Our Rabbi would, in any case remain pure when he carried the strip of cloth on his knees.

In heaven, however, the rules of Rabbi Eliezer prevailed,[78] and in his opinion the woman was ritually impure. According to the laws of the *Beraitha d'Nidda* any object touched by a menstruating woman (not only *Midras*) imparts impurity to a man.[79]

As surmised above, the mystics considered these stringent laws as binding on any man who wanted to be admitted to the precincts of heaven. Rabbi Neḥunya carrying the strip of cloth on his knees became impure and consequently dismissed from his seat. The group of rabbis achieved their purpose without violating any principle of the *Halakha* valid on earth.

This passage of the *Heikhaloth* demonstrates that the Jewish mystics were not רבנן דאגדתא (rabbis who dealt with *Aggada* only), but were scholars also at home in the subtle intricacies of the *Halakha*.

---

77 See TP *Ma'asser Sheni* IV, 55d, TB *Sanhedrin* 109a, *Bereshith Rabba* XXVII, 3, p. 257. Compare also Gruenwald's note in *Tarbiz* XXXVIII (1969), p. 370, n. 48.

78 See TP *Mo'ed Katan* III, 1, 81d, TB *Baba Mezi'a* 59b. Comp. also *Pesikta de Rav Kahana* IV, ed. Mandelbaum, p. 73, and parallels. *Beraitha d'Niddah* (p. 21) claims that in heaven they follow the rules of the school of Shammai.

79 See p. 50: דילמא נגע במידי דנגעה היא ואתי לאטמויי

INDICES

A. GENERAL

Abraham, 55-57, 100, 138, 157
Adam, 239
Aggadah, 244
Alphabet, Letters of, 203, 322
  Assyrian, 70
  Combination of, 11
ʿAnan ben Ner, 222
Angels, 13, 23, 25, 26-29, 31, 35-38, 42-44, 50-51, 53, 58, 60-61, 65-67, 70-71, 83, 89, 94, 101, 104, 109, 113, 119-120, 129-130, 139-140, 152, 155-156, 159, 169-170, 181, 188-189, 193, 198, 200, 206, 212
  Angelic revelation, 123, 200, 205-207, 210-211, 214
  Etymology of names of, 206
  Song of:
    Benedictus, 215
    Celestial song, 55
    Doxologies, 39, 40, 67, 152, 184
    Hymns of, 31, 41, 55-56, 67, 103, 139-140, 152-155, 191-192, 207, 216, 232-233
    Incantations, 150-151
    Qedushah., 55, 139, 154, 159, 190, 207, 216, 233
    Sanctus, 69, 154, 215
  Classes of:
    Cherubim, 35, 44, 54, 114, 154, 201
    Hayyot, 54, 56, 57, 67-69, 94-95, 103, 114-116, 139, 141, 148, 153, 155, 160, 167, 176, 211, 214-215, 233
    ʿIrim, 44
    Ofanim, 44, 154, 176, 204
    Serafim, 44, 56, 68, 103, 115, 206-207
    Thronos, 59, 60
  Proper Names of:
    ʿAgmitiya, 186
    Akatriel, 168
    ʿAnafiel, 121, 167-168, 202-205
    Arpedes, 109
    ʿAza, 198
    ʿAzael, 198, 207(43)
    Dubiel, 206
    Dumiel, 165-166
    Gabriel, 44, 51, 166.
    Gedudaya, 183-184
    Gevuratiel, 206
    Jaoel (Yhoel), 52-57, 103, 144, 194, 196, 202
    Lailael, 204
    Metatron, v. Metatron
    Michael, 44, 51, 65
    ʾOfafaniel, 206
    Padkeres, etc., 109, 186
    Panuel, 44
    Qaẓpiel, 121, 165-166, 192-193
    Raguel, 38
    Raphael, 44
    Raziel, 227
    Samael, 206-207
    Sarafiel, 206
    Satan, 206-207
    Suriya, 105, 184
    Synadelphon, 65-66, 168-169, 177, 183 (5)
    Uriel, 9, 12
    ʿUza, 198, 207 (43)
    Yofiel, 184
Apocalyptic, 14, 22-28, 48, 50, 55, 69, 72, 90, 94, 127, 135, 144, 156-157, 227-228
  Christian, 61
  Jewish, 9, 16, 27, 29, 45-47, 50, 59-60, 100, 109, 123, 132, 162
Anthropomorphism, 215
Astrology, 227-230
Astronomy, 227

Babylonia, 80, 81, 172

Chaos, 112
Chiromancy, 218, 219, 224
Cosmology, 9, 14-18, 19, 48, 98, 118, 134-135, 148, 155, 162
Crystal, 33, 35

Day of Atonement, 96
Deification, 129
Dualism, 27, 119

B. PROPER NAMES (TALMUDIC SAGES)

C. MODERN SCHOLARS

D. HEBREW AND ARAMAIC TECHNICAL TERMS